The
Story
of
Avis

The Story of Avis

Elizabeth
Stuart
Phelps

Carol Farley Kessler,
editor

Rutgers University Press

New Brunswick, New Jersey

Library of Congress Cataloging in Publication Data

Phelps, Elizabeth Stuart, 1844–1911.
  The story of Avis.

  Bibliography: p.
  I. Kessler, Carol Farley.   II. Title.
  PS3142.S7   1985   813'.4   84–27538
  ISBN 0–8135–1098–8
  ISBN 0–8135–1099–6 (pbk.)

❧ CONTENTS

🌿 ACKNOWLEDGMENTS

Over one hundred years after its first publication, like a phoenix *The Story of Avis* regains a life. Many of us have waited a decade for this novel to become easily available. I personally am delighted at the opportunity to help place it in your hands. But many others deserve thanks for help and support along the way. As initiators of the project my thanks go to Sally Mitchell for urging that *Avis* be next and to Leslie Mitchner for listening, reading, and more than space permits. I also extend hearty thanks to Joanne Dobson, Sarah Elbert, Judith Fetterley, Annette Kolodny, Marjorie Pryse, and Elaine Showalter for their confidence in me. For permission to use "Female Life Studies" as the cover, I thank Robert Arthur Harman of the Pennsylvania Academy of Fine Arts. I gratefully acknowledge the help of Professor Frank Paul Bowman, University of Pennsylvania, for writing to Professor Jacques Seebacher, Université de Paris, who located the lines from Victor Hugo's "Regret," in the epigraph to Chapter 18. To John D. Vairo, Campus Executive Officer, and Edward S. J. Tomezsko, Director of Academic Affairs, at the Delaware County Campus of the Pennsylvania State University, go special thanks for providing the many supports that facilitate the functioning of teacher-scholars on a two-year campus. Sara Lou Whildin and Susan Ware, and their staff at Delaware County Campus Library, responded eagerly to numerous requests for reference support, as have Charles W. Mann, Jr., and Linda K. Rambler at Pattee Library, University Park. And David Kresh, Reference Specialist at the Library of Congress, solved several esoteric puzzles. The Liberal Arts College Fund for Research has made possible professional typing by Jean Patrick, whose cheer, interest, and above all expertise I appreciate. Finally I thank all generations of my very tolerant family for permitting me to get on with my work by becoming effectively self-dependent.

1815   Mother, Elizabeth Wooster Stuart, born in Andover to
       Moses Stuart (b. 1780), professor at Andover Theological
       Seminary, and his wife Abigail Clark (b. 1783); a fifth
       child and first daughter surviving to adulthood

1820   Father, Austin Phelps, born in West Brookfield, Massa-
       chusetts, to Eliakim Phelps (1780–1880), a revivalist
       preacher, and his wife, Sarah Adams (1783–1845); a sec-
       ond child and first son

1842   Marriage of parents, Elizabeth and Austin; subsequent
       residence in parsonage of Pine Street Congregational
       Church, Boston

1844   Born 31 August, Elizabeth Stuart Phelps, a first child and
       daughter, christened Mary Gray for a maternal friend;
       followed by M[oses] Stuart (b. 1849) and A[mos] Law-
       rence (b. 1852)

1848   Move to Andover where father was appointed professor at
       Andover Theological Seminary

1851   *The Sunny Side; or, The Country Minister's Wife* pub-
       lished, establishing her mother's reputation as a popular
       writer; Harriet Beecher Stowe and family arrive in An-
       dover (depart 1864)

1852   *A Peep at "Number Five"; or, A Chapter in the Life of a
       City Pastor*, mother's next novel, published, largely auto-
       biographical; death of paternal grandfather; death of
       mother from "brain fever"; possible assumption of
       mother's name

1853   *The Last Leaf from Sunny Side*, mother's posthumous
       collection, published, including "A Memorial of the Au-
       thor" by A. Phelps

1854   Father's second marriage to aunt, Mary Stuart (b. 1822)

1855   Death of maternal grandmother

1856   Death from tuberculosis of aunt/stepmother; possible
       assumption of mother's name

1858   Father's third marriage to Mary Ann Johnson (1829–1918), followed by births of two stepbrothers (1860; 1863, the prototype of her juvenile character "Trotty")

1860   Read Elizabeth Barrett Browning's *Aurora Leigh* (1857); completed unusually thorough education for women at that time at Mrs. Edwards's School for Young Ladies in Andover

1864   *The Gates Ajar* begun

1868   *The Gates Ajar* published, establishing her literary career

1870   *Hedged In* published, a novel exposing society's mistreatment of single mothers

1871   Feminist articles published in *The Independent* and republished in *The Woman's Journal; The Silent Partner* published, a novel concerning social reform as a woman's alternative to business

1874   Rebuttal written to Dr. E. H. Clarke on women's health

1876   "George Eliot" lectures delivered at Boston University; Gloucester cottage built

1877   *The Story of Avis* published, her best novel, concerning the dilemma for a woman of combining career with marriage

1878   Austin Phelps's first essay against woman suffrage, "Woman-Suffrage as Judged by the Working of Negro-Suffrage"

1879   *An Old Maid's Paradise* published, sketches exuding feminist humor, partially autobiographical

1881   *Friends: A Duet* published, a novel concerning a woman being drawn into marriage with her deceased husband's best friend; Austin Phelps's second essay against woman suffrage, "Reform in the Political Status of Women"

1882   *Doctor Zay* published, a novel concerning a female physician and her courtship by a male patient; *My Portfolio* by A. Phelps published, including his misogynist essays

1883   *Beyond the Gates*, a fantasy depicting a heavenly Utopia for women, published; accidental death of brother Stuart

1886   *Burglars in Paradise*, a detective-fiction parody, published; death of friend, Dr. Mary Briggs Harris (b. 1847)

1887   *The Gates Between* published, a Utopian fantasy show-
        ing a male physician's heavenly education to humanhood

1888   Marriage to Herbert Dickenson Ward (1861–1932), a
        journalist

1889   Next-door neighbor until 1893 to maternal aunt S[arah]
        S[tuart] Robbins (b. 1817)

1890   Death of father

1891   *Austin Phelps: A Memoir* published

1893   Move to home built in Newton Centre, Massachusetts

1895   *A Singular Life* published, a temperance novel, whose
        hero is martyred

1896   *Chapters from a Life*, her autobiography, published

1901   *The Successors of Mary the First* published

1902   *Avery*, a dream vision concerning a husband's lack of
        consideration for his wife, first published as "His Wife,"
        in *Harper's New Monthly Magazine; Confessions of a
        Wife* published under pseudonym Mary Adams, a novel
        revealing an unhappy marriage

1904–   Magazine short stories and serializations, themes be-
1910   ing antivivisection, marriage, sickness, and women's
        strength; *The Man in the Case* (1906), *Walled In: A
        Novel* (1907), *Though Death Us Do Part* (1908) published

1909   *Old Andover Days* by Mrs. S. S. Robbins appears, a remi-
        niscence not fully flattering to the Stuart family

1910   Death of Sarah Stuart Robbins, maternal aunt

1911   Death 28 January in Newton Centre, of heart disease;
        cremated and ashes interred on hillside in Newton
        Cemetery beneath a stone having a lily motif of her
        design

~ INTRODUCTION

First appearing in October 1877,
The Story of Avis by Elizabeth Stuart Phelps [Ward] (1844–1911)
depicts the *artiste manquée*, the would-be woman artist who
never realizes her potential.[1] If we understand that a character cast
as an artist symbolizes human creative potential in general, then
the novel speaks to each of us concerning those conditions that in-
hibit creative self-expression. One such condition is the often
incapacitating expectations held by family, friends, and society, as
the life and death of Clover Hooper (1843–1883) illustrates. At the
time Phelps was writing *Avis*, Clover Hooper and Henry Adams
(1838–1918) had just embarked upon their thirteen-year marriage—the richest years of his life, Henry would later claim. To
Henry James (1843–1916), Clover was "the incarnation of my native land," whose spirit and values would inform *The Education of
Henry Adams* (1907).[2] Yet Clover's talent—she was an accom-
plished photographer—and her marriage to Henry did not prevent
her suicide. Among the conditions that Henry created which could
have contributed to this end were his inability to praise, his dislike
of her relatives, and his disparagement of her aesthetic taste. Her
death later permitted Henry to understand that women can pay—
with their lives—for men's achievements.[3]

Phelps does not exact so momentous a price from her character.
Rather, she models Avis Dobell upon *Aurora Leigh* (1857) by Elizabeth Barrett Browning (1806–1861), a book read by both author
Phelps and character Avis at sixteen. This blank verse epic lionizes
the career of a woman poet, a female hero who surmounts being
orphaned and being reared by an uncomprehending aunt. Aurora at
first refuses to marry her cousin Romney, a disparager of women's
poetic capacities:

> Women as you are,
> Mere women, personal and passionate,
> You give us doating mothers, and chaste wives.
> Sublime Madonnas, and enduring saints!
> We get no Christ from you,—and verily
> We shall not get a poet, in my mind.[4]

But where Barrett Browning stresses a career successfully launched,
Phelps asks why many talented women seem to have produced so
little. Not lack of talent, Phelps makes clear, but the absence of
emotional supports prevents creative work from emerging. Typi-

cally, women provide rather than receive such nurture. Romney's words to Aurora express the conventional expectation that children and husbands will receive this sustenance.[5]

Both historical and fictional antecedents existed for the situation of the *artiste manquée* that Phelps depicts in *The Story of Avis*. First, the negligible position of women artists and the wide-ranging critique of marriage by the women's movement inform *Avis*: we must see this novel as an expression of feminist social activism. In addition, *Avis* is part of a women's literary tradition existing in Britain and in the United States. Finally, Phelps's biography and literary work provide additional contexts that illuminate this novel.

Early in *The Story of Avis* (chaps. 1, 4), Phelps establishes Avis's artistic talent by sketching the training available in Italy and France for United States women. A female life class, as depicted in a grisaille by Alice Barber [Stephens] (1858–1932), had been available on a limited basis since 1868 at the Pennsylvania Academy of Fine Arts in Philadelphia. However, like Mary Cassatt (1844–1926) in the 1860s, the character Avis Dobell turns to the Masters, whom she must seek in European studios and galleries.[6] Women were following this path in sufficient numbers for May Alcott [Nieriker] (1840–1879), sister of Louisa May Alcott (1832–1888), to publish in 1879 *Studying Art Abroad, and How to Do it Cheaply*.[7] Like other woman students, she found closed doors and higher fees.[8] Phelps takes Avis to Florence, Naples, and Paris over a period of about five years, but omits the hardships women faced. Rather, Phelps reveals the constraints to creative self-expression that women typically must confront. To this end she omits the arduous training that might lead to artistic success; for this we must wait for *The Song of the Lark* (1915) by Willa Cather (1873–1947). Instead, Phelps depicts minutely how the institutions of marriage and motherhood could undermine one woman's developing her creative potential. Phelps anticipates, by demonstrating the cost of straitened circumstances, the 1929 claim of Virginia Woolf (1882–1941) that "a woman must have money and a room of her own if she is to write fiction"—or pursue creative work of any sort.[9]

This focus was not unique to Phelps. The women's movement flourished during the 1870s. And although suffrage was an issue, the great M's—money, marriage, and motherhood—were equally important, marriage being central. The reigning domestic ideology of the nineteenth century included the beliefs that 1) money-making was the realm of the man, as suited to his competitive instincts as homemaking was to the woman's maternal instincts; 2) heterosexual marriage leading to the establishment of home and family offered the best refuge from a hostile world; 3) the mother, given her assumed moral superiority, was the natural guardian of innocent children, as well as of their father, against worldly evil; and 4) man could experience erotic need and pleasure, while the sexuality of woman was solely reproductive, this being her mode of creative self-expression.[10]

These beliefs elicited critiques from various segments of society, ranging from women's rights advocates to socialist anarchists. Among feminists, how centrally to place marriage within an array of reforms became a divisive issue. Although pre–Civil War feminists agreed that marriage was a problem (and disagreed about remedies, depending upon whether they saw marriage as a "contract," a "relation," or "an institution"), the women's movement split in 1869.[11] The more radical members of the newly-established National Woman's Suffrage Association (NWSA) saw suffrage as the means to the end of women's social and economic emancipation. But while the American Woman's Suffrage Association (AWSA) made suffrage the central concern, NWSA continued to stress pre–Civil War issues as well. Elizabeth Cady Stanton (1815–1902) never withdrew her 1853 comment to Susan B. Anthony (1820–1906): "I feel this whole question of woman's rights turns on the point of the marriage relation, and sooner or later it will be the question for discussion."[12] During the 1870s, a flurry of antimarriage commentary appeared. Lasting egalitarian marriages were expected to lead to a reconstructed society, while inequality in marriage was believed the source of larger social inequality.[13] In an article on "Home Life" (c. 1875), Stanton acknowledged that "the secret of the opposition to woman's inequality in the State and in the church [is that] men are not ready to recognize it in the home."[14] Feminists, both men and women, sought economic independence for women, denied the centrality of motherhood in women's lives, accepted the control of births, understood that both sexes experience sexual need and pleasure, and expected the full participation of women in public life. In 1889, upon the occasion of the merger of AWSA and NWSA into NAWSA, Stanton wrote: "Lucy [Stone (1818–1893)] and Susan [B. Anthony] alike see suffrage only. They do not see woman's religious and *social bondage*" (my italics).[15] Of such bondage, Matilda Joslyn Gage (1826–1898) declared,

> Like Adolph under St. Clair, in *Uncle Tom's Cabin*, [a woman] has freedom because a good master allows her to take it; under a bad master she suffers as Adolph when falling into the hands of Legree. Personal rights are the basis of all other rights; personal slavery is the root of all other wrongs. Neither freedom of the intellect or conscience can exist without freedom of person.[16]

Women's movement theorists constituted one part of the critique on marriage; anarchists provided another. In fact, their critiques could appear strikingly similar. Individualist-anarchist Voltairine de Cleyre (1866–1912), referring to the views of a then-imprisoned colleague, noted that "he beheld every married woman for what she is, a bonded slave, who takes her master's name, her master's bread, and serves her master's passion; [and] who passes through the ordeal of pregnancy and the throes of travail at *his* dictation."[17] Where AWSA fought for suffrage and NWSA stressed political, social, and economic reforms, the anarchists in their critique of marriage sought to exchange monogamy for sex varietism or free love. They considered church and state regulation of private sexual behavior inappropriate. During the 1860s and 1870s, anarchists expected free love to lead to a higher moral standard; the anarchists of the 1880s and 1890s thought happier, healthier children would result.[18]

All of the elements of the anarchist critique of heterosexual marriage (except free love) appear in Phelps's radical novel, *The Story of Avis*: maternal instinct is questioned; marriage, though sacred, is seriously flawed, offering little refuge to any woman or man. Even a freer sexuality is hinted: we are made aware symbolically of Avis's sexual interest. Although Phelps would agree with de Cleyre that individual growth is stifled by marriage, she would not go de Cleyre's next step to claim marriage wrong, as did some women utopians.[19] And although she would not have said with the socialist Aleksandra Kollontai (1872–1952) that women's inferiority derives from heterosexual erotic relationships,[20] *The Story of Avis* offers evidence in Kollontai's support, as does Phelps's earlier novel, *The Silent Partner* (1871), where no woman accepts the silent partnership of marriage.[21] Phelps's radical critique of marriage still holds and warrants our consideration, as research into women's position within marriage continues to suggest.[22]

Phelps forged a new plot to accomplish this critique of marriage. To show the marital constraints upon a woman's growth toward creative self-expression, she blended elements of two novel types: the woman's (or sentimental) novel, and the *bildungsroman* (apprenticeship novel), with its subtype, the *künstlerroman* (artist novel). According to Nina Baym, the woman's novel flourished from 1820 to 1870, but many of its features continued to appear after that period. In *Avis* (1877), Phelps follows the "trials and triumphs" plot as her heroine overcomes the handicaps of a deceased mother, an unsympathetic aunt, and an uncomprehending father—but in order to attain the reward of art study abroad, rather than the conventional marriage. Also unlike the woman's novel, men exist not as potential spouses but as Avis's mentors, teachers, and admirers of her talent; however, she has no female friends who fully understand her. Avis's refusal of Philip's first proposal is an atypical triumph, though once he is battle-wounded, she succumbs to his pressure to marry. This strong heroine typical of the woman's novel plunges on, but she will miss the happy ending of a successful, equal marriage.[23] Instead, her marriage will be to her "like death" (in contrast to a Utopian heaven where death for the heroine becomes life)—what Annis Pratt considers the "archetypal enclosure," which removes the possibility of authentic self-expression.[24] Marriage for a woman ends her growth, and for the artist blocks her development. Phelps's courageous honesty as the first writer to portray a failed marriage opened the way for Henry James's *The Portrait of a Lady* (1881) and William Dean Howells's (1837–1920) *A Modern Instance* (1882).[25] In addition, her inconclusive end anticipates James's *Portrait*: where his novel contains a heterosexual innuendo, hers suggests the future possibility of authentic and self-actualizing womanhood, given supportive conditions.[26]

Phelps's treatment of marriage in the novels just preceding and following *Avis* is unconventional and innovative, without the standard happy ending of woman's fiction. In *Hedged In* (1870) marriage ends a friendship between two women, the death of one concluding the novel. *The Silent Partner* (1871) contains marriage refusals from an upper- and a lower-class woman, both of whom will work together beyond the novel's close for the betterment of mill workers. *Friends: A Duet* (1881) moves a friendship into a marriage, but with no promise of future happiness and with evidence of the woman's resignation. *Doctor Zay* (1882) concludes with the promise of marriage between a patient and his physician; despite the innovative gender role reversal, Phelps offers no evidence that the venture will succeed.[27] As in woman's fiction, marriage for Phelps was never a proper or sufficient goal: women should grow toward other ends. Louisa May Alcott came to a similar conclusion in her novel *Moods* (1865; rev. 1882), where a young woman learns she must give herself time to become an individual before entering marriage. As Alcott noted, "The duty we owe ourselves is greater than that we owe others."[28]

The bildungsroman, or the apprenticeship novel, depicts a character's growth and development—the "duty" Alcott means. The British novels by women that influenced Phelps either show a heroine blocked in her growth by circumstances that she lacks the power to control, or make her obtainment of this control the measure of her growth—rather than the sexual initiation typical of a male hero.[29] Dorothea of George Eliot's (1819–1880) *Middlemarch* (1872) exemplifies a thwarted development, a "meanness of opportunity."[30] Although *Middlemarch* itself is a novel of manners, the development of Dorothea exemplifies the journey of a female apprentice in wifehood. In 1873 Phelps wrote Eliot that Dorothea should

> never accept wifehood as a metier. The woman's personal identity is a vast undiscovered country—with which Society has yet to acquaint itself, and by which it is yet to be revolutionized.
>
> I cannot tell you how earnestly I feel that it will require a *great novel* to proclaim the royal lineage of the Coming Woman to the average mind, nor what a positive personal longing it has become to me, that you should write it—if for no other reason to prevent my writing a small one![31]

Avis is of course Phelps's answer, though Phelps permits her heroine a clear sense of her own capacity (in contrast to Dorothea's dependence upon marriage to provide her métier). Barrett Browning's *Aurora Leigh* offered a verse precedent for a woman artist, but where Aurora makes her reputation and then marries a blinded man (thus to prevent his domination), Avis marries a wounded man before achieving artistic maturity. Phelps reveals more clearly the cost to a woman of even an unhealthy husband, if he is socialized to imperious (patriarchal) ways. By such disablements, men may be educated to accept a limited dependence and to yield dominant ways, as Philip's second disabling suggests.[32] But Phelps would also reveal how maimed men could acquire a new mode of control in requiring women's care.[33] For the heroine, development was at best precariously unpredictable.

Just as British writers explicated women's potential for growth, numerous United States women writers also made a heroine's developing artistic creativity central in their künstlerroman. Unlike Henry James's *Roderick Hudson* (1875), a novel depicting a successful sculptor who commits suicide over a failed love affair, artists in novels by women writers are survivors though conditions may not permit the fruition of their talents.[34] Even before *Aurora Leigh*, *Ruth Hall* (1855) appeared by Sara Payson Willis Parton (1811–1877) ["Fanny Fern," pseud.], much praised by Hawthorne as a commendable exception to work by the "damned mob of scribbling women."[35] This angry woman's novel shows how one author overcomes the trials put upon her by men who will not help and triumphs professionally to support her eager and proud daughters Katy and Nettie. In *Earthen Pitchers* (1873–1874) by Rebecca Harding Davis (1831–1910), heroine Audrey is like Avis in her love of the sea, dislike of housekeeping, longing for a deceased mother, and "look of a caged animal" upon admitting her love for a man.[36]

Davis contrasts Audrey's untrained voice—submerged in her family—with the lesser but well-nurtured talent of a neighboring man, doted upon by his wife. No sustenance exists for Audrey; her energy supports her family. In contrast, artistic recognition comes to the heroine of *Mercy Philbrick's Choice* (1876) by Helen Hunt Jackson (1830–1885), who in choosing to live alone can nurture her own talent.[37] In a recently published fragment, *Diana & Persis* (written in 1879), Alcott struggles with the possibility of artistic growth within a woman's life.[38] Of the two artists, staunchly unmarried Di continues to develop as an artist; Percy, burdened with the care of husband and baby, finds little time. Not until after the turn of the century can women imagine female artists both successful in their art and emotionally sustained by those around them. Mary Austin's (1868–1934) actress Olivia Lattimore in *A Woman of Genius* (1912) and Willa Cather's operatic diva Thea Kronberg in *The Song of the Lark* both rise to a success with costs as well as rewards. Not marriage, but the circle of women and men around each provides the needed support. No künstlerroman better shows the potential reciprocal fit between creativity and human relationships than May Sarton's (b. 1912) *Mrs. Stevens Hears the Mermaids Singing* (1965): Hilary Stevens's poems are the artistic fruits of intense feelings for the women and men she loves.[39] These more recent examples carry out *Avis*'s concluding hope—Avis for her daughter Wait's life, Phelps's for all of womankind. Olivia, Thea, and Hilary reveal who Wait may become, models whom we today may seek out to support and emulate.

The Story of Avis points the way from the nineteenth- to the twentieth-century female-artist novel. Avis's experience of a divided self differs from that of the typical male artist. Where he feels the split between himself and society, the female artist feels it within herself. If creativity—both its power and its freedom to formulate a universe—is considered to be a God-like capacity and if God is male, then any woman aspiring to artistic self-expression finds herself in conflict with a basic social concept. Hence, in her vision Avis seeks Goddesses to validate her genius (chap. 8). Hence, she sees that creation in an androcentric social world requires her separation from it: experience in such a world would lead to self-alienation through her having to accept God- rather than Goddess-centered theories of creativity.[40]

The social world of the 1870s in which Phelps lived and within which she wrote *The Story of Avis* included widespread urbanization and industrialization, with resulting human dislocations. With men increasingly taking over the centers of power, women experienced a more separate sphere than ever before. No longer were women's connections with each other acceptable: historians

Nancy Sahli and Carroll Smith-Rosenberg have shown that women's homosociality received increasingly less approval, and instead heterosociality was confidently expected to meet women's relational needs.[41] But women and men were socialized to different ways of being, and to the average woman in the nineteenth century, men appeared to be naturally more brutish and less sensitive than women.[42] Emotional support essential to women's creative effort was less available with women's networks broken and men absent in a nondomestic workplace.[43] Phelps both experienced these changes in attitude and possibility in her life and reflected them in her work.

Left motherless at eight years, the eldest daughter with four younger brothers, Phelps early felt the difference that gender could make. (See Chronology). She had no mother to advocate her cause and saw younger brothers given privileges withheld from her. For example, at the time of the 1860 Pemberton Mill disaster in Lawrence, Massachusetts—the incident that informs an early short story, "The Tenth of January" (1868)—her younger brother Stuart "being of the privileged sex, was sent over to see the scene," but she "was not allowed to go."[44] Nor was a college education open to her in the 1860s. In 1864 she did not even have a place at home where she could work undisturbed by the boys—save "on the chilly bed in the cold room" under her mother's "old fur cape, or pelisse."[45]

Not having had a mother, Phelps had to become her own. Two stepmothers followed. Her mother's sister—Sarah Stuart Robbins—may well have been a substantial influence, as she too was an author, even a neighbor for a short time later in Phelps's life.[46] At some point Phelps took on her mother's name, although she had been christened Mary Gray for a maternal friend. Sources are divided concerning whether this occurred at her mother's death or upon her joining the church (at about twelve years of age). Nor do we know whether *she* chose to "wear" her mother's name or whether it was given to her.[47] Whatever the reality was, her self-identity was complicated by her nominal identity and by an absent mother, an ideal of memory never to be corrected by reality. The mother-daughter relation, always problematic in a society that devalues the female and places in her hands the socializing of future females, became especially complicated for Phelps. In *Avis*, she draws upon the lives of both her mother and herself.

Her mother was a successful popular writer, and Phelps notes that "it was impossible to be her daughter and not to write."[48] She believed that her mother "fell" beneath the multiple demands of her roles as wife, mother, and author. And she accused her father, Professor Austin Phelps, of seeing only her mother's "fireside graces."[49] That he also could not appreciate her own support for the "enfranchisement and elevation of her own sex" must have caused her additional stress.[50] The parental vacuum notwithstanding, with professional and sororal support, Phelps mustered the strength to write her best and most socially explosive novel. But a six-year silence occurred between *Avis* and *The Silent Partner* (1871).[51] In May 1877 she wrote George Eliot that this silence was "enforced . . . (from illness)." Of *Avis*, she noted, "I do not hope much for it now; I am physically too far spent ever to do what it is a bitter comfort to hope I might have done." The book was a "compromise with fate."[52] While health can become a convenient way to control an implacable environment, it can also reveal stress through the outer manifestation of inner malaise.[53] The latter course seems to have been true for Phelps. She was plagued by insomnia throughout her life and suffered occasional lameness and eye fatigue.[54] In the mid 1880s she lost several intimates and also experienced failing health. At this time she married a young man about the age of the two younger brothers who had just left the Andover home. With this marriage, her writing turns from a direct confrontation of women's wrongs to such concerns as temperance and antivivisection.[55] In a 1903 letter to Harriet Prescott Spofford (1835–1921) she wrote that "the married are hampered in what they can say. I remember that when I wrote *Avis* I said 'were I married, I could not write this book.'"[56] Phelps's individual retreat occurs, of course, within the context of a society that was coming to define gender roles more rigidly and narrowly. It was not Phelps alone who retreated. The whole women's movement changed its strategy from a demand for rights to a claim of social-housekeeping superiority.[57]

Phelps's writing, of course, recorded these changes in attitude. May Sarton has noted, "My own feeling is that the only possible reason for engaging in the hard labor of writing a novel, is that one is bothered by something one needs to understand and can come to understand only, as the psychiatrists would say, 'by acting out' through the characters in the imagined situation."[58] The observation is especially cogent with respect to Phelps and *The Story of Avis*. We need first to see the novel within her overall literary output and then to examine its pages.

From the 1860s to 1880s, Phelps's characters—mostly women—fall into three types—the benefited, the benefactress, and the self-supporter. These characters show that young women need strong support from other women in order to achieve independence. Early fiction makes the heroine a young woman, as in "Jane Gurley's Story" (serialized in *Hours at Home*, 1866), where Jane—taken in by Miss Granger—learns that she can use her talent for design to become a commercial artist and thus earn a living for herself and her younger brother.[59] During the 1870s the heroine becomes a public benefactress who demonstrates female moral potency in righting wrongs against women and other powerless members of society. With *Avis* in 1877 Phelps first depicts a married woman and continues until 1887 to depict her heroines as self-dependent women. Although the characters before 1877 refuse marriage proposals, in 1874 Phelps did publish a model "marriage service" that placed identical marital obligations upon each spouse: not full rejection but reformation of the institution appears her stated goal here.[60] But in *An Old Maid's Paradise* (1879), much of the humor derives from the superfluity of the male to female welfare, his absence creating her paradise. Heroines feel threatened by marriages in the 1880s: *Friends: A Duet* (1881) and *Doctor Zay* (1882) as well as *Beyond the Gates* (1883) and *Burglars in Paradise* (1886) depict heroines who doubt their "free will absolute" to pass through life alone and who reluctantly capitulate to male wills.[61] In novels after *The Gates Between* (1887) men gain in marriage compliance and emotional support from women. The martyred pastor Emanuel Bayard of *A Singular Life* (1895)—Phelps's "dearest hero" as was Avis her "favorite heroine"—lives surrounded by wife, housekeeper, and nurse.[62] Of him Phelps notes, "The best of men may work his share of heart-break, and the better he is the less he will suspect it."[63] The pattern in Phelps's fiction for heroines was away from singular paradise to uncomfortable subordination in marriage.[64] And her strongest depiction of the discomfort— the clearest rationale for the existence of a singular paradise for women—occurs in *The Story of Avis*.

In an 1877 speech called "Homes of Single Women," Susan B. Anthony observed, "'The logic of events' points, inevitably to an *epoch of single women*. If women will not accept marriage *with subjection*, nor men proffer it *without*, there is, there can be, *no alternative*. The women who will *not be ruled* must live without marriage. . . . And during this transition period, wherever . . . single women make comfortable and attractive homes for themselves, they furnish the best and most efficient object lessons to men."[65] Ironically, the age of singular women was passing. The "Boston marriages" of post–Civil War New England were on the wane as the proportion of heterosexual marriages increased from 1890 to 1910,[66] this emphasis upon heterosexuality implying a devaluation of homosociality.[67] Therefore, *Avis* appears just before the homosociality tide turns and women's relations with each other begin to ebb.

The novel arrived at the tide's highwater mark, when women received social approval at least as moral guardians of society and when women together could form such a guard without stigma. In October 1877 *The Story of Avis* rolled from the Franklin Press to the publishing offices of James R. Osgood, Boston, and thence to the nation's parlors. Reviewers clearly liked or clearly disliked *Avis*. If they disliked it, they stressed stylistic infelicities, weak male characters, unhealthy and abnormal attitudes toward marriage, and a dangerously unappealing heroine.[68] One *Atlantic* comment in "The Contributors Club" suggests that such findings may be "wholly evolved from the minds of the critics"—who resist accepting a "'women's rights' creation."[69] If reviewers liked *Avis*, the very flaws become strengths: husband's shortcomings, marital burdens, and stifled creativity provide a corrective view; style, though often correctly seen to be flawed, was viewed as an incidental rather than as a central problem.[70] (See Contexts: "The True Woman" essay by Phelps and Four Contemporary Reviews of *Avis* reveal the critique Phelps developed in essays as well as novels and readers' varied responses to her viewpoint.)

Phelps has been criticized consistently for her language, but a novel that challenges cultural norms could hardly have been written easily or smoothly. The style documents Phelps's effort to force her voice from hedged-in silence. Stylistic grace must rest as much upon calm self-confidence as upon conscious care; Phelps's style reveals an anxious but failed search for the *mot juste*, the graceful phrase. Where *Avis* succeeds is in its innovative social vision, a literary capacity underrecognized and underexamined.[71] Phelps communicates her social vision through imagery, although she sometimes lacks adequate control. Even if at times exaggerated, her metaphors emerge from the novel's action, ranging from the bird and lighthouse combination for the artist and her goal (see chap. 3, n. 7; chap. 13, n. 5); the Sphinx for the difficulty of breaking silence and finding a voice (chap. 6, n. 14; chap. 7, n. 3, chap. 8, n. 9); the goddess Isis whose carmine red attire parallels Avis's gown (chap. 8, n. 7); to floral, geological, and battle imagery as indices of relations between the sexes (chap. 6, nn. 11, 15; chap. 5, n. 1; chap. 10, n. 3).

By incorporating social issues into her plot, Phelps also reveals her social vision. In *Avis* marriage stifles creativity. Although Phelps shows us a sensuous and sensual young woman in the opening chapters, although the landscape itself becomes an objective correlative for her sexual passion, sexual expression brings her not pleasure but pain—neither sweetness, nor safety, as the lines from George Eliot forbode (chap. 7, n. 1). Where for the male artist, a spouse smoothes the way, for the female artist, the way becomes strewn with obstacles. Wifehood, homemaking, and motherhood—for which Phelps shows a woman to have no particular instinct—use all energy, all time. Philip's emotional immaturity is such that Avis must resort to training him maternally, as if another child. Her maid's irresponsibility requires her shouldering household duties. And children, she finds, are "*a great deal of trouble*" (p. 152).[72] Little time remains for art. No matter if the master Couture himself expected "two years to make a reputation" (p. 37), no matter if she had already envisioned a masterwork that would give voice to the Sphinx (p. 83). (So central did Phelps consider the subject of this painting that she had originally considered calling the novel "The Story of the Sphinx.")

For creative work to emerge, a woman requires abundant emotional support—a living mother, understanding women friends. These Avis lacks. She does have about her several men who help—a father who tries to imagine what his wife would have wanted for her daughter, mentors who challenge her to be her best, a neighbor who buys her work and allies her with other women. And she feels the strength of her-story summoned as an inspirational vision to spark creation, revealed as a unity of affliction. Finally, she looks with faith toward the future her daughter Wait will inhabit, the splendid result of three generations of evolution away from a dumb "sad Sphinx" and toward "the true woman earth has never seen" ("The True Woman," 1871). Here in the character of Wait, Phelps constructs a fantasy of a life she might have enjoyed, had her mother been at hand like Avis.

Phelps's social concerns also emerge through character development and framing of the novel. The developing characters who shape the novel's structure are, of course, Avis Dobell and Philip Ostrander. As the novel opens, they stand as equals, and both are independently self-directed. But marriage and its consequences for personal development move Avis and Philip in opposite directions: Avis loses power in the relationship as Philip gains it. Unlike the characters in woman's fiction examined by Baym, Avis triumphs over her trials until marriage; thereafter, the trials triumph over her. It is not, in Phelps's view, that women and men inherently cannot get on together: it is that the conditions for woman to be her natural self—whatever that may mean—do not exist when she is defined by those around her. In this instance, Avis's family encourages her to paint Philip's portrait—exactly the work her mentor told her not to do. As a result, the spark ignited in the Parisian Church of the Madeleine, where Avis and Philip first meet, bursts into flame. The Civil War almost permits Avis to escape from this battle between the sexes over her self-direction, but the civil war between woman and man resumes when Philip returns wounded and engages her pity. Her generous concern for the well-being of *others* leads her astray from attending to her *own*. The nurturing strength for which her era lauded women, Phelps shows to be Avis's very downfall. A further irony emerges from Avis's aesthetic sense, which attracts her to Philip in the first place: her great gift does not permit her to look deeply enough behind Philip's "remarkable face" (p. 38). Not until too late does she perceive that Philip's concern is mere show: she misses the omens of the deceased bluejay, his failure to visit his mother, his lack of candor about Susan Wanamaker and his debts.

Up to this point, Phelps might be accused of misandry and inconsistency in her development of Philip. Neither is true. She well knew of women marrying men younger than themselves, the better to equalize a relationship.[73] She knew that women and men are first human, each having access to the same array of possibilities. Women may be maternal or not, men beautiful or not: she deliberately chooses the gender-atypical trait. The Florida interlude, where Avis and Philip retreat after the death of their son, clarifies Phelps's position.[74] Here she makes clear that were society constructed differently, its people would differ as well; that no necessary connections exist between sex and gender behaviors. Society, not humanity, is flawed and thus ruins people. The observation made about autobiography suits *The Story of Avis* as well: "a grim tale of a woman's claustrophobia when she cannot get out of the prison of the self or of her nightmare when she is kept from coming into her own self through the proximate existence of another or others."[75]

But the novel is not solely negative. Phelps frames her revelations of the hedges surrounding women with allusions to Spenser's Red Cross Knight of *The Faerie Queen* at the beginning of *Avis* and the Grail Legend from King Arthur's Round Table at the end. Spenser's tale foreshadows Avis's capitulation to Philip and her acceptance of the traditional male hegemony over the female; his definition of her is disastrous for the development of her creative talent. The heterosexual coupling which is based in his domination destroys her. The plot shows one human (male) obtaining another human (female) for his own use. Rather than follow man's myth for women, as here, women should consider man's myth for himself. The Grail Legend shows an older human (male) parenting a young human (male) in such a way as to enable the younger to be more successful than the older at completing a spiritual quest. Lancelot and Galahad parallel Avis and Wait. The title page epigraph—"Now, all the meaning of the king was to see Sir Galahad proved"—reveals Phelps's wish for woman's future access to a self of her own definition, the Grail of womanhood. Phelps develops the connection with care. Spenser in the legend of the Knight of the Red Cross uses red. Avis appears in gowns of carmine red, a color associated with the goddess Isis, thus, a reference to woman's creative potential. Woman must not be rescued by the Red Cross

Knight but must become him—not in a quest to win another human, but to find the spiritual self, as in the Grail Legend where again a red cross appears.[76] She must become the rescuer of her own self, the maker (Avis as parent) of like future selves (Wait as daughter). In 1983, Gayle Graham Yates, a theorist of religion, noted that where men's characteristic sin is pride or egocentricity, women's is denial of development of the self.[77] In 1893, Matilda Joslyn Gage concluded *Woman, Church & State* by observing,

> But woman is learning for herself that not self-sacrifice, but self development, is her first duty in life; and this, not primarily for the sake of others but that she may become fully herself; a perfectly rounded being from every point of view; her duty to others being a secondary consideration arising from those relations in life where she finds herself placed at birth, or those which later she voluntarily assumes. But these duties are not different in point of obligation, no more imperative upon her, than are similar duties upon man.[78]

The artist as creative person is metaphoric for human creative potential. Creativity can only exist within the context of authentic self-definition and the self-development that thereby proceeds; authenticity and inequality cannot co-exist.[79] The voice of Elizabeth Stuart Phelps, coming from a woman's pulpit of the past century, provides us with equipment for living on into the twenty-first century. In *The Story of Avis* she has named for us conditions that block human creativity. We are her future, for whom the novel was "made to be used" and who must now prove ourselves able to attain our individual Grails.[80]

Delaware County Campus   Carol Farley Kessler
The Pennsylvania State University

NOTES

1. Elizabeth Stuart Phelps [Ward], *The Story of Avis* (Boston: James R. Osgood and Company [Late Ticknor & Fields, and Fields, Osgood, & Co.], 1877).
2. Quoted by Eugenia Kaledin, *The Education of Mrs. Henry Adams* (Philadelphia: Temple University Press, 1981), p. 13. Alice James, Henry's sister, provides another example of unfulfilled talent.
3. Kaledin, *Education of Mrs. Henry Adams*, pp. xv, 3, 70 and chaps. 4, 5. The whole study deserves a careful reading.
4. *Aurora Leigh*, Book II, ll. 220–25. On reading *Aurora Leigh*, see Elizabeth Stuart Phelps [Ward], *Chapters from a Life* (Boston: Houghton, Mifflin, 1896), pp. 65–66; see notes to *Avis*, pp. 30, 32, 34.
5. For example, Susan Macdowell, student and eventual wife of artist Thomas Eakins, made her "first concern . . . her husband's art rather than her own." After his death, she "almost never left the house. . . . It was as though she had years of painting to catch up with, and every minute counted" (Seymour Adelman, *Susan Macdowell Eakins 1851–1938* [Philadelphia: Pennsylvania Academy of Fine Arts, 1973], pp. 10, 13).
6. Christine Jones Huber, *The Pennsylvania Academy and Its Women, 1850 to 1920* (Philadelphia: Pennsylvania Academy of Fine Arts, 1973), pp. 16–17.
7. May Alcott [Nieriker], *Studying Art Abroad, and How to Do It Cheaply* (Boston: Roberts Bros., 1879); see also Caroline Ticknor, *May Alcott: A Memoir* (Boston: Little, Brown, 1928).
8. *The Pennsylvania Academy and Its Women*, pp. 16, 30 n. 36; Charlotte Streifer Rubinstein, *American Women Artists from Early Indian Times to the Present* (Boston: G. K. Hall, 1982), pp. 92–93.
9. Virginia Woolf, *A Room of One's Own* (1929: reprint New York: Harbinger/Harcourt, Brace & World, 1957), p. 4.
10. For background, see Ellen Carol DuBois and Linda Gordon, "Seeking Ecstasy on the Battlefield: Danger and Pleasure in Nineteenth Century Feminist Sexual Thought," *Feminist Studies* 9 (1983): 7–25; Glenda Gates Riley, "The Subtle Subversion: Changes in the Traditionalist Image of the American Woman," *The Historian* 32 (1970): 210–227; Kathryn Kish Sklar, *Catherine Beecher: A Study in American Domesticity* (New Haven: Yale Univ. Press, 1973); Barbara Welter, *Dimity Convictions: The American Woman in the Nineteenth Century* (Athens, Ohio: Ohio Univ. Press, 1976).
11. For one instance of diverging views on marital remedies, see "Debates on Marriage and Divorce" (1860), Document 18, in *The Concise History of Woman Suffrage*, ed. Mari Jo and Paul Buhle (Urbana: Univ. of Illinois Press, 1978), pp. 170–189. The respective views belong to Elizabeth Cady Stanton, Antoinette Brown Blackwell, and Ernestine L. Rose; Susan B. Anthony makes a final comment.
12. Ellen Carol DuBois, ed., *Elizabeth Cady Stanton/Susan B. Anthony: Correspondence, Writings, Speeches* (New York: Schocken, 1981), p. 56.
13. For a thorough discussion of the debates about marriage during the 1870s, see William Leach, *True Love and Perfect Union: The Feminist Re-*

form of Sex and Society (New York: Basic, 1980), especially Parts 1 and 2; but see also review by Eli Zaretsky, *Signs* 7 (1981): 230–233. In addition, marriage received center focus in Utopias by women: see *Daring to Dream: Utopian Stories by United States Women, 1836–1919*, ed. Carol Farley Kessler (London: Pandora/Routledge & Kegan Paul, 1984), especially Introduction, pp. 1–14.

14. Elizabeth Cady Stanton, "Home Life," in *Elizabeth Cady Stanton/ Susan B. Anthony*, ed. DuBois, p. 132.

15. Quoted in Sally Roesch Wagner, Introduction to *Woman, Church & State* by Matilda Joslyn Gage (1893; reprint Watertown, Massachusetts: Persephone, 1980), p. xxxiii.

16. See Gage, *Woman, Church & State*, p. 144, note 15.

17. Quoted in Margaret S. Marsh, *Anarchist Woman, 1870–1920* (Philadelphia: Temple Univ. Press, 1981), p. 77, from *The Selected Works of Voltairine de Cleyre* (New York: Mother Earth, 1914), p. 344; see also Marsh, "The Anarchist-Feminist Reponse to the 'Woman Question' in Late Nineteenth-Century America," *American Quarterly* 30 (1978): 533–547.

18. Marsh, *Anarchist Women*, p. 91. Utopian fiction provides a critique of marriage covering the full historical range. For a sampling, see Kessler, ed., *Daring to Dream*, note 13. The fictions mirror in reverse the omitted needs of historical women's lives: heterosexual marriage left them much yet to desire.

19. Quoted in Marsh, *Anarchist Women*, p. 92, from "They Who Marry Do Ill" in *Mother Earth* 2 (Jan. 1908), which communist-anarchist Emma Goldman edited.

20. Cited by Marsh, *Anarchist Women*, p. 169, from Barbara Evans Clements, *Bolshevik Feminist: The Life of Aleksandra Kollontai* (Bloomington: Indiana Univ. Press, 1979), p. 69.

21. Elizabeth Stuart Phelps [Ward], *The Silent Partner* (1871; reprint Old Westbury: Feminist Press, 1983). Dorothy Tennov, a psychologist, shows how emotional attachments can be overwhelming. She distinguishes among sex, friendship, affection, love and "being in love." She has analyzed this last as "the course of limerence" in *Love and Limerence: The Experience of Being in Love* (New York: Stein and Day, 1980). Phelps's description of the early recognition and attraction between Avis and Philip exemplifies the experience of limerence.

22. For current research on women and marriage, see Jessie Bernard, "Homosociality and Female Depression," *Journal of Social Issues* 32 (1976): 213–238; Jan Roberts Chapman and Margaret Gates, eds., *Women into Wives: The Legal and Economic Impact of Marriage* (Beverly Hills: Sage, 1977); Elaine Walker, *The Chronicle of Higher Education* 28 (8 Aug. 1984): 6.

23. Nina Baym, *Women's Fiction: A Guide to Novels by and about Women in America, 1820–1870* (Ithaca: Cornell Univ. Press, 1978), chap. 2.

24. Quoted by Kessler, ed., in *Daring to Dream*, p. 105, from Phelps [Ward] *Beyond the Gates* (1883) and *The Gates Between* (1887) (see pp. 104–116 for Phelps's excerpts); Annis Pratt, *Archetypal Patterns in Women's Fiction* (Bloomington: Indiana Univ. Press, 1981), pp. 45–48.

25. Alfred Habegger, *Gender, Fantasy, and Realism in American Literature* (New York: Columbia Univ. Press 1982), p. 54. In addition to discussing Phelps, Habegger offers informative re-evaluations of James and Howells.

26. Habegger, *Gender, Fantasy, and Realism*, chap. 8; see also perceptive discussions by Rachel Blau DuPlessis, *Writing Beyond the Ending: Narrative Strategies in Twentieth-Century Women's Writing* (Bloomington: Indiana Univ. Press, 1985) and Annette Niemtzow, "Marriage and the New Woman in *The Portrait of a Lady*," *American Literature* 47 (1975): 377–395, especially p. 393.

27. See Carol Farley Kessler, *Elizabeth Stuart Phelps*, TUSAS #434 (Boston: G. K. Hall, 1982), pp. 83–100, on Phelps's treatment of marriage in her fiction. The Twayne volume condenses "'The Woman's Hour': Life and Novels of Elizabeth Stuart Phelps (1844–1911)," Ph.D. diss., University of Pennsylvania, 1977.

28. Louisa May Alcott, *Moods* (Boston: Roberts, 1882), chap. 11. For a recent discussion, see Sarah Elbert, *A Hunger for Home: Louisa May Alcott and "Little Women"* (Philadelphia: Temple Univ. Press, 1984), chap. 7.

29. Baym, *Women's Fiction*, p. 30. See also Elaine Showalter, *A Literature of Their Own: British Women Novelists from Brontë to Lessing* (Princeton: Princeton Univ. Press, 1977), p. 13, for developmental phases in a women's literary tradition. In the United States, the first "feminine" phase ends about 1870; the second "feminist" phase concludes about 1960, with hints during the 1940s of the third "female" phase to follow.

30. George Eliot, Prelude to *Middlemarch*.

31. Elizabeth Stuart Phelps to George Eliot, 26 February 1873, The Beinecke Rare Book and Manuscript Library, Yale University; Eliot's response appears in *The George Eliot Letters*, ed. Gordon Haight (New Haven: Yale Univ. Press, 1954–1955), vol. 5, p. 388. See also Kessler, *Elizabeth Stuart Phelps*, pp. 85–86; and *Avis*, chap. 7, n. 2.

32. See Showalter, *A Literature of Their Own*, p. 150, on male characters' education. Phelps likely had read at this time Charlotte Brontë's *Jane Eyre* (1847) as well, and thus Jane and Rochester may be predecessors as well as Aurora and Romney (see chap. 9, n. 5). Showalter notes the "blinding, maiming, blighting" of the "feminine heroes." The purpose, Showalter convincingly suggests, is "emotional education through symbolic role-reversal," what she calls a "limited experience of dependency, frustration, and powerlessness—in short, of womanhood" (p. 150). Helen Papashvily, in *All the Happy Endings* (New York: Harper Bros., 1956), discovers women writers in the United States mentally or physically handicapping male characters (p. 91). Nina Baym, in *Woman's Fiction*, finds that United States women writers strive for economic independence and marital equality for heroines (pp. 39–41).

33. See Phelps's later works: *The Man in the Case* (1906), *Walled In: A Novel* (1907), *Though Life Us Do Part* (1908). All are discussed in Kessler, *Elizabeth Stuart Phelps*, chap. 5.

34. An exception may be *The Awakening* (1899) by Kate Chopin (1851–1904). In this novel, however, art is less central and reasons other than a failed love affair exist for the suicide.

35. Caroline Ticknor, *Hawthorne and His Publisher* (Boston: Houghton, Mifflin, 1878), p. 141.

36. Rebecca Harding Davis, "Earthen Pitchers," *Scribners Monthly* 7 (Nov. 1873–Apr. 1874): 73–81, 199–207, 274–281, 490–494, 595–600, 714–721; here p. 719.

37. *Mercy Philbrick's Choice* by Helen Hunt Jackson, published as the lead volume in the "No Name Series" (Boston: Roberts, 1876). See chap. 11, n. 1.
38. Louisa May Alcott, *Diana & Persis*, ed. Sarah Elbert (New York: Arno, 1978).
39. Compare to *Avis*, p. 244 and see note to chap. 25, n. 3.
40. See Maurice Beebe, *Ivory Towers and Sacred Founts: The Artist as Hero in Fiction from Goethe to Joyce* (New York: New York Univ. Press, 1964), Part I; Jean Shinoda Bolen, M.D., *Goddesses in Everywoman: A New Psychology of Women* (New York: Harper & Row, 1984); Linda Huf, *A Portrait of the Artist as a Young Woman* (New York: Ungar, 1983); Milton C. Nahm, "Creativity in Art," in *Dictionary of the History of Ideas* (New York: Scribners, 1973), 1: 577–589; Grace Stewart, *A New Mythos: The Novel of the Artist as Heroine 1877–1977* (Brattleboro, Vermont: Eden, 1979).
41. Nancy Sahli, "Smashing: Women's Relationships before the Fall," *Chrysalis* No. 8 (Summer 1979): 17–28; and Carroll Smith-Rosenberg, "The Female World of Love and Ritual: Relations between Women in Nineteenth Century America," *Signs* 1 (1975): 1–30. They discuss the intricacy, longevity, and depth of these relationships.
42. Leach, *True Love*, chap. 5. Note, however, distinctions among "sentimental love," based upon sex differences of male breadwinning versus female breadmaking; "romantic love," upon passion; and "rational love," upon knowledge, the first two being the object of feminist critique.
43. Jessie Bernard, "Homosociality and Female Depression," and *The Female World* (New York: Free Press, 1981); Rosalind Rosenberg, *Beyond Separate Spheres: Intellectual Roots of Modern Feminism* (New Haven: Yale Univ. Press, 1982).
44. Phelps [Ward], *Chapters from a Life*, p. 91. See Chronology.
45. Ibid., p. 103.
46. Mrs. S[arah] S[tuart] Robbins wrote the fictional works *My New Home: A Woman's Diary* (New York: Carter & Bros., 1865) and *One Happy Winter; or a Visit to Florida* (Boston: Lockwood, Brooks, & Co., 1878). See Chronology.
47. Kessler, *Phelps*, pp. 16, 136 nn. 28, 29.
48. Phelps [Ward], *Chapters*, p. 15. For a discussion of her mother's influence, see Kessler, "A Literary Legacy: Elizabeth Stuart Phelps, Mother and Daughter," *Frontiers* 5, no. 3 (Fall 1980): 28–33.
49. Phelps [Ward], *Austin Phelps: A Memoir* (New York: Scribners, 1891), p. 87.
50. Phelps [Ward], *Chapters*, p. 250.
51. Kessler, *Phelps*, pp. 85–87; Tillie Olsen, *Silences* (New York: Delta, 1978), pp. 9, 10, 17.
52. Elizabeth Stuart Phelps [Ward] to George Eliot, 27 May 1877, The Beinecke Rare Book and Manuscript Library, Yale University.
53. Carroll Smith-Rosenberg, "The Hysterical Woman: Sex Roles and Role Conflict in Nineteenth Century America," *Social Research* 39 (1972): 652–678.
54. On Phelps's invalidism, see Kessler, *Phelps*, pp. 51–52, 73, 80, 85–87.
55. Kessler, *Phelps*, chaps. 4 and 5.
56. Elizabeth Stuart Phelps [Ward] to Harriet Prescott Spofford, 2 February 1903, The American Antiquarian Society, Worcester, Massachusetts.

57. Aileen S. Kraditor, *The Ideas of the Woman Suffrage Movement 1890–1920* (New York: Columbia Univ. Press, 1965), especially chap. 3.

58. May Sarton, *Writings on Writing* (Orono, Maine: Puckerbush, 1980), p. 26.

59. See Kessler, *Phelps*, pp. 24–29, 83–85, 92–95, on characters and marriage.

60. Phelps [Ward], Marriage Service of "A Dream within a Dream," in *Daring*, ed. Kessler, pp. 109–111.

61. Phelps [Ward], *Chapters*, p. 29.

62. Phelps [Ward], *Chapters*, pp. 157, 273.

63. Phelps [Ward], *A Singular Life* (Boston: Houghton, Mifflin, 1895), p. 197.

64. Kessler, *Phelps*, chap. 4. For discussions of relevant short stories on marriage, see Lori Duin Kelly, *The Life and Works of Elizabeth Stuart Phelps, Victorian Feminist Writer* (Troy, New York: Whitston, 1983), chap. 5; on work as artists, see Susan Ward, "The Career Woman Fiction of Elizabeth Stuart Phelps," in *Proceedings, Nineteenth Century Women Writers International Conference*, ed. Rhoda Nathan (Westport, Connecticut: Greenwood, forthcoming). Ward could also include "Old Mother Goose" (actress) and "Doherty" (singer), both in *Sealed Orders* (Boston: Houghton, Mifflin, 1880). Of course fictional portraits of marriage are more stereotyped than they are historical: see Polly Longsworth, ed., *Austin and Mabel: The Amherst Affair and Love Letters of Austin Dickinson and Mabel Loomis Todd* (New York: Farrar, Straus & Giroux, 1984) and Phyllis Rose, *Parallel Lives: Five Victorian Marriages* (New York: Knopf, 1984) for instances of individuals who freed themselves from expected practices, a choice sometimes terrifying in causing anxiety over taking responsibility for the possibility of painful error. In any historical moment, more options exist for the courageous chooser than for those who follow trodden paths.

65. Susan B. Anthony, "Homes of Single Women," in *Stanton/Anthony*, ed. DuBois, p. 148. Note Louisa May Alcott's comment in her journal that she knows little about marriage save few are happy. See *Louisa May Alcott: Her Life, Letters and Journals*, ed. Ednah D. Cheney (Boston: Little, Brown, 1892), p. 166.

66. "Boston marriages" were between two women—homosocial couples—who lived together as a household; such relationships may or may not have included sexual expression. A well-known example within Phelps's network of friends was Annie Adams Fields (1834–1915) and Sarah Orne Jewett (1849–1909). See also Bernard, "Homosociality and Female Depression," p. 230 n. 6: from 1890–1910, "the proportion of males married rose from 52 to 54%; of females from 55 to 57%."

67. Adrienne Rich, "Compulsory Heterosexuality and Lesbian Experience," *Signs* 5 (1980): 631–660.

68. Kessler, *Phelps*, pp. 126, 150 n. 14. See also *New York Times* (15 Oct. 1877), p. 2, col. 1; *Philadelphia Inquirer* (13 Oct. 1877), "New Books"; *Chicago Tribune* (10 Nov. 1897), "Literature"; Gail Hamilton (pseud. of Mary Abigail Dodge, 1838–1896), *New York Daily Tribune* (2, 5, 9, 12 Feb. 1878), "Gail Hamilton Once More. The Story of Avis—A Review in IV Parts"; Scrapbook [n.d.], Alderman Library, University of Virginia, p. 5.

69. *Atlantic Monthly* 43 (February 1879): 258.

70. Kessler, *Phelps*, pp. 126, 150 n. 14. See also [Harriet Waters Preston], "The Story of Avis, and Other Novels," *Atlantic* 41 (Apr. 1878): 486–489; James Herbert Morse, "The Native Element in American Fiction. Since the War," *Century* 26 (Jul. 1883): 370–371; Sojourner, "Miss Phelps and Howells," *Woman's Journal* 18 (8 Oct. 1887): 322.

71. Kessler, *Phelps*, pp. 87, 132–133.

72. Phelps was among the earliest to argue on the side of learned vs. instinctual mothering. The debate continues, but feminist research weights it toward the latter. For recent discussions, see Nancy Chodorow, *The Reproduction of Mothering: Psychoanalysis and the Sociology of Gender* (Berkeley and Los Angeles: Univ. of California Press, 1978); Dorothy Dinnerstein, *The Mermaid and the Minotaur: Sexual Arrangements and Human Malaise* (New York: Harper & Row, 1976); Adrienne Rich, *Of Woman Born: Motherhood as Experience and Institution* (New York: Norton, 1976). See *Avis*, pp. 150–151.

73. Kessler, *Phelps*, pp. 79, 143 n. 8.

74. See chaps. 22–24. Unfortunately in her depiction of the black servant Jeff, Phelps shows the patronizing attitude typical of members of her society. See *Avis*, pp. 234–240.

75. Mary G. Mason, "Autobiographies of Women Writers" in *Autobiography: Essays Theoretical and Critical*, ed. James Olney (Princeton: Princeton Univ. Press 1980), p. 234.

76. Thomas Bulfinch, *Age of Chivalry* (1862; reprint New York: New American Library, 1962), p. 161. Galahad receives a white shield in the middle of which is a red cross.

77. Gayle Graham Yates, "Spirituality and the American Feminist Experience," *Signs* 9 (1983): 65.

78. Gage, *Woman, Church, & State*, pp. 239–240. For an incisive evaluation of Gage's contribution, see Dale Spender, *Women of Ideas and What Men Have Done to Them: From Aphra Behn to Adrienne Rich* (London: Routledge & Kegan Paul, 1982), pp. 226–252.

79. Jean Baker Miller, *Toward a New Psychology of Women* (Boston: Beacon, 1976), p. 98.

80. Kenneth Burke, "Literature as Equipment for Living" in *The Philosophy of Literary Form*, 3rd ed. (Berkeley and Los Angeles: Univ. of California Press, 1973), pp. 293–304; Rachel Blau DuPlessis, *Writing Beyond the Ending*; Marge Piercy, "To Be of Use" in *Circles on the Water: Selected Poems* (New York: Knopf, 1982), p. 106, l. 24. On relationships as a mode of creativity, see Rose, *Parallel Lives*, pp. 5–6: "living is an act of creativity" as we "decide upon the story of our own lives."

✒ SELECTED

BIBLIOGRAPHY

Auerbach, Nina. Review of *The Story of Avis. Nineteenth-Century Fiction* 33 (1979): 476–478.

Bennett, Mary Angela. *Elizabeth Stuart Phelps.* Philadelphia: Univ. of Pennsylvania Press, 1939.

Donovan, Josephine. *New England Local Color Tradition: A Women's Tradition.* New York: Ungar, 1983.

Douglas, Ann. *The Feminization of American Culture.* New York: Knopf, 1977.

Habegger, Alfred. *Gender, Fantasy, and Realism in American Literature.* New York: Columbia Univ. Press, 1982.

Huf, Linda. *A Portrait of the Artist as a Young Woman.* New York: Ungar, 1984.

Ives, Ella Gilbert. "Elizabeth Stuart P. Ward: A More Intimate Sketch of Her Personality." Boston *Transcript* (4 Feb. 1911).

Kelly, Lori Duin. *The Life and Works of Elizabeth Stuart Phelps, Victorian Feminist Writer.* Troy, New York: Whitston, 1983.

Kessler, Carol Farley. *Elizabeth Stuart Phelps.* Boston: G. K. Hall, 1982.

———. "Legacy Profile: Elizabeth Stuart Phelps [Ward]: 1844–1911," *Legacy: A newsletter of nineteenth-century American women writers,* 1, no. 2 (Fall 1984): 3–5.

———. "A Literary Legacy: Elizabeth Stuart Phelps, Mother and Daughter," *Frontiers* 5, no. 3 (Fall 1980): 28–33.

Pratt, Annis. *Archetypal Patterns in Women's Fiction.* Bloomington: Indiana Univ. Press, 1981.

Stansell, Christine. "Elizabeth Stuart Phelps: A Study in Female Rebellion." *Massachusetts Review* 13 (1979): 239–256.

Stewart, Grace. *A New Mythos: The Novel of the Artist as Heroine 1877–1977.* Brattleboro, Vermont: Eden, 1979.

Welter, Barbara. "Defenders of the Faith." In *Dimity Convictions: The American Woman in the Nineteenth Century.* Athens, Ohio: Ohio Univ. Press, 1976.

Westbrook, Perry D. *Acres of Flint.* 2nd ed. Metuchen, New Jersey: Scarecrow, 1984.

A Note on the Text

The text has been reset, following the 1877 edition of *The Story of Avis* by the original publisher, James R. Osgood and Company (Late Ticknor & Fields, and Fields, Osgood & Co.), Boston

The
Story
of
Avis

"Now, all the meaning
of the King was
to see Sir Galahad
proved."

*"Pray you, say nothing;
pray you, who neither feel
nor see the rain,
being in't."*

ᔍ THE STORY
OF AVIS

CHAPTER I

*"And all I saw was on the
sunny ground,
The flying shadow of an
unseen bird."*

What *was* it about her?

Coy Bishop at the Poetry Club that night, while a theological
student with a cold in his head was declaiming from the second
canto, sat perversely wondering. It was becoming to Coy to wonder; she did not very often,—being a blonde, with a small mouth
and happy eyes.

She changed the accent of her thoughts as they pursued her; out
of irresistible sympathy, perhaps with the reader, who experienced
some elocutionary difficulty in changing his; though, indeed, she
found her own revery so much more to the purpose just then than
her desire for literary culture, that she conceived a distaste for the
young gentleman as a tiresome interruption, and hoped that some
of the girls would refuse him before the winter was over.

What was it then *about* her? There was more sense than syntax
in Coy's question; at least a sense perfectly clear to herself, who, as
the only person concerned in this mute discussion, had obvious
rhetorical rights therein.

This was in the days when young ladies had not begun to have
"opinions" upon the doctrine of evolution, and before feminine
friendship and estrangements were founded on the distinctions between protoplasm and biplasm. Yet, even fifteen years ago, the resemblance of the human face to different types of animals was no
novelty to any thoughtful fancy. So, too, the likenesses in the human body to forms of life incident to the vegetable world, were surprising only to people ignorant of the anatomy of the nervous and
arterial systems.

Coy was not ignorant. Harmouth[1] girls never were. Her mind
was stocked with facts sufficient to bring these correspondences

before it. But there she stumbled upon a dense idea across which neither the diploma of the Harmouth Female Seminary, nor the "course of study" in which all Harmouth girls engaged, could strike a light. Had anybody ever said that people resembled metals? Was it Galileo, or Socrates? Newton perhaps. Or—or—could it have been John Rose?

The theological reader at the other end of the room just then, suddenly observing Miss Bishop's averted face, floundered into an acute embarrassment upon seeing that she blushed swiftly, and wondered if he had read from the love-passages too long. His mind gathered an immediate accretion to the conviction that light literary work was unsuitable to the preparation for the gospel ministry.

Coy was not blushing about John Rose: young men are too common in Harmouth to be easily blushed about. She was aware of a certain incongruousness in that fancy about the metals. What was the use of reading-clubs, and suffering such anxiety about the coffee, when one took one's turn, if one could not tell whether one owed an idea to an old Greek, or an evening caller? That she could have originated it, Coy never for an instant conceived. She left ideas to Avis.

What she meant about the metals was this. All people in their physical natures are akin to some form of inorganic existence. Some, for instance, are clay, sheer clay, mud. Certain metals enter into the composition of certain temperaments: brass or iron, gold, silver, or steel, stratifies in the nature, and gives character to body and soul. "Who knows," Coy would have said if she could,—"who knows but a skillful soul-geologist may learn to detect these metallic traces in men and women, and can act upon the character of a soul's topography accordingly, can map it with some accuracy, can fathom its wealth, or measure its barrenness, indicate the presence of its mines, discover its fossils, account for its deluges, prophesy its earthquakes, its volcanoes?" It was surely in the old creed of the alchemists, that metals were endowed with sense and feeling, and possessed of either masculine or feminine qualities. Then why not the man or the woman with the sense or the trait of the metal?

Now, Avis was a magnet.

Coy's metallic theory had by this time rather run away with her. But of so much she was sure: when Avis was a baby, mother-earth yielded pure perfect magnet up into her composition. Shrewd Nature, never to be cheated out of her control over her children, held back her gold, her gems, her silver, and her fine, dumb pearl, and wrought into Avis just the one thing more precious than they all.

People, to be sure, were artificially magnetized to a certain extent. Barbara Allen, for instance, turning the exact intellectual pose of her head (there was but one intellectual pose to Barbara's head) towards Philip Ostrander, while he read his paper on Spenserian metres, was a species of electromagnet.

But Avis was, without alloy, loadstone. In Avis there existed that attribute—no, that quality; which was it? Coy remembered hearing one of the Professors say at a supper that there was a difference between these two things; but she did not remember which was which: she seldom did. At all events, Avis had that one particular coloring about her (Coy decided to call it coloring), which is, in a woman, powerful above all beauty, wit, or genius,—that subtle something which we name *charm*.

Now, it was true and tender in Coy to sit thinking this about Avis. That was a wise word which said, that, when we have ceased to enjoy the superiority of another, we have ceased to love him. Hence it may be the self-defensive strategy of affection, that we feel our friend's advantage long before we allow ourselves to perceive it; nay, in proportion to the depth of our feeling under it; are we not apt to have a frost-bite of the intellect, which makes its distinct acknowledgment a matter of hard thawing? And Coy was not by any means a girl of liquid moods. She sometimes felt it proper to judge Avis very severely; else what was the use in having grown up with her?

For instance, she had reproved her for staying so much by herself since she had come home. Barbara, now, thought that affectation, it was plain to see (and affectation it would have been in Barbara), though, of course, she was too well bred to say so. Coy knew better than that. It was only morbidness. Coy had the glibness of most unaccentuated natures in the use of this convenient word, which is without a rival in its adaptability to cover all forms of character differing from one's own.

There had been a ripple of surprise when Avis came into the club that night. The club met at Chatty Hogarth's. Chatty was the president's daughter, and an invalid. Avis did not like to refuse poor Chatty. It was the first time that Miss Dobell had appeared in Harmouth society since her return from Florence.

At this rate, it was plain that Miss Cora Bishop's Spenserian culture would be very deficient. Coy, with a pretty change of mental attitude, which had a pretty bodily expression down to the very tips of her fingers, tightening, like growing shells, about the covers of her book, brought her intellect to bear severely upon the busines of the evening.

> "But fly, ah! fly far hence away, for feare
> Lest to you hap that happened to me heare."[2]

A low and singularly musical voice was pronouncing these words as Coy looked up; not the catarrhal theologue, surely? He had finished his contribution to the evening's entertainment, thank the Muses! and Mr. Ostrander was reading,—Philip Ostrander, the new tutor. There was always a new tutor to be considered in Harmouth University: he had not always, however, a musical voice.

"And to this wretched lady, my deare love;
O too deare love,—love bought with death too deare!"

Clearly Mr. Ostrander was an effective reader; "a cultivated reader," Coy said. Miss Dobell, from her corner opposite the gentleman, sitting a little in the shadow, and giving equable and earnest attention to the performance of each member of the Poetry Club, in turn, said only, "an effective reader," but hesitated at the word, and listened thoughtfully.

"With sudden feare her pitcher downe she threw,
And fled away,"

sang on the reader.

"Full fast she fled, ne ever lookt behynd,
As if her life upon the wager lay."

Musical was the word assuredly. Mr. Ostrander's voice held rather melody than harmony, but music, beyond a question. There was a modesty and simplicity about its accent not common to young men in those stages of growth in which Harmouth knew them; perhaps a little uncommon in any young man. It suffused a penetrative sense of pleasure, of unexplained organic joy, like that of Nature in her simpler moods: it had an effect not unlike that of an unseen brook or a flying bird. Though the brook chanted, it ran; though the bird sang, it flew; its sweetness was measured by its evanescence. People often noted Mr. Ostrander's voice. Young ladies had been heard to declare that it was "like Mozart."

Avis Dobell, sitting in the shadowed corner of the president's parlor that night, had happened to place herself against some very heavy drapery, which clasped two warm arms of intense color across the chill of a bay-window. The color was that called variously and lawlessly by upholsterers cranberry, garnet, or ponso; known to artists as carmine. The material held a satin thread, which lent to the curtains the lustre of jewels in a dark setting, or of water under a flaming sky. In the gaslight and firelight of the room, the insensate piece of cloth took on a strange and vivid life, and seemed to throb as if it held some inarticulate passion, like that of a subject soul.

Coy or Barbara would have known better than to have ventured their complexions against this trying background. Avis went to it as straight as a bird to a lighthouse on a dark night. She would have beaten herself against that color, like those very birds against the glowing glass, and been happy, even if she had beaten her soul out with it as they did.

She had a fierce kinship in her for that color, of which she seldom spoke. She did not expect it to be understood; she did not care that it should be; perhaps she imperfectly understood it herself: she only knew that it made her happy to be near it. To-night, for instance, though she had felt this Poetry Club rather a bore, a positive wave of pleasure flowed to her from the sight and contact of that curtain, which she felt in every sense of soul and body.

Avis was affected by color as the more sensitive musical temperament is by sound. Color divorced from form, crude and clear, was to her what the musical notation is to the composer, who, without striking a note, reads the score by the hour as other men read printed text.

Besides, she knew perfectly well that the curtain became her.

Against this background of the passion of carmine, Avis, sitting silently the evening through, had a solitary look. There was a certain aloofness in her very beauty, if one chose to call by the name of beauty the kindling of her face: it was somehow unlike that of other handsome women. It cannot be said that she was quite without consciousness of it; no woman could have been: it might be rather that she made no effort to appear unconscious of it. She had nothing of that wide-eyed, infantile look of distraction, which, in a grown woman, indicates the very quintessence of egoism.

She carried about her an indefinable air of having been used to the love, or admiration probably, of men as well as women, which the most exquisitely modest women will sometimes wear, and which is as unmistakable as it is alluring to the eye. Her dress, made in the fashion of the time, fitting closely, and without trimming, was of a negative tint, something toning upon black, else she should not, and so would not, have sat by the carmine curtain. She wore, as all well-dressed women wore at that time, a very full white undersleeve, which completely concealed the outline of the arm. Over her shoulders a shawl of Fayal lace, white, and very delicate, hung like a thistle-down. She had a fresh but fine and restless color, and brown, abundant hair. She had a generous mouth and a delicate ear. Her profile, when the carmine curtain took it, had the harmony of a strong antique.

"Avis," said Mrs. Hogarth, when Mr. Ostrander had finished his canto, and the little party of young people had fallen into that general discussion of the topic of the evening's study, which was usual in Harmouth "Clubs,"—"Avis, my dear, are we to hear nothing from you to-night?"

"Oh, yes, Avis!" urged Chatty.

"You must excuse me," pleaded Avis in a voice more timid than one would have looked to hear from a young lady of so much presence. She spoke faintly, like a shrinking child: indeed it made her feel like one, coming, from the strange changes of her life, suddenly back here among her old playfellows; being called out by Mrs. Hogarth so, as if she were to recite a lesson. Mrs. Hogarth was one of those people who always made her feel as if she were a little girl, always would: it would not matter to Mrs. Hogarth if she had painted the Sistine Mary.

There were others, however, in the Spenser Club, strangers, across whom stirred a visible wave of interest when Avis, speaking for the first time, drew all the eyes in the room towards the carmine curtain. Coy remarked it, and felt proud of her; for Avis had got into the newspapers. It was seldom that a Harmouth woman got into the papers. It was only men—at Harmouth: indeed, the University existed, she supposed, for the glorification of men. This was all right and proper. Coy had never been conscious of any depressing aspirations towards the college diploma; but she took an aromatic enjoyment, after all, in the fact that one of the professor's daughters had adopted "a career." She was glad it was precisely Avis, and not Barbara, or some of the other girls, who had painted a good picture, and sold it in London. She enjoyed having it thoroughly understood in Harmouth that people who knew about such things (Coy was not quite sure who; but that did not matter) had predicted a "brilliant future" for the modest young lady who made that picture.

"May I not be pardoned," repeated Avis, "if I do not bring my share of the work to-night? I have been busy in other ways so long, it is not possible that I could find any thing to say worth your hearing, on a subject which the rest of you have been studying all winter."

"Avis!" said Coy suddenly from across the room, "if I had done a real mean thing, should you want to know it?"

"No," said Avis: "if anybody I cared for *could* be mean, I should rather never know it." She spoke in the graceful surface-tone through which the serious instinct of an earnest nature can no more help penetrating than the sun can help shining through ornamented glass.

"You have turned over two leaves, Mr. Ostrander," said Barbara Allen, who was looking up footnotes with him. "And do you incline to Upton's conjecture? It seems to me, if we grant the Henry VIII. theory, then Una"—

"It's about Una that I've been mean," said Coy rather loudly.

"Avis, I brought your sketch of Una that you gave me. I know you'll let me show it. You never were a bit of a shirk, now, Avis; and this is just your fair contribution to a Spenser evening. Please, Avis?"

Avis did not please, that was plain; but she consented without any fuss; and the young people gathered about Miss Bishop to see the sketch.

It was a sketch in charcoal, strongly but not roughly laid in, and preserved by a shellac, which lent a soft color, like that of a very old print, to the paper. It bore marks of the artist's peculiar style; for it was already recognized in art-circles that Miss Dobell had "a style."

The sketch was expressive of the lines:—

"Ere long he came where Una traveild slow,
And that champion wayting her besyde.
. . By his like-seeming shield her knight by name
Shee weend it was, and towards him gan ride:
Approaching nigh, she wist it was the same;
And with faire fearefull humblesse towards him shee came."

Miss Dobell's Una was a spirited figure; did not ride the lion like a donkey, neither did she pat him like a dog, in the approved manner: he followed her in a shadow almost as heavy as that which hides the Jupiter in Correggio's Io,[3]—dark, vague, and inscrutable as fate. She had been walking swiftly: the lethargy of collapse from motion had settled on every limb. Arrested in the full light, the woman curved one fine hand inward, like a shell, as if to warn the creature back. It was impossible to look upon this woman, and not say, "She sees the man she loves." Her eyes leaped to him; her lips leaned to him; her whole being gravitated to him.

"Pretty girl," said John Rose, who dared say any thing to anybody; and, besides, he used to know Avis in college,—"very pretty girl; but how she holds her head! Put her into a Harmouth Senior party now, she'd freeze a fellow into a sherbet."

"Was Una so easily won, my dear?" asked Mrs. Hogarth, with a little matronly smile.

"Easily won!" A voice behind the young artist repeated these words in a protesting whisper; then, gathering distinctness, said,—

"My dear Mrs. Hogarth, do you not see? Every nerve and muscle is tense for flight. She will turn and run before that clumsy knight gets up to her—if she can."

Avis, turning with a grateful look to see who had interpreted her picture, felt Coy's hand laid upon her arm.

"Avis, may I present Mr. Ostrander?"

Avis very ceremoniously bowed. As she did so, there flitted across her eyes, like the shadow of an unseen object, an expression which Coy found it so difficult to understand, that she even made up her mind to ask her afterwards if she had objected to the introduction.

But probably Avis had met far more interesting men in Florence, where it was understood that she had been much sought.

"May I?" urged Ostrander with hesitancy, putting out his hand for the sketch. On the back of it was written, with a brush dipped in a crimson water-color, these words,—

> "She speakes no more
> Of past: true is that true love hath no power
> To looken backe; his eie be fixt before."

"I am glad not to have blundered," he said simply in handing the picture back.

The weight of talk had by this time slipped from the picture, and he and the two young ladies stood slightly apart.

"But, after all, you see," said the young man musingly, "your Truth is subject to Love, omnipotently subject."

"I am not responsible for Spenser's theology," said Avis, laughing evasively; "and an artist has such gloriously lawless moods! Why should I trouble myself to think about Una every day? I had a pretty girl to draw: so I drew her. But I put the lion in, so people shouldn't make a mistake. 'It is better to be dumb than to be misunderstood.'"

"Who said that?" asked Ostrander, with a fine smile. But he was conscious of feeling some curiosity over this superficial little speech of Miss Dobell's. There was not a superficial stroke in the picture,—nor in the speaker, to his mind.

"How do you know that *I* did not say it?" returned the young lady.

"Mr. Ostrander," said Coy, "Miss Hogarth wants you to bring Miss Dobell the oysters. Do it gracefully. She'll sketch you while you are gone!"

When Ostrander returned, Coy had been called away, and Avis was alone. As he handed her plate, their eyes met in a long, full, grave look. Avis's eyes were neither brown nor black, yet they were very dark. One sometimes sees in the lining of waves on which the full sun shines, and in which the bright weeds are thick, a color that resembles them.

Philip Ostrander said,—

"I have seen you before."

Avis hesitated: she hesitated perceptibly before she answered.

"Yes."

"Had you forgotten it?"

Now Ostrander spoke with hesitation: he felt a little alarmed at his own intrepidity. This young lady in the Fayal shawl, with the slightly disturbed carriage to her head, had suddenly acquired throughout her face and figure a beautiful protest, which he felt it would be the easiest thing in the world to mistake.

Should he go on, or stop exactly where he was? After a moment's silence, he said, with an accent of renewed decision,—

"*Had* you forgotten it?"

Avis lifted her eyelids very slowly, and in her honest, even voice, said,—

"No."

❧ CHAPTER II

*"We rejoice in hunting Truth in
company as in hunting game."*
—Themistius[1]

*"For mervaille of this knight
him to behold,
Full besily they waiten, young
and old."*
—Chaucer[2]

Coy and John Rose walked home
together in the dear, old, foolish country-fashion, which Harmouth was too full of young people to outgrow.

It was a night of many stars. The two, as they stepped out into
the April weather, in deference to the constitution of the Spenser
Club, at the stroke of half-past ten, had involuntarily stood for a
moment with uplifted faces in the thin, half-frozen snow. Great
pulses of light beat before the eyes, where stars that our Northern
atmospheres know only in their happiest moods, were aflame that
night; and arteries of fire ran along wastes of space, quivering as
they ran: the very ether in which they hung seemed to be crossed
with fine lines, shadow drawn on shadow, like the nerves of a mute
and infinite organism, whose heart only—beating somewhere, im-
passioned, imprisoned—was hidden from the sight.

But Coy and John Rose did not talk about the stars: it was not
their way. The young man, if he had said any thing, would have
wrenched a pun out of them perhaps, or propounded a conundrum,
for no better reason than that the sight of them had moved him.
And the first thing that Coy said was,—

"Avis wishes us all in Guinea."

"But why?"

"She hasn't seen so much astronomy since she was in Italy. She
wants to be by herself, and reduce it to Prussian blue and Naples
yellow. I think it must be very uncomfortable to be an artist. You're
always looking at Nature with a professional squint: you can't put
yourself on any sort of terms with her, I should say, more than a
photographer can with a complexion, or a dentist with front-teeth."

It was true enough, that Avis, coming out of the close room into
the freshening April night, had thrilled beneath the sudden throbbing of the stars, with an impulse which those only know whose
life in its more poetic stages has been passed under the ardors of a

Southern sky. Some slight disturbing element which had entered into the evening for her, served only to make the coolness and calm and vastness more marked and reposeful. She had drawn a deep breath as one does in re-adjusting one's self to a momentarily suspended action. She would have liked Mr. Ostrander better if he had not exclaimed, "Almost Florence!" as he turned to take Barbara home. She was glad it was nobody but Barbara's brother, poor fellow! who was to walk with her, and that he did not expect her to talk about the stars, and that Coy and John Rose seemed so very comfortable together just in front of them. Her mind was pre-occupied in ways to which the little inner life of a Harmouth reading-club was as foreign as—ah, well!—as foreign as the car-mine curtain to the cold north star. She felt no less annoyed than perplexed by the slight pressure of circumstances which seemed to have drawn her to-night into the exact atmosphere of that half-expressed life. She longed for the poise which solitude only can give, and half wished that she had not invited Coy to spend the night with her, and see the Venetian views to-morrow.

Her fancy about the curtain and the light-house came before her with a strange, pictorial vividness, as she walked on, talking common-place to Barbara's brother.

Out beyond the little sheltered town the great sea swept. She could hear the far beating of the tide upon the receptive April air. While the currents of these delicate human lives swept softly on in their elected channels, long waves thundered against the Harbor Light. Miles away through the night, some homeless bird took wing for the burning bosom of the reflector, and straight, straight— led as unerringly as instinct leads, as tenderly as love constrains, as brutally as Nature cheats, with a glad fluttering at the delicate throat, with a trustful quiver of the flashing wings, like the bend- ing of a harebell, like the breath of an arrow—came swaying; was tossed, was torn, and fell.

She had been out when she was a child, after many a storm, and seen them dead there by hundreds on the rock. The light-keeper gathered them up into a bushel-basket once, for the scientific professor.

They had strewn the shores of her young thought with untold and ungathered suffering,—those birds. No one thing had been more responsible for the attack of universal scepticism which she had successfully weathered at eighteen, in common with the ex-isting senior class of college-boys in her father's lecture-room.

Sometimes in Florence, on a radiant night, when across the roofs, against the setting sun, the sparrows stood twittering in Ital-ian (no New-England sparrow could have rehearsed in that accent if his engagement for the season had depended on it), and the voices of children, whose parents' eyes had never questioned Fate, poured their pliant chirrup into the Arno's monotone beyond the studio window,—then suddenly, like a drop of sleet upon a flower, would fall a vision of the Harbor Light at home, and towards it, through the freezing night, a bird fly to its death.

She had not thought about the light before, since she had come home.

But Coy and John Rose were walking together beneath the April stars. They did not talk of the Spenserian metres, nor the Utopian theory. They discussed the oysters and the last engagement, the coming concert and the impending battle, the hazing scrape, and the Mission Sunday school.

Then they talked a little about Barbara, and a little of the new tutor, and then about Miss Dobell, and then a little about art and life, and earnestness, and about a man's understanding himself, and about the beauty of high purposes, and the preciousness of sympathy, and the uncertainty of the future, and many other original and impressive themes. And the young man made no conundrums now, and grew so grave, that Coy took fright, and asked him, Was he going on a mission? But he answered, gravely still, Did she think him fit? To which she told him promptly, No; that he would set the cannibals to making bad puns before a week was out; and then he said he was afraid he should, and that he must be content with some obscure position among educated Americans who read the charades in the religious weeklies Sunday mornings. And by that time they were at the gate of Professor Dobell's old-fashioned silent house, and stopped to wait for Avis.

"Poor Mr. Allen!" said Coy, turning the curve of her cheek in the starlight.

"I don't know about that," said the young minister perversely.

"But Avis will never, never"—

"I wouldn't grant that any woman I cared for would never, never, as long as she allowed me upon terms of friendship at all," persisted the young man.

"But," said Coy hurriedly, "Avis is not like other women. She never was."

"Then you admit"—began John Rose.

"I admit that I'm cold, and here she is," shivered Coy. Coy was half frightened. If Mr. Rose had said any more about sympathy and friendship just then, she would have gone into the house without waiting for Avis. The color had heightened in her young face. Her foot tapped the snow sharply in her impatience for Avis to come up. It seemed to her as if she and John Rose, standing there in the professor's snowy, shaded yard, had been left alone, the only two people on the breathing earth.

"I never saw a woman have a latch-key before," said Coy, as the two girls, having dismissed their escorts, lest so many voices should disturb the professor, stood together upon the door-step.

"Father is in the study," said Avis; "and I begged aunt Chloe to go to bed; and the girls are tired, poor things! Why shouldn't a woman have a latch-key?"

This was one of those propositions of which the burden of proof certainly lies with the negative; and Coy replied only by an amused smile as they passed into the large and silent house. It was lighted only in the halls; for aunt Chloe was of an economical, old-fashioned temper, and thought it rather snobbish to waste good kerosene, when there was not brandy enough for the soldiers in the hospitals. Aunt Chloe had attacks of benevolent parsimony very peculiar to herself. When these overtook her, she resolutely denied herself her cup of Oolong tea at night for months at a time, and relinquished butter on her buckwheats of a morning. It was never quite clear to the rest of the family exactly how the United-States army was the better for that tea or butter.

"But aunt Chloe has that sense of superior personal sacrifice, which is the most useful element in our charities, beyond doubt," laughed Avis, as she and Coy went directly to her own room, treading softly past the study-door.

It was abundantly light and warm in Avis's room. The fire was in the grate; the curtains were drawn; Avis's easy-chair and slippers were before the hearth. It was a plain, rather a grave place, that little bedroom; would have been prim with Avis out of it; such a room one would look for in a house of which Professor Dobell's sister had been the mistress for eighteen years. Aunt Chloe believed in good blankets and towels, and a plenty of them; and, when you bought a piece of furniture, buy "the real" always; but, as long as there were home missionary boxes[3] to be made up spring and fall, she could not see that the New Testament recommended a fashion in carpets, or that St. Paul could possibly have been sensitive to any lack of harmony in upholstery or mantel ornaments. There was one fine bit of marble,—the Melian Venus.[4] This, with the few foreign trinkets and engravings which Avis had scattered about the room, seemed to be there only by tolerance, till she herself came into it. Then a fair congruousness settled upon the air. Every thread of color left in the old rug, and antiquated chintz, and faint wall-paper, seemed to shake itself, and begin to shine. The firelight leaped to her feet like a lover. All the room budded and opened like a flower about her, as the two girls threw themselves in lithe attitudes upon the old rug to "toast their feet" like children at the fire.

I find that I am talking rather lawlessly about these "girls." Avis

Dobell was a woman of twenty-six, and Coy not many years the younger. But they were girls still to each other by that pretty trick of speech and fancy common in the comradeship of all women before marriage. Sometimes we find it in our way to smile at this illusion; but, like all illusions, its pathetic side is its deepest and its truest one. Within the soul of every unwon woman abides eternal youth. Though the snow be on her hair before the King may claim her, yet shall he not find violets and the birds of spring, when at last, at last, his coming feet shine beautiful upon the mountains of her ungarnered heart?

It was quite the proper thing in Harmouth, as I have intimated, for young ladies to be somewhat seriously intelligent; and so when Avis had got her long hair down over her white merino wrapper, and Coy, with a gay silk shoulder-robe thrown across her night-dress, was crimping her short front-locks before the deepening fire, she began,—

"What do you think about the Club, Avis?"

"I thought you called it a Chaucer Club," said Avis.

"Oh! so it is," said Coy. "We've been the whole mortal winter poking over Chaucer. We only got into Spenser last week. For my part, I hate him."

"Which?"

"Why, Chaucer! I never did like old-fashioned poetry, and I never shall. I'm a terrible modern, Avis. I *like* Tennyson and Whittier and Longfellow, and the Brownings, and so on. And that Scotch-woman, Jean Ingelow,[5] cultivates *me* more than two Spensers. I've just had to set to on the old fellow like a Latin prose-lesson all winter. We've really worked very hard," said Coy, with a sense of high literary virtue. "I never worked so hard in a club in my life. That is Mr. Ostrander's doing. They say he's very talented. But, then, talented tutors are so common in Harmouth! I wonder we don't hear more of them afterwards, don't you?"

Coy wound her small fingers in and out of her crimping-pins with a sinuous motion; her two lifted bare arms enclosing a face as innocent of sarcasm as a mocking-bird's. Coy was one of the immortal few who can look pretty in their crimping-pins.

"I suppose you've gone on having clubs," mused Avis, leaning her head back against the seat of the easy-chair, and clasping both arms above it, "every winter, just as we did when we were girls."

"Just the same," said Coy, "as we did when you were at home six years ago. You know how it is with people: some take to zoölogy, and some take to religion. That's the way it is with places. It may be the Lancers; and it may be prayer-meetings. Once I went to see my grandmother in the country, and everybody had a candy-pull: there were twenty-five candy-pulls and taffy-bakes in that town that winter. John Rose says, in the Connecticut Valley, where he came from, it was missionary barrels; and I heard of a place where it was cold coffee. In Harmouth, it's improving your mind. It comes hard on me," said Coy plaintively. "It comes rather hard on me. Generally I have an intellectual conviction that I ought to improve my mind. But nothing comes of it, you know, till there's a club. Then I groan; but I go in for it hardest of them all. Improving your mind is as bad as old poetry. I don't *take* to it," said Coy mournfully. "I ought never to have been born in Harmouth. If I'd been just a downright society girl now, I could have been a dunce, and nobody ever have known the difference: I know I could. But the amount I've read this last four years! It positively makes my head swim to think of the titles of the books. And, strictly speaking, I'm not in the Faculty either, you know, Avis; for father resigned when I was— Why, it was the year I was going on with Jim Snowe: I couldn't have been fourteen. I wish, when he took to patenting his discoveries, he had taken me with him. I *think* I could have patented a crimper that would make a simpler system of punctuation in your finger than this."

"And so," added Coy, turning one bare foot slowly around from side to side, before the deep-red fire, as if she were baking an exquisite bit of porcelain, "and so we run to reading-clubs; and we all go fierce winter after winter to see who'll get the 'severest.' There's a set outside of the Faculty that descend to charades and music and inconceivably low intellectual depths; and some of our girls sneak off, and get in there once in a while, like the little girl that wanted to go from heaven to hell to play Saturday afternoons, just as you and I used to do, Avis, when we dared. But I find I've got too old for that," said Coy sadly. "When you're fairly past the college-boys, and as far along as the law-students"—

"Or the theologues?" interposed Avis.

"Yes, or the theologues, or even the medical department; then there positively *is* nothing for it but to improve your mind."

Coy pathetically turned the other foot to the fire, and watched it with an attentive air, as if there were danger of its being overdone.

"And so we have the clubs. Sometimes it's old poets served hot, and sometimes it's plain history cut cold, and it may be a hash of the fine arts, or even a *ragout* of well-spiced science. One winter it was political economy. I had my first gray hairs that winter. But the season we took the positive philosophy, they thought I was going into a decline. And we all fight, to begin with, in the politest possible way, every year, as to who shall be in, and who sha'n't, and what we shall be allowed to have for supper. And the wrong people are always let in, and the right ones are always left out; and we have the usual number of flirtations, and the usual set of jokes; and we get off the old one about Barbara Allen's name regularly, for each new club. And there are about so many engagements, and the usual number of offers; and so it goes. I think I must be growing old. I only had two last winter." Coy drew both feet back from the ardor of the fire, and folded them in the plaid-silk robe. There was a silence, which she broke by saying,—

"Mr. Ostrander is tutor in Latin."

"Is John Rose going to settle over the Central Church?" asked Avis.

"Probably. Father says he will have the call."

"It seems unspeakably funny to me to see John turn into a minister," said Avis. "He was such a little scapegrace in college! I remember his telling me he should like to preach; but it would never do, he was too fond of slang; should say, 'Wot larks, my brethren!' before the sermon was over."

"Oh, yes! Well, he's got past that," said Coy. "He's very good, I think: he's a great deal better than I am. *I'm* not good at all. But I think myself he'll make a peculiar minister, he is so much like other men. Did you know there was talk of making a professor of Mr. Ostrander?—professor of geology."

"But I thought he was teaching Latin," said Avis.

"So he is; but there's no vacancy in Latin, and he is said to have a very versatile mind. He was once educated in medicine, besides. Father says he has a very broad grasp."

"I should think so," said Avis, with an inscrutable look. "How old, pray, is this Mr. Ostrander?"

"Oh, he's very old!" said Coy: "he's almost thirty. He teaches German too," she added persuasively, after a silence. "He has a class of young ladies. Barbara is in it, and I'm going to join when I get round to it. I should think you would like to go. What pretty arms you have, Avis!"

Avis had risen from the old rug, untwining her arms from the locked position above her head, which they had steadily retained while Coy was talking. The sleeves of the white wrapper fell away in the abrupt motion.

"They're not fat, like mine," said Coy, with a critical air. "Did anybody ever tell you they were like the arms of Mme. Recamier, in David's picture?"[6]

"Yes," said Avis: "I have been told so. Let us go to sleep now, Coy."

Avis was a light sleeper, and she lay long awake that night, watching the glow within the grate, and listening to the beat of the surf upon the shore, almost a mile beyond her father's house. She lay, rather she sat, perfectly still, bolstered against aunt Chloe's generous pillows, with one hand thrust through her long hair, and her strong young eyes fixed undazzled upon the white-heat of the coals, till it had died to a delicate blush of color, until the blue ashes had crept like the hue of death upon a human cheek across it. The window towards the sea was open, and the rhythm of the tide beat a strange duet with Coy's gentle, happy breathing on the pillow at her side. It seemed to her a great song without words, full of uncaptured meanings, deep with unuttered impulse. She would have liked to fit expression to it; but Avis never wrote "poetry," never had, even when she was in her teens. That was not the baptism with which she was baptized. Certain words, as sleep overtook her, adjusted themselves in a disjointed fashion to her thoughts; but when, starting, she roused and wakened, staring about the darkening room, from which even the starlight was now gone, she found that they were only these:—

> "Full fast shee fled, ne ever lookd behynde,
> As if her life upon the wager lay."

CHAPTER III

*"By nature a philosopher, spirited,
swift, and strong."*
—Plato

*"Young, and a woman; 'tis thus
she was mine."*
—Goethe's *Pandora*

When Hegel Dobell, Professor
of Ethics and Intellectual Philosophy, thirty-five years old, and a
bachelor, brought home one day to the old-fashioned house set
apart for the incumbents in his department a bride of nineteen
New-York summers, all Harmouth shook its highly intellectual
head.

In the nature of things, it was argued, a man of years and reputation, a man pre-eminently a scholar as well as a student, a man
capable of writing the celebrated brochure, "Was Fichte a Mystic?"
to say nothing of the correspondence with the Berlin professor
whose name Harmouth never could remember, on the subject Harmouth always found it difficult to recall; even throwing out of
the question the pamphlet on the "Identity of Identity and Non-
Identity," which that other celebrated German (name also gone for
the moment) was understood to have discussed at one of his Sunday dinners, before his mind gave way,—such a man, it was urged,
must find a slender stock of conjugal promise in the choice of a
society girl known to have been gay, and understood to be peculiar.
Any man, in fact, filling the metaphysical chair in Harmouth University, must discover that he had mistaken the premises of his syllogism in marrying a spoiled child, whose parents had experienced
difficulty even in restraining her within polite circles at all.

This pretty young thing, who peeped shyly as an anemone out of
her stylish hat at the congregation in the college chapel, looked
demure enough, and delicate, as if a waft of wind or sun would wilt
her. Yet it was distinctly understood, below the bated breath of
Harmouth, that the great professor had won this little lady but just
in time to prevent her from running away to go upon the stage.

Perhaps, indeed, it was a trifle gossipy to call it "running away;"
and Harmouth never gossiped. Miss Mercy had suggested as much
as this, and the phrase was decorously amended. Miss Mercy was a

mild and matronly power in Harmouth always, even before her marriage. In fact, Harmouth had privately selected *her* as the proper Mrs. Dobell long before the New-York girl was met or thought of. Was she not a lady of unexceptionable antecedents, whose family had been "professional" for as many generations as a good American could conscientiously count at all? Could it be denied that she was healthy, handsome, and thirty-one? Could one fail to recall her marked (and lucrative) success as principal of the Harmouth Female Seminary? and if you chose to consider her known interest in the university scientific endowments?—And where else *was* there a woman who had read the professor's lectures on Spinoza through?

It was not for a long while, indeed, not until Miss Mercy had become the second Mrs. Hogarth, and the president's wife had avenged the spinster, that Harmouth was comforted for this highly-educated lady.

But perhaps she was right. The little bride had not exactly run away. Yet there was certainly a freak for the stage, intercepted somewhere. And clearly she was a restless, glittering, inefficient thing, like a humming-bird turned radical. Would the great professor bend his well-salaried powers happily now to investigating the varieties of honey which his quiet garden-roses might have and hold for a petulant beak?

At all events, it was as clear as the Law of Excluded Middle, that the great professor—like any small man who delays marriage till he has reached the age when his neighbors should choose for him—had made a serious blunder.

The professor, however, like every other genius, had a touch of obstinacy about him, and persistently delayed, as time ran metaphysically on, to discover that he had blundered at all, was an inexcusably tedious while in beginning to be disappointed in his marriage-venture, and ended by flatly refusing altogether to be miserable. This was an unscientific evolution from precedent, which tried Harmouth to the soul's depths. We can forgive our friend much. All true allegiance deepens in geometrical proportion to his deserved misfortune, and a crime can only test the temper of sound loyalty; but who can pardon him for not being unhappy when we have foretold him that he would be?

If the professor's little wife were a humming-bird, she was a very tender and true one: she loved the great hand that had lured her from the fields on which the wild dew lay, and sipped his grave domestic honey with happy, upturned look.

Once in a while, when the professor, strolling about the house in the play-hour which rigorously followed meals, saw through the

window Mrs. Hogarth walking intelligently and plumply by upon
the president's arm, a fine scintillant gleam of fun twinkled in
his deep-set eyes. He said nothing,—he never said any thing of
any matter which kindled that rare spark under the cavern of his
brows,—but he strode across the room to where his wife was sitting, pulled his nervous hand out of his pocket, and bending his
gaunt, awkward shoulders, gently laid a finger under her chin, and
turned her young face up to his; and then she said,—

"Do you want any thing, Professor?"

And then he said,—

"Only to see if you look happy and well, my dear."

Perhaps after that they looked into one another's eyes a moment
with something of the gravity which is inseparable from all deep
happiness, before she stirred, and put up both lithe arms to be
caught, to be clasped, to be devoured against his heart.

For it was the old imperious story that we know so well,—this
story of the scholar and the woman: who can explain the witchery
by which it pulls at the hearts-strings of us all? As alive as Faust,[1]
as old as Abelard,[2] as tender as Petrarch,[3] as eternal as Dante,[4] it
keeps pace with our calmer passions and our serener time.

In the sweep of pre-eminently well-regulated affections that ed-
died through the real life of that decorous university town, there
was probably none more constraining, there certainly was none
more controlling, than the love which had settled upon the quiet
home where the rebellious little society girl had passed her honeymoon, and begun to extract from joy the elements of rest.

It was the same old intense, delirious story,—the overwrought
mind captured by the unused heart, the monarch will bent to the
subject emotion, the great purpose gone suppliant to the great passion,—a wise man become as a fool for a pair of velvet arms; and
the author of the Identity of Identity and Non-Identity was the
elected priest or victim of the ancient and honorable experience.

That was as one chose to look at it. Harmouth might call him a
victim; but, in the glamour of his own vision, he was the awed
priest chosen for an imposing and sacred service.

No college-boy in his class-room, struggling with his first fancy,
struck wilder currents than this grave man in his late, impetuous
love. There was no girl, dreaming with shy eyes in the twilight before a folded and glorified ideal, who had a simpler or more romantic faith in it than the metaphysician held in his. In his pure and
studious life Hegel Dobell had been blessed above his own deem-
ing or dreaming in this,—that he had never spent his nature upon
unworthy, or even mixed or insufficient feeling. The great passion
of his life was one with its great love. The forces of both overtook

him with the swiftness of a freshet. He yielded to the torrent with the childlike and ecstatic surprise that he would have felt at the discovery of a new axiom.

It was Eden in the old-fashioned house; and the tremulous amazement of the first man and the first woman filled it. To them was given dominion over a world as unreal to souls incapable of sublimation by a great love, as the Paradise of Milton,[5] or the Palace of Kubla Khan.[6]

They were not of dull fancy, after all, who nicknamed the professor's wife. There was something bird-like in her; in her buoyant attitudes, in a way she had of turning her head sidewise to look at her husband as she perched upon the arm of his chair, in the cooing tones of her clear but uninsistent voice, and especially in a certain reserve that was very marked in her.[7]

We are apt to think of a bird as rather an open-hearted, impetuous creature, telling all she knows, pouring out her private affairs to the whole world's hearing by simple force of her nature. In fact, perhaps no creature is more capable of concealment. Naturalists load us with stories of her little stratagems. We have but to look intently in her eye to be made conscious that she has her mental reservations about many matters; in particular, opinions about ourselves, which it is not worth while to explain.

The robin at your door on a June morning seems to be expressing himself with lavish confidence; but, to a patient listener, his song has something of the exuberant frankness which is the most impenetrable disguise in the world. The sparrow on her nest under your terrace broods meekly; but the centuries have not wrung from one such pretty prisoner a breath of longing for the freedom of the summer-day. Do her delicate, cramped muscles ache for flight? her fleet, unused wings tremble against the long roots of the overhanging grass? She turns her soft eye upon you with a fine, far sarcasm. You may find out if you can.

It was in memory, perhaps, of some of the sweet nonsense of her honeymoon, that Mrs. Dobell had selected for her little daughter the name of Avis.

"Mamma," said the child one day, not coming to her mother's knee, but sitting in the sunlight at some distance from her on the floor, "what shall I be?"

"What shall you *be*, Avis?"

"Drayton Allen is going to keep a dog-store; and Ben Hogarth is going to be president of some college. What shall *I* be?"

"What will Coy be, my dear, and Barbara?"

"Coy is going to be a lady, she says, mamma."

"Very well," said mamma.

"And Barbara is going to get married."

Mamma made no reply.

"I think I'd rather keep dogs," said Avis gravely, after a silence. After some moments, receiving still no answer, the child rose to her feet, pushing back her thick hair from her eyes, standing in the full sun.

"Mamma, did you run away?"

"Did I *what*?"

"Barbara says you ran away. She says you ran away in a stage."

"Barbara told you a very wrong story, my child. Come here."

Avis threw down her playthings, and went slowly to her mother's knee. The mother put her arm expressively about the child; but still she did not speak.

"Mamma," began the little girl again, "I have never seen anybody in a theatre."

"Some day you shall, when it is right and best."

"Mamma," slowly after a pause, "did *you* ever want to keep dogs?"

"Not exactly, Avis."

"I thought not. You know you didn't like that dog I had who drowned himself. Now, what I'd like to know is this: if you wanted to keep theatres, why didn't you?"

Mrs. Dobell, with some signs of agitation, laid aside her sewing, and drew her little daughter upon her lap. She looked into Avis's eyes for a long moment, with that instinctive assurance of sympathy and impulse of confidence, which, from the hour when the baby's face is first upturned to hers, a mother feels at times in the presence of a woman-child.

"Avis," she said gravely, "I married your papa: that is why I never acted in the theatre."

"Oh, yes! Well, I didn't know. Did you never want to run away after you had married papa? Did you never care about the theatre again? Mamma, what is the matter? Are you cold? I don't want to go away and play. I haven't talked enough. I had a great many questions to ask you. I like you better than I do Barbara's mother. You're so much prettier, mamma."

But long after that, after her pretty mother had become a thin, sweet vision, like a fading sketch to the young girl's heart, she recalled with incisive distinctness the way in which she had been put down from her mother's knee that morning, then impulsively recalled, snatched, kissed, and cried over with a gush of incoherent words and scalding tears. She never saw her mother cry before or after that. But all that she could understand of what she said was,—

"Oh, my little woman! Mother's little woman, little woman!"

This glimpse into her mother's heart, the child, held by some blind and delicate sense of honor, never shared with any other human eyes. When she was herself a woman grown, and not till then, she asked her father once, if he supposed her mother to have possessed genuine dramatic talent.

"Unquestionably," said the professor, lifting his head. "My wife was not like most women, given to magnifying every little aesthetic taste into an unappreciated genius. She had, beyond doubt, the histrionic gift. Under proper conditions she might have become famous."

"Why, then, should she never have cultivated such a gift?" ventured Avis.

"Because," said the man simply, "she married me."

"But do you not suppose," persisted Avis, "that in all those years, shut up in this quiet house, she ever knew a restless longing in that—in those—in such directions?"

Avis faltered beneath the old man's sharp and sudden look, bent upon her in a kind of deep, indignant pity.

"Your mother was my wife," he said superbly; "and my wife loved me."

One other morning spent in the sunlight with her mother became pictorial in Avis's memory,—one other only; and whether the first threw the more powerful focus upon the last, or the last against the first, it were difficult to say. Avis was nine years old that morning. It was winter; and her father waked her in the freezing dawn, while as yet only a single feather of gold flecked the east, where snow-clouds were piling high.

Her mother had been ailing, ill: none knew exactly why. It was quite certain that she had no disease; only the waxing and waning and wasting of a fine, feverish excitement, for which there seemed to be neither cause nor remedy.

Last night they told her she was better.

They had called her now in hot haste. Swift feet passed to and fro across the halls; and voices broke and whispered at the doors.

The child, in her little night-gown, pattered across the entry, shivering with cold; but, when her mother asked her why she cried, she said papa had hurt her hand when he took hold to lead her in.

The light had broadened when she climbed upon the high, old-fashioned bed, and pulled aside the clothes to get in upon her mother's arm. Some one objected to this; but some one else said, "Let the child alone." The color in the east unfolded, and hung against the windows like a wing, she thought, as she lay down, and curled against her mother's heart.

"Mamma," began the child, "I am sorry you are sick. Sha'n't I bring you a little picture that I drew last night?"

But her mother answered only, "There, my daughter! Mother loves her; there!"

"It is a picture of a bird, mamma, with trees. I thought you'd like to see it. And—O mamma! the wing!—see the wing the sun has made upon the sky! It looks as if it meant to wrap us, wrap us, wrap us in."

As Avis, leaning on one little arm, uttered these words in the dreamy monotone of an imaginative child, the sun-burst broke full against her face.

It was then that there rang throughout the room a tense and awe-struck cry. It was not in any sense a cry of pain; rather surcharged with a burden of wondering joy. Then there followed words resonant and vibrant:—

"Under the shadow of His wing shalt *thou* abide."[8]

But when Avis, dazzled by the sunrise, turned her head, some one came from behind, and swiftly laid a gentle hand across her eyes. And though she begged them, till the day was dark again, to let her go back, just for once, and hear mamma say, "Mother loves her," none would give her leave.

The professor's sister was a homeless widow, of excellent Vermont intentions, and high ideals in cupcake. In the course of a severe and simple life she had known one passion, and one only,—the refined passion for flowers, which makes the sole poetry of many a plain, prosaic story. She accepted her calling and election conscientiously, when she was summoned to that most difficult of human tasks, the training of another woman's child. When Hegel's letter came, beseeching her to bring the presence of the "ever-womanly" into the desolated house of a heart-broken man, she prayed over it for a week. And then she spent another in wondering what it would be her clear duty to do by that child in regard to pickles and hot biscuit: her poor mother had never attended to her diet. She held it to be the first business of any woman who undertook the management of a literary family, like her brother's, to attend properly to its digestion. And then she wrote her brother simply—saying nothing of either prayers or pickles—that she would come and do the best she could. Her sole stipulation was, that she might be allowed to bring her geraniums.

Her best—to her glory be it said, from the day when she first unpacked in the professor's house the rather rural-looking trunks, to which Avis's town-bred sensibility immediately objected—aunt Chloe faithfully, evenly, and nobly did; and what could angels or mothers more?

Yet when she had been in her brother's family a year, she came to him one day with a sunken look about the temples,—a family look, indicating sternly-repressed feeling, in which she bore at times a marvellous likeness to the professor.

"Hegel," said the childless woman, with a quivering lip, "I should *like* to have your little daughter love me: but I'm afraid she never will."

"What's the matter now?" The professor brought his black brows together, looking up from the copy of Hamilton's[9] Logic, in which he was trying, with the "patience of genius," to keep six places open with five fingers.

"Nothing very new," sighed aunt Chloe. "The same old story. She had to rip her seam out in the—the undergarments, and she *would* not stir the jelly. And, when I went to ask her why she had not made her bed, I found her putting tinfoil over the medallions that you brought from Mantua; making impressions of them with her finger-nail. And the noses, Hegel! It will displease you very much to see the noses. The Laocoön is as black as the register; and the Apollo"—

The professor strode across the room, and into the parlor where Avis sat, deep in the broad cushioned window-sill, with the medallions on her lap. A vein on the child's temple began to throb as she looked up.

"Papa, I never *meant* to hurt their noses! I didn't know they were so tender,—just like sugar. I wanted to make a statue out of the tinfoil. Poor Apollo, papa! He's just a snub."

Avis brought the medallions to him with a swift, sweet gesture of appeal, which too frequently converted her clearest faults into her most irresistible claims upon one's sympathy; or, as aunt Chloe put it, "turned her from a sinner into a sufferer" at once.

"Never mind the noses!" said the professor, irritably tossing the medallions to one side. "Avis, don't you love your aunt Chloe?"

"Why, yes!" said Avis, with wide eyes. "I like aunt *Chloe*. It isn't aunt *Chloe* that I hate."

"What *do* you hate?"

Her father looked at her across the great black Logic, as a depressed garrison might look at the progress of an enemy whose movements it was utterly unable to forecast.

"Aunt Chloe says it's unladylike to hate," said Avis. "If it is, then I'd rather not be a lady. There are other people in the world than ladies. And I hate to make my bed; and I hate, hate, to sew chemises; and I hate, hate, *hate*, to go cooking round the kitchen. It makes a crawling down my back to sew. But the crawling comes from hating: the more I hate, the more I crawl. And mamma never cooked about the kitchen. I think that is a servant's work. I'm very ugly to aunt Chloe sometimes, papa. And then I'm sorry. But I don't tell her, unless I think of it. On the whole, papa," added the child gravely, "I have so many sorrows in this world, that I don't care to live."

"But," said her father, with rather a gymnastic sternness, "it is shirking not to attend to your work. There's nothing meaner than a shirk."

"I'm not a shirk, papa!" cried Avis, with hot, indignant eyes. "It isn't the *work* I hate. I raked up the leaves for you last fall, and you said I did it most as well as Jacobs. And I go to the post-office every day. It's not the working, but the hating and the crawling, that I mind."

"It is proper that little girls should learn to sew and cook," said the professor of intellectual philosophy faintly. He turned the leaves of the Logic; he groped blindly among the marginal annotations. His two hundred unruly boys in the college class-room he could manage; but all the wisdom of Sir William was as the folly of a fool to teach a great man what to say to a little girl who did not like to sew.

There was a vein of broad tolerance in Hegel Dobell's sturdy nature. He knew that it would give *him* "a crawling" to sit for fifteen minutes at that slow, nervous, precise drawing in and out of the needle, at which his little daughter, with flushed cheeks and twitching fingers, sat by the hour at a time. "A crawling?" Call it a brain-fever.

Yet it was unquestionably proper for all women, certainly for all women belonging to himself, to be versed in those domestic accomplishments to which the feminine nature was created to adjust itself happily at some cost. So he only said,—

"Well, well, my dear; do as aunt Chloe bids you, and hate as few things as possible. And now, if you want to make statues, spare my medallions, and put the tinfoil on your dolls' faces in the play-room."

"My dolls!" said Avis. Her color came swiftly: she lifted her little head with the helpless look of one who receives a perfectly unavengeable insult. "Why, papa! I haven't had a doll since long before mamma died. You *know* I buried my last one under the tool-house, and Coy came to the funeral."

But papa and Sir William the Wise were gone.

"It is an admitted principle in all systems of education," said the professor plaintively to his sister, "that some concession shall be made to the moulds of individuality. In point of fact, all theories cool off in such moulds at last. There certainly is this element of justice in the electoral system which is in danger of becoming so threatening to our universities."

"Do you want Avis to give up learning to cook?" asked aunt Chloe, with a puzzled face.

"Certainly not," said her father, retreating promptly and safely behind the cover of the Logic.

Aunt Chloe sighed. In her heart she thought, that if Avis failed in the end to grow up like other girls, and be a credit to her, it would be owing chiefly to her poor mother's city-bred, unthrifty system of allowing servants to manage their work with so little personal supervision.

It has been said that every human opinion is strong enough to have had its martyrs. Aunt Chloe would have gone to the stake cheerfully for this conviction.

🐦 CHAPTER IV

"Yet thoroughly to believe in
one's own self,
So one's self were thorough,
were to do
Great things."
—Tennyson[1]

The illuminated hours of life
are few; but those of our first youth have a piercing splendor which
neither earlier nor later experience can by any chance absorb. Avis
was, perhaps sixteen, when one of these phosphorescent hours
flashed upon her.

To the day of her death she will recall the last detail that expressed it to her. As most of us revive the sunrise of love, or the
first assault of grief, it is given to a few to individualize the moment when aspiration lays a coal of fire upon our young dumb lips.

She was down in her father's apple-orchard, where the low, out-
skirting branches yield the outlook to the sea. Between her and the
shore swept placidly the expanse of the farm, for whose sake the
professor clung with syllogistic precision to the old-fashioned
house so far from the centre of the town. The ripening grain had a
sinuous, feminine motion under the light wind. The stalks of the
young corn turned their edges in profile towards the sun; and the
short silk hung like the hair of babies, tangled and falling: it seemed
to Avis that she could see a stir now and then, and tiny green hands
put up to push it out of winking eyes. In the meadow the long grass
rioted; and black and brown and yellow bees made love to crimson
clovers. How they blushed! She should think they would. They
were too lavish of their honey, those buxom clovers, like an un-
taught country lassie with a kiss. But the daisies that skirted the
old gray stone walls—the slim, white daisies with the golden
hearts—looked to the young girl's fancy like the virgins in the
Bible story, carrying each a burning lamp.

She had climbed into the highest, airiest branch of the highest
tree in all the orchard, principally because aunt Chloe said it was
unladylike to climb. Any thing, every thing, that aunt Chloe did
not want her to be, she would like to become that morning. It was
purely because all things had gone narrowly wrong in doors that
day, that she had taken her little blue-and-gold girls' copy of "Aurora Leigh,"[2] and rushed out fiercely with it into the wide June

weather. Because aunt Chloe had made her late to the drawing-lesson to get that parlor swept; because she had been rude and wrong about it, and aunt Chloe had been polite and right; because aunt Chloe had said she would never grow gentle and womanly like other girls, and she had retorted that she hoped she never, never, never should; because, too, she had told aunt Chloe hotly, to that good lady's extreme perplexity, that *"carpet-dusting, though a pretty trade, was not the imperative labor after all,"*[3] and so had run up to get the poem, and see in secret if she had her quotation right,—because of all this, here they were, she and Aurora together, tossing like feathers in the apple-bough, high, still, safe from all the whole round, rasping world.

Besides, aunt Chloe never could find her, and would have to make the pudding by herself.

So near our pettiest motives do our largest inspirations lie!

She had easily thrown off the annoyance of the morning, with the blessed, elastic temper of her young years; flinging herself upon one elbow, in that way of hers, pressing her fingers against her temple and under the girlish fillet of her closely braided hair, balancing herself dexterously by her feet upon the tremulous bough, and so plunged into that idyl of the June, that girls' gospel, which will be great as long as there are girls in the world to think it so.

As few poems are ever read, as only an imaginative girl can read those few, Avis in the apple-bough read on and on. She had always meant to take just some such June morning, and find out to her satisfaction what the woman really meant to say who wrote that book, but had only nibbled at it hitherto indiscriminately, after the manner of girls.

Full of the vague restlessness which possesses healthy young creatures, and the more definite hungers natural to a girl of her temperament, Avis was ready to be fed with any full, rich nutriment which seemed to promise fibrine to a growing soul.

Poison or nectar, brimstone or manna, our lips slake at the nearest, be it what it may, in the crisis of that fine fever which comes but once in life. Avis was not without capability of relishing a certain quality of poison, not too fully flavored, of prismatic tints, and in a lily's shape, like hyacinths. But it was silent as a convent in the apple-boughs; the growing day drew on a solemn veil of light; upon the sea the steps of unseen sacred feet were stirring—and so the manna fell.

I like to think of this young thing, coiled there, like an oread, in the apple-tree, with the shadow of a leaf set like a seal upon her parted lips, and her eyes leaping now and then, dumb prisoners, from her book to the horizon of the summer sea; her heart arising with the sweet imperiousness of girlhood to solve the problem of her whole long life before that robin yonder should cease singing, or the next wave break upon the shore, or the lamp of one of the virgin daisies go out under the shadow of the overflying cloud that swept across the meadow.

"The June was in her, with its nightingales;"[4]

and are there not those of us who would yield our lives to know their Junes once more?

Avis, long years after, used to remember with a positive thrill how she said aloud that morning, throwing back her head, and turning her eye through the close leaves to the vivid sky,—

"I am alive. What did God mean by that?" And then was frightened lest the very orioles should understand her. It seemed to her to be the first time that she had ever really thought she was alive. But no one could understand: no one *should* understand. She sat up, and looked at the birds with her finger on her lips.

Despite our most conscientious endeavor to "go on cutting bread and butter," it is on ideals that the world's starvation feeds. And to most of us who must perforce live prose, there is a charm beyond all definition in the development of a poetic nature. In the budding of all young gifts, in the recognition of all high graces, in the kindling of all divine fires, we feel a generous glow upon our own colder and serener fates, like the presence of the late evening light upon a drift of snow. When the passion of our lives has long since wasted into pathos, and hope has shrivelled to fit the cell of care, we lean with increasing ardor on the hearts of those in whom purpose and poetry were permitted to be one.

On Monday when the fire smokes, on Tuesday when the bills come in, on Wednesday when the children cry, it is not more smoke, more debt, more tears, we want: tell us, rather, how a statue grew, or how a poem sprang, or how a song was wrought, or how a prayer conceived.

Avis climbed down from the apple-tree by and by, with eyes in which a proud young purpose hid. It had come to her now—it had all come to her very plainly—why she was alive; what God meant by making her; what he meant by her being Avis Dobell, and reading just that thing that morning in the apple-boughs, with the breath of June upon her,—Avis Dobell, who had rather take her painting-lesson than go to the senior party,—just Avis, not Coy, nor Barbara.

She climbed down, and went straight into the house to her father. The orioles looked kindly after her; and the maiden daisies held their lamps aloft to light the going of her impetuous feet; and perhaps either birds or flowers came nearer to the young girl's heart just then than our tenderest imagination can ever take us.

Aunt Chloe had made her pudding alone, and the professor had eaten it. Avis thought of it as she went into the study. Very well. Other women might make puddings.

She went straight to her father's knee, and, standing with her straw hat hanging by the strings between her crossed hands, said as simply as if she had been asking for a kiss,—

"Papa, I should like to be an artist, if you please."

The professor looked up from the "Critique of Pure Reason"[5] with a faint, appealing perplexity, like a child waked from a nap in a strange room.

"O Avis! you have come. Your aunt missed you at dinner. I am sorry that you have made her more trouble about your domestic duties."

Avis stood for a moment perfectly still. She seldom entirely lost the delicate, fluctuating color which lighted her face. At that moment she became, for one of very few times in her life, absolutely pale.

"But, papa," she stretched out both her hands a little towards him,—"papa, you do not understand me.

"I have decided this morning that I want to be an artist. I want to be educated as an artist, and paint pictures all my life."

"Poh, poh!" said the professor. "Nonsense!"

Ah, well! we must forgive him. What should he know of the apple-trees and the orioles, the daisies, and the blue-and-gold poem, and the way of a June morning with a young girl's heart?

"Nonsense, nonsense!" repeated Professor Dobell. "I can't have you filling your head with any of these womanish apings of a man's affairs, like a monkey playing tunes on a hand-organ." He spoke with a rude irritability not common with him in his treatment of his little daughter; and under that cavern of his brows glittered the rare spark which his wife had known so well.

Avis, by some subtle law of association, thought at that moment of her mother, and wondered if papa were thinking of her also; but she said nothing, only turned miserably away.

"But my child," called her father more gently, "come here, come here! What is all this about? I don't understand. If you want to go on with your drawing-lessons, nothing is to prevent, that I know. Make yourself happy with your paint-box, if you like. That was a very pretty little copy which you made me of Sir William. The likeness was really preserved."

Still, still, and forever, Achilles will have his one little vulnerability. When he was a young man, Hegel Dobell had been told that he resembled Sir William Hamilton. Perhaps he did: at all events, it was the pride and delight of his gentle life to think so. A portrait engraving of the great philosopher always hung above the study-table. To be invited into that study was to be expected to observe with more or less promptness that remarkable likeness. His college-boys understood this so well, that he used frequently to remark, after a visit from some more than commonly promising young man, how much that resemblance seemed to be thought to increase with years.

"It was a very pretty little copy," repeated the professor.

"I do not want to make pretty little copies," cried Avis with quivering lip. *"'I who love my art would never wish it lower to suit my stature.'"* [6]

The professor of intellectual philosophy, not being well read in "Aurora Leigh," stared at this alarming quotation. But Avis went headlong on,—

"I want to be educated. I want to be thoroughly educated in art. Mr. Maynard told me, when I drew the Venus, that I should go to Florence."

"Certainly," said her father, "you shall go to Florence in due time, like other educated young ladies. And, when you have had enough of Mr. Maynard, I will send you to the Art School, if that will make you happy. But fret no more about 'being' this or that. Your business at present is to 'be' a studious and womanly girl. Now kiss me, and run and beg aunt Chloe's pardon for being late to dinner."

So lightly do we dispose of the instincts of the young thing lifting the first startled, self-concentrated eyes to ours. We pat the sleeping lion at our feet as if it were a spaniel, offering milk and sugar to the creature that would feed on flesh and blood, and settle, after the trifling disturbance, to our after-dinner nap.

There was little enough of the lion in poor Avis's composition. She had all the self-consciousness of the artistic temperament with but a small share of its self-confidence. After this little scene with her father, she shrank and shrivelled into herself for a long time. She must be spurred, applauded, to her possibility, or it was possible no longer. It seemed to her an arrogance not to measure her belief in herself by the belief of others in her. Above all, she craved at this time the daily stir and stimulus of an idealizing love. She wondered sometimes, if in the feeling that other girls had about their mothers lay hidden the wine which she found missing from her youth. For a soul which loved her so that it could not *help* believing in her, Avis could have dared the world. But only mothers, she supposed, ever cared for a perplexed and solitary girl like that. Still, because her hour had come, and because "the June was in her," she bent blindly to her young purpose, in her young and groping way.

But she quoted no more Mrs. Browning to her father; and, if he praised her crayons, she sat politely silent. It is possible that this poised reserve excited in the professor more respect than a man may naturally be supposed to feel for the mental processes of his daughter at any age.

When Avis, being nineteen, and having finished, as one was careful to say in Harmouth, her *school* education, thus delicately expressing the true Harmouth compassion for those types of society in which post-graduate courses of reading were not added to a young lady's accomplishments,—when Avis was sent to Europe with the Hogarths and Coy to stay a year, she kissed her father good-by as innocently and quite as charmingly as any young lady who was travelling to improve her accent in French. But, when the year was out, he received from her a serious proposition, that her friends be allowed to return without her, and that she be permitted to remain for an indefinite time, and study art.

"She hasn't underclothes enough," said aunt Chloe decidedly. "I only fitted her out for a year."

When the professor, with a slow smile, suggested that possibly this was a difficulty which time and talent could overcome, aunt Chloe looked very much depressed. If Hegel were going to give in to Avis at last, after all the good sense that he had shown in managing her, the poor girl would never be a credit to her, never, and *her* life's work would simply be thrown away. Aunt Chloe was of quite as unselfish a temper as the most of us; but she found it hard sometimes to trace the exact distinction between Avis's good and her own glory.

"Besides," urged aunt Chloe, "what is to become of her when she is married?" Aunt Chloe held it to be impossible that any woman could make home happy without being able to make good Graham bread; and Avis's last remarkable experiment in this direction was yet vividly in mind. How a course of instruction in oil-colors was to help the matter, it really was not immediately easy to see. But the professor strode about his study a little while, and then sat down and wrote,—

"It is the custom, in the training of carrier-doves, to let them all loose from their places of confinement into the upper air; but those which do not return readily without interference are cast aside as too dull to be worth the trouble of further education.

"I let *you* go, my dear daughter, not without misgivings; but omnipotent Nature is wiser than I. I should be duller than the dullest bird among them all, if I could not trust you at her hands."

Avis had now plunged into a life which extremely few women in

America, twenty years ago, found it either possible or desirable to lead. Those who know any thing of art-circles in Italy at that time will recall the impression made upon them by her superb perseverance in mastering the difficulties of her position long before her gift had been distinguished from a grace. The shy American girl of the unquestionable breeding and the yet half-blossomed beauty, trod the mazes of Florentine life with an innocent rapture which protected her like a shining veil.

The prospect of commanding proper surroundings to her venture had seemed, at first, a hopeless one; but one day her friends looked about to find that the little Yankee girl had brought her circumstances, like spaniels, to her feet. She had even provided herself with a *chaperone* of Mrs. Hogarth's own selection. She had then armed herself with a new palette, Coy's last kiss, and a single introductory letter, and, with the sublime assurance of twenty, gone headlong to work.

With a dumb joy, such as some world-sick soul of us may feel in the actual, long-delayed presence of death, this young thing now began in soul and sense to live.

Now, indeed, she knew that she had never lived before. She read her life backwards, like the Chaldæans, translating all its suppressed text by the light of her aspiration, as happy lovers view their past by the illumination of their love, grudging to time every hour they have spent apart. We find that most of the traits of a great affectional passion exist in the young genius which is making the first use of its antennæ.

Her letter, over the signature of Frederick Maynard, was addressed to Alta Mura,[7] once—as the Harmouth drawing-teacher was used to say with lifted head,—once his master.

"Go over to Naples," said the scrutinizing artist to whom the young lady had been advised to carry it; "go and ask Alta Mura what he wants done with you."

Avis went to Naples, and Alta Mura sent her back again.

"Are you ready, young lady," he had said, "to spend two days copying a carrot that hangs twenty feet away from you against the wall?"

"Two hundred, if I must," said Avis.

"Then throw away every thing in your very pretty portfolio. Maynard has taken to copying from the flat. Go back to Florence, to a man whose name I'll give you, in a street that I will tell you. Do exactly as he bids you for two years; then come back to me."

"She will get tired of it in six months," said aunt Chloe; "but I'll knit her some woollen stockings, for I'm told the Italian winters are quite rheumatic." Aunt Chloe was still so old-fashioned, that she would not say, "neuralgic," even of a young lady's bones.

And the professor paced the silent study, beneath the portrait of Sir William, wondering sometimes, when the sun got low, where it was he found that rather touching anecdote about the carrier-doves.

Avis, in the little bare studio,—high, high, so high that it seemed, by putting her hand out of the window in the roof, she could touch the purple wideness of the Florentine sky,—had her own thoughts about those doves, perhaps.

But she stooped to her task with a stern, ungirlish doggedness. In the little attic studio, Pegasus kicked at the plough now and then, but, on the whole, behaved himself somewhat remarkably. She was young to have been so docile; but she thought nothing about that. She did not know that she was in any sense unusual in coining the fervors of twenty to secure that most elusive of human gifts,—a disciplined imagination. The self-distrust which had shrunk at the first rebuff of ardor was her preservation now. She abandoned herself to the grating drudgeries involved in mastering the *technique* of art with a passion of which it were not discerning not to say that it added to the fire of the artist something of feminine self-abnegation.

In short, Avis shared the fate of most American art-students in Italy at that time. She simply spent two years unlearning, that she might begin to learn.

When these two years were over, she went back to Alta Mura. He said,—

"Now I will see if you can be taught," and took her, with her *chaperone*, into the *atelier*, under his protection. She went to her place on the front settee before the students entered, and left it after they had gone.

When two years were gone again, Alta Mura sent her to Paris; and Paris sent her to Couture.[8]

When she was in Paris, her father came out to see her.

"I think I would let the dove fly," he said, "a little longer."

One day Couture came into the studio, and said,—

"Mademoiselle, I will give you two years to make a reputation."

Avis, standing with her slender thumb piercing her palette, and her brushes gathered with it, thrust out her empty hand with a gesture which the great artist admired more thoroughly than he understood. Her magnificent, rare pallor swept over her face, and the quality of her features heightened. Her face and head looked larger when she was pale. She reminded him at that moment of Soddoma's Roxana, in the Alexander's marriage at Rome.[9] Copies from the fresco sometimes had that colossal look, and her face had taken on the tints of a deep engraving. If the Archangel Gabriel had said, "Mademoiselle, I will let you into heaven, be but so good as to wait an hour," Avis might have looked at him with just that widening of the eyes and parting of the lips.

She went back to her apartments that morning with a dazzled face; but she walked weakly, and for the first time for nearly six years of hard work and hard homesickness, burst into a passion of hysterical tears. She had worked so gently and so humbly, with such patient service of her possibility, that success overtook her with more the grip of a paralysis than the thrill of a delight. For two days she lay actually ill upon her bed. For a week she did not enter the studio, but wandered about Paris like a spirit in a vision. The monarch of her young future had turned lover, and kneeled at her feet. His resplendent promise humbled her. Like the beggar-maiden in the story, she stretched no hand out towards her crown, and stood with downcast eyes "before the King Cophetua."[10]

It was under the glamour of these blinding days that she found herself one afternoon wandering into the Madeleine.[11] The blessed Christian habit by which an over-full heart relieves itself in prayer to an unseen God, was on her.

But just then the tropical Catholic atmosphere came more kindly to the New-England girl than any other could. In the college chapel at home, perhaps, she would have found an audible public prayer at an arctic remove from the seething necessities of her mood. She kneeled at vespers in the Madeleine in that temper when a religion of emotions assumes a sacerdotal authority over the intellect, and even a superstition takes on the sacredness of faith. Avis often found in such hours a certain positive physical repose, which only the reverent can understand, or even, perhaps, respect. It seemed to her that these prayers, which bore the burden of centuries of half-inarticulate human longing, surrounded her like everlasting arms; and upon the chant which held the cry of ages she leaned her head, as John did upon the bosom of his Lord. It would be impossible, of course, to explain to any other than a believer that this was something as much deeper than a physiological effect as the soul is finer than the body.

It was when Avis rose from her knees, with the halo that John himself might have worn upon her face, and was about turning, with the few stray Parisians who surrounded her, to leave the Madeleine that afternoon, that she found herself arrested by a pair of eyes fastened upon her in the twilight, across the nave.

They were the eyes of a fellow-countryman, as it took but the flash of an instinct to see.

Avis, in that flash, said, "There is a remarkable face!" Perhaps any one would have called it a remarkable face: certainly, in the impressive background of the dim-lit church, it blazed like an amber intaglio.[12]

We see occasionally in women, but very rarely in a man, that union of the Saxon and the Southern which weds the fair hair to the dark eye. This face was set in a nimbus of bright hair, which, in a boyhood not too long departed, must have been of deep, unusual gold. A beard which had never known a razor quite concealed the outline of what seemed to be a sensitive mouth; but of that it was impossible to tell. The young man wore his hair a little long, perhaps with either the carelessness or the affectation of a student. Avis liked the shape of his head, which her artist's glance had caught simultaneously with the color and character of his eyes. These were black, with a large iridescent pupil, which she felt concentrated upon her—upon her lifted face, her arrested motion, her responsive attitude—like a burning-glass.

The telegraphic signal-system of the human soul runs now and then in a cipher blank to the most imaginative of us all. It is not easy to explain, but most of us will admit, the effect which people may produce upon one another by the outleaping eye in the prison of a chance crowd. I do not think that I am overstating the case, in saying that these two, man and woman grown, going out from the Madeleine that afternoon to the world's wide ends, would have thought of one another, as we think of an unread poem, or an undiscovered country, as long as either lived.

In Avis this was very natural. The artist's world is peopled with the vanishing of such mute and unknown friends; and the artist's eye is privileged to take their passports as they come and go.

But when, standing with her gloved hand upon a column, her face, draped in the dark veil of her little Parisian hat, bent slightly forwards and upwards, and her eyes gone rebel to all but the instinct of the moment, starting, she stirred and turned away, she felt a great tidal wave of color surge across her face. If the eye of that amber god [13] across the Madeleine had caught an artist, it had held a woman.

Avis became aware of this with a scorching, maidenly self-scorn. She dropped her veil, and hurried from the church.

❧ CHAPTER V

*"My saul, ye maun blythe-bid
the Lord, ettlin' his carriage
the cluds; on the wings o' the
win' making' speed:
Errand-runner he make o' the
blasts, and loons o' his ain,
the bleeze o'lowe."*
—Scotch Psalms

If Philip Ostrander expected Miss Dobell to join his German class, he was doomed to what it is not exactly correct to call a disappointment. Probably he did expect it. The other young ladies had all joined. Young ladies were apt to join any classes which he chanced to open without undue reluctance. He had been in the frequent way of this sort of thing, in the natural course of that griping struggle with ways and means which had brought the keen-eyed, poverty-ridden boy from an uncultivated New-Hampshire home to one of the most brilliant positions which New England had then to offer.

For it was now considered, as Avis heard from her father when she had been at home a little while, quite assured that Mr. Ostrander would ultimately take the geological chair through the probation of the assistant professorship. True he was not a Harmouth graduate, this the professor regretted keenly; but his shining talents burned the more conspicuously for this disadvantage. And that he had refused a position in his Alma Mater to compass those two years in Germany, by which a promising young man expected, with some confidence, fifteen or twenty years ago, to become immediately "distinguished," had naturally recommended him to the Harmouth perceptive Faculty.

Coy was right when she said that Mr. Ostrander was thought in Harmouth to be remarkably versatile.

At all events, a versatility which can be converted into a dollar an hour is not to be despised by a Harmouth tutor; and Ostrander held the rudder of his yet unanchored craft with a very easy hand.

In this matter of the German lessons—which, requiring but the slightest type of attention, left him space for a good deal of revery,—he was conscious of watching narrowly to see what Miss Dobell would do. During the afternoons which he spent in the sunny parlors of the Harmouth ladies, with the prettiest girls in the city chirping gutturals at his feet, or in the evenings which he devoted to Barbara Allen's fine renderings of Schumann, he made no attempt to deny that the young artist occupied certain large un-travelled spaces upon the map of his fancy. It is more than possible, that if Avis had drifted into the German class; if there had been established between them that time-honored relation of master and pupil, which, always fraught with the sweetest possible perils to man and woman, is more stimulating to the imagination of the pupil than of the master; if Avis, too, had sat and chirped at his feet, then—well, *what* then?

Possibly Ostrander assumed that then the delicate poem opened one day at vespers in the Madeleine would hardly have been found worth the reading, and the radiant, undiscovered country would have scarcely compelled the explorer over the threshold.

Possibly, too, both nature and experience would have taken his brief, had he been tried for this assumption. Ostrander, at this pe-riod of his life, protected himself against the ambuscades of his own temperament with that forethought which an unmarried man of thirty is clearly expected to have acquired. But he experienced a singular sense of relief and expectancy, when several weeks had passed, and Miss Dobell did *not* join the German class.

That sibyl of the Madeleine perhaps possessed the fine old clas-sic instinct which every year he thought grew rare and rarer among women. She must, it seemed, be absolutely sought.

Some pressing Faculty business took him, before the vacillating April days were quite over, to Professor Dobell's house. He called at dusk, and aunt Chloe invited him to tea. He hesitatingly re-fused; but when she said,—

"Then come next Friday, Mr. Ostrander: it is a long time since we have had the pleasure, and I notice my brother is always in good spirits when you have been to see us," he accepted the invitation at once. He did not in the least attempt to wrestle with his motive in this innocent bit of scene-shifting, but allowed himself to be led blindfold by it. His wish to see that girl again had become impera-tive. Ostrander had the deepest respect for whatever he found really imperious in himself.

With Friday, the New-England April weather had assumed one of the caprices which we tolerate so tenderly in any born coquette; and snow fell heavily. The day before had been as gentle as a baby's dream. Avis worked in the studio in the garden without a fire; and one of the college-boys brought Ostrander a tuft of saxifrage from the pale-green promise of the meadows. That morning the wind lay in the east sleepily enough; but by noon the air was blurred with the large, irregular spring flakes, as if Nature had taken a wayward fancy to fold herself in a Japanese screen. In the afternoon, when Ostrander had strolled out of town, and down the shore to see the surf, the drifts were already piling high. He tramped through them lightly enough, in the rubber-boots which are the chief end of man in New England, and with his soft silk cap drawn over his eyes, and his powerful figure bent a little with the first languid action of a wrestler upon it, yielded himself to the intoxication of the winter shore.

Few greater passions pass more readily into the permanence and fidelity of love than the passion for the sea. Ostrander had an elemental kinship with it in himself, which every year of his life had intensified. He sometimes wished that he was quite sure he cared as much for any human creature as he did for Harmouth Harbor. He struck off down the drifted beach toward the Light. The wind was in his face. Through the opaque air he could see rudely defined, like the values of a vast, unfinished sketch, the waves leap and slip and fall upon the glazed cliffs, and across the narrow reef from which the light-house shot sheer against the sky. He pushed on down, perhaps a mile, to find a shelter; and there, with the tide at his feet and the spray in his face, flung himself upon the freezing rocks, possessed with a kind of fierce but abundant joy.

The Light stood just across the bay where the Harbor widened to the sea; it might have been a dozen rods or so from where Ostrander sat. The reef, traversable at low tide, ran from it to a gorge within the cliff.[1] The well-defined metallic tints common to the New-England coast—the greens and reds and umbers, the colors of rust, of bronze, of ruins—covered the reef. The gorge was a vein of deep purple lava, which to Ostrander's educated eye told the story of a terrible organic divorce.

The wave that tore its heart out at his feet was throbbing green; but, beyond that, the inrolling tide, the chalky outline of the Light, the harbormouth, the narrowing horizon, the low sky, all the world, lay gray beneath the footsteps of the dizzy snow. The wind was rising from the sullenness of a blow to the anger of a gale; and the crash of the breakers which he could see had a shrill, petulant sound set to the boom of those unseen across the bay.

Was it the lawlessness of all this, or the law of it, that thrilled Ostrander? Was it the passion, or the purpose, which commanded him? Was the eternal drama of unrest an outlet, or an inlet, to his nature; an excitant, or a sedative? It were hard to say. The young man asked himself the question, but found a shrug of his fine shoulders the most intelligent answer at his command.

Or perhaps we must admit that there was as much rheumatism as philosophy in that shrug. It certainly was growing very cold, and darkening fast.

Ostrander had been somewhat sheltered by the cliff at whose feet he sat; so much so, that he was quite unaware of the extent to which the wind had risen. A man does not sit very long upon an ice-covered rock; but a few moments will suffice to let loose the prisoned temper of an April gale. When he turned to get back to the beach, he found the wind racing through the lava-gorge at the rate of perhaps eighty miles an hour, and the snow seething under his feet before the first oncoming of the heavy, breeze-swept tide.

He stopped to pull up his coat-collar, as he would now have the storm at his back; as he did so, the fog-bell began to toll from the Light, and he turned instinctively at the sound.

At that moment he saw a figure between himself and the light-house, moving slowly shorewards along the reef. It was the figure of a woman—it was the figure of a lady, slight and delicately dressed. It was not so dark but that he could see that she moved with great difficulty. The reef was jagged as a saw, and glared with the thin, blue, cruel ice. It ran at an angle to the northward, and took the whole sweep of the easterly gale.

Ostrander, as he watched her, felt the blood tingle about his heart. He believed that there was but one lady in Harmouth who would have taken a walk to the light-house on such a day. Did Miss Dobell know that not one woman in one hundred could get across that reef in a blow like this? The light-keeper must have been mad to let her start.

It seemed that the light-keeper himself was coming to that late and useful conclusion. Dimly through the snow Ostrander saw the flash of the lantern with which he had accompanied her to the reef's edge. There was still much sickly light in the air, and the lantern shone pale and ghastly. The man gesticulated violently, and seemed to be shouting unheard words. Ostrander remembered suddenly how shallow the rocks grew in sloping to the little island. The rising tide had probably cut between the keeper and the lady, and by this time distinctly severed them.

Ostrander hesitated no longer, but ran swiftly out upon the reef.

She was making her way valiantly enough, perhaps without any more than a vague and not unpleasant consciousness of possible peril. The gale took the heavy drapery of her skirts and long water-proof cloak in a cruel fashion, winding them about and about her limbs. She looked very tall in the waning light, and there was a certain grandeur in her motions. She stood out against the ice-covered rock like a creature sprung from it, sculptured, primeval, born of the storm.

As Ostrander ran along the reef, he saw her stop or stagger, hesitate, then stoop slowly, and take to her hands and knees. She rose again in a moment, and stood cowering a little, afraid or unable to stretch her full height to the force of the gale, which seemed to Ostrander something satanic, now that he was in the teeth of it upon that reef. Could a blind, insensate force of Nature, so many feet of atmospheric pressure to the square inch, obedient to a powerful, and, on the whole, kindly-disposed Creator, set the whole weight of its brute organism to work with this devilish intelligence, to beat a delicate woman, blow by blow, to death? There seemed something so profoundly revolting to Ostrander's manhood in this idea, just then, that it did not occur to him, that he was not the only man in the world who had ever experienced his first genuine defiance of fate in some stress of peril sprung upon the woman whom he would have given— What would Ostrander have given to save her?

It seemed to him at that moment that he would have given his young life; for as he crept along the reef—now swiftly, that he might reach her, and then slowly, that he might not startle her— she threw up her arms, and fell.

He came leaping from rock to rock, and would possibly have plunged into the water; but through the dusk he heard her voice.

She said, "I have not fallen into the water. Can you get over to that great purple rock?"

She spoke so quietly, that he was completely re-assured about her until he crawled over under the pounding of the gale, and, dashing the snow out of his eyes, looked down. She had slipped from the edge of the reef, and hung at full-length along the slope of a huge bowlder. The slope was perhaps twenty feet long, and very gradual: it was covered with ice. The spray froze in his face as he looked over. The water was breaking across her feet. She clung with both hands to the polished edge of the bowlder: there was blood upon the ice where she had clutched and beaten it away. But perhaps the fact which came most distinctly to Ostrander's consciousness was, that the tips of her fingers were absolutely without color.

The first thing which he did was to tear off his fur gloves, and, leaning over the reef, stretch both his warm hands upon hers. The water sucked between the reef and the bowlder in a narrow, inky stream.

"You are right," she said: "they *were* getting frost-bitten. There. Now I can hold myself easily enough as long as I must. Mr. Ostrander, do you find it very slippery upon the reef?"

"Not in the least," said Ostrander grimly, grinding his heel into the ice.

"Can you brace yourself sufficiently to put one foot against the bowlder?"

"I should hope so."

"Only one foot, please, and only one hand. Do not try to get upon the bowlder, and do not step between the bowlder and the reef. Do you understand?"

"Miss Dobell, give me one hand now—slowly. Raise your fingers, one at a time, and put them into mine.

"Do you understand that you are not to come upon the bowlder?

"If you do not give me your hand immediately, I cannot possibly answer for what I shall do."

"Promise me, that, if I slip, you will let go."

"I promise nothing. Give me your hand!"

"Promise that you will not let me drag you after me."

"I promise any thing. For God's sake, give me, this instant, the fingers of your right hand!"

She gave them to him with that, obediently enough. She lifted them one by one from the ice; one by one he slipped his own under them, slid the palm of his hand slowly under the palm of hers; so cautiously, but with the full prehensile force of her own supple touch to help him, reached and grasped her wrist. Avis had firmer fingers than most women; but they were as supple as withes.

"Now, the other!"

They managed it with the other more nervously, for the water was now dashing freely in their faces.

"Now I am quite firm upon the reef. I shall draw you easily up. Do you trust me perfectly that I know what I am about?"

"Perfectly. Do you remember, that, in case of an accident, only *one* must slip?"

"I remember."

"Very well."

"Are you ready?"

"Quite ready."

It seemed to Avis but a moment's work; and they sat crouched and panting side by side upon the broad surface of the reef. She could not possibly have said how she came there. Her most definite thought was a perfectly new conception of the power of the human hand. Ostrander's controlled, intelligent grasp challenged the blind mood of the gale: it was iron and velvet, it was fury and pity; as if the soul of the storm had assumed the sense of a man.

As soon as might be, for the tide was rising fast, they made their way across the reef, and sat down for a moment's breath upon the shore. Neither had yet spoken. Ostrander had not, indeed, released the grip which he had of Miss Dobell's hand. Avis was the first to break the silence which had fallen upon them. She said,—

"I am afraid I have killed the bird."

"I beg your pardon?" said Ostrander, staring.

"I went over to the Light to see about the birds that are brought by the storm," said Avis, exactly as if nothing had happened. "The keeper gave me a little blue-jay that he picked up under the lighthouse. He thought it might live; and I wrapped it in my cloak-pocket. Ah, see! No: it is alive."

"Give it to me," said Ostrander, adopting the young lady's tone very quietly. "You are too much chilled to keep it. And now are you able to get on a little? The tide is becoming really troublesome; and the walk is longer than I wish it were."

He took the bird, and, unfastening his coat, wrapped it in his breast. Avis, looking up through the dusk, thought how tenderly the little act was done.

"The poor thing flutters against my heart," said Ostrander in his exquisitely-modulated tones. He had one of those voices into which all the tenderness of the nature flows readily, like the meadows which are the first to receive the freshet of the river. And then Ostrander was really sorry for the bird.

Avis made no reply. She took his arm in silence, and in silence they passed through the lava-gorge, and out upon the drifted beach. There she stopped and looked back. The fog-bell was tolling steadily, and under the gray sheen of the snow the grayer mist stole in.

"I have always wondered exactly what made this gorge," she said, quite as if she and Ostrander had only come out on a little geological expedition. "What was torn out of the heart of the rock?"

"Nothing was torn out," said Ostrander. "The two sides of that gorge are thrust apart by flood or fire. They were originally of one flesh. It was a perfect primeval marriage. The heart of the rock was simply broken."

Avis stood for a moment in the purple shadow of the cleft, into which the water was now bounding high. A certain awe fell upon them both as Ostrander spoke. Instinctively they glanced from rent side to rent side of the divorced cliff, and then into one another's faces. Stirred by the strain of peril and the thrill of safety, Avis's excited imagination took vivid hold of the story of the rock. It seemed to her as if they stood there in the wake of an awful organic tragedy, differing from human tragedy only in being symbolic of it; as if through the deep, dumb suffering of Nature, the deeper because the dumber, all little human pains went seething shallowly, as the tide came seething through the gorge. In some form or other, the motherhood of earth had forecast all types of anguish under which her children groaned; had also thrilled, perhaps, beneath all forms of joy. Suppose the bridal gladness or the widowed pathos of a rock. Suppose the sentient nature of a thing adapted to its reticence. What a story, then, in sea or shore, in forest, hills, and sky, in wind and fire, in all things whose mighty lips were sealed! Suppose she herself, gone mute as the mutest of them, cognizant of their secret, joined to their brotherhood, were dashing on the tide across the lava-gorge.

As they turned away, she leaned rather heavily upon his arm, and tremulously said,—

"I suppose, Mr. Ostrander, if it had not been for you"—

"Ah, no, no!" interrupted Ostrander quickly. "The light-keeper would have got out the boats. I have only saved you a pretty cold bath. Pray let us not talk of that.—But indeed," he added, abruptly changing his tone, "I begin to understand why the people in the novels always *are* saving each other's lives. It is just another instance of the absolute naturalness of much that we are all used to call unnatural in fiction."

"And why?" asked Avis, without the least apparent awkwardness.

"Because nothing acquaints two people like the unconventionalities of danger. It seems to me—pray pardon me—as if I had known you for a long time."

Avis made no reply; and they struck out upon the drifting shore. They seemed to have been taken up now, and driven by the gale behind them, as if they had been scooped into the hollow of a mighty hand.

"And nothing isolates," continued Ostrander, "like the interchange of emotions which any such experience involves. See now," added the young man, looking about the desolate shore, "how lonely we seem. It would be easy to think that there was no other life than ours in all this world."

He turned as he spoke, and would have stood to face the wind; but the mighty hand which had gathered them swept them imperiously on, as if it conceived them to have been bent upon some terrible errand of its own.

Perhaps Ostrander, too, had received quite his share of the excitement of that April afternoon. He was in some sense rather a guarded man in his habit of speech among women, sufficiently cautious not to involve himself in those little ambiguous sallies of the lip to which young ladies attach an importance which a man reserves for affairs. He caught himself in thinking that he did not know another woman in the world to whom he could have made that speech without a savage and humiliating fear of misinterpretation.

With a little of the madness of any rarely-tasted license, he plunged on,—

"How like you it was, in the midst of all that, to tell me to get upon the *purple* rock!"

"How do you know it was like me?" laughed Avis, as they struggled through the snow.

"I think I have always known what would be like you," said the young man in a lower voice, "since I saw you in the Madeleine."

There is a certain shade of expression peculiar to a man's face, which every woman knows, but few understand. It falls as far short of the flash of over-mastering feeling on the one hand as it does of self-possession on the other. Its wearer is at once constrained to admire, and predetermined not to love; and precisely in so far as he is unconscious even of that predetermination does this delicate play of the features take on the appearance of the strongest emotion.

It was not so dark but that Avis, looking up through the storm, saw that sensitive expression dart across Ostrander's face. Then the lines about his mouth subsided, his eye cleared, he lifted his head, and it was gone. She need not be a vain woman, only an inexperienced one, who reads in such a facial change a tenderness which it by no means bespeaks. Avis, being neither the one nor the other, suffered nothing more than a slight feeling of surprise.

"I suppose," he added, after a few minutes' profound attention to the problem: given darkness, a lady, and a snow-drift four feet high, how to flounder through the latter with that grace which it will be a pleasure to reflect upon to-morrow,—"I suppose *you* now went home, and thought what a rude American you had seen. I was glad when I saw you come into the Chaucer Club. I have always felt that I owed you an apology for that stare."

He said this with the manner of one who is conscious of having said an uncommon thing, and hastens to wrench out of it a common-place significance.

"Not in the least," said Avis with composure. "I owe the making of a very satisfactory little sketch to you. I put you into sepia, on a neutral gray. Couture took a great fancy to that sepia."

"If I have been in any sense the cloak across which your royal feet have stepped upon the muddy road to glory, or the royal road to glory, or—my metaphor is gone mad, and I give it up," said Ostrander, with the carelessness which conceals rather than expresses meaning. "At all events, I am glad you made the sketch. We are getting along bravely. Are you very cold?"

"Not much. Only my hand which I bruised. Thank you! No, I should be very unhappy to take your glove. How is my bird, Mr. Ostrander?"

"I forgot the bird!"

He sought for it very gently with his free hand, and said,—

"It lives. It is quite warm. But it does not stir."

"Why," said Avis as they drew in sight of her father's house— "why should we disturb my father by telling him about that slip upon the rock?"

"Why, indeed? You are very wise and right. We will not talk of it."

"I have been away from him so many years," said Avis in the almost timid way she had when her gentlest feeling was aroused, "that, now I am come back, I find I like to spare him all possible pain, even a little one like this. And *now*, Mr. Ostrander, how is my bird?"

The light from the hall fell full upon his face when they stopped without the door. The snow lay lightly on his beard and bright hair. He looked like a young Scandinavian god.

He slipped his hand very tenderly under his shaggy coat as he stood there looking down at her.

"I hope all is well with the poor thing," said he. But the bird upon his heart lay dead.

Avis was in no possible sense what we call a woman of moods: her mouth and eyes were too harmonious, and her chin too broadly cut. Yet she had as many phases as the moon. So (as unconscious of the lack of originality in his fancy as most excited young creatures to whom all earth's dull, old figures are sublimated by the moment's fever) Ostrander thought, when she came down to supper that night, gone, by some ten minutes' magic, out of her wet wrappings into a wonderful warmth and delicacy. Even the scent of her dress as she swept past him—a fine French perfume, but one which he could not associate with any pretty Parisian whom he had ever met—added to this impression. At once she had become a housed, sheltered, hearth-loving creature. The soul of the storm lingered only upon her hair and eyes. There was a certain native daintiness about Avis, distinct from the inevitable elegance of a young lady recently returned from Paris, and hardly to be expected of the artistic temperament. She had her mother to thank for that, aunt Chloe said. It was still well remembered in Harmouth that the professor's wife wore colors that no reading-club would have thought of combining, and laces of a very unintellectual character.

Ostrander did not recollect having seen any other woman in such a dress as Miss Dobell wore that evening. It was of white French flannel, very fine and soft, somewhat loosely worn, and unornamented. She was standing by her father's open fire when he came back from his room at the college, and was ushered by aunt Chloe into the study. Her eyes only moved to meet him. She looked slender and shining as a Doric column.

"Ah," said the professor, "I am more than glad to see you here. I do not recall, Mr. Ostrander, whether you have been in my study before. So? Then you will have seen my engraving of Sir William,—Avis, be good enough to turn on the gas a little,—the only copy from that plate, sir, to be found in this country, I believe."

Ostrander was hastening to say that there was, he fancied—or was it fancy?—a remarkable likeness, when Avis interrupted him by saying, with an irrelevance which surprised the professor in a girl of Avis's really coherent mind, that aunt Chloe had sprained her wrist; had tried to lift her great ivy-jar. Aunt Chloe tended her flowers as if they were all orphans, and loved that ivy like her own soul.

"I have never thought myself lacking in the commoner forms of humanity," observed Avis, her eyes electric with merriment; "but I certainly could not sit up nights with a sick ivy."

"It was a German ivy," said aunt Chloe plaintively; "and I thought it would freeze. I can't sleep warm if I know my plants are cold. Did you never notice, Mr. Ostrander, how an arbutelon, for instance, will shiver? It will shiver like a thoroughbred spaniel at a draught of air. But the ivy *was* heavy. And Avis, I think you must pour the tea, if you please, my dear."

Ostrander was not sorry to see Avis pour the tea; but he recommended an arnica bandage to aunt Chloe with much graceful sympathy, discussing the continental pronunciation with the professor, meanwhile.

Ostrander had no deeply preconceived repulsions to women with "careers," holding it the first duty of an educated man to cultivate a tolerance of opinion, especially in matters in which opinion most unconsciously cooled into prejudice; but he had, without doubt, his preconceived ideals. Among these he found that he had never placed a young woman in a white French evening-dress, pouring tea at a cultivated table, with a singularly pretty arm.

After tea—for the simple habits of the Christian family were not often disturbed for a quiet guest, and especially not for any pet of the professor's, like this young man,—Avis went to her accustomed seat upon a low cricket at her father's feet, and, sitting in the full firelight with bent head, read the Psalm for evening prayers. A beautiful womanliness was upon her. She seemed to be wrapped in it like a Naiad in a silver shell.

Ostrander yielded himself to the domestic spirit of the evening with the rare relief which a homeless and restless man alone can know. He sat with his hand above his eyes, and listened to her reverent young voice.

After prayers, the professor monopolized the conversation, to the exclusion of the ladies,—a Harmouth habit of which his wife had nearly succeeded in breaking him; but aunt Chloe supposed that was the way in all literary families, and a lady could always take her work while gentlemen talked.

Ostrander did not object to this form of parlor etiquette, however, just then. He would have been quite satisfied if he need not have exchanged another word with Miss Dobell that evening. It suited his mood to steal a look at her now and then in silence. Even to watch her, almost reduced his thought of her to garrulousness. In the beautiful scholastic sense which wise men give to our common phrase, he had become *conscious* of her. He was made aware of the variations in her voice, her attitude, her glance, as he was made aware of the fluctuations of his own breath. He felt her presence in the room as he felt aunt Chloe's rose-hyacinth in the atmosphere.

Was the repressed excitement of a shared and unspoken experience upon her as upon himself? She spoke but little, and wandered about the room, when aunt Chloe, from over her knitting, recommended some light crochet-work, which she was sure Mr. Ostrander would excuse.

How superb she was in that white wool! as if she had wrapped herself in a snow-cloud; as if the very soul of the storm, gone mad as a lover to infold her, turned warm as the June to win her, had followed her in from death and the freezing sea.

She was standing with her face bent, and buried in the hyacinth, when aunt Chloe presently called her:—

"Avis, Mr. Ostrander wants to get a portrait done for a birthday present to his mother."

"Mr. Ostrander, then, is a devoted son?" said Avis, lifting her face.

"So I was telling him. And we have so few! Good sons have gone out of fashion, like hollyhocks. I hope you will be able to give him the sittings, Avis. The studio will soon be quite comfortable with the May sun."

"How is it, Avis?" said the professor, thrusting his hands into his pockets, and stopping in his walk across the room to look at her. "Can you gratify Mr. Ostrander, my dear, do you think?"

It was when Ostrander was wading back to his rooms, beating his way through the damp and heavy drifts with the good temper of a man who has passed an exhilarating evening, that he saw, turning the sharp corner upon the college green, a slight figure struggling before him in the snow. It staggered with the helplessness of a creature encumbered by heavy swathing of the limbs, as only a woman mummied in her skirts can stagger. The poor soul was slightly dressed, and carried a little bag such as is carried by agents or female peddlers,—a sight much less common fifteen years ago than now. As Ostrander approached, she tripped, and fell heavily across the snow, bruising her head, he thought, against a lamp-post as she fell. Inwardly wondering of how many more damsels in distress he was elected to be the knight-errant before that storm was over, with a lurking smile upon his lips, but instant pity in his eyes, he sprang, and lifted the young woman to her feet.

As she turned to thank him, the light from the street-lamp fell full upon her face and his. They looked steadily at one another before she spoke.

❧ *CHAPTER VI*

"The clearest skies are those
That farthest off appear
To birds of strongest wing.
The dearest loves are those
That no man can come near
With his best following."
—R. K. Weeks[1]

The subtle footsteps of the spring stole on.

The Chaucer Club adjourned till the "months with the r" should reinstate the oyster-suppers. The German lessons—since now a yachting-party offered its own peculiar type of culture, and a little wider variety in those forms of stimulus which no intelligent young lady is ashamed to admit receiving from the masculine mind,—the German lessons flagged. The deepening sun upon the picture of Sir William wandered through the open window by which the professor had wheeled his study-chair. Aunt Chloe's geraniums were promoted to the garden, and aunt Chloe's soul to the seventh heaven of tender garden cares and hopes and fears, which those only know whose nature bourgeons with "the green things growing," and with these alone.

And in the studio, Couture's pet pupil sat painting the very successful portrait of her first American sitter.

Her great master, if he might have strolled through the old-fashioned garden, and into the snug summer-house which Avis had levied for her uses, would possibly have said, with a keen glance from face to face,—

"Très bien! You give Mademoiselle a long-haired student. She gives you Thor, Odin, Balder.[2] Mademoiselle idealizes. Mademoiselle has a future."

It seemed to Mademoiselle, meanwhile, that in strange senses, tingling as an unmastered science, and blinding as an unknown art, and solemn as an untrod world, her future, through the budding of that spring, advanced to meet her.

She became electrically prescient of it. She throbbed to it as if perplexing magnetisms played upon the lenient May air. It was as if she held it in her young hand as she held the violet-buds that Ostrander brought her. He brought her only buds.

"I am so glad to be at work!" she said,—"so gravely, greatly glad!"

She said this to herself. It was necessary to say something. She did not remember to have worked so excitedly before. She thrilled to her task as the violet thrilled to the sun. Never had she seemed to conceive or to construct, with her imagination so recipient and docile to her inspirations. Never had she seemed before to be in such harmony with the infinite growing and yearning of Nature.

She stood like the child of the desert, with her ear at the lips of the sphinx.[3] The whole world had leaped into bloom to yield her the secrets of beauty. She spread the spring showers upon her palette, and dipped her brushes in the rainbow.

As for her sitter, he served as well as another to pass the mood of the May weather; better, perhaps, with that stimulating, legendary type of beauty. She found much beauty—and more, the better she knew it—in Philip Ostrander's face. She told him so one day, with a *naiveté* which enchanted him.

"I rarely meet," said the young artist, "with beauty in men. I have known several beautiful women."

"And other women, it seems, know beautiful men," urged Ostrander, gracefully evasive of the compliment, though he felt to the bottom of his soul the utter absence of that which would have given it a distinct value to him. This young woman regarded the contour of a man's face precisely as a physician regards a hectic flush or a bilious eye-ball. It was the intricate strife of the artist with the woman in her which had been the bewitchment of that look surprised in the Madeleine. He rather hoped some sudden, abashed consciousness would overtake her calm, professional scrutiny: he had often wished so while the portrait had been in progress. Just now he would have been glad to see her blush, perhaps. But she went serenely on.

"I know, I know! But I never could understand it. When I was a girl, and the other girls talked about the handsome college-boys, I was greatly puzzled. I did not know but I was color-blind about it, or that my eyes were made with different lenses. I am afraid I am not just like other women," added Avis simply, dipping her brush with deep absorption in the madder-rose.

"Thank Heaven!" said Ostrander, in a low, delirious tone.

Avis lifted her eyes with a startled change of expression, holding the tube of brilliant color like an arrested thought upon the air.

"I did not understand you," she said gravely.

"I said you were in danger of dropping the madder-rose. There! Allow me. Do not stir: it will hit the hem of your dress."

He stooped to pick it up, her dress, as he did so, falling with a faint electric touch against his hand. Raising his head suddenly, he surprised her eyes upon him. They were wide, grave, imperious. They made him think of a Juno that he knew, and thought the grandest in the world. Was it the sensitiveness of a young man's wounded vanity that led him to fancy that her lips parted with something of the dumb and delicate scorn that the lips of that Ludovisi Juno,[4] alone of all sculpture that he had ever seen, commanded?

In truth, Avis had come home with large segments of her nature not altogether occupied by young Scandinavian divinities; and it is doubtful if all the gods of Olympus would have appealed to her sensibilities on any sustained scale, just then, other than as affording more or less fresh material for "a charcoal," "a memory," or "a sienna."

As the souls of the dead are said, in the hideous fable, to suck the heart's blood of the living, so, without doubt, a great purpose sprung too early upon a young life may dehumanize it,—sometimes does. It is impossible to over-estimate the effect of substituting an intellectual for an emotional passion in the absorbent phases of a woman's life which are covered by the decade from sixteen to twenty-six. Such an experience may prune the nature, as we are told that hardship does that of certain savage races, retarding their tenderer impulses. While the other girls talked of love and lovers, Avis sat and sketched their shy, expectant faces. Yet nothing could be more fatal to horticulture than to mistake the retarded for the stunted or the sterile growth. Avis's abundant being had suffered no depletion. She was alive to the nerves of her soul. She was still an unwon woman. She felt even glad sometimes, that there were men in the world who loved her. She liked to think that they loved her because they could not help it. She wondered why it was, that, the swifter the retreat of her nature from them had been, the surer had been the advance of theirs. She was sorry about it when it happened; but she had no coquettish consciousness of having been in fault. And she thought very humbly of her power to mar the music of any other life. Men usually married. And it was pleasant to remember that she was not unlovely or unlovable. Sometimes, when she sat before her easel, forecasting her fair future, she felt suddenly glad, with a downright womanish thrill, that she was so sure of the beauty and patience of her purpose; that she was not to live a solitary life because no other had been open to her. Perhaps the woman does not live for whom the kingdoms of earth and the glory of them could blunt the tooth of that one little poisoned thought.

And Avis did not mean to marry: that was a matter of course. It was not necessary to talk about it: young women were apt to say something of the sort, she believed. She had never meant to marry, and she knew that she had never meant to. She acted upon this consciousness as reticently as she did upon the combinations of her palette, and as naturally as she did upon the reflex motion of her muscles.

But the silent footsteps of the spring crept on. It was pleasant in the garden studio. The square little building with the Gothic door and porch, and long, low windows, stood within call of the house, yet was quite isolated by the budding trees, an island in a sea of leaves. It gave a sense of solitude to the fancy, which was rather heightened than lessened by the close presence of unseen life. When aunt Chloe, who had the best intentions in the world in the matter of matronizing Avis through this portrait, trotted in and out in her short garden-gown, it seemed somehow only to deepen their isolation. When she suddenly remembered that the lilies were to have been bedded this morning, or wondered if Jacobs had let the cows into the corn-patch, or was afraid the newspaper over the wisteria had been blown away, or was sure Julia would get the dumplings underdone, or the professor get home from lecture before the study was dusted, and, begging Mr. Ostrander to excuse her for a minute, vanished for an hour, Avis, looking gently after her, used to think of some odd, old words: "*Then she departed into her own country by another way.*"[5] Turning to Ostrander, she would find his eyes upon her; but his lips said nothing. The robins came and peered at them with curious glance upon the window-ledge; a ground-sparrow who had built her nest just beneath the wooden doorstep twittered in a tender monotone; the boughs of the budding apple-trees hit the glass with slender finger-tips, and reddened if one looked at them; the dumb sunlight crawled inch by inch, like a creeping child, across the steps, and in upon the floor; the air was full of the languors of unseen buds; far and faint upon the shore summoned the rapture of the hidden sea.

He could understand, Ostrander thought, why it was given to the first man to woo the first woman in a garden. Out of all the untried moods of the new heavens and the new earth,—the gloom of the forest, the strength of the hills, the stir of the moors, or the glory of the sea,—what could have taught that perfect primeval creature the slow, sweet lesson of love's surrender, like the temper of one budding flower?

Eve, he had always fancied, was rather hard to win.

And now the hurrying footsteps of the spring swept on.

In the ripening grass the clover-buds appeared, bursting into color impetuously, like kisses that a child throws to the sky. In the pansy-bed beside the summer-house, aunt Chloe's old-fashioned lady's-delights lifted their impressive faces, and sat like philosophers in the sun, asking forever a question to which no man could reply. The imperfectly defined scent of buds faded from an air gone drunk with yielding blossoms. One day, as Avis sat painting busily, there came a stir upon the apple-tree, as if a spirit had troubled the soul of it. A fine, almost inaudible sound, like a murmur of appeal or remonstrance, crossed the boughs; and a shower of blossoms fell in upon her.

"Every petal is a perfumed shell," said Avis, drawing her breath.

"See how they drift to their places, drawn by the currents, compelled by the currents, of an unseen tide!" answered Ostrander.

His voice had the tense resonance which precedes tremulousness.

"This means," he said, as he stooped to gather a leaf which had fallen from her hair, and was sinking with a reluctant motion to the floor,—"this means that May is past, and June has come to us."

He said this in his penetrative undertone,—that tone which may mean any thing or nothing, but which, in Ostrander, gave one the impression that he spoke in a delicate, spiritual cipher, to which it were a dulness amounting to grossness not to find the key. He thought, as he spoke, that a faint flush stirred across Avis's listening face; but, if so, it was transparent as the color of the petal in his hand, and as swift to fade.

"I have been very slow about the portrait," returned Avis, hastening to speak. "I worked more rapidly with a master. At the first plunge into a solitary struggle, a self-distrust, which I can neither explain nor avoid, comes upon me now and then, like the cramp upon a swimmer; yet I am quite sure I am doing better work. If we had multiplied the sittings a little, the picture would have been— should have been—finished before the apple-blossoms fell."

"Pray do not misunderstand me," urged Ostrander gently. "How could you for one moment think"—

"Mr. Ostrander," interrupted Avis, with a sudden piercing candor in her eyes, "I did not misunderstand you."

"Then tell me," pleaded Ostrander, caressing the apple-blossom which lay quivering across his hand like a thing that might fly,— "tell me what I would have said. I am struck dumb to-day."

"I think you meant to say that there is a calendar for all kind thought that people acquire of one another," said Avis quietly. "All friendliness is a progression. A friend is a marvel, a creation, a discovery, a growth like a year; and June will follow May."

"A friend, a friend!" said the young man, bringing his hand slowly across his eyes. "How often do you find the June in the soul of a friend?"

"I am not sure," said Avis, laying down her brushes, "that we either of us quite know what we are trying to say. Strictly, since you ask me, I must think my life has been barren of that which, it seems to me, a friend would put into it. Of course, one is always giving and receiving a sort of service and tenderness. But I see many women find the closest sympathies and the deepest comfort. Perhaps I have been necessarily too much absorbed in my own affairs to cultivate that divine self-oblivion which is the first condition of friendship."

She took up her brushes with a solitary look; but, before Ostrander could answer, it had turned into an expression which deterred him from speech, like an outstretched hand. He had never seen her look so seriously annoyed, nay, disturbed. He had heard women talk about friendship before: he had never seen one who did not mellow under the subject like a September afternoon. But Miss Dobell froze before the sunbeam fell.

In truth, Avis was bitterly annoyed with herself. She recoiled from her little innocent impulse as if it had held the compromising power of an imprudence, and felt the scathing hurt which a delicate nature receives from the re-action of all misplaced ardor.

She had not reached the age—perhaps with those serious eyes of hers would be long in doing so—when we can catch only the ludicrous angle in the sight of a woman talking friendship with a man.

But a friend—, a *friend*. She had allowed this man a momentary privilege, sacred and mystical to her as her maidenly dim vision of the rights of plighted love. He had overtaken her upon the boundary of a country holy as heaven, and human as Eden. Avis Dobell, in her nurtured, loved, and eventful, but, as she truly said, most solitary life, had dreamed of the heart of a friend with more passion and more reserve than most women dedicate to the lover of their young ideal. But, like Frigga, the wife of Odin, who foreknew, but never foretold, the destinies of men, she had the silence of her inspirations.

She had never told anybody that she felt solitary before; she had never chattered about sympathy, or cackled about being imperfectly understood; an obstinate weakness in people, which she hated as she did some of her tubes of paint, always telling on the colors of character, killing superior values by its terrible encroachment. All forms of self-pity, like Prussian-blue, should be sparingly used.

A friend? Her friend? What was this that she had done?

She felt a sudden sick emptiness of soul, as if an artery had been opened there, which no human power could ever bind. Her whole nature crouched, as if it would spring upon this man who had severed it.

She had returned to her painting quietly enough. Ostrander watched her between his half-closed, guarded eyes. "Beautiful leopardess!" he said; but he did not say it aloud.

And now it was June in the garden studio.

Coy was privileged one day to come in when Avis was working alone, and criticise the picture.

"I suppose I must make a fish-horn of my fingers?" said the young lady plaintively. "I never knew an artist who didn't go about the world with one hand curled up at his eye like the tin fish-horns that we find in galleries to see the pictures through. I always use them devoutly, of course; but I never knew what they were there for.—Yes, Avis, that is a likeness. His eyes are too big, and his nose is too little, and there's too much—what do you call it?—action? in the left mustache; but it is a very good likeness. How much you have improved! As Mrs. Hogarth says, 'It will be quite a step for Avis.'"

"I do not mean to paint portraits," said Avis, coloring slightly, "though Couture said I probably must, in America. But I have different plans: at least I have different hopes. Is the hair too highly lighted, Coy?"

"No." Coy uncurled her hand like a long spiral shell, and bent her two keen, unaided eyes upon Avis. "No: your portrait is alive. Flattered, of course: that is the first duty of a portrait-painter. I didn't know before, that Mr. Ostrander had a mother. I wonder if she gave him his light hair. He looks like the people with the horrid Norse names in the poems Longfellow's taken to writing,— Frigga, and those."

"Wasn't Frigga a woman?" suggested Avis.

"Oh, well! it's all the same. He has the antique, Icelandic style. Mrs. Hogarth is much interested about it."

"Ah!" said Avis.

"And Barbara," added Coy. "But then Barbara isn't in the Faculty." Avis made no reply.

"In fact, Avis, I may say that the greater part of Harmouth is familiar with the history and progress of this portrait."

"Oh! I suppose so," said Avis wearily. "It is just so if a woman writes a poem, or does any thing less to be expected than making One-Two-Three-Four Cake. I must submit to that: I work so busily and so happily, that I seldom think about it. But I suppose the woman never lived who would not rather work in the shelter of a desert or a star."

"Very true," said Coy with her most motherly air. "And you know, Avis, you never even knew till you got home, that Harmouth had engaged you in Florence to two sculptors and one artist—no, two artists and a sculptor, besides the Italian count."

"You are wrong: it was a German baron," said Avis in a tone of scientific precision.

"At all events," said Coy, with a swift glance from the portrait to Avis, and back again to the portrait, "it is a good subject. Mr. Rose says they call him the beauty of the Faculty,—the belle of the Faculty, I think he said. Isn't that good? The Antinous[6] of a college Faculty! I should as soon look for a Belvedere[7] in the third tertiary strata. Now, there's my father. If it hadn't been for mother's kind interference, I suppose I might have looked like him; probably should have been proportionately intellectual. Brains and beauty, as some one was saying the other day of the critic and the creator,— but I don't *think* that was Mr. Rose,—seem to be born enemies."

"O Coy!" cried Avis, lighting. "Schiller and Goethe and Burns! And see that print of Robertson behind you."

"Very likely," insisted Coy. "Indeed, I know girls who are more in love with a photograph of Frederick Robertson[8] to-day than they ever were with a live man. But all the same I stake my point, and refer you to any good album of the poets—or the clergy. As a rule, a man can't cultivate his mustache and his talents impartially. There's apt to be something askew or deficient in handsome men. They don't do great things, I think, more than flowers do—or women."

So, with a pretty ingenuity that she had, Coy worked out the chance barbs which had annoyed Avis. She knew. Avis never sat so still with just one vein throbbing in her temple, unless she were annoyed. And yet the June budded in the garden studio; and one day the portrait was done.

Avis, feeling the inevitable strain which falls upon the portrait-artist with the completion of a work, had slept lightly and little for several nights. The moment when the subject and the picture are first brought face to face, she thought no experience could ever make other than one of refined nervous trial to her. She had often heard artists speak of this; and some of them never outgrew it, as some great orators are found never to outgrow the sudden sick bounding of the heart, and trembling of the muscles of the face, which the first sight of an audience produces.

The artist's public, narrowed for the moment into one pair of human eyes, acquires a kind of omnipotence, like that of the sliding wall in the old story of martyrdom, which, towering higher as each day brings it nearer, creeps to crush the victim at the appointed hour.

She once heard Alexander[9] say that he could tell across the studio, by the look of a man's back, whether he liked his picture.

She would have been sorry not to have Mr. Ostrander like the portrait, but more sorry, she thought, if it failed to please that lonely old mother in New Hampshire. Mr. Ostrander had said that he was not able to visit his mother as often as he would like; the state of his health requiring a different climate in the brief vacations which an over-worked man cannot afford not to expend to the best physical advantage. He had said this so sadly, that Avis felt very sorry for him. It did not occur to her till afterwards to be very sorry for the old lady.

As the day drew on when she was to show him the picture, her repressed excitement deepened. She must have lost more sleep than she had supposed, so taut a tension seemed to have been sprung upon her nerves.

During the night she lay with wide eyes, seeing the souls of un-wrought pictures, like disembodied spirits, sweep by, vision upon vision, electrotyped upon the darkness with the substance of wine or opium fantasies; an experience which chanced to her only in her most fertile moods. When day broke, a strange buoyancy overtook her. Her veins seemed filled with a fine fire, like an intoxication which she had seen follow the use of certain rare *liqueurs* among Parisian women,—juices expressed from subtle fruits, or the flowers of fruits, after which the Lachrymae Christi[10] seemed gross.

Ostrander came after tea to see the picture. Her father and aunt Chloe had just been in, finding themselves sufficiently pleased with the work: but a Faculty meeting, involving a pet quarrel with the Theological Chair, absorbed the professor; and aunt Chloe had an oleander to water before the sun had set. The artist and the model were left alone.

It was still quite light. The birds, in unseen nests, were singing themselves to sleep with a lessening, crooning cry, as children do, one by one falling smothered in silence. The surf upon the beach had died; only a slight sob came from the Harbor, like that of a creature in whom a great struggle had worn to a peaceful close. There was not wind enough to take the pollen from a lily. But the bees were awake, and hummed dizzily among the flowers.

"My picture must be the final cause of this evening," said Ostrander lightly, as they approached the easel; for he felt her strained nerves beneath her quiet manner, as sailors feel the prophecy of a storm upon a sleeping sea. "Such a coloring will define it like a frame. . . . Ah! There. Do not move it. The light is perfect—and so is the portrait. Miss Dobell, my mother will be satisfied."

"You are very good to think so," said Avis, drawing her breath. "But shall *you* be satisfied?"

"More than satisfied," said Ostrander, after a pause. He stood for a few moments, silently looking at the picture, before he added in a lower tone, "Much more. Do I really look like that? Out of the kind eyes of a friend? . . . Why!" turning suddenly, so that his eyes swept her face and figure, "are you so tired? You are worn out. I have wearied you. Pray do not stand."

In truth Avis trembled heavily, and sank into the chair which he had brought.

"Did you mind *me* so much?" murmured Ostrander, with a daring rapture in his voice.

"I am ashamed!" she cried impetuously; "but it is a nervousness I have when a picture comes to an end. It is like the ending of a life."

Her chance words fell with a sudden dreary significance upon them both as they sat looking across the little room, which seemed to be absorbent of the intense evening light, and to throb like a topaz about them.

Avis looked up at him with timid, candid eyes. It would be lonely in the studio to-morrow: he must know that. She had nothing to conceal from this man,—nothing, nothing! She repeated the word to herself with a sharpening emphasis.

But she rose with a swift motion, as if she discarded some encroaching thought, and, going to the doorway, stood there, looking out across the garden.

Ostrander followed her, and gently said,—

"Do you see the bees on the wigelia?"

As he spoke, one circled away from the blush of the shrub, and hovered over her with a slow, intoxicated swing.

"You have flowers about you," he said.

"No—yes: I had forgotten. It is the rose[11] in my hair."

She flung it away as she spoke with a startled gesture.

"You did not listen," said Ostrander, "to the bee. Have you forgotten the pretty thought about the growing of the grass and budding of the flowers?[12]—that it is only because our eyes are not fine enough, that we do not see a lily open, or a clover bloom; and only because our ears are not delicate enough, that we do not hear the sap circulate in a rose-leaf, or the heart throb in the insect that alights upon it."

"I have thought of that," said Avis in a low voice, "every day. Sights that I never saw, and sounds that I never heard, it seems to me I have heard and seen this spring. Something ails the June. I have felt as if I had her heart beneath a microscope all the time. It is the being at home, I think, and finding my father so well, and content to see me hard at work. And I am always excited when I am at work."

"No," said Ostrander in a changed voice. "No, that is not it. I believe you are the only woman in the world who would not understand. You do not, will not, *will* not. Ah, hush! For all that ails the June is, that we love each other."

The young man had hardly uttered these words before he would have given a ransom to recall them.

There is something appalling, at times, to the dullest fancy, in the inexorable nature of human speech. The word that has leaped from the lips has gone, as the soul goes from the body; it has taken on the awful rebellion of a departed spirit; to recall it is like recalling the dead. A moment ago your friend was yours, to have and to hold, to kiss, to clasp. Now, whose is he? and what? and where? An instant past, your thought was your slave, mute, subservient, safe: now it defies you.

Ostrander had felt himself blindly driven, that evening, towards some riot of expression, circling slowly to it as the bee circled to the flower in her abundant hair. He had struggled against this impulse stoutly. As long as his love was his secret, he felt himself to be, in a certain mystical, exalted sense, the master of this beautiful, defiant creature. He could love her. She could not help that. Deeper than all the moods that the subtle June night could ever strike, he knew now that he loved her. It was no riot: he was not the man to mistake a revolution for a riot; he knew the difference.

He had been spurred into speech by an instinct, daring as all instincts are, and as full of danger.

And his instinct had told him that this was a woman to be surprised, not wooed. He felt, that, if he came suppliant to her, her whole being would have gathered itself like a queen, and receded from him. He could not have dallied with her, or pleaded with her, or sighed before her: that seemed to him an artificial process, adapted for the winning of other women, in whose tenderness there was usually an element of art. They might melt beneath it: it would be like the administration of ether to the grand simplicity of her soul; the influence meant to subject her into a gentle dream would prove a powerful excitant; she would freeze under it, like ice mechanically formed at mid-summer.

He could not think of her as a woman to whom a man would ever say, "Learn to love me. Permit me to teach you. Suffer me to be near you." He would as naturally have said to a beautiful torrent, "Seek to love me;" or beckoned to some sweet, wild creature of the woods, expecting it to fawn at his feet.

The young man's nature had leaped to entrap her, as the hero in the old mythology crossed the ring of fire that surrounded the daughter of the gods.[13] When he had made the plunge, he found indeed a woman sleeping; but it was a woman armed.

Avis lifted her eyes slowly, like one struggling with a fugitive dream. He would have given years of his life at that moment to see her lip tremble, or her eyelash fall, or her commanding figure shrink. She did, indeed, change color, but it was to take on the color of white fire. And then the antique cast of her features came on. She looked like a great, dumb, protesting goddess, whom some light hand had just dragged from the bosom of the earth to the glare of day.[14]

As they stood there, the humming of the bees in the wigelia-bush[15] reverberated, and seemed to fill the world. One crawled out of the rose which she had cast away, and reeled against her foot. They stood just as his broken words had arrested them, fastened by each other's eyes. Suddenly in hers there dawned a far, startled look: she began to turn her neck a little from side to side, like a deer stirred by the sound, but not as yet by the sight of pursuit, and secretly preparing for flight.

Then she thrust out both her hands.

"I deny it!" said the woman.

"I assert it!" said the man. They faced one another, flashing like duellists.

"You assume," she blazed, stammering, and struggling with her words,—"you presume—what no man"—

"I presume to say that I love you," he urged, swiftly scintillating into a dazzling tenderness. "I quite dare to say that I love you. I know what I am saying. I love you, love you!"

At that moment his words seemed to her a kind of unendurable liberty, like personal approach, as if he had touched her dress or hand. Her startled maidenhood felt a wild rebellion in just stand-ing there, and knowing that his eyes were on her. Her own had now fallen. She began to quiver and flush, but it was not with tender-ness. She was caught between two fires. She could not have told just then for which cause she felt most repellant of him,—that he loved her, or that he had told her she loved him. A kind of wide recoil from him, such as she had never known from any man, made either of these suppositions seem to her like usurpations; like infringements of some blind, sacred law, which she felt about her, like the evening air, and would seek to understand at a calmer time. But it was not an instinct of repugnance that had spread in a moment—there, through the calm June afterglow—a sudden im-passable distance between herself and this man (an antipathy would have been less complex, and so more tractable, than this feeling): it was a rebound of dismay; it was at once blindly instinc-tive and rigidly measured, like that which one makes before a plunge.

No man had ever spoken to her like this man. His words had the character of events. She felt as if she had in one moment put a great fact behind her, whose effects the whole of life could not undo. What was the weakness in her nature that had made this experience possible? and what the tumult there which made it memorable, stamped it upon her like the mould of a great sorrow, or a wild joy?

Her startled look had broadened now, and brightened, like a light coming near and nearer to one through the undergrowth of a dense forest. There was even a kind of appeal in her voice, though it was with ceremonious dignity that she said,—

"I hope, Mr. Ostrander, that you may find yourself as much mistaken in your own feeling as you have been, so extraordinarily, in mine. It will undoubtedly be so. Nothing is easier than to overestimate the depth of a passing influence."

"I have over-estimated nothing," persisted he doggedly. "And I am mistaken in nothing. Ah, hush! Let me speak; let me explain. You do not understand yourself or me. You recoil; you are angry with me. I was abrupt, I was uncouth, I was unreasonable; but before God I believe I was right. Turn to me one moment. Let me see your eyes. Let me beg of you to listen"—

"I wonder, Mr. Ostrander," said aunt Chloe, panting up across the pansy-bed, "if I *might* so greatly trouble you as to help me one moment with the grape-vine.—And, Avis, I am sorry; but there are callers: I think it is Mr. Allen and his sister; and the grape-vine will get a sprain if I leave it as it is. I thought—if they'll excuse the garden-gown—you would like to bring them out, and get their criticism upon the picture."

CHAPTER VII

ARMGART:
"I accept the peril;
I choose to walk high with
sublimer dread
Rather than crawl in safety."
GRAF:
"Armgart, I would with all my
soul I knew
The man so rare, that he could
make your life
As woman sweet to you, as
artist safe."
—George Eliot [1]

He sought her the next day without preface or apology, and like a man demanded his hearing out. There was a perfectly new element in his manner to her, that had almost the dignity of a claim or right; but to resent this seemed like resenting the sacred incoherencies of grief. Avis received him gently.

He found her wandering in the fields about the shore. She could not work. She, too, had not slept, and looked well-nigh as worn as he. They did not sit down, but walked restlessly to and fro through the long, impeding grass.

He could not catch her eye; but the expression of her mouth when he began to speak disheartened him. He had never seen her put her lips together so. Avis felt that a battle was impending. Even her gentleness had a kind of strategical character. Her foot fell upon the bruised clover with a martial rhythm. The whole force of her, soul and body seemed to garrison itself.

He began by telling her in a tone of proud humility that he had been too hasty yesterday; that though it was not possible that he could be mistaken in his own feeling, as she would know, if she knew him better, yet that it was never easy for a man's imagination to employ itself upon the nature of a woman.

"And you," he said, with a lover's ingenious gravity, "are like no other woman,—no other that I ever saw. I do not believe the world contains another. You perplex me like the Sphinx; you awe me like the Venus; you allure me like the Lörelei! I have dreamed of such women. I never saw one. I love you!"

He turned to her with a kind of solemn authority, as if in those three words all the swift, sweet arguments of his heart had so clearly culminated, that it would be as impossible for her to combat them as it was to advance any thing more compelling or convincing; as if he had said, "The sky is blue fire," or "The daisy turns to it," or "The tide leans to the shore."

He looked at her a little blindly, with half-fallen lids: there was a hazy radiance in his eyes, from the full force of which it was as if he shielded her. Glancing up with some unspoken protest on her lips, she seemed to feel this; she put her hand across her own eyes as if she had been dazzled.

"When a man loves a woman as I love you," he said quietly, "he expects to be loved; he has a right to be; he must be."

"You do not know what you say!" she cried: "you don't know what you ask. I am not a woman to make you—to make any man happy. Even if I"—

"Ah, what? Even if you what? Rest here a minute in the shade, and tell me. You shut your heart away from me. Let me stay here till I find it."

"Then you will stay forever!" flashed the woman, off her guard. He threw himself at her feet, in the shadow of the stone wall, and, across a little cordon of tall daisies that leaped uncrushed between them, looked over at her.

"Even if you"—

"That does not matter now. It was nothing. Let that drop."

"Even if you—what? Pray finish your sentence. You are incapable of small coquetries. If you do not finish your sentence, it must be that you really prefer me to finish it for you."

"No, no! I would rather finish it for myself. I meant to say, that even if I loved you."

"And what then? Suppose—just suppose it that you loved me. Suppose that all this spring, the feeling—you have called it artistic fervor; the sympathy—you have thought it friendliness; the sweetness,—I believe you thought that had something to do with your father; all the glory that has come into life; all this delicate intoxication that has been between us two, man and woman, created by heaven, to love, to yield, like other men and women"—

"I will never yield, like other women!" cried Avis, quivering across the daisies.

"But suppose," he continued, his tone gaining in quiet insistence as hers lost strength in emotion,—"suppose that all this *had* meant that you loved me?"

"Then I should be very sorry," she said tremulously.

"Why sorry?"

"You compel me to repeat an unpleasant thing," she replied

more faintly yet. "I said, even supposing it were as you wish, I could never make you happy."

"I have the right to judge of that,—rather a comfortless right; but I shall not overlook it, nor any other right you give me."

"I have given you none, none!" She rose in much agitation, and, sweeping down the daisies, turned from him. It were hard to say whether it were his eyes or his voice that restrained her,—surely his touch had not fallen upon so much as the hem of her garment,—but she stood swaying and uncertain, and then slowly, as if tender, compelling hands had drawn her, sank down against the wall again.

Perhaps there was a momentary consciousness of weakness in this little act, which stung her; for her whole mood seemed suddenly to gather and defend itself.

"Mr. Ostrander," she said with a gentle distinctness, "we are making a long and painful scene out of a matter which a dozen plain words will settle."

"Then," said he," let us speak the plain words."

She sat for a moment with her face turned towards him, in the attitude of one who waits for expected speech. But the young man, with his elbow in the daisies, and his head upon his hand, lay watching her in a kind of trance. His eyes had gone quite dull and blind, as if the force of his repressed feeling had been an objective presence, like a mid-day sun. Turning, she saw this memorable look, for the first, but not the last time in her life. Her resolution seemed to gather courage from it; and she said with increasing quietness,—

"The plain word is, that I do not, and I must not, think of love, because the plain truth is, that I cannot accept the consequences of love as other women do."

"Oh, I see! I was a brute to make you say that," cried Ostrander impatiently. That blind look broke suddenly, and scattered into an uncertain, darting gleam, like a ball of quicksilver crushed. "You mean that you do not wish to marry?"

"Certainly I mean that. But it was a little hard to be made to say it. Now it is said, I don't care. There is an end to it."

"It is not love, then, that you feel a disrespect for, but marriage? You prefer to marry Art, I suppose," he said perplexedly. "You are happier so?"

"I feel no disrespect for either, that I am conscious of; but surely I am happier as I am." That sensitive vein on her temple throbbed painfully. What did this man take her for? Painted canvas, perhaps; or a marble antique; a torso, possibly; something mechanically constructed on the principles of the highest art, content to gather the dust of her studio without a heart-throb; a fleshless, bloodless thing. A great impulse surged over her to rise, and cry out to him,—

"I am human, I am woman! I have had my dreams of love like other women!" But that was not a matter to chatter about. When she found the man who could both understand and reverence these dreams—but in her wildest vision she had only seen his face as we see the loved faces of the dead, sacred, safe, and snatched from her. God gave her the power to make a picture before he gave her the power to love a man.

And this man, *this*, who had confused and agitated, nay, half blinded her, with whom her nature found escape or surrender equally impossible,—what should she do with him? She thought of him with a kind of terror which only a woman can understand, because he had come so near, but failed to come nearer, to her; because he had startled her into putting her whole soul in arms which he had failed to conquer. She almost wished at that moment that she could have loved like other women, and that she could have loved him. That experience, at least, would have had the beauty of holiness: this bore the bruise of sacrilege.

His thoughts, like a witch-hazel, seemed to follow and command the spring of hers; for just then he said abruptly,—

"So, then, if you loved me, you are sure you would not marry me? We might be so happy! Did you never think of that?"

He drew a little nearer to her. Both the words and the motion had something of the nature of unconsciousness. The tall white daisies swayed delicately in the golden air between them.

"A woman never thinks—I never thought—of such a thing in such a way," said Avis, with recoiling eyes.

"I beg your pardon. A man is so different! and *you* are so different from most women! But, if you loved me, you would marry me all the same. You should be happy. You should paint. I should be proud to have you paint. I used to think I should be wretched with a gifted wife (all young men do); but you have taught me better. It would be the purpose—do not think it the ravings of a lover if I say it would be the passion—of my life to help you realize your dreams of success."

Avis smiled sadly; but she said, with the evidence and the consciousness of feeling more deeply shaken than any he had yet seen,—

"How can you know what my dreams are? Did I ever tell them to you? You are using a language that you do not understand. My ideals of art are those with which marriage is perfectly incompatible. Success—for a woman—means absolute surrender, in whatever direction. Whether she paints a picture, or loves a man, there is no division of labor possible in her economy. To the attainment of any end worth living for, a symmetrical sacrifice of her nature is compulsory upon her. I do not say that this was meant to be so. I do not think we know what was meant for women. It is enough that it *is* so. God may have been in a just mood, but he was not in a merciful one, when, knowing that they were to be in the same world with men, he made women."

"But suppose," interrupted Ostrander, thrilling with hope in proportion as she fired with rebellion,—"suppose two people had been born to show that this need not be so. That would be very much like God, on the whole, to let the whole world suspect, if it dared not accuse, him of injustice in a given course, and then spring the abounding mercy of it on us at the brink of faith's surrender. Suppose a man and woman had been made and led and drawn to one another, just to show that the tolerance of individuality, even the enthusiasm of superiority, could be a perfectly mutual thing."

"There may be such women in the world," said Avis: "I have never seen such a man. Only lovers think it to be possible."

Nothing could have disheartened him like the delicate tooth of perfectly unconscious satire biting through those last few words; not even her lapse into her wonted self-command, nor the sealed eyes which she was turning away from him to the restless sea. He understood, as perfectly as if she had said so, that the tide of an emotion stronger than he had ever witnessed in her had turned, and was setting out from him. He was only half comforted when she added, in the calmer tone of one who brings a discussion to an inexorable close,—

"I never said to any one what I have said to you to-day, if that is any pleasure to you: it will be none to me."

"I suppose," he said, after an oppressive silence, "if I had been more of a man, a man of genius for instance, I might have commanded your love by this time. Whatever my abilities are, they are untried. Your future is so far established. It is all so different from the way a man and woman usually meet! A man of my sort must seem to you so young. To your inspirational atmosphere what a plodding dog a college tutor is! I suppose a gifted woman dreams of a great man. I shall never be a great man; but—with you—I might do some worthy work. I feel a unity in all aims, all hope, since I have known you; life seems symmetrical and coherent, and worth while. It does not always. I am a restless fellow."

"I am sure you will do worthy work," said Avis with ringing earnestness,—"sure, sure!"

"Are you so sure? Thank you for that. I wish I were."

"And you mistake me," she continued eagerly, "in what you said just now. I don't think I could love a great man, if I tried."

"Why not?" asked Ostrander, a faint smile encroaching upon the deepening pain of his face.

"I never asked myself why, any more than I ask myself why I thrill to paint a picture, and suffer to sew a seam. It is enough to feel such things, if you feel them as hard as I do. But I suppose it is the moral nature of a man a woman needs—I mean I should need— to find great. That is noble, I think,—to be a man, and be great in goodness; to have faith and tenderness and truth, and whiteness of soul. I should care much less for what was in a man's head than what was in his heart. And a great man is absorbed: he is not so apt to think of little things; he is too busy to be tender, I should say."

"But that is the way," said he, "that men feel about women, not women about men."

"Is it?" asked Avis, sighing: "I do not know. I should think all women would feel so. But I have told you more than enough, Mr. Ostrander, of what I think and feel. It cannot help us any. And no man's love can be meant for me."

"Now that," he said musingly, "is what I cannot quite understand. I never knew a woman in my life who could love a man so much—if she would. Pray forgive me! Ah, you do not—you dare not—deny that. You would perjure your own nature if you tried."

"God forbid that I perjure my own nature!" answered Avis, beginning to grow pale. "But, as I live, I should perjure it if I said to you to-day that I believed love and marriage were meant for me. And whatever it would be to me—this life that other women seem to be so—happy in; this feeling that other women—have—to offer to the man they"—

She broke off abruptly: her voice had fallen to an awe-struck whisper.

Her solemn reticence and reluctance before this experience which he had been used to see women enter upon both readily and irreverently, affected Ostrander as the flash of a new planet affects the astronomer whose telescope misses to-day what it has discovered yesterday. He brought his dry hands together, and wrung them,—a silent, eloquent gesture.

"Marriage," said Avis, not assertantly, but only sadly, as if she were but recognizing some dreary, universal truth, like that of sin, or misery, or death, "is a profession to a woman.[2] And I have my work; I have my work!"

"But suppose," he suggested, "that your future should fail to fulfil its—present promise— Be patient with me! You cannot think I am capable of underrating that promise. As I see it, it is a splendid one. But fate is so false to genius!—perhaps most of all to women, as you say. A thousand things may baffle you. You dare the loss of what nineteen centuries of womanhood has held as the life of its life; you dare the loss of home and love for—God forbid that I say an unproved but as yet untried power."

"At least," she said, after a silence in which she had sat not unmoved,—"yes, at least I can dare.[3] There is that in me which will not *permit* me not to dare. God gave it to me."

"Amen!" said the young man solemnly. Just then he could add no more. He had, perhaps, never thought till that moment that God really did give such things to women. How right she was about it! How true, how strong! His reverence for her grew with his sense of loss. His ardor deepened under her denial. He had always thought he should learn to hate a woman who had been too easily won. It seemed to him at that moment that he would rather be scorned by her than loved by any other creature in the world.

"May I not come another day?" he pleaded; for she had risen as she spoke, and, carefully stepping around the daisy cordon, turned her face towards her father's house.

"What could be gained?" said Avis sadly. "We can neither of us spare the strength needed for our life's work—you or I—on scenes like this. They take strength. How tired you look!"

She looked up at him with a sudden womanly quiver on her face, and held out her hand.

"You won't mind it, if I say that I shall—miss you? Or that I shall always like to know you are my friend?" she added timidly. "And by and by, when all is different . . . and we can talk of other things . . . you will come back to me?"

"If ever I come back to you, it will be to stay," said Ostrander under his breath. "You will not get rid of me so easily, if you beckon me back." But he turned haggardly away; and, leaping the wall with a mighty bound, strode off alone upon the beach.

Avis stood as he had left her till he was out of sight; then slowly, as if each nerve and muscle in her body yielded separately, sank down among the daisies, throwing her arms above her head, among their roots. She was worn with the strain of the last few days. She thrust her cheek down into the cool, clean earth, and let the grass close over her young head with a dull wish that it were closing for the last time.

As she lay there, prone as a fallen Caryatide, steps crushed the clovers; Ostrander had returned, and stood again beside her.

"Pardon me," he said deprecatingly. "I have no right, but the right of my misery, to intrude in this way. I thought you would have heard me. Do not stir. I have only come back to ask you a single question."

He parted the long grass that had closed above her, and looked down. She had sprung, half leaning on her elbow, and lifted her face, which gathered a chill from the dull green shadow in which she was.

"In your soul's name and mine," he said, "will you answer what I shall ask?"

"I will try," she said solemnly.

"Tell me, then," he proceeded with a dizzy feeling, wondering whether it were madness or inspiration that possessed him, and why a man must find in either an iron necessity like this that flogged him into speech, "tell me,—it is all you can do for me now, and I dare believe you would relieve the pain you must inflict so far as you can,—tell me if I am the man you would have, might have, loved?"

All her face and figure, which had been suffused while he spoke, with a beautiful compassion, grew tense. She flung out one bent elbow as if she had been warding off a blow. But she said still solemnly,—

"For your soul's sake and mine, you are the man I *will* not love."

It was not long, possibly it might have been a week or ten days, after the completion of the portrait, when one evening, as Avis came in rather wearily from the studio, she found aunt Chloe beckoning mysteriously to her from the piazza-steps. Aunt Chloe had on the purple-and-wood-colored garden-gown that she had bought at a Harmouth bankrupt sale, since three cents a yard was a saving worthy the attention of any woman who handled money often enough to know the value of it; and the difference would exactly get one and a half of those religious mottoes so pretty in the Soldier's Hospital. Aunt Chloe beckoning on the piazza, behind the woodbine, bloomed like a large and rather stumpy pansy. Avis remembered the pattern of that calico, and remembered the outline that the woodbine mercifully dropped upon it, for years after it had gone to adorn some Georgia freedwoman of an undoubtedly deserving, but, it is to be hoped, not an aesthetic cast of mind.

"I wanted to see you, my dear," said aunt Chloe, "about the lemon cream. Can you step into the pantry a minute? There. Just taste it, will you? Too much sugar? I thought so. For a woman who can *not* cook, you are the most faultless taster I ever knew. Thank you. I wonder if you'll shut the door—it blows the cream. That will do. If you've got the paint off your hands, suppose you skim a little for your father's berries. Your father is quite put about, to-night," added aunt Chloe, who seldom dropped into the expressive old Vermont phrase unless the Harmouth anxieties were over-keen.

So that was it. Of course it had not been the lemon cream. Since aunt Chloe had sadly, but, as she hoped, resignedly and finally admitted the glaring culinary deficiencies of Avis's nature, these pantry *matinées* had been rare.

Avis asked, rather listlessly, what was the matter with father this time? Was it the sophomore hazing, or the senior rush? the dangerously lax position taken by the Theological Chair? or had somebody taken the liberty to differ from him about the *non-ego*? Poor father! His nervous irritability grew upon him a little.

"Yes," said aunt Chloe, "I think it does. We must watch him more carefully. We must see that he is kept amused and exercised."

This was said in the tone which aunt Chloe always adopted in discussing this time-honored subject,—the tone usual with the women of a literary man's family; one of calm and gentle superiority to a race of beings, and to a class of weaknesses, which must be tolerated, but might not be cured or improved. Aunt Chloe said he must be kept amused and exercised, exactly as if she had been speaking of a fine terrier or blooded racer, for whose physical nurture she was professionally though affectionately responsible.

"I wonder," went on aunt Chloe, with placid irrelevance, "why we none of us gave Mr. Ostrander his title?"

"His title?" Avis held the skimmer suspended at a rash angle over a plate of bread-cake.

"Yes, his medical title. You know he graduated somewhere in medicine; but I believe he found it distasteful or injurious; I think it was injurious to his health. And I should no more have thought of him as a doctor than I should think of him as a—porpoise," said aunt Chloe, finding her imagination suddenly bankrupt of scientific similes. "But, now he must needs go into the army, it comes into play. It shows the great usefulness of a liberal education, I suppose; but your father is just as much worked up about it. You are dribbling the cream on the breadcake. Your father says the country needs superior young men to preserve the tone of her colleges as much as she does at the front just now. And he says there's a plethora of surgeons. Mr. Ostrander was such a pet with him! What have you done with the skimmer? And the worst of it is"—

"Well," said Avis, "what is the worst of it?" For aunt Chloe had suddenly set her sentence away to cool in the ice-chest, into which she had dived bodily on one of those mysterious domestic inspirations which Avis had long since ceased attempting to fathom. Aunt Chloe's face and shoulders had quite disappeared; but the back of the pansy-gown presented a broad and impressive front, if I may be allowed the expression. Avis's eyes traced the pattern up and down. There seemed to be nothing but a brown palm-leaf and a purple stripe in all the world.

"You were saying, aunt Chloe, the worst of it was"—

"The berries are withered," said aunt Chloe, slowly exhuming herself from the refrigerator. "Oh, yes! the worst of it is about the professorship. Mr. Ostrander received the call last night, and this morning he enlisted for three months. That is what has put your father out so. I told him, if the young man was worth any thing, he was worth their waiting for. But he said three months was long enough to kill a man, and that he liked to see a young fellow have a mind, and stick to it. Now, if you'll call Julia, we will have these picked over."

The next day Coy and Barbara came over to beg some of aunt Chloe's flowers to send out to camp, whither, they said, Mr. Ostrander was going in an hour. The next night the professor laid a letter upon Avis's plate at tea, from which, when she opened it, there dropped out a check, drawn in Philip Ostrander's name, upon the Harmouth Bank. It was enclosed in a letter-sheet, on which was written only, in the pencilled camp-scrawl which quickly takes on something of the sacredness of death,—

"I have made it payable to your father's order, thinking it may be more convenient or agreeable for you to cash."[4] Nothing more. It was the price of the portrait.

❧ CHAPTER VIII

"Touch is the sight of the
body. . . . Sight is the touch of
the soul."
—Charles Blanc[1]

Read us at length,
Read this transcendent thing
  Neither angel nor human;
Alert with a lion's strength,
Plumed with an eagle's wing,—
  But still with the face of a
woman.

July kindled slowly but fiercely, like the heart of a furnace. The delicate edges of each nervous leaf on the famous Harmouth elms curled and blackened. The much-gravelled sidewalks burned the dignified feet of the professors on their patient way to lecture. The much-expanded cotton umbrella gloomed gracefully above their heads. The college-boys fitted for biennial under the tutelage of the ice-cream vender, and became the abject preys of the soda-fountain and the lemonade-boy. The yachting-parties drew in their idle sails. Aunt Chloe's anxious watering-pot made no tours among the stifling flowers till the scorching sun had stooped. The blinds of the garden studio were closely drawn.

At the front, hale soldiers dropped from the ranks with sun-stroke, and the wounded died of thirst upon the field. It was the summer of battles,—Fair Oaks, The Seven Days, Cedar Mountain, Bull Run, Harper's Ferry, Antietam.[2]

Avis, that summer, seemed to herself to be turning her life through her fingers, as we turn the pages of a book whose purpose we foreknew, but whose construction is blind: its action moved slowly and almost painfully, like the motion of superfluous details muffling the stir of events. She read on and on and on, with fixed eyes, but with a sense of expectance difficult to explain or justify: by and by the text would be clear; by and by she should live in terse sentences.

She had set herself, with more patience than power, resolutely to work; but she found the lips of her visions muttering in a foreign tongue. She sat entire days before an untouched canvas. She stared entire nights upon untapestried darkness. Her father found her one day, burning the sketches in her studio in a fever of self-despair. He said nothing, except that he thought the sketches were promised to him, gave her a keen look, patted her cheek gently, and went away. He could not help her. He supposed that was the way the "fine frenzy" worked upon the feminine nature.

Perhaps her mother would have known what to say to the child. If she must live this life, she needed her mother. The professor had long since tabulated his daughter as a glittering syllogism whose premises were incorrect, though its conclusion was perversely attractive, and so, like a philosopher, peacefully given her up. It must be admitted that Avis's pictures were better than her biscuit. And man did not live on bread alone. And sometimes, when he came out from the studio, a dimness like faint mist stirred far within his cavernous eyes. She would have been proud of this dark-eyed, deft-handed, undomestic girl. She had never wanted a boy.

Beyond two or three really fine things done in Paris, the landscape which had attracted so much notice in London, a sketch or so in the spring exhibition, and Philip Ostrander's portrait, Avis had as yet done little towards giving form to her ideals; and more than one year of Couture's golden probation was gone.

Her return to America had been in itself one of those stimulating experiences whose immediate effect is a sedative one.

The elemental loves of kin and country had been stirred in her to the finest fibre of their wide-reaching roots. She had come home to find that the afternoon sun in her father's study, on the picture of Sir William, thrilled her as no glory or story of Vatican, Pitti, or Louvre,[3] had ever done. It meant more to her, at first, just to go out into the garden and bury her face in the young grass, and listen to the squirrels scolding in the pear-trees, and the trustful call of the cows waiting for Jacobs down the field, than it seemed as if the fair young picture before her could ever mean. Especially she was moved by the spring scents; the breath of the earth, where the overturned loam lay moistly melting shades of brown together,—amber, umber, sienna, madder, bitumen, and Vandyck,—with that tenderness which is so inexpressibly heightened by the gravity of the color; the aromatic odor of the early bonfires with whose smoke the languid air was blurred and blue; then by the exhalation of small buds, the elm and the grape that borrowed the mantle of the leaf, as wild things do that of the forest, to escape detection. Every sense in her quivered to homely and unobtrusive influences.

It was a long time before she could look at a certain faded cricket in the parlor that her mother worked, without the strange, hot tears. She would not have exchanged the choirs of St. Peter's for the sound of the old chapel bell calling the students to evening prayers.

And then—ah well! and then there had been that slip upon the light-house reef; that had cost its own proportion of dumb days. And after that she had painted the portrait. And then it would have been impossible to forecast the precise personal effect of this war. Life, she thought, had pressed too near her, since she came home, for her to tell the world what it meant; clung too close, and with too sweet insistence, like the friend who stops the mouth with kisses.

All those studies which had stood with their faces to the wall while Ostrander had been in the studio, she would have liked to put out of the wide world, if her father had not cared. She wanted a clean, cold, barren start, like a racer in a moor. There were some pleasant little things among them too,—a Florentine sunset, five poplars on the crest of a hill against a sky of dull metallic red; a Neapolitan girl tossing her *bambino* into the air; a study of breakers under an advancing fog, the mist stalking in about a headland, licking up the deep undertones of a great green wave; figures,—a man and a woman peering over the edge of a precipice under an intense tropical moon; a woman's head, the eyes quite turned away,—a study from some Parisian model,—unfinished.

But Avis put them all back with their faces to the wall, sat an hour longer before her blank canvas, then laid down the charcoals, and went wearily out into the hot air. The sultry evening had settled upon the sultrier day. The college-boys over on the green were singing army songs.

"The studio is too hot," said aunt Chloe with conscientious sympathy. "I wonder if it wouldn't help you out to go down cellar, and stir the ice-cream."

"I shall get to work to-morrow," said Avis, who never liked her studio to be under family discussion. But to-morrow Coy came over to take her to the chapel, where the women of Harmouth sat with hushed voices, rolling bandages and picking lint. The butchery of Bull Run had fallen upon the mangled land.

This meant that it was August in the garden studio. Avis had meant to have a picture—had hoped to have a good picture—well under way by the time that the copper-colored sunlight struggled through the August murk upon the easel.

She went up to her bedroom that night with dogged eyes. She had fallen into one of those syncopes of the imagination in which men have periled their souls to stimulate a paralyzed inspiration. By any cost—"by virtue or by vice, by friend or by fiend, by prayer or by wine"—the dumb artist courts the miracle of speech.

Angel or devil, who is it that troubleth the torpid waters? Equally the soul makes haste, lest another should step down before her.

Avis shut and locked the door of her bare, old-fashioned room, looking about it with a kind of triumphant rebellion. She was a woman. Those four walls shut out the world from the refined license of her mood. She wanted nothing of it,—the great unholy world, in which seers struggled and sinned for their visions. Let them go fighting and erring on. God spoke in another way to women,—in no earthquake, in no fire of the soul, but in still small voices. What would her escaping nature with her? Perhaps by and by, when all the house was still, she would go bounding down through the long grass, and dash herself full-length upon the shore, and let one wave—just one—break its white heart upon her. Or she would push her little boat off from the beach, and row out alone a mile or two down the Harbor, till she was exhausted (and so calmed) by the wooing of the faint moonlit shores. The only thing she could think of that she wanted, out of all the intoxications that the round world held that summer night, would be a room full of hyacinths,—rose-hyacinths,—and some one to play Schumann in the sultry garden. Then, by morning, she might paint her picture.

Was that what the work of women lacked?—high stimulant, rough virtues, strong vices, all the great peril and power of exuberant, exposed life?

Dreamily across the current of her thought, floated the pathetic sound of the boys's voices in the street, still and forever busy with those army songs:—

> "In the beauty of the lilies
> Christ was born across the sea."

She turned from the window with an abrupt, dejected motion. Who could make a picture till the war was over?

> "Since he died to make men holy,"

sang on the boys,

> "Let us die to make men free."[4]

She stood for some moments quite still, in the middle of the room, her arms thrown down, and her fingers clasped together at the tips. Suddenly starting, with a firm step, and half-amused, half-curious lighting of the face, she unlocked a little French dressing-case that stood upon the bureau, and took from it a slender bottle, bearing the trade-mark of a house in the south of France, and the label, "*Eau de Fleurs d'Oranger*."[5]

She poured the liquid out, holding it to the light. Each drop was an amber bead, sluggish and sweet.

Leave men their carousal, their fellowship, the heart's blood of the burning grape. In the veins of the buds that girls wear at their bridals runs a fire of flavor deep enough for us. The wine of a flower has carried many a pretty Parisian to an intrigue or a convent. Could it carry a Yankee girl to glory?

So, half laughing, half credulous, wholly excited, Avis swallowed a cautious dose of the innocent-looking *liqueur*, darkened her room, threw wide her blinds, and went to bed.

In the course of perhaps ten minutes she experienced a slight swimming of the head: she bolstered herself high upon the square pillows, and threw her arms down by her side; they fell heavily, and she found it a task not quite worth the undertaking to stir them again from their places. A dull but not painful pressure set slowly in the brain, and a slight but not disagreeable ringing, in the ears. The most distinct thought that she had was now a sense of relief that she could not hear the army songs. Suddenly the room began to reel. Then, as if a Titan had taken her by the feet, and swung her through infinite space, she felt herself spin round and round. As suddenly all motion and all sound ceased. She sat up agains the pillows. The world was still, cool, calm. If she had been foolish to try the experiment upon so warm a day, she thought she was lightly punished. Her head was quite clear and strong. She got up, and bathed her face and bare arms and neck. All her motions were free and full; only a faint sickness remained. Nothing had happened. She drained a tumbler of ice-water, and went back to bed. The moon had now set. Nothing had happened, except that the darkness had become alive.

That which she saw appeared at the remote wall of the room,—a panorama extending from floor to ceiling, stirring slowly, like Gobelin tapestry which unseen hands rolled and unrolled. She roused herself, sitting with her hands clasped about her knees, giving, as was her habit, a more iron attention to these fictions of her own nature than to any thing which those of others had made fact in the world. Neither Raphael nor Titian could have taught her what she learned in one such self-articulate hour[6] as this.

The first thing which she saw was a huge earthen vase, standing by itself against the wall, raised a few inches from the floor, thus, and thus only, indicating to her eyes that it was not what we are used to call a reality. It was of an antique Egyptian mould, with which she must have been unconsciously familiar; but the pattern of its decoration was one perfectly unknown to her. Through a maze of lotus-leaves Isis went seeking Osiris,[7] the figures moving faintly before her eyes till they had adjusted themselves with what seemed a voluntary motion to their attitudes upon the clay. The figures were black, expressed by gray lights. The leaves were of an opaque green, without veining or shadow. A raised design of silver and steel surrounded the neck, lips, and pedestal of the jar. If it had been light enough, she could have taken her pencil, and accurately copied this design, which was very intricate, and which pleased her. At the mouth of the jar a bronze crocodile lurked, with fore-feet and jaws only raised above the edge, lolling like a tongue.

This appearance, which lasted but a few moments, was the signal for a kaleidoscope of beautiful and soulless form to stir before her, slowly and subtly, like the outer circle of a whirlpool into which she was to be drawn. Pottery, porcelain, furniture, drapery, sculpture, then flowers, fruits,—a medley of still-life,—swept through strange, half-revealed, but wholly resplendent interiors, which glided on indifferently, like languages that said, "What hast thou to do with us?" Now and then, out of the splendid maze, a distinct effect seemed to pause, and poise itself, and woo her through the dark. An open hand, raised, and turned at the wrist like a flower on its stem, held water-lilies drooping and dripping. A sunbeam, upon an empty chair in a student's alcove, focussed upon a child's shoe and a woman's ribbon. A skull ground a rose between its teeth. Bees, upon a patch of burning July sky, wooed a clover. In a pool in a cliff, a star-fish defined the colors of a tangle of weeds and shells. In a thicket of wild-briar a single rose-leaf had fallen upon a gray stone, across which, and over the miniature clearing in the mimic forest, the tattered and fringed light lay.

These passed. Avis nodded at them like the children at the visions in Hans Anderson's tales. It was all a kind of bric-à-brac. She had not the ceramic nature. Let them go.

They were succeeded by an uplifting and sweeping on of perspective, by means of which great distances seemed to become measurable in the little room. Through them the generous moods of nature stirred, and earth turned herself about like a beautiful creature half awake. At first it was the cactus on the campagna which shot up against the dark, scarlet, blazing, having a pulsation like a heart; it towered heaven-high, as if to the eyes of one who sat below its level; and low through, and far beyond it, the sun had set, shrinking under a purple cloud.

Then out of a cool, green shadow faint outlines grew, sharpened, swept; and a world of ferns arose. She could see spiral buds uncoil delicately, like the opening life of a silent girl, and the fine fronds sway and aspire. These, too, shot high, as if she had been prone upon the ground among them; and on them the light lay low. From the gold to the cold, every chromatic shade due to them was there. It was a melody in green.

From this there slowly gathered itself, and leaned towards her, one Titantic wave. It was a mid-ocean wave. It reared its full-length from foot to head. The colors which are seen only at the ocean's core settled upon it. Not a shoal tint was in it. It was both the science and the art of a wave. It held both the passion and the intellect of the sea. Above its crest there was flung one human hand, and a strip of pearl-white sky.

A medley of outlines followed,—caravans crawling through a desert; sunsets behind palmettos; twilights in forests "wherein no man had been since the making of the world;" a silver fog curling from a harbor pierced by the masts of anchored ships; wastes of snow, blue-cold, and wan, unbroken by human foot, defined by the loneliest of all horizons,—the horizon of pines; then one mountain-peak, swathed below in gloom, swiftly broken at the summit into glory, on which "God made himself an awful rose of dawn."

But Avis bowed her head before these things, and said, "Only the high priest enters in."

When she raised her eyes, they fell upon forms and faces grown gaunt with toil,—an old man sowing sparse seed in a chill place; the lantern-flash on a miner's stooping face; the brow and smile of a starving child; sailors abandoned in a frozen sea; a group of factory women huddling in the wind; the poisoned face of a lead-worker suddenly uplifted like a curse; two huge hands knotted with labor, and haggard with famine, thrust groping out upon the dark.

But her heart cried out, "I am yet too happy, too young, too sheltered, to understand. How dare I be the apostle of want and woe?"

Even with the word the vision changed, and slowly as she leaned to look, swiftly as her heart beat in gazing, there grew the outline of a Face. It was a Face dark, dim, brightening, blinding, beneath a crown of thorns; but she dashed her hand across her eyes, and said, "I am unworthy."

The night might have been now well worn on, and she was conscious only of that exhaustion of the nature which comes from a highly-excited but impotent imagination. The repose of creation had failed to relieve the fever of vision. She was thinking so, dejectedly enough, listlessly looking in one corner of the room, where two or three slender, bright harebells seemed to be springing from a cleft in a rock, when, as she looked, a girl in the garb of a peasant stood stooping to pluck them. Instantly the room seemed to become full of women. Cleopatra was there, and Godiva, Aphrodite and St. Elizabeth, Ariadne and Esther, Helen and Jeanne d'Arc, and the Magdalene, Sappho, and Cornelia,[8]—a motley company. These moved on solemnly, and gave way to a silent army of the unknown. They swept before her in file, in procession, in groups. They blushed at altars; they knelt in convents; they leered in the streets; they sang to their babes; they stooped and stitched in black attics; they trembled beneath summer moons; they starved in cellars; they fell by the blow of a man's hand; they sold their souls for bread; they dashed their lives out in swift streams; they wrung their hands in prayer. Each, in turn, these figures passed on, and vanished in an expanse of imperfectly-defined color like a cloud, which for some moments she found without form and void to her.

Slowly but surely at last, and with piercing vividness, this unfolded, and she saw in curt outlines, like a story told in a few immortal words, this only:—

She saw a low, unclouded Eastern sky; fire to the horizon's rim; sand and sun; the infinite desert; a caravan departing, faint as a forgotten hope; mid-way, what might be a camel perished of thirst. In the foreground the sphinx, the great sphinx, restored. The mutilated face patiently took on the forms and the hues of life; the wide eyes met her own; the dumb lips parted; the solemn brow unbent. The riddle of ages[9] whispered to her. The mystery of womanhood stood before her, and said, "Speak for me."

Avis lay back upon her pillow with a sudden, long, sobbing sigh. She was very tired; but she had seen her picture. To-morrow she could work.

Up to this point there had been nothing unprecedented in the character of these fantasies, excepting in their number and variety. Her creative moods were always those of tense vision, amounting almost to optical illusion, failing of it only where the element of deception begins; but now when, exhausted and satisfied, she turned upon her pillow, nestling her check into her hand like a child, for sleep, none came. Still before her closcd eyes the panorama swept imperiously; but it had become a panorama of agonies. For a long time she perceived only the suffering of animals, an appalling vision of the especial anguish incident to dumb things. She saw the quiver of the deer under the teeth of the hound, the heart-throb of the pursued hare, the pathetic brow of a dying lioness, the reproach in the eye of a shot bird, a dog under vivisection[10] licking the hand that tore him. Sharply, without transition or preparation of the fancy, this changed to—O heavens! What?

Avis started, with a cry that rang through and through the sleeping house, beating her hands against her eyes, as if she would beat out the very retina on which the shadow of such sight could fall. For now she was pursued by a vision of battles. Martial music filled the room; bright blood-streaked standards waved and sank and rose again; human faces, like a wind-struck tide, surged to and fro; men reeled, threw up their arms, and fell; the floor crawled with the dead and dying; wounded faces huddled in corners, came and vanished on the ceiling, entered and re-entered through the door, gasped their life away upon the bed. The glazing eye, the whitening jaw, the clinching fingers, the ineffectual, hoarse effort to breathe a broken name,—all were there: nothing was hidden, hinted, or veiled; nothing was spared her.

"O terror! O pity! Have mercy, have mercy, have mercy!"

Aunt Chloe came panting in (in an amazing wrapper that outdid the pansy-gown), and shut the blinds before she struck the light. No good housekeeper would let in the mosquitos, whatever the emergency.

"Nightmare, Avis, or colic? I thought the blackberries were sour. Never mind, we will have a light directly. Why, what is this broken glass? Pieces of a bottle on the window-sill! Are you hurt—cut? I was sure I heard your voice. But, fortunately, it has not waked your father. Now, my dear!"

"Aunt Chloe," said Avis, passing her hand blindly across her eyes, "where is the military music?"

"Music? There's no music, but those boys: they've kept it up till now, the worse for them! There'll be some business for the Faculty to-morrow. I always thought the objection to a university town was the students. So that was what waked you, was it? I don't see why your father doesn't put a stop to these midnight carousals. Army songs, indeed! I suppose the cats in the back-yard think they're patriotic, and I *had* one in Vermont that used to start 'America;' but he never got beyond the second bar. There, my dear. All right now? Why, Avis!"

For Avis, like any broken-hearted woman who was not going to paint a great picture to-morrow, had fallen back upon the pillows, and crying, "Auntie, auntie, O auntie! let me cry a minute," lay shivering and sobbing in the chill dawn.

Aunt Chloe and the professor sat in the study in the August sunset. Aunt Chloe had meant to take the first opportunity to recommend to the Faculty a stricter *régime* of night police for those boys; but she had forgotten all about the boys. Her knitting-work (blue stockings for a theological student destined for the Bulgarian field) lay idly on her broad, benevolent lap. Now and then the rare, honest tears of her Puritan race fell: it was too dark for Hegel to see them. Under the Bulgarian stocking lay the evening paper, folded with the particular crease indicative in aunt Chloe's family that a newspaper was sacred from the waste-basket, and elected to go upon file in the left corner of the third shelf from the top in the little what-not in the study alcove.

"What," asked the professor, bringing his more than commonly nervous pace to a halt, "what, by the way, did Avis say to this?"

"Nothing."

"Nothing at all? I should have thought—they were thrown so

much together—that the young man's fate would have been something of a shock to her. Where is she?"

"She has been in the studio all day, except a while when she would go rowing. I found her with a terrible headache this morning, what with the blackberries and the boys. I don't believe Avis has had a headache before since she had the measles. But directly after breakfast she dragged herself out into that hot summer-house, and there she's been. I carried her the paper. I thought she'd better read it herself. She thanked me, and went on drawing. Oh, yes! she asked if I knew where he would naturally be carried."

"To his home in New Hampshire, I should suppose," said the professor sadly. "I believe there is an old father—or mother. I should have thought Avis would have been more touched by this."

"No doubt she feels it," said aunt Chloe, with a certain reserve; "but you know when she is in that studio, nothing is to be got out of her."

"True," said the professor, "any close occupation, indeed, is literally a pre-occupation: the absorbed mind is inhospitable to intrusions. Sir William says"—

"Are the Faculty going to do any thing?" interrupted aunt Chloe, who seldom found Sir William as much to the point as might have been expected of a really intelligent-looking man who resembled her brother.

"What can be done? But you may be right. There ought at least to be some formal action, some expression of sympathy. Now you remind me of it, I will just step over to the president's, and see if the matter has been broached."

"Poor fellow, poor fellow! Tell Avis I will be back in season to say good-night," added the professor gently, coming back after he had closed the door.

Aunt Chloe sat for a few minutes in the dark, still idly, thinking how long it was since she had seen Hegel so much moved. Then she rolled up the Bulgarian stocking, and went to put away the paper in its place, stopping only by the window to be sure that the marked passage lay folded on the top. The faint and now rapidly dying light enabled her to read, with her comments spectacles, very clearly,—

"Ostrander, Philip, surgeon: in the lungs."

It was perhaps a week after the battle of Bull Run, and Avis had found herself quite undisturbed at her work, left, indeed, in a rather exceptional solitude, at which she wondered. She liked to see Coy now and then; missed her, as we miss the sunlight whose presence we are yet too absorbed, or too miserable, to note. Harmouth without Coy would have been like Harmouth without the elms or the chapel bell. She clung to Coy with the almost pathetic loyalty of a woman whose twenty-six years had given her no comradeship of a fibre against which her own could lean. In all her young and later friendships Avis had been used to bring, not to receive, the elements of support. Deeper than all chance in this, some unconquerable instinct lay. In the relations of girlhood she had been marked for a certain sweet but unapproachable reserve. She kissed the girls politely, since it was expected of her; but, in their indiscriminate caressing, she found no part, no lot: her nearest intimate could not recall an hour of weakness, of pain, or of excitement, which had surprised Avis into it. As for Coy, she would as soon have thought of petting the Faculty as of offering any of these little feminine eccentricities as an expression of her feeling of Avis.

Now, Coy had never voluntarily staid away from her a fortnight before in all he life. When, therefore, she came into the studio one morning after this temporary defalcation, Avis turned the sphinx to the wall, and received her with unusual warmth.

"Avis," began Coy at once, "you are pale,—pale as the higher mathematics."

"And you," said Avis, closely scrutinizing her, standing at arm's length, with both hands on her shoulders, "you are as radiant as a Neapolitan rose."

"So she said in a novel, I think," said Coy. "Be original, Avis, if you must be complimentary. You don't ask me, either, why I radiate. If you don't keep a cricket in your studio for me, I shall have to sit in your lap; and I've gained five pounds this summer. Well, the classical dictionary will do: it is quite as hospitable. Avis?"

"Very well, Coy."

"If you were like other women,—which you know you never, never will be, as I've said in your defence a hundred times,—but just to suppose it, as you might suppose you could make Parkerhouse rolls, or a tatting collar, or any other *chef d'oeuvre* of which your nature is incapable: what I want to know is, if you liked a man,—let me sharpen that crayon for you: I hate to sit doing nothing,—if you liked a real, live, dreadful man, do you suppose you would be *all* summer finding it out?"

"O Coy! Ask me some conundrum with which my education has made me familiar. But what is it, Coy? Who is he? What have you come to tell me?"

Avis laid down the crayon, pushed the sphinx a little away from her, and, gently clasping her hands around Coy's neck, looked with a solemn tenderness at her.

"I said if there were," nodded Coy perversely. "You generalize from insufficient data, Avis,—a mistake said to be common to women and reformers. But speaking of men—you know all about Mr. Ostrander? If you don't, I have a lovely bit of gossip for you,—a kind of Sèvres specimen,[11] very rare. I like to gossip in Harmouth: it is considered so unintellectual."

"I knew that there was some hope of Mr. Ostrander's recovery." Avis removed her arms from Coy's neck, and took up her charcoal. "Father said so this week. I have heard nothing else."

"You didn't know that he was in Harmouth?"

"In Harmouth?"

"He was brought here last night." Coy, on the dictionary, waited with a pretty, expectant look, perhaps to be questioned further; but Avis asked no questions. She replied that she had supposed him to be in New Hampshire, and finished sharpening the charcoal slowly.

"Guess now, Avis, where he is staying. Just guess."

"I never guessed any thing in my life."

"Your superior women never can. Don't mind it, dear: it's a deficiency common to your class. Give it up? At Mr. Stratford Allen's."

"Mr. Allen is very kind," said Avis, after a momentary silence.

"And so," said Coy, "is Barbara,—very kind."

"Barbara *is* a good-hearted girl," urged Avis honestly. "I don't like to hear women speak of one another in that tone, Coy."

"Mr. Allen went on as far as Washington to bring him home," proceeded Coy, ignoring the rebuke. "Mr. Ostrander had no brother or father to depend upon, and Stratford Allen is always doing such things. He wouldn't let him go to those hot college-rooms. And I believe, in point of fact, it was thought the mother was too old to be any thing but a burden in a sick-room: so New Hampshire was just put quietly out of the question. And here comes in the advantage of being your brother's housekeeper. All that Christian self-sacrifice and grateful patriotism can do, Barbara will see to it is done, you may depend. There hasn't been such a dainty bit of household art-decoration as that in Harmouth circles this many a day. Meanwhile, poor Mr. Ostrander is still very ill, and greatly exhausted with the journey."

Avis put away her charcoal, and, rising, hunted in her portfolio for a model of her sphinx, then for a blender, then for the chamois-skin and chalk. After a little delay she sat down again, and began touching in the values of the sketch with a firm and conscientious hand.

"Now," she said gravely, "since we cannot help Mr. Ostrander,—you or I,—what is it about that other man, Coy? Am I not fit, not enough like other women, to hear?" The point of the blender trembled a little against the sphinx's chin.

"And you haven't been to see me for a fortnight, Coy!"

"Avis," said Coy with judicial solemnity, "I have done the best I could by you. We weren't engaged till last night; and I haven't even told my mother yet. I'm going to make John do that. It is with falling in love as it is with religion,—your parents are the last people to know when you've been converted. At any rate, that's the way at our house. It's a family awkwardness we have. I'd rather be disinherited than tell my mother I loved a man. *She* married father because she RESPECTED him. I've heard her say so. So I poked John in at the front-door this morning, to have it well over with, and I ran out across lots, and over here to you. It was mean, but unavoidable. John will have no trouble: he's precocious, patriotic, and pious,— three harmonious p's. He got one very becoming scar in the army. He's several years too young to have been called to the Central Church. And there's been a revival already since he was settled.[12] Mother will cry a little, and be as happy as a kind-hearted old lady with a funeral to go to."

"And you," said Avis, laying down her work, and once more bringing the tips of her fingers together about Coy's neck, "*you* are happy, Coy? There. Hush! I see. It wasn't fair to make you look like that."

Avis's sense of awe increased. It seemed to her a kind of rudeness for her to sit and watch this young, transfigured face. She had almost a consciousness of indelicacy, as if she had usurped one of John Rose's new and sacred rights, in having surprised Coy into the expression with which—half kneeling, with both arms about Avis's waist, and her face uplifed—she regarded her.

The two women sat for a little space in silence; Avis still with that delicate action of the hands which hovered about, but did not rest upon Coy, as if she had become a holy object that she might not touch. There was something very noticeable in this reticent and reverent motion. She was thinking how far apart, all at once, and by one little word, she and this other woman, scarcely younger than herself, scarcely more full of unexpressed life, seemed to have been thrust.

"How natural," she said rather wistfully,—"how natural it must seem to be so happy!"

"It is as natural as life," said Coy, suddenly starting to her feet,— "so natural, that I think John will expect me by this time. I'll tell you more about it all some other day. But there's really nothing to tell, Avis. He propounded the conundrum, and I gave it up. We just loved each other, and so we're going to be married. That's all," added Coy simply.

"It sounds a simple matter, as you put it," said Avis, smiling in rather a lonely way.

"And I don't mean to make fun of John's revivals," said Coy, turning in the doorway. "If there were more like John in the world, there'd be less like—mother, perhaps. When he was in college, don't you know how he used to say he should have to be a minister to keep himself straight? It sounded mean; but it was only brave. And now there isn't a thread, not a shred, of cant in him. To the bottom of his soul he means what he says, and says what he means, when he tries to save a soul. John believes people have got to be saved. So I have given him a chance to try his hand on me. But I shall never be half good enough for him, never!"

When Coy had crossed the garden, she came back, and, putting her face in at the half-open door, said,—

"Avis, there's only one little matter that troubles me."

Avis, uncovering the sphinx, looked interrogatively around.

"It is Barbara Allen's curls."

CHAPTER IX

"What's death? You'll love me yet!"
—Browning[1]

"Loved for we did, and like the elements,
That know not what nor why."
—Two Noble Kinsmen[2]

Now and then a feature, an atti-
tude, an accent, gets a mathematical hold of our imaginations, as
far removed as is possible from the aesthetic or magnetic way, yet
more imperious than either; like the pattern of the wall-paper in
the room which has known some tragedy or ecstasy of our lives.
We sit enchained by a trick of speech in the man we hate, or the cut
of the brow in the creature we despise, the shadow under the lip of
the stranger we neither expect nor care to meet again, or the glance
of the friend in whose broken faith eternity could not tempt us to
confide. These things happen as the comets march and counter-
march, by laws deeper than, though apparently subservient to,
caprice.

Something of this sort occurred to Philip Ostrander as he lay
through the long September days in Stratford Allen's luxurious
guest-room, wooing, more slowly than might have been expected
of his youth and health, an escaping soul to remain in a mutilated
body. He had been very near death.

Of this, though no one had told him so, he was fully aware. He
had enlisted in a reckless temper, like—who can count how many
other young men? to whom the war offered the quickest and most incisive road to a glorious solution of inglorious personal difficulties.

Ostrander had the refracting, not the absorbing nature, in which
ambition kindles under emotion, like the maple-leaf, whose heart
the autumn seeks earliest, and earliest deserts. A keen passion like
vanity, a strong one like love, or a subtle one like that of immediate
personal sway, transfigure the resolve of such a nature, only so long
as they may focus upon it. He would have felt himself humiliated
to own to another man how impossible he had found it to dedicate
to a science of which he believed himself to be enthusiastically ap-
preciative, the life which a woman's foot had bruised. Yet he felt no
more degradation in admitting this to himself than he did at ad-

mitting the beating of his heart. Perhaps we may say he made as little resistance to it.

The position reserved for him in Harmouth College ceased to possess those elements of attraction which he considered conditions of success for himself in any thing, as soon as he found himself compelled to undertake it in teeth of the precise experience awaiting the man who has to adjust the hunger of a strong nature to the famine of a denied love. This, as he assumed, was the fault of his temperament. He yielded to it as he would to a distaste for a poem or a pie.

The world was wide. A Harmouth professorship was not an undue part of it. One man would answer about as well as another to fill any mould, unless, perhaps, the chalices of life; and it could hardly be said that the veins of his nature throbbed with sacramental wine, only a serviceable secular brand. It was, indeed, he thought, indicative of a narrow, if not an arrogant fancy, to suppose that it made much difference, in the end, who undertook any given little portion of the work of his age: these youthful enthusiasms were interchangeable. If he were shot, there would be one indifferent geologist less in the world, possibly one grieving woman more. He had moments in which he had dared believe that she would mourn for him. He found these inexpressibly and mystically sweet. Regret in a nature like hers might easily turn into tenderness, when her beautiful, fierce maidenhood was forever safe from its encroachment. Death would not be a costly price to pay for that subtle and constraining mastery of her soul which repentant grief and virgin widowhood would give him. Nay, the barren chance of this seemed worth far bitterer than a soldier's fate. There would be a few robust physical pangs, more or less, perhaps the inevitable homesickness to be expected at first from entering an unknown life, the relief consequent upon leaving one with which he was at present thoroughly dissatisfied, then the wide spaces and free chances of a spiritual economy in which to make his nature worthy of approach to hers, as, by an instinct deeper than the reverent humility of newly-awakened love, he felt that it was not likely to become, in the conditions of this. For Ostrander believed in another life. Fifteen years ago, an educated young man did not find it absolutely imperative to doubt the immortality of his own soul. He had, therefore,—for it was thus that he loved this woman, with all the strength and the weakness, with the heights and the depths, of his nature,—gone into the army, moved by a profound and intelligent hope that he might never come out of it.

When, however, the shot struck, he had grappled with death as manfully as most life-sick young creatures do, if given the chance; for, as he fell, his major's horse toppled over on him. It was the struggle consequent on the effort to free himself from so hideous a death, rather than the wound (not in itself deadly), which had made the nature of his peril. The pierced lung was badly bruised.

Through the sultry days and cooling nights in which the first breath of autumn crept, his mind had stirred sluggishly towards the positions in which death had met it. His medical training told him that this was his most hopeful symptom, and one to be fostered. He yielded himself peacefully to the little eddies of a sick-room existence. He would have been glad to forget that the whole round world was not bounded by the daintily-decorated, scented, and soothing spot in which his recovery met him. He would have been glad to forget that there was any other woman in the world than this excellent sister of a good fellow whose kingly hospitality was likely to save his life. He experienced a peculiar sense of relief in the presence of a simple feminine nature lending itself to these delicate cares with which he felt himself surrounded unobtrusively, as he was with the pale, cool pearl-tint of the walls, the select engravings, the luxurious knick-knacks of the toilet or the medicine-table, the exquisite service of his breakfast, or the pattern of ferns on the lace, to which the Venetian blinds lent a suffusive woodland tint.

Awaking one morning, several days after his return to Harmouth, from the state of semi-conscious exhaustion into which the hot journey had thrown him, he had been made aware of a distinct and new sensation of optical pleasure. For the first time, he perceived within the hazy lighting and shading of the room a soft outline upon which his eye wandered, rested, and remained, with the wide, blind impulse of a baby's on a sunbeam. It was the outline of a woman's neck.

It was a delicate neck, of not too muscular nor yet too full a curve; of the sensitive fairness which accompanies umber tints in the hair, eyes, and brow. The hair was brushed well up from it, lingering reluctantly in little rings, of which it was difficult to express the images of endearment that they presented involuntarily to the mind, as it is difficult to explain those which we receive from tendrils or from the shadow of tendrils upon a ripe leaf. Thrown high over a comb, two or three curls fell, leaning lightly, and yielding with an almost imperceptible stir to the motions of the wearer's breath.

The sick man's fancy had from that time found itself curiously, but not ungratefully, subject to the outline of those curls; pursuing it idly in his weakest hours, with interest in his stronger ones; tracing the exact course of a lock that defied him like the pattern of an old lace; watching for the resumption of certain broad lights or warm shadows that he saw yesterday; disappointed if they did not re-appear; nervously fretful sometimes if he could not understand why, when she turned her head, one curl would fall, and another only nestle closer to its place; busy now and then in putting them into imaginary order upon his finger. He once heard a celebrated beauty say, that, if she could possess but one physical attraction, it should be that of pliant and abundant hair.

"Miss Barbara," he had said one day, "do you ever arrange your hair in any other way?"

"Do you not like it?" she answered, turning her neck slowly. She generally sat with her profile towards him.

"Amazingly."

"Does it have a nervous effect on you in any way,—to see the curls fly, I mean? I can change it if it annoys you."

"It does not annoy me in the least. But I should like to see it changed—for once," he demanded, in the idly autocratic tone of the spoiled convalescent.

"Certainly," said Barbara. "I will do it up plainly some day, if you wish. I will try and remember it."

But she never did, it chanced, remember it.

Certainly there never was a better nurse than Barbara Allen,— soft of step, and quiet of dress; sure of the right word at the right time, yet mistress of long silences; never taxing a weak and wearied attention with chatter about her china, yet capable of bringing the English breakfast-tea in a lotus-leaf, and the ice-water in a pond-lily; competent to adjust the color of the doyley to the prevailing tint of one's supper; throwing an atmosphere of domestic frankness about a homeless man when her brother was in the room; just brushed in his absence by a poised reserve; perceptive of the precise moment when speech is a strain, and silence an oppression, and a song of Schubert's, touched in the twilight, should stir like a spirit through the quiet house; full of those delicate and pictorial resources of which returning strength is least likely to become ungratefully critical.

"You have been so kind to me!" said Ostrander, the day that he took his first step into the cool hall, and she drew out the white linen ottoman for him from the direct draught, and took the cricket at his feet, there being no other seat there for her,—"so kind, that it seems a sort of rudeness or affectation for me to express a gratitude that must only deepen with time."

"Stratford and I are so glad!" said Barbara warmly. "It is the only very visible way we have had open to us of doing our little share for the men who are imperilling their lives for us. The obligation is all on our side, Mr. Ostrander. And you have been such a delightfully romantic invalid, it has been like having a poem or a story alive in one's own house. How do you think we are going to get along on plain prose when you are gone?"

"Shall you miss me?" asked Ostrander, leaning back upon the white ottoman, and watching her dreamily. It was a graceful pose she had upon the cricket; and the low wind was busy with her hair. Barbara lifted her brown eyes; but they fell, and she said nothing. She was content to be watched like that. Why spoil an innocent pleasure by talking?

"So much?" continued Ostrander in a lower tone, clasping his hands behind his head, and bringing his lips together under his bright breard. "I don't know but it is worth a man's being shot, to be first cured, and then missed—so."

Now, as Ostrander could never have sat with downcast eyes listening to his own voice, its effect could hardly have been a measurable thing with him. And then he was very grateful, and at that moment he was filled with the tender flood of returning life—and Barbara happened to be there.

Tea, to which, for the first time, Ostrander staggered down, was late that night. Barbara always waited tea for her brother. Stratford Allen, who had failed to develop that naturally superior manner to be expected of the business-man who is known to have endowed a university, came in with, perhaps, an unwonted touch of his habitual, modest, sad reserve. When Barbara asked him why he was so late, he said he had been at the treasurer's office.

"Did you ask Professor Dobell about those German books for his department?" asked Barbara.

"Yes: I stopped at his house a moment," said her brother, coming up to give his cordial hand to Ostrander. "I think you had better run over there to-morrow, Barbara. Miss Avis has got hurt rowing."

"Oh! Much hurt?—Mr. Ostrander, not in the draught, please: take this chair."

"Nothing serious, I hope; but a troublesome bruise. She was pulling her boat in through a heavy sea, and brought her thumb between the rock and the bows somehow. She made light of it; but it will cripple her for a while, I am afraid.—Ostrander, how pleasant this is! Shall I help you to the very last huckleberry that was to be found in New England?"

After tea, Ostrander said that he wished to try a step or two upon the piazza. Stratford objected; but Barbara said it was her rule that sick people (of any thing beyond a common-school education) should be allowed to do as they liked. She came up to him with a rose-bud in one hand and his overcoat in another,—his winter coat: Barbara's lightest sentiment had a sufficiently practical ballast. She pinned in the rose, a plump, hot-house bud of a sturdy color; one long sinuous curl fell over it. Ostrander drew his furred lappel over the flower with an exquisite motion which an artist or novelist would not have wasted upon any thing less than a Madonna lily. With his peculiar tenderness of touch, and with his eyes fixed upon her, he folded it slowly against his heart.

"As if it had been—a woman," thought Barbara with a discreet vagueness of imagination. Barbara had a high respect for a man who could receive a favor of hers with a grace so princely. But she did not wish she were that rose. Ostrander, still touching his coat with a certain gentleness, crept out into the rapidly chilling air.

He had come out to try his strength. He meant to know for himself about that hurt hand. He crawled along with a suppressed fierceness when he found how weak he was. The fat rose-bud slipped and fell. He did not see it, and stepped on it twice in crossing the piazza-floor.

It was impossible to have better intentions than aunt Chloe's, when any member of the family was by illness or otherwise thrown defencelessly upon them. When Avis had been for three days incapacitated for work by her little accident, aunt Chloe resolutely took her sewing, and went to find her. It was nonsense to be moping out there like a chilled blue-jay. Avis must be entertained. The first condition of recovery, were it from a broken thumb or a broken head, aunt Chloe held, was to be got out of one's self. And, in the nature of things, we find those people to be self-absorbed who are not occupied in our own particular forms of benevolence, precisely as we find those irreligious who are not of our own especial faith. The main trouble with Avis, aunt Chloe reasoned, was, that she did not go out of herself.

What if she could not paint for a week or two? A soldier's box could be packed, at all events a Harmouth soup-ticket could be distributed with any energetic left hand. It may be that aunt Chloe's stout impulse, like that of many another outflowing heart, sometimes struck nearer to a truth than the richer but less objective fancy.

But Avis in the orchard, flung upon the short September grass with her Ruskin and Hawthorne, and Mrs. Jameson,[3] and other resources not so immediately telling upon the needs of the age as the soup-tickets, responded to aunt Chloe's sympathy with the assurance that she was not in pain, and fully occupied, and hoped to be at work again in at most a fortnight.

"I hope so, my dear, I'm sure," said aunt Chloe, laboriously seating herself beside her, and unrolling a package of metaphysical shirts; "for it must be very lonely, having so few resources as you do. I came out because I thought it bad for you to be so much alone."

"Thank you, auntie," said Avis in a sincere tone, closing her book.

"How odd all this is about Mr. Ostrander and Barbara!" began aunt Chloe, carefully fitting a gusset. (Why was it, that it always made Avis frantic to see aunt Chloe fit gussets?) "It is the last thing I should have thought of. Should you have thought of it?"

"Perhaps not," said Avis; "but it is very natural."

"I hope, for her sake, it will prove a *bonâ fide* engagement," buzzed aunt Chloe: "it will be so awkward for her otherwise! Though it isn't a choice *I* should have made for Mr. Ostrander. I sent him some nasturtiums[4] this morning. Avis, let me see that hand once more. I don't understand why you should look so fagged out over it."

"A little hurt sometimes causes a good deal of pain," said Avis rather wearily. She threw herself back upon the brown grass, and closed her eyes while aunt Chloe talked. It irked her, this enforced idleness, more than she could remember to have been irked by any thing since she sat cutting out night-clothes with aunt Chloe, on the dining-room table, at sixteen. Just now, it seemed as imperative to be busy, as action to the swimmer; and her efforts to exchange her palette for her books had been purposeless and spasmodic, like the motions of the sinking. She seldom read while she was at work, and could recall many a sketch which had been ruined by the morning paper. She could not set the fire of creation to boiling the tea-kettle of acquisition. Especially had this experience proved untimely and unmerciful. There seemed to be great spaces in her nature, into which she neither cared nor dared to look, and which the events of the summer had imperceptibly enlarged, like the boundaries of a conquering country. She found herself now with a kind of terror thrust into them against her will.

"My dear," said aunt Chloe with unwonted abruptness, folding the gusset, however, before she laid it down, "I don't know but there is a providence in this accident, after all. I have been troubled about you for a long time. It is always a pity for a woman to become dependent upon any excitement outside of the sphere to which she must, of course, in the end, adjust herself. And really, Avis, I don't see how you are going to marry in that studio. I do not wish to speak of such matters with any indelicate freedom," added aunt Chloe with her old-fashioned womanly reserve, which Avis, in all her life, never remembered to have seen broken in this way before; "but of course, my dear, you will expect to marry."

"No," said Avis gently, with the perfectly hopeless feeling one

has under the necessity of an explanation which kindliness demands, but which is sure to be only a deepening mystery to the
auditor.

"No, auntie, I do not expect to marry."

"In a certain way," replied aunt Chloe with grave hesitation,
"that is the way a woman should feel. I had refused your uncle
twice before I thought of marriage. I am glad you preserve so much
modesty about such matters. Young girls now-a-days are generally
so different! Of course, no *lady* will ever allow herself to become
interested in a gentleman till he has positively sought her in
marriage."

Aunt Chloe rolled up her work as she uttered this first and great
commandment, upon which all the law and prophets of womanhood hung, with the serene dignity which only an absolute inability to conceive of two sides to a question can give. What a lady
ought not, that, of course, a lady never did. It was scarcely necessary to remind any niece of hers of that. But aunt Chloe had almost a sense of immodesty in having spoken, as she had felt it her
duty to do, to Avis. Marriage was not a thing for women to chatter
about. But equally it was not the thing for women deliberately to
put themselves beyond the reach of that honorable institution,
which, we must admit, was ordained of Almighty God, and necessary to weak-minded man. And, when a poor motherless girl had
reached the age of twenty-six without any apparent appreciation of
this fact, it was clearly the duty of somebody to remind her, with
that delicacy belonging to the old-time breeding, of the mistaken
and undesirable position into which she was drifting.

"Not," said aunt Chloe, hastening to a virtuous qualification of
her unwonted indiscretion,—"not that a maiden lady cannot live a
very useful and unselfish life, my dear. I have known many instances. But I think *you*, Avis, would be happier in the married
state; and so I thought I would take an opportunity to caution you
a little. You seem to be so absorbed in that painting, that somebody
must think for you. And now Coy has gone, and Barbara will soon
follow, you will be left very much alone. I cannot deny that I feel
some anxiety for your future."

"Thank you, auntie," said Avis again. A dull sense of disturbance
mingled with her surprise at aunt Chloe's unprecedented expression of feeling. She was glad when the last gusset was rolled away,
and Julia called to ask if she should scald over the marmalade.

She wandered away restlessly, when aunt Chloe had gone,
through the orchard, over the meadow, across the field. She crushed
the crisp grass idly. The brown butterflies circled over her head;
and the grasshoppers rose and fell in their short autumn riot,
which lends almost a pathos to a creature that is alternately re-

pulsive and absurd, as the throb of any ephemeral life must do in its last delight. Avis watched them with a sudden, fierce envy: they would die of the bitter frost; but they had leaped to the summer sun.

She stopped—from a feeling too ill defined to be called a purpose, perhaps hardly conscious enough to be named an impulse—at the spot where she had last seen and spoken with Philip Ostrander. It was broad, white September noon. The narrow shadow crept crouching against the feet of the stone wall.

The direct touch of the sun fell gratefully; for the morning had been chill. There was a rising, but as yet unagitated wind, which appealed to, but did not stir, the purple heart of the sea morning-glories that sprang from the sand across the wall. The water had the superlative and unmated meaning of a September sea. The near waves broke weedless and kindling, clean to the heart's core, like a nature burnt holy with a consecrated passion. All the colors of the tide and of the shore compelled attention, as if one must create a vocabulary to express them, as if one struggled to say, A blazing brown, a joyous gray, a restless green, a reticent red, a something never seen before: in every tint there was a subtle contradiction. The life and death of the year wrestled upon the face of the water. The whole harbor looked to Avis like some large soul, in which a conflict old as time, and young as hope, and eternal as nature, and sad as fate, was impending. By and by the harbor, too, must freeze.

A pace or two down the wall, two little stunted spruces grew,—sparse, wind-beaten things, shivering away from the sea with the touching action of all trees upon an easterly shore. Avis, stepping along to help herself up by the assistance of their shrinking branches, climbed the stone wall, and stood for a moment between them, looking across the cliff, and down.

In her full lithe length there, a perfect panel against the sky and sea, she was still standing, when she heard her name spoken under breath; and immediately the speaker added,—

"Do not move, I pray you; do not even turn your head just this moment."

Neither starting nor stirring, without comment or inquiry, she obeyed. Perhaps her breath came with some swiftness; for she seemed to sway a very little in standing. In her pale straw-colored summer dress, she looked like a delicate flame, slender, and ascending against the sky.

Still without turning, she gently said,—

"This is long enough, I think, Mr. Ostrander."

"Is it? Are you tired? Ah! Well, I am selfish. I would have kept you there much longer. Well, then, if you must. Shall I help you down?"

Then she turned. Slowly, like a statue on its pivot, she circled towards him between the dark lines of the two trees, and slowly opened her grave eyes upon his face.

Perhaps she was not thinking that he would be so sorely changed. It was so long since she had seen him! Silence had been heavy between them, and the shadow of death had overhung. In all the strain of this summer she had thrust herself back upon her own quiveringly-poised imagination—a terrible companion. Upon the battle-field, beneath the shot, within the blazing hospital, upon the scorching journey, and at the door of death, she had followed him as one follows afar off, exchanging the terror of that which is for the horror of that which may be. Her mind had not been at any time laggard in its apprehension of the fact that he lay, at a stone's throw from her, grappling with life, and that another woman rendered him the tender offices of friendship and of compassion.

But her pictorial instinct, cruelly loyal to her thus far, had failed her at last. This face, *this*, which he lifted to her now, haggard and gray, tense with that enforced patience, so foreign to a man, that a woman instinctively gauges the extent of his physical suffering by his acquisition of it,—against this, her saddest vision had not fortified her.

Astronomy happened upon a beautiful and significant phrase when it gave us "energy of position," and meant us to understand by it that certain separated bodies are far apart, with great spaces to travel to reach each other.

At that one moment the energy of position between these two seemed an immeasurable thing. Avis, perhaps because she had just obeyed him in standing still to be looked at, had turned a little coldly. Where she stood high upon the wall, her health and youth and color seemed to cut themselves like articulate words before his eyes. He, upon the side of the ascending field, crawled weakly towards her. He was shattered as a broken column. For that moment they looked steadily and silently upon one another.

Then slowly, furtively as an unacknowledged motive or a rebel fancy, there crept over her face a change. It was the marvellous and magnificent change wrought upon a woman's face only by that compassion which steals a regent to the palace where Love the King has been dethroned. Nothing is more beautiful, because nothing is more womanly, than that subsidence of the muscles, that quiver of the nerves, that kindling of color, and luminous entreaty of the eye.

The young man held his breath before it, stirred with a perfectly new and daring hope. He felt, that, had he come to her again in the power of his manhood, he might again have gone as he came. It was his physical ruin and helplessness[5] which appealed to the strength in her. He would have died to see that lip of hers tremble so—for him. Now he saw it—and lived. He had exchanged nothing but a shot lung and life-long feebleness—for heaven. He drew a weak step nearer to her, and held out his arms.

She wavered for an instant. The morning-glory behind her, across the wall, wavered as much in the now rising wind. Then, with a low, inarticulate cry, she stretched both hands down towards him.

He took them, and she slid down from the wall, and stood beside him. She did not·offer to remove her hands. He thought she was unconscious of his touch, for she had not yet taken that broken, piteous look from his face.

"Oh!" she said indistinctly. "I did not think—I did not know"—

"You did not know I was so changed?" He gently took her hurt right hand by the wrist as he spoke, holding it like a drooping water-lily by the stem. "There, I must have hurt you. I was cruel; but I was dazzled. Poor little hand! There is a great deal of suffering in a little hurt like this. A bruise is so much worse than a cut—in hearts or hands. *I* have had the cut. You have almost drawn the life-blood out of my soul, I think; but you—*you* have been bruised."

A wild flash of dissent or protest shot across her eyes; but the quiver of her lip increased.

"All this time," he went on in the pathetic accent which mortal illness leaves lingering so long upon a man's voice, "you have sent me no word, no sign."

She silently shook her head: her eyelids looked heavy, as if a distinct effort only prevented them from drooping.

"You never expressed to me the commonest sympathies of friendship."

Imperfectly she said, "No."

"I lay, pretty weak, watching, day after day, thinking perhaps you would come, or speak one little word. I went down into the valley of the shadow of death without you. You never extended a finger-touch to help me."

"I never did."

"You did not dare!"

Then her eyelids fell; then her quivering lip melted; then her whole face broke and blazed. She snatched away both hands, and covered it.

"Let me hear you say it," he demanded with a kind of solemn authority which seemed, for the moment, to be that of one who dealt with a divine, not a human, passion. "You dared not!"

"I—dared—not."

"Let me know why not."

"*Because you did not—ask me to.*"

Scarlet behind her shielding hands she flung out the words.

He took one blind step towards her.

"If I had asked you—would you have come? Did you care? Did you *want* to come—when I was suffering—to me?"

"Oh! every day, every hour—there was not a minute—for so many cruel weeks. It was so hard! Oh! don't think I am crying: it's only that I cannot get my breath—and I couldn't go—I was afraid"—

"You were afraid you loved me!" he cried. "You are afraid of it now."

As long as he lived, Ostrander saw in dreams the expression of exquisite pain with which she dragged her hands away from her face, and met his eye. She seemed like a creature whose throbbing heart was torn out of her live body.

"If this be love," she slowly said, "I am afraid I love you now."

He staggered, he was still so weak: he staggered, and, putting out one hand upon her shoulder, sank slowly to the ground.

"Oh!" she cried, "I have hurt you!"

"No, oh, no! Hush! You have healed me. I am well. Only let me rest a minute, till my breath comes." He leaned panting against the wall, under the scant shade of the storm-tormented spruce.

"Oh! I *have* hurt you," she repeated, kneeling beside him. "What can I say? Is there any thing that I can do?"

She had melted into a gentleness under which he felt his head spin giddily. There was a suppressed, appealing accent in her voice which he had never heard: it was faint as the first golden outline of land to one long in mid-ocean. He put his head back, and closed his eyes. He would not for life's sake, just then, have seen more than that mistily throbbing boundary. It was as much as he could bear. If this was her pity, what would her tenderness be?

When he had grown a little stronger, he turned, and silently looked at her. Already upon her rested that indefinable change, on the hither side of which, when once it has touched her, all time cannot put a woman's face. In yielding her confession, she seemed already to have yielded some impalpable portion of her personality. In the words of the old story of chivalry, "her soul had gone out of her." Her blinding consciousness of having taken the first step in a road which led to some indefined but imperative surrender of her nature had an effect upon her incalculable to one familiar only with a simpler type of woman. She did not look subdued, only startled. And, when he reverently extended his thin hand again towards her, she shrank, with widening, fear-stricken eyes.

Just then Ostrander thought her beautiful terror of him more precious than her love.

He did not press any expression of his feeling upon her, and they sat quite still, and the live noon pulsated about them.

Presently she said tremulously,—

"You are so weak! And you walked across this long field: how will you ever get back? I am troubled that you came."

"I can go anywhere," said Ostrander in an intoxicated tone, "do any thing. I can go the world over; for you will go with me."

He turned to her, leaning his head upon one wan hand on which the sunlight drew out the veins. She turned away. She could not just then say the word which would darken sun, moon, and stars in the face of a man who looked like that. Her own grew tense and pinched.

"But still, as you say," said Ostrander,—whether wilfully or not unconscious of this movement,—"I am not yet very strong. Indulge me. Let me hear you say once more—I'll not ask for it but once to-day—that you are afraid you love me."

"Oh! I *am* afraid I love you! There, hush!" She sprang to her feet, putting her finger on her own lips.

"And can you not love me without being afraid?"

She shook her head, her eyes beginning to wander from side to side.

"But why?"

"I do not know. I am made so," defiantly. "Let me go. Let us go now—home, somewhere. Oh, I forget! I am cruel." She broke into a penitent tenderness. "Are you rested? Can you walk so far yet? Can you go?"

"One moment." Ostrander rose feebly, and stood beside her. His startling pallor burned as marble does if thrust into the full sun, as if it were lighted, not from without, but from within. He folded his arms with the resolute action of a man who thinks that is the safest thing to do with them, before he said,—

"You will not leave me, I think—to-day—like this. I am almost too sick a man yet to be left—so."

"Do you appeal to my pity?" she flashed, drawing a step back.

"No. I appeal to your love."

The scorching color slowly rose, lighted, sped, fired her face, brow, and neck: when he saw it, he knew that he had never seen her blush before. She seemed to stand imprisoned by that blush, as if it had been a physical paralysis or pain.

"My love," she said under her breath,—"*my* love! Do you know to what you are appealing?"

"Hardly,—yet," said Ostrander deliriously. "I am not strong enough to know to-day. I only ask that you will give me the right to know another day—to-morrow—when you will. Is it too much to ask?"

She made as if she would have spoken some impetuous word; but a glance at him restrained her. He was trembling heavily, and his breath had visibly shortened. He looked very ill. Her heart leaped with the deep maternal yearning over suffering that is more elemental in women than the yearning of maiden or of wife. Had he spoken no word of that other love to her, she could have gathered his faint face in her arms, and brooded over it with leaning cheek and sobbing voice; but this other, this encroaching, appalling love, which she felt in herself, as yet, only as the presence of a vague, organic dread,—for this, nature gave her no speech nor language but the instinct of flight. Yet flight now would be either coquetry or cruelty, and of both she was incapable.

"I will see you," she said after a moment's grave silence—"yes, I will see you again."

Ostrander was sensitively conscious that her transparent honesty could not wrest even from her compassion a distinct mortgage to his now blinding hope. But he felt himself as physically unequal to enduring just then any possible depression of that hope, as he was to yielding any larger allowance of the scant breath with which he must compass that widening distance across the dizzy field. He paused, however, to say with a certain authority,—

"You understood what I asked in asking that we may talk of this, that we may talk of our love, again?"

"Yes."

"And you distinctly grant that we may speak of it, so?"

She said, "If you stand another moment, you cannot crawl home."

"I shall stand till you grant what I ask."

"Oh, I grant it! Come! How shall I—how can I help you over this rough ground? I wish I were a man!"

"I am sorry not to sympathize with any wish of yours," said Ostrander, breaking into a boyish laugh as they turned, striking down into the brown stubbly field. "And now, if you will permit me,— just a hand upon your shoulder. It shall be a light one; and I shall get along famously. I am already stronger than I was."

She lent him her strong young shoulder simply and readily, and, he leaning upon it with radiant eyes, they passed over the conscious meadows in the white September noon.

CHAPTER X

"Are there not . . .
Two points in the adventure of
the diver?—
One—when, a beggar, he
prepares to plunge;
One—when, a prince, he rises
with his pearl.
Festus, I plunge!"
FEST. *I wait you when you rise!*
—Browning's Paracelsus.[1]

There now began in Avis a memorable conflict, which only a woman, and of women perhaps only a few, can articulately understand.

Ostrander felt that it was only accelerated, but did not believe that it was in any other sense affected, by the state of extreme exhaustion into which that morning by the shore had plunged him.

He had struggled up through the orchard and the garden, and as far as the studio, where he sank upon the steps. The professor and aunt Chloe came out and got him into the house; and he lay for the rest of the day upon the study sofa, sorely spent.

Nothing would have suited aunt Chloe better than to keep him beneath her motherly wing; she had small secret respect for Barbara Allen's nursing. What could a girl with red curls know about gunshot wounds? And she understood that Mr. Ostrander had been kept too long in a dark room: men, like flowers, waxed strong in the light of heaven. Undoubtedly, Barbara could play opera music for him down stairs; but meanwhile, who was to rub the poor fellow's feet? or exert an authoritative influence in the question of wet or dry heat in an attack of pain?

And now that he had really gone back to the college (too soon, as it had clearly proved), she could surely take him in hand without any discourtesy to the Allens. Aunt Chloe's hospitality expressed itself with the touch of dignity, which, though it makes acceptance easy, leaves denial graceful. She did not press the matter, when Ostrander, growing stronger with the heavily cooling evening, said only that it was best for him to go; and he returned to his old quarters, upon which he held some lien by courtesy until his health should admit of a definite settlement of his relation to the university.

Avis was in her room when his carriage drove up, and did not come down. She had presented herself through the day only so much as was necessary to prevent remark. She hovered about him distantly. In her eyes smouldered a dangerous light. When once they had been left for a few minutes alone together, as the afternoon shadow was stooping to the study-floor, she had fanned him conscientiously, to be sure; but she had not broken by a breath, the expressive silence which settled like a third personality between them. He did not watch her, but lay with closed eyes: he perceived the shining of her slender wrist, the faint scent from her dress and hair. When aunt Chloe came in, she felt his pulse anxiously, and said she had given him too large a dose of the elderberry-wine.

For that next day he left her to herself. And for yet another he stood afar off from a struggle upon which he felt it unchivalric to urge, more than need inevitably be, the appeal of his physical wreck and disordered future. Upon the third day he came, leaning upon John Rose's arm. Rose had found him down the street, crawling along home. But John Rose had an appointment with a lady, and would not come in.

Aunt Chloe stood in the hall with her bonnet on. She was going to a very special female prayer-meeting (of which far be it from me to speak sceptically), appointed to further the discontinuance of the war. And the professor would not return from the lecture-room till after the Alpha Delta Phi dinner, which would be a late (and dyspeptic) affair. Aunt Chloe thought the parlor too damp for Mr. Ostrander, and would send Avis into the study.

He went in, and awaited her with such nerve as he could command: he would not have turned his transparent hand over either way upon his chance. He waited what seemed an immeasurable, and really was rather a cruel time.

When at last she came in, down the long, sunlit, home-like room, between the rows of books, he was shocked to see the traces of a sleepless and joyless struggle that she bore.

He met her with some indistinct, impetuous word of endearment, and drew her beside him upon the old mahogany sofa.

"You suffer!" he cried, with the helpless bewilderment of the strongest man before the nature of a strong woman. "I would make you so happy; and I have made you miserable! Why do you suffer?"

He held her fast now by the delicate crossed wrists. She lifted her tender face.

"I suffer," she said, "because I love you."

"Oh! Is *that* all?"

"I never loved any other man. I did not know what it was like."

She gently drew her hands away, and folded them one into the other.

"And what is it like? Can you tell me?"

One might have said of Ostrander's voice at that moment, what was said once, and said perfectly, of music, that it was "love in search of a word."

"It is like—death,"[2] said the woman slowly, with a deepening shade on every feature.

"Then," said the young man lightly, "I am ready to die."

But he was sorry to have made her smile so; for her smile did not encourage him.

"It is civil war,"[3] she said.

Spurred by a momentary stinging sense of having retraced his own footsteps, he leaped on,—

"Do you remember that you were to give me an answer,—that you were to talk with me of our future, to-day?"

"Yes."

"And I may know—now—what it is you have to say to me?"

"Mr. Ostrander, in all my life—since I was a little girl—I have never known one hour in which I expected—like other women—to marry."

"You could not be like other women," he murmured; but she waved his words away with her bruised hand.

"I don't think you understand what that means. I never could conceive of myself as expecting it. I cannot now. I do not wish to marry any man. It seems to me a perfectly unnatural thing that any man should look me in the face, and ask me to be his wife: it always did. And that a man of your superior intelligence should actually *expect* it is really incomprehensible to me."

She pelted these words at him over her shoulder. Ostrander heard them too anxiously to smile. It was the irrational outcry of a creature rasped and wrung by the friction of her own nature upon itself. Only a woman terrified by the serried advance of a mighty love upon an able and discomfited resistance, could have spoken those words in that way. But only a few men in the world would have instinctively understood this. Ostrander was not one of these few. It seemed to his dizzy eyes that her face receded as she spoke, growing larger but dimmer with every word.

"I never said this before," she added, with the rapid, incisive utterance of one who is expressing what is so long familiar, and so long suppressed, as to have become a functional part of the being, and to exhale involuntarily like the breath. "I never cared enough—for any one—to try to explain it. But I must tell you. I had rather not be happy than to be happy at such a cost as marriage demands of women."

"Ah! then you own that you would, that you could, be happy." He hastened to entrap her in her sweet admission. She gave him one transcendent look. As if she had given him some matchless wine never before unsealed for human lips, his head grew light. But then there fell a swift and great withdrawal upon her; and her face gathered itself together like a garrison, while she said,—

"I told you something about this long ago, before you went into the army, that day by the shore; but I could not explain it then, for I could not explain myself then. Every thing that I felt then has intensified. With my feeling for you has deepened this other feeling. The more I care for you, the more I shrink from what you ask."

"Let us talk of this quietly now, and reasonably," said Ostrander in his low, vibrant way. "I will urge nothing upon you. Only let us reason about it. Marriage is not to be treated with such personal irreverence or rebellion, I think. It is really the best plan Almighty God could contrive for us. It is his will that men and women should love one another, and, loving, marry."

"But I do not see it to be his will for me," urged Avis. "He has set two natures in me, warring against each other. He has made me a law unto myself—*He* made me so. How can I help that? I do not say, Heaven knows! that I am better, or greater, or truer than other women, when I say it is quite right for other women to become wives, and not for me. I only say, If that is what a woman is made for, I am not like that: I am different. And God did it."

There was a solemn but yet submissive arraignment in these words, and in the tone with which they were uttered, to which, at that moment, Ostrander found no ready lover's argument of a texture large enough to be laid against them.

"Even if I had no work, no life, of my own," she continued less calmly, "I think it would be the same, though I cannot tell. But I have my work, and I have my life. I was not made to yield these to any man. I was not made to absorb them in his work and his life. And I should do it—if I married him. I should care so much—too much for what happened to him. . . . Mr. Ostrander, if I were a man, I would not stoop to ask such a sacrifice of any woman!"

"And I stoop to ask for no more than I give," he said with a haughty humility. "I will take from you only what I can yield to you,—the love of a life. I do not want your work, or your individuality. I refuse to accept any such sacrifice from the woman I love. You are perfectly right. A man ought to be above it. Let me be that man." Ostrander uttered this daring sentiment as ardently as if he had ever thought of it before, and as sincerely as if it had been the watchword of his life. He felt himself at that moment in the radiation of a great truth that blazed from her ringing voice and her intrenched beauty. He seemed to himself to be the discoverer of a new type of womanhood, to which, as we do in the presence of all ideals, he instinctively brought his own nature to the rapid test: he

would have scorned himself if his manhood had not rung responsive to it. He ventured solemnly to say,—

"Only let us love, and live, and work together. Your genius shall
be more tenderly my pride than my little talents can possibly be
yours. I shall feel more care for your assured future than you ought
to feel for my wrecked one. Try me if you will; trust me if you can.
I do not say that I am worthy. But you shall make me so. If I did not
believe you could make me so, before God, I would go out from
your presence to-day, and never seek it again." He spoke in an agitation now, that extended itself, like the air they breathed, to her.
She rose, and walked across the study-floor two or three times,
with something of her father's attitude, the long, nervous step soft-
ened to a sinuous grace in her clinging dress.

"I wish I had a different past and a different future to offer you,"
pleaded Ostrander, throwing one weak arm up over his head restlessly. "But the one has at least been clean, I believe; and the other
must be—what God and yourself will it."

She stopped her rapid walk, and looked at him standing in the
middle of the floor; and in what seemed a half-unconscious tone,
as if she had not been listening to his last words, she said,—

"I have wondered sometimes if there were such a man in the
world. I always knew," whispering, "how I should feel. I knew it
would be all over with me when I found him." Then, still softly,—

"Oh, how pale you are! All this excitement—is so wrong for
you! I should be so glad to see you happy—to help you to get well!
Oh, I think I could make you happy! I would try—there is nothing
I would not do, would not suffer"—

With a swift motion she stirred towards him, saw him reach his
arms out dumbly, wavered and turned, then,—

"Oh, no, no, no!" she cried. "*Help* me to say no! Come another
time. I must think. I must take time—because"—

"Because what?" he demanded, sorely shaken by the prolongation of this strain.

"Because I care too much for you to make you miserable. Every
thing would be so hard for you! Don't think it is that I care so
much about myself! *I* could bear it,—to grow poor and sick and
worn-out, and never to paint, and to have to sew so much! When
you look at me, (oh, you are so pale!) I could bear it all. But I can't
forget how it would be—and the coffee wouldn't be right. And men
mind such things—you would mind. You would be sorry we had
done it. It is not right for us to marry. Don't *let* me do what is not
right! You should see—you should be merciful to yourself and me."

She seemed to slip and slide before his still extended hands like a
wraith, and he heard the door open and close, and the afternoon
sun bent placidly upon the rows of books, upon the portrait of Sir

William, upon the decorous mahogany sofa, and the dull figure on the carpet where she had stood.

He took his hat, and crawled away in the bright sunshine. Avis up stairs held her hands upon her ears as if she were trying to shut out the sound of her own words; and the professor at the Alpha Delta Phi dinner sat discussing representative perception with that New-York clergyman who had written so intelligent a review of the Identity of Identity and Non-Identity; and aunt Chloe at the prayer-meeting poured out her good soul for the benefit of the country.

He did not seek to see her after this, but wrote to her several times, expressing more fully both the burden of his love and the reason of his hope, crystallizing calmly all a lover's sublime conviction of the practicability of his wishes. He had no answers; but he wrote bravely on. Perhaps a fortnight passed in this way. All this while, Ostrander had said nothing of his health.

One day Coy came in and said,—

"Poor Mr. Ostrander! He doesn't seem to get up. John goes over there almost every day. He doesn't walk out now,—hasn't for a week; and the Allens take him to ride. But I hear his chum is very good to him, and he won't go anywhere else. And John says he can't see why he doesn't gain. John is very good to him. And John says"—

But Avis did not seem to be granting her usual tender attention to what John said; and Coy changed the subject—to bias ruffles.

It was when Ostrander was lying alone in the dusk, on his college lounge, the next day, that a little note was brought to him, the first he had ever received from her. With shaking fingers he struck a light, and read, in her large, defined hand, this only:—

> "MY DEAR MR. OSTRANDER,—I should like to see you, if you are strong enough to drive to my father's house. Do not come till you are quite able. I have nothing to say that cannot be said as well at one time as another.   Yours sincerely,
> "AVIS DOBELL."

His chum came in at that moment; and Ostrander, who had not ventured into the evening air for weeks, fiercely demanded a carriage and his overcoat, and got them. He usually got what he sought in that reverberating tone. Men were almost as pliable as women to the quality of Philip Ostrander's voice.

As luck would have it, there was a Faculty meeting in the study, and a City Relief Society in the parlors. He asked distinctly for Miss Avis, and was bidden into the long, empty dining-room. There was faint firelight in the Franklin stove; and the moon, which was full, looked in over aunt Chloe's ivies. There was heliotrope[4] in the room somewhere; but it could not be seen. She came, before the lights, not knowing how it was, and stopped in the doorway, uncertain. He was standing at the other end of the room. It seemed as if he leaned against a column of straight moonlight. His height and pallor were thus both emphasized.

Avis, looking in through the darkened room, leaning forward a little, hesitating, thought of the Harbor Light, oddly enough, and of the birds.

The lamps came in while they were standing so: the servant went out and closed the door. Avis had on something scarlet over a thick white dress that blazed out with the lighting of the room. She spoke first, and she said gravely,—

"Mr. Ostrander, I have decided"—

"Oh! do not decide—yet."

"It is quite necessary. I have tried your patience overmuch. I have decided; and I pray you pardon me for the lateness of the decision, and for all the trouble I have been to you, and all the pain—but—I have decided that I cannot resign my profession as an artist."

He was hastening impetuously to remind her that they had both decided she need resign nothing, when he perceived a tender merriment that he had never seen before, dawning far within her eyes.

His voice and face sprang towards her; but she motioned him back.

"And—I forgot to tell you that I hate—with a fervent hatred—to keep house."

"I did not ask you to be my housekeeper!"

"And," suddenly serious, "I make very sour bread."

"You will bring me," he said reverently, "the bread of life."

He looked so wasted, standing trembling there, with his hand upon the long table, that his words seemed less the rhapsody of love than the cry of famine; and the reply, which in the telling has almost a touch of the ludicrous, in the solemn saying was almost sublime.

"Come," he said feebly, "I am starving. Come!" Slowly at first, with her head bent, as if she resisted some opposing pressure, then swiftly, as if she had been drawn by irresistible forces, then blindly, like the bird to the light-house, she passed the length of the silent room, and put both hands, the palms pressed together as if they had been manacled, into his.

CHAPTER XI

"Wine sweeter than first wine
She gave him drop by drop;
Wine stronger than seal could
sign
She poured, and did not stop."
—H. H.[1]

Never was there such a wooing. So, with the simple assurance of that glorified time in which we seem to ourselves to be the originators of each new emotion that overtakes us, Ostrander thought. And, indeed, many a lover's sweet fallacy has been farther from the truth.

Had she not been of a tissue to which caprice was as impossible as crime, he would scarcely have felt, for a day's space, confident of his new and dazzling claim. Her betrothal fitted upon her impatiently, like the first articles in a treaty of capitulation only looking askance as yet towards a dreaded surrender in which a passionately defended lost cause was to go down. He felt his way painfully with her, careful not to startle her, as if she had been a bird poised with tender, receding feet, and fluttering wing, uncertain whether it would nestle at his heart.

The abrupt and cavalierly form of wooing with which he had at first, as was inevitable, shocked and temporarily estranged (but thus ultimately strengthened) the leaning of her feeling towards him, had given place to a definite persistence, to be sure, but to one so tender and cautious, that she seemed to be scarcely more conscious of it than of the temperature of the morning.

For the first few days she received him with a distance which would have disheartened a less perceptive man. Even her anxiety for his recovery seemed to have retired from the foreground of her thoughts. Neither the future nor the past, apparently, occupied her imagination much more than they do that of the caged creature who has just become percipient of the existence and the nature of bars. She sat by him silently, or they talked of matters of wide interest, or aunt Chloe came in. She had steadfastly refused so far to acquaint her family with the state of the case between them, saying decidedly,—

"I must get a little used to it first." Secretly, Ostrander blessed the sturdy American sentiment which made this possible. It seemed to him just then as much as he could bear, that they two, they only out of all the world, should know that the almost inconceivable future was possible to him, which would give him the right to call her his wife. To share the first blush of this knowledge with any human creature was like bruising the velvet on the petal of an iris.

"Aren't you sorry yet?" she asked one day, when this first mood had passed. "Don't you think we had better not do this? I can't do any of the things men expect."

"Oh!" he cried, "you shall not be what other men expect. I don't want you like other men's wives. You Lorelei! sphinx! you Cassandra, you! rebellious—beautiful"—

"But they thought Cassandra was mad," interrupted Avis. "Except"—

"Well?"

"The king loved her," said Avis softly.

It was perhaps a week since he had received her promise, when one evening, as they were alone together, he went resolutely yet gently over to the window where she stood behind the heavy curtains, restlessly shifting aunt Chloe's flowers about to no very definite end, that he could see, and said,—

"Avis?"

He had not called her so before. She started with leaping eyes, moved her lips as if she would have spoken; said nothing.

"Avis," he repeated, "do you know that we have been engaged a week—a whole week?"

When she looked up, he was smiling quietly, and he spoke in that unimpassioned, matter-of-course tone which most quickly disarms the dismay of such a woman; as if that which he sought were as natural as the drawing of the breath, and in no sense more suited to create an exciting scene; or as if he dealt, indeed, with a thought too lofty and too grave to be reduced to the level of an excitement.

"A whole week, my darling. Ah, hush! Can you not bear so much as *that*? And you have not yet given me one kiss. Don't you think it is a little hard on a poor wreck of a wounded soldier?"

"I don't mean to be hard," she said, slowly receding from him with unconscious steps that twisted in her long dress.

"But you *are*—very hard. It doesn't seem to me worth while exactly. Why should you mind so much, if you really love me?"

"I love you!" she murmured, standing quite still.

"Ah, how much? Dear, how much?"

"Do you think I can—*say*, what I have not dared—yet—to"— Her voice sunk.

"All the same," said Ostrander, shaking his head, obstinate with joy, "I'm tired of living on faith. I don't feel sure of you."

She began to stir again, still receding, her outline growing fainter in the shadowed corner of the room. He advanced as slowly, but with a reverent attendance on her wish, towards her.

"You don't undestand!" she cried. "No man could. This is all so new, so strange, so terrible, to me. You don't remember how it is. I never expected to *be* in such a position as this: in all my life I've never thought I *could* be! If I am more foolish than other women, that is why. I don't mean to be foolish. Be patient with me! I love you!"

"If I had not been patient"—he began impulsively, but checked himself.

"I don't know what to do, how to act, how to adjust myself to what has happened," she said in an entreating, childlike way, as if she sought his tolerance for some radical fault of hers. He was intoxicated by this peculiarly beautiful lowliness into which her unstooping spirit now and then surged over, and spent itself, like the foam upon the crest of a wave.

"Only let me teach you!" he urged, drawing, unforbidden, nearer her. "Only say that you will try to learn!"

He thought for a moment that she would have fled; her hands held her very dress away; she seemed to draw even her breath back from him. There was a solemn deprecation, almost of the character of a rebuke, upon her face. But she did not deny him. A sense of sacramental awe, such as he would not have believed it possible for him to be so penetrated with at such a moment,—penetrated almost to the exclusion of the sense of joy,—possessed him; and his own hand with which he touched her seemed to the young man to alter, and become transfigured, like the hand of a spirit stretched to meet him across the kneeling room.

Then, indeed, he walked about with resplendent eyes. He trod on bounding air. Then, at last, he felt that he should win her. He was no longer afraid of any mood, or re-action, or recoil of hers. She might withdraw herself as she would, or grieve over her sweet, lost liberty as she must; she was his.

All our pleasure is said to be nothing more than the consciousness of some one or other of our perfections. Ostrander wore the self-gratified smile of successful love. But one's personal share of acidity must be flavored with gall, if one would be untender with this form of complacency.

It was the next day after the little scene just related, that she went to aunt Chloe. She had preferred to go, and to go alone. Aunt Chloe heard her in silence, and rounded off her stocking (for the little feet of the State orphans, this time), before she said,—

"My dear, he's consumptive! However," after a long pause, in which she knitted and winked with violent rhythmic harmony, "your father will be pleased. And in these days it isn't every talented young man who takes a decided stand. Mr. Ostrander doesn't think he's too smart to believe the Bible, so far. Of course you wouldn't marry any but a religious man. And he will go into the professorship as soon as he recovers. I don't see, on the whole, what could be better. You might take that house of the Perkinses on High Street. But I confess, I thought you'd tug away at that painting a while longer."

"I do not intend this to make any difference with my painting," said Avis quickly: "my marriage, if I marry, is not to interfere with my work. Mr. Ostrander does not wish it."

Aunt Chloe laid down the little stocking, and regarded her niece with that superior matronly smile, under which, above all earthly afflictions, a young woman feels herself a helpless rebel. But all aunt Chloe's reply was a long, low, significant,

"H-u-m-ph!"

"Certainly not," repeated Avis very distinctly. "I would not marry, if I must give up my profession. That is understood."

"When a—woman becomes—a wife," said aunt Chloe, taking to the little stocking again with her generous, dogmatic hands, "her husband's interests in life are enough for her. When you are once married, you will no longer feel any of this youthful irritation against the things that other women do. Women," added aunt Chloe solemnly, "are *not* men. God made us."

"Well, I," said Avis, laughing, "am like the boy in the Sunday school, whom God didn't make. We'll play that somebody else made me, auntie.—Aunt Chloe,"—she suddenly changed her tone to one of grave and searching appeal,—"tell me now,—tell me the holy truth (for I need all the truth I can get just now, auntie), did *you* never in all your life want to be any thing else but my uncle's wife? Is there nothing in all the world that you,—a woman of overflowing energy and individuality, and organizing power,—able to carry a Christian commission or a national commissary on your shoulders,—is there nothing that you ever wanted to *be*?"

The little stocking gently sank to aunt Chloe's broad knee, and there was a pause, in which her soft, brown, benevolent eyes filled with a slow light. In the window-sill the September sun fell upon her geraniums. They turned their burning faces to her solemnly, like visions which said, "We will never tell." Aunt Chloe arose, went over and stroked them, then came back.

"My dear Avis," she said in a subdued voice, "I suppose all of us have times of thinking strange thoughts, and wishing impossible things. I *have* thought sometimes—if I could begin life over, and choose for my own selfish pleasure, that I would like to give myself to the culture and study of plants. I should be—a florist, perhaps, my dear; or a botanist."

Aunt Chloe uttered these words under her breath, as she might have some beautiful heresy, then took to her knitting with a fierce repentance; and that one particular orphan had a pair of stone-china colored stockings before tea-time. It would be difficult to follow the precise chain of mental influences which led aunt Chloe to put in Turkey-red toes.

The interview between Avis and her father was, like all deeply-fraught scenes between them, a brief one. She went in, and, sliding away his books, knelt beside him, and, without looking upwards, said,—

"Father, I have promised to marry Mr. Ostrander. I never meant to marry."

The professor pushed back his spectacles, then his lexicon, then his daughter; held her at arm's length for a moment.

"The conceivable," he murmured, "lies always between two inconceivable extremes. Such we find in the law of the conditioned."

Then gently,—

"And so my little girl—has come to—*that*! I can hardly understand. It seems such a short time since you were playing about; and your mother"—

The professor laid his nervous, scholarly hand upon his daughter's head; she felt it suddenly tremble. But he collected himself, and said,—

"I have a high regard for Mr. Ostrander. I think your mother would have liked him—but it was not quite easy to prophesy whom your mother would like. She was a woman of rare penetration into human character. I wish she were here—just now. But there, my child, is the lecture-bell. I have mislaid the fifth lecture on the Cartesian *dictum*, somewhere, Avis: I think your aunt must have been dusting to-day. Look under those three volumes of Dugald Stewart.[2] Try Reid on Aristotle.[3] No, that is the refutation of Hobbes. Have you shaken the Duality of Consciousness thoroughly?"

He dropped his hand once more upon his daughter's head in passing out, but only said,—

"*Et in Acadia ego.*[4] How like your mother you are looking in these days, my dear!"

He strode away to lecture at a more jagged pace than usual. Across the Cartesian *dictum*, which he clutched with reverent tenacity under one gaunt elbow, the Duality of Consciousness (whatever was to be said of the argument) carried every thing before it that afternoon. If hands had touched him, clinging by the sensitive finger-tips to his lonely old arm—but the bloodless September air was wan and empty. If a voice had spoken—but there was only a sulky wind to say,—

"*Did you want any thing, Professor?*"

And clearly only the Duality of Consciousness could reply, with the leaping pulse of eternal youth,—

"*Only to see if you look well and happy, my dear;*" while the boys upon the college-steps were shouting within his mild, objective ears,—

"Here's the old fellow himself!"

That afternoon, too, Avis sent a little note to Coy. It ran thus:—

> "DEAR COY,—I have said, that, sometime or other, I will marry Mr. Ostrander. But, Coy, if you talk to me about this as most women do about such things, I'll break the engagement.   Yours,
>
> > "AVIS.'

And Coy answered,—

> "DEAR AVIS,—You'll streak his cake with saleratus. His biscuit will taste of yeast. His wristbands will be wrinkled. But you know, if I were a man, Avis, I'd live on johnny-cake and paper cuffs to get you. You'd better be married Christmas, when we are.   Yours,
>
> > "COY.'

And now the marvellous medicine of joy began its subtle work; and fast, with the glamour of the autumn days, the wounded man waxed strong. Avis, looking up sometimes with timid, astonished eyes, trembled to see the work that love had wrought upon him. She was frightened that she could make him so happy. Perhaps for the first time in her young, untroubled story, she had a glimpse into that mysterious truth which no story is long enough or sad enough to penetrate,—that joy *is* life, as misery is death, as the sun is organic warmth, or the night inherent blackness. There may be deeper significance than we always fancy in the sacred figures which familiarize our lips with the everlasting life of heaven and the everlasting death of hell.

In brief, Ostrander, being in heaven, proceeded to immediate, and let us never say, amazing recovery. He received, and before November was able to accept, the renewed overtures from the university. He became the junior colleague of the old geological professor, whose death or resignation (and the Board of Trustees generously allowed him his choice of these alternatives), undoubtedly to take place in a few years' time, would slip the young man into an assured and commanding future.

"I can hardly understand," said Avis: "a month ago you were a failing man. We thought—I thought, Philip, you would die."

She had but just learned, slowly and hardly, to make music of his name for him upon her bewildered lips. The "little language" in which lovers are usually profuse, he heard but scantily. An exquisite reticence hung over her, which he would not, if he could, have shaken. Her expressions of endearment, like her caresses, were rare, rapturous, and rich. His hungry mood waited on them: they surprised his imagination like the discovery of a new art, which all time would not be long enough for him to make his own.

"The man who has won *you*," he would answer, with that unconsciousness of possible exaggeration which makes the very folly of young love sublime,—"such a man *could* not die."

Then, indeed, she turned her strong head towards him, in that way of hers, with a kind of lofty wonder at the new conditions in which she found herself, making it possible for her to sit and hear a radically feeble assertion without any intellectual revolt. Upon this grave wonder a gradual tolerance grew; then, perhaps, if she were in her gentler temper, she melted into some sign of tenderness, which overtook him like a beautiful stratagem of her nature, yet which expended itself as unconsciously as the smile of a child, or the nodding of an anemone.

Or perhaps she sat wrapped in some maiden revery of silence, or fear, or retreat, which he found it impossible to understand or to share with her: he sat shut out, as if he had tried to lift the veil of Isis, or to woo the Sphinx of the desert to open her stone lips.

One day he asked her to play to him, for he had never heard her. She told him, what was true enough, that her execution, which was always poor, had not been improved by six years of exclusive art-study. But she went to her mother's old piano, and played for half an hour,—fragments from the Andante of Beethoven's Fifth Symphony, a serenade of Schubert's, the Adelaide,[5] some Scotch melodies, and one or two improvisations, unscientific, powerful, and magnetic.

Ostrander threw himself upon the sofa, and listened, with his hand above his eyes, as if he were shutting out a light.

"Oh," he said under his breath when she had finished, "what a touch!"

Avis heard this gratefully. Ostrander's taste for music was highly cultivated: she would have felt it to be an unkind insincerity if he had said she played well. She was moved by the delicate and honest fervor of his tribute; as if he—he first and only in the world—had recognized some dumb side to her nature. She cherished the memory of this recognition with a peculiarly coy happiness, which she had afterwards occasion to remember.

She long remembered too, and he—what lovers would soon forget?—their first shared experience of the rapture of the dying year. It seemed to her that the heart of spring could never beat to stir her own like this October pulse.

What was the vigor of a violet? the fire of a snow-drop? What did the young grass know of hardly-yielded and sternly-encroaching love? One red leaf understood her better than they all. They walked one day far out of the town, into a forest of young oaks, and stood clinging together, awed by the sea of subdued color that broke against their feet, and down the knoll, to the crown of which they had climbed. In the violet distance the maples splashed into shallow tints, bold vermilion and transparent yellow, like emotions quickly stung and healed. But the infant oaks, mere shrubs yet, gathered themselves in deep shades, blood to the heart's core. All the gales of winter could not stir their leaves. They would cling like the unclasped fingers that death had overtaken; they appealed to the imagination like some superb constancy towering above all lesser story, as strength must, perforce, tower over weakness, and unity above disintegration.

Avis, standing with her straw hat thrust hanging down her shoulders, and her head bent as if she listened, turned suddenly, with an appealing gesture, towards Ostrander, and said,—

"I never loved another man. What should I do if you had loved another woman?"

Instantly, for her only answer, she was swept to his heart, with an impulse more daring and authoritative than she had ever witnessed in him, as if some impalpable power had been arrayed to snatch her from him, or as if her mad supposition were beneath the respect of articulate reply.

The young oaks throbbed about them dizzily for a moment, before, moved by his continued silence, she drew her face back, that she might look up into his. She was a little surprised to find, for the second time, that look which she had marked upon the June morning by the shore. He seemed to have become, for the moment, perfectly blind, and to regard her with the blank, narrow gaze of a person whose brain was stealthily diseased. Then swiftly it darted as before, and his deep eyes burnt it out before he said,—

"Avis, never say that again! It frightens the man—who has won the right to hold you here—to remember that it might or could, but for God's mercy, have been some other woman. And you—you would have still been in the world,—in the same world with him!"

Avis said nothing. A man, after all, was so different! She, for instance, had never thought that it might or could have been some other who should have so much as touched her hand. One does not waste the fancy upon the incredible. It had not occurred to her as a special interposition of Providence, that she should love Philip Ostrander. What man cometh after the king? Her great love was simply the condition of existence, like the action of her heart. She had never felt called upon to thank God for that.

Just before his assumption of his new duties in the college, Ostrander left for a few days' visit in New Hampshire. He expressed much regret, in which Avis, with a tenderness which she shrank from expressing, fully shared, that he had been obliged to defer seeing his mother for so long. She felt sorry that this had been, and must have been so. Her heart yearned towards that solitary old mother—Philip's mother. She did not care how rustic, or old, or ignorant she might be. ("My poor mother is not exactly a cultivated woman," Ostrander had said once in his tender way.) Her own motherless youth reached with a peculiar longing after this unknown woman who had borne the man she loved. She wondered sometimes if the old lady would not find it less lonely to live in Harmouth. But of course her son would be the best to know, and should be the first to speak of that. She contented herself with sending a timid but tender little message when Ostrander went, in response to the cramped, old-fashioned postscript—her only welcome from his only living kin—in which Mrs. Ostrander had once sent "her kind respects to the young lady of whom her son had written her."

When he was gone, for the first time since the injury to her hand, she resumed with stiff, strange fingers, her work in the studio. It was not easy to estimate, perhaps, the precise effect which that disabled hand had borne upon her lot. Avis found herself wondering, with a kind of terror, if she should ever have promised to be Philip Ostrander's wife, if she had been through those idle, enthralling days doggedly at work.

A stiffness and strangeness deeper than a bruised muscle could strike, came upon her when she closed the door of the long-deserted place, and, striking a fire in her little grate, sat down to warm her hands. The autumn sun stepped in, and stood cool and calm against the wall, like the friend who never forgets, or suffers us to forget, the resolve or the aspiration which we once expressed. The dust had collected upon her sketches; the boughs of the apple-tree were bare; upon the easel the sphinx hung, covered and dumb.

Avis looked about her with a singularly self-defensive feeling, as if she were summoned by some invisible tribunal to answer for an impalpable offence. A radical confusion, such as her young life had never known before, obscured her thoughts. She had something of the self-recoil which a man has in turning to his books or his business after a night's dissipation.

She went up and uncovered her sketch. The critical, cool sunlight fell upon it. The woman and the sphinx looked at one another. Avis glanced at the ring that fettered her finger. Her whole figure straightened and heightened: she lifted her head, and out of her deepening eye there sprang that magnificent light which so allured and commanded Philip Ostrander.

"What have I done?" she cried. "Oh! what have I done?"

With an impulse which only a woman will quite respect, standing alone there in the silent witness of the little room, she tore off her betrothal ring.

Then with one of her rare sobs, sudden and sharp as an articulate cry, she flung her arms about the insensate canvas, and laid her cheek, as if it had been the touch of one woman upon another, against the cold cheek of the sphinx; and solemnly, as if she sought to atone to a goddess for some broken fealty, she whispered,—

"I will be true."

When Ostrander returned, he found her nervously at work. A marked unrest enveloped her. But she stood quite still, when, pushing open the studio-door eagerly, he met her with the accumulated fervors of a lover after a first separation. A chill crept over him even while he touched her—beautiful, reluctant, mysterious—this strong, sweet woman, wooed, but not yet won.

"Are you not glad," he pleaded, "to see me back?"

"I did not think I should be so glad."

"And you missed me—a little?"

"I had no idea," complainingly, "that I should miss you so much. I can't understand it. I ought not to have minded. I have been at work." She spoke with protesting significance, glancing at her hand, which he held—palette, brushes, and all—fast prisoner. He followed her glance, and changed color swiftly, before he said,—

"Avis, where is your ring?"

"I took it off. It made me uncomfortable."

"Made you uncomfortable—my ring—our engagement-ring?"

Ostrander released her hands, and stood looking at her with a perplexity which struck, as indeed it seemed to, the very core of his imagination.

"I do not understand this at all," he said with some displeasure. "Where is the ring?"

"On the shelf, behind the Lake of Como, at the left of father's portrait, on the right of the charcoal newsboy," replied Avis, laughing. Ostrander brought the ring, and stood with it balanced between his thumb and forefinger, looking from her to it, thoroughly uncertain what to do or say.

Turning with one of her sudden, supple motions, she saw how deeply she had pained him. She put down her brushes, and held out her firm finger at once.

"Shall I put it on again?" he hesitated.

"If you think I deserve it," she gently said.

He put it on; and they talked no more about it. Ostrander was thoroughly uneasy. He ventured for the first time, that morning, to speak quite distinctly of their future; said that he was going with her father, when his inauguration was well over, to see the available houses in Harmouth; spoke of his improving health, and of his desire to be quietly settled; but more especially of his wish to see her at work more to the purpose than she could be, as things were at present, than she could indeed, he feared, well be until after their marriage.

Avis, while he spoke, painted busily. Still painting, and without looking round, she said below her breath,—

"Philip, don't *want* me to marry you yet!"

But, when he left her, she crept up to him, timid as a hare, and besought him to be patient with her; for she was sorely tried in ways she said, that she knew she could not expect him to understand. He would have waited half a lifetime for the tone and the touch with which she said those words.

After this she painted with great steadiness. Ostrander spent most of his spare hours in the studio. Aunt Chloe had an easy-chair wheeled out for him, and set beside the little grate.

"Why not leave that picture," he asked one day, as he stood silently watching it, "until by and by?"

"Why do you want me to do that?"

"I think you would make a greater picture of it after we are married," he answered, disregarding her disturbed expression. "You will have more leisure, more calm. It is going to be a great work, Avis. I wish to be as proud of it as possible. I wish it to be grand and full, without deficiency. I want the world to know you by it, in some sense,—in its sense,—for what you are."

She was touched by his generous interest in her work and fame. She thought how true was that wise man's word who said that a friend is he who makes us do what we can: she pitied with the calm compassion of joy that woman, wherever she might be on the earth, who would not find in this beautiful sense a friend in the man whose wife she was to be. Down through the years she suddenly saw herself transfigured by happiness. She saw her whole nature deepening, its lightest grace or deepest gift illuminated, herself idealized, by love. This man—so tender, and so noble above his fellows, so true that he could be proud of the woman he loved, so great that he could make himself small beside her, so anxious rather for her success in doing the thing God had made her to do than for his own, so simply and superbly recognizant of the truth that this thing was not done when she had become his wife, and ordered his house,—this man brought her, she thought, that transcendent experience which is so often given to a man, but alas! so unknown to women, in which the sternest aspiration is strengthened by the sweetest joy; in which love shall be found more a stimulus to than a sacrifice of the higher elements of the nature.

Hand in hand with this man whose generous humility had exalted him—as what else could?—to the kingship of her, she should climb to see "how life looked behind the mountains."

She longed to make herself worthy of so royal a love. She began to be glad with a proud pleasure that it was in the nature of things that she should sacrifice more for Philip than he for her. It seemed that, by slow and kind degrees, a reposeful spirit crept upon her. The inevitable conflict between her art and her love, which had diseased her happiest hours, shrivelled from an organic to a functional thing. She began to consider it now without alarm.

She began to understand how natural is joy. Her sequestered tenderness peered out more frequently. She became a radiant creature.

Ostrander watched her in a kind of ethereal trance, which, for a long time, he guarded from the disturbance of his own more impatient moods as jealously as he guarded herself from them. He felt it a barbarism now to mar the unforecasting nature of her sweet impulse, as it would be to hasten mechanically the budding of a flower. He felt that he was living that which few men ever live at all, and no man ever lives but once. He held the cup of his happiness to a delicate and slowly-tasting lip.

But the autumn met its blazing death, and the calmer colors of the winter set in.

The tenser nerve and the clearer brain kept time to the strong step that crushed the flakes of first-fallen snow. Now, on nights when one's solitary feet rang upon the walks of the little town, shadows flitted on drawn curtains, and lights beamed out from the hearts of deeply-colored rooms. All the sacraments and sacrifices that go to make up human homes, began to gather upon them the vigorous solemnity of the winter.

On Christmas Coy was married; and the two young people began, with the touching confidence of the young and the very happy, the sacred work which we are wont to call "saving souls." The phrase is well-rasped, not to say worn, but indestructible as an atom, and poetic as a fossil.

It was not long after this, that aunt Chloe began in a vague and abstract manner to drop a variety of remarks upon the family ear, which Avis failed to find interesting, but did think singularly inconsequent.

"What is it," she said to Coy one day, sitting in the cheerful parsonage-parlor, "that *has* happened lately in the cotton-market? Aunt Chloe keeps telling me how cheap unbleached cotton is. I think it is twenty-five cents,—or really, perhaps it was five. Is that a fact so vital to the interests of the country, that I ought to care about it?"

"My dear child," cried Mrs. Rose with her most matronly smile, "it is the servants' sheets!"

"Servants'—sheets?"

"Why, yes. O Avis—Avis Dobell! Who but you would be so divinely dull? I suppose you expect your servants to *have* sheets, when you go to housekeeping?"

"I never thought," said Avis faintly. "And is that what she meant, too, about towels? She's been exhausting the subject of towels, Coy. There is something very remarkable about them. I think you cut the fringe, or else you fell—let me see. No, I think you overcast it. I think it was very ill-mannered in aunt Chloe."

"A roller-cloth would do, dear," suggested Coy soothingly. "And *no* New-England servant would mind camping out. I wouldn't trouble myself, if I were you."

But Avis sat looking at her with wide eyes, like an injured goddess. Women upon whom domestic details sit with a natural, or even an acquired grace, will need to cultivate their sympathies with this young recoiling creature. Across her picture or her poem, looking up a little blindly, she had listened to the household chatter of women, with a kind of gentle indifference, such as one feels about the habits of the Fee-jeeans.[6] Unbleached cotton, like x in the algebra, represented an unknown quantity of oppressive but extremely distant facts. How had she brought herself into a world where the fringe upon a towel must become a subject requiring fixed opinions?

She bade Coy good-by abruptly, fled to her studio, and worked till dark.

But, when she went into the house, she found aunt Chloe advancing a new theory about comforters. In Vermont they were quilted at home. But there were advantages in purchasing them outright, not to be under-estimated, unless—as in the case of Miss Snipper, a worthy young woman who had put two brothers through college, and one into the Hawaiian field (he died in six months, poor fellow!)—you really felt it a duty to employ a seamstress; and the professor made so much less trouble about having her at the table; which was the more to his credit, as her teeth were set by so inefficient a dentist, and make that peculiar noise, especially with biscuit. But aunt Chloe thought milk-toast would remedy the difficulty.

CHAPTER XII

> *"It should be remembered that*
> *the p'îng is a 'calling' or*
> *'exclaiming' tone; the shàng is a*
> *'questioning' tone; the kú is a*
> *'despairing' tone; and the hiá-*
> *p'îng, an 'assenting' tone; the*
> *jă-shūng is an 'abrupt' stop."*
> —Chinese Grammar

It was in the heart of the happy winter that Ostrander, sitting one day by the study-fire with Avis, after a long walk over the frozen beach, said quietly, as if resuming a broken conversation,—

"But, Avis, is this to last forever?"

"*This!*" She turned to catch his meaning, dull with happiness. "It is pleasant enough to last forever, I think," she said, throwing herself back in her deep chair. She sat drowned in her furs and partially loosened cape: her cheek had the vivid flush that a winter-night paints upon faces, and the fine excitement which accompanies it, hovered in her eyes.

"But our own home would be like this always," persisted he, with the vague and blessed fatuity of a lover's imagination, which, while it may perceive the trail of the serpent over Adam's Eden, or Tom Smith's, or yours, or mine, hears in its own only the rustle of the leaf upon the tree of life.

Avis, who had now lost her brilliant color, and sat quite dull and still, said,—

"I wish a man and woman could be always engaged! What are you laughing at, Philip?"

"Should you really like it to be so—for you and me?" asked Ostrander, with a smile that was grave enough.

"Certainly," said Avis promptly. "Of course I should. I am perfectly happy as we are. I think most women would be."

"But I," suggested Ostrander, "am not happy. I am tired of a homeless life; I have lived one so long!" He had never so distinctly urged his own need upon her before. Avis listened attentively. Her precious freedom—wild rebel that it was! petted, perhaps, and over-indulged—took on to her mind for the first time, faintly, the aspect of a selfish delight. To be sure, Philip had no home, like herself, no consonance of household repose and love let into his life. She had not thought sufficiently of that.

"I do not wish to press any claim or want of mine unduly," he went on gently; "but there *is* my work. I have my future to make; I don't want it to be one that my wife shall be ashamed of. Situated as I am, I cannot command my best conditions. With his home and his wife, a man must develop himself, if he ever can. With you, Avis, with *you*," he paused, much agitated, "there are no bounds but those of my own nature that will prevent my life from becoming at least a worthy if not a noble deed."

Long years after, these words came back to Avis Dobell's memory, like the carven stone into which time has wrought meanings that the sculptor's mind or hand was impotent to grasp.

"Come, now," he continued more lightly, "an honest word for an honest word, Avis! Do you suppose, if I let you go on just as you like, you would ever make a definite step towards our wedding-day?"

"No," said the woman, after a long pause. "*Never!*" She threw back her wrappings with a suffocated look, and paced for a few minutes back and forth before the brilliant fire, a silhouette in her falling feather and dark winter-dress. Ostrander watched her with compressed lip and guarded eye. He was prepared for a long and serious contest, in which he had fully made up his mind not to be worsted. By gradations as fine as the shades in a woman's fancy— too fine for any man but a determined lover to be patient with—he expected her to taunt, torment, allure, baffle, but yield to him now. He had not understood (what man ever understood a complex woman?) the immortal element of surprise in her nature. He sat dumb with delight under the look and the motion with which she presently turned to him. As beautiful is the pliability of a torrent meeting its first unconquerable resistance; it surrenders as mightily as it defied.

"You are perfectly right," she said with a grave, sweet dignity; "and I have been very foolish. If you leave me to myself, I shall never make any change in any thing. If I am ever to become your wife, let it be all over with as soon as possible."

They were married in three weeks.

If ever the Christian character deepened under discipline, aunt Chloe's should have been that character at the end of this memorable time. We are all of us a little incredulous of our neighbor's affliction; but among the radical trials of life, who could fail to rank the rearing of a motherless child to a marriage in which neither the trousseau nor the upholstery commanded the proper respect of the bride? Unless, as some one has told us, deficiency of charity be deficiency of imagination, we must feel sorry for aunt Chloe.

Avis positively refused, at the outset, to investigate the deeps beyond the lowest deeps that underlay the nature of unbleached cotton; asked why, if a woman had money enough to buy blankets, she must sit an hour discussing the wadding of a comforter; and failed utterly to see why the marriage-certificate would not be valid without the intervention of Miss Snipper and the milk-toast. There was a compromise upon these fatal questions. Aunt Chloe retained the privilege of seeing to it that Avis entered upon the holy estate of matrimony as a lady ought, with a dozen of every thing, upon sole condition that Avis herself should not be consulted. Instead, therefore, of a heavy-eyed, exhausted woman, whose every nerve was stitched into her clothes, Avis came to her wedding-day brilliant with health, and calm as the sky.

This little fact was the more memorable because it left her to her instincts, and no one knew quite how those led her to dispose of these three weeks. She was much in the open air, pacing the shore and the snowy fields; or she worked intently in the studio; or she sat alone with unshared, inscrutable moods. Ostrander would have said that he scarcely saw her in all that time. She received him quietly, but with a withdrawal which he dared not disturb. It was evident that she preferred her solitude to himself. He left her to her fancy, not altogether, perhaps, without some comprehension of it. A man does not live a celibate till thirty-one without becoming fully as conscious of the perils as of the pleasures of a wedded future. Ostrander would not have thought it possible, however, that he could put his broad shoulders beneath this sweet yoke with so slight a protest. His feeling that he accepted a sacrifice radically so much deeper than any he could ever make, overswept the superficial shrinking from change, which perhaps all but the youngest lovers feel in more or less degree upon the immediate eve of marriage. He felt impressed by his dim conception of the strong individual struggle in the nature of this woman whom he loved. His whole soul concentred itself, with a unity not habitual to him in all things, upon the effort to adjudge himself worthy of the acquiescence of her life with his. He tried to tell her so the day before their marriage. But she gave him one look which stopped the breath of his soul, for joy; and he tried no more just then.

It was the simplest of weddings. Mr. and Mrs. John Rose were there, and Barbara; but her brother was out of town on business. Barbara looked at Ostrander, and remembered the tea-rose. Ostrander looked at Barbara, and forgot it. Poor Chatty Hogarth was got over with her wheeled chair; and Frederick Maynard came to see what he was known to have pronounced "the burial of the

most promising artist in New England;" and at Avis's request the
family servant came in; and her father (who, as is so usual with
the collegiate instructors of America, had begun life in the pulpit)
married them; while aunt Chloe, with a mind at peace with God
and man upon the subject of the wedding-cake, which no New-
York caterer had been allowed to handle for *her* niece, protected
her silver-gray silk from her honest, sparse tears, and made it
clearly understood among the guests, that Mrs. Ostrander's health
had not permitted her attending her son's marriage, and that the
young people would visit her in New Hampshire upon their brief
little wedding-tour.

They had a relenting February day, in which the prophecy of the
near spring was audible, as the whisper of one dear to us across a
darkened room. The windows were flung open in the house, and
the well-worn path to the studio was without frost, yielding timidly to the touch of the foot that loved it.

Avis slipped away somehow, and was missing after the wedding:
her husband went in search of her. He found her, as he had expected, in the studio. The disarray of packing put a chill desolation
into the room. The pictures were boxed or gone; the easels folded
against the wall; only the sphinx was left. There had been no fire
in the building that week. Avis, in the middle of the cold little neglected place, stood shivering in her wedding-dress.

He held his arms out, smiling, but with an emotion which he
found it difficult not to call sad even at that moment. He was so
sorry to startle, to grieve, or distress her, by the inevitable presence of his feeling. There seemed to him just then something inexorable, like a Pagan Fate, in the nature of a mighty love. They two,
standing there in the yielding winter sunshine, seemed like children swept and lost within it.

"Tell me," he said, seeking to dissipate the almost oppressive
solemnity which the moment had assumed for him, and coming
up behind her where she stood before the still incomplete but now
strongly-indicated and impressive picture, "what would you do if
you had to choose now between us,—the sphinx and me?"

"A man cannot understand, perhaps," said Avis, after a long silence, "or he would never ask a woman such a bitter question."

"Oh! we will have no bitter questions *to-day*," he murmured,
taking a step back to look at her. There seemed to him something
strangely select and severe in her unornamented dress. Only an
artist could make such a bride. Her silk drapery hung about her
like the marble folds upon a statue.

"*Can* you understand," continued Avis, ignoring or unconscious
of his look, "that I might—perhaps—choose to stay with the sphinx
to-day—and not mind it much?"

"I think I can," he said, hesitating. "No, I will not mind. I can't be jealous even of the sphinx just now."

"And then," she added, turning sharply, so that she stood with her face averted from him, "another day,"—

"Oh! and what the other day?"

Avis did not answer. Impetuous words bounded to her lips; but they were checked by an instinct that she herself did not comprehend. Her nature recoiled on itself in the discovery that she had begun to tell him that she could think of no price too costly by which to purchase her way back to him.

She stood in her white dress with burning cheeks. She wondered if, when a woman had been for half a lifetime a happy wife, she could let her husband understand how much she loved him. Her love seemed to her an eternal secret. Her soul spoke to his in whispers. It were unwomanly, unwifely, to lavish herself.

After a silent moment, she glided to him like a goddess, and for the first time of her own unguided, or it might be unguarded, will, his wife lifted her lips to his.

They passed out together into the pliant air; and aunt Chloe came calling about the carriage and the people; and the sky, when they looked up to it through the garden trees, lifted itself, and widened, like a joy whose nature knows no end. They passed on through the golden weather, in the solemn separateness from all our little common cares and pleasures, which to have known is to have lived, and to have missed is to hope for life beyond.

🜆 CHAPTER XIII

*"In the opinion of the world
marriage ends all, as it does
in a comedy. The truth
is precisely the reverse. It
begins all."*
—Mme de Swetchine [1]

*"Who hath most, he yearneth
most,
Sure as seldom heretofore,
Somewhere of the gracious
more.
Deepest joy the least shall
boast,
Asking with new-opened eyes
The remainder."* . . .
—Jean Ingelow [2]

The reluctance with which we turn from any intense feeling, whether of pain or pleasure, to a lower level of emotion, is a psychological study for which the curriculum of Harmouth University unquestionably finds a proper place in the lecture-room, where all well-classified feelings go, but strictly in view of which, it does not regulate the academical year. Granting that the corporation agreed to honor him by the offer of a chair, Harmouth would have summoned Adam out of Eden, had the Lord chosen to create him in term-time.

It lacked still some weeks to the spring vacation, and Ostrander's bridal tour was necessarily compressed almost between two sabbath sunsets. They did not get up into New Hampshire, after all. He found himself suffering somewhat from the capricious weather; and it would be really worth more to his mother, he said, to see them in July.

The two young people came dreamily to their own home. The afternoon that they were to come, Coy and aunt Chloe held confidential counsel in the expectant house, a passable place, which had been selected in the perplexed patience with which we adjust ourselves to all depressed ideals. Avis in the town was like a bird that has flown through a window by mistake. The sea could be heard, but not seen, from her chamber-window. The noise from the street interrupted the library. It was not quite clear where the studio was to be, unless in the attic. But there were elms in the yard, and crocuses in the garden, and the house stood at three minutes' walk from the college green. This, in view of the New-England winters, and the delicate health of the young professor, was decisive.

"I can arrange about the studio somehow," Avis had said.

"Certainly," said Ostrander, "*that* must be managed." He meant to manage it, of course. There should be no trouble about the studio. And aunt Chloe said approvingly,—

"You do quite right, Avis, my dear, to consult Mr. Ostrander's interest first."

Avis vaguely resented this, she could not have told why. She had no principles but the instinctive code of daily love, about deifying her husband's interests, and had found women singularly weak upon this point. But it was quite reasonable that Philip should be near the college: she thought she had done no more than good manners required.

"Poor Avis," said aunt Chloe plaintively, as she and Coy put the touches to the small dining-room, where tea was spread for the travellers, "*would have* pink doyleys. Of course, the first cooked huckleberry will ruin them. And I told her they never could be used with English breakfast-tea, and they fade in washing beyond all belief."

"Yes, they fade like a sunrise," said Mrs. Rose demurely; "but Avis is precisely one of those women of whom you *can* say that she never will be married again. And salt sets them. Is this the china she painted? How like Avis! At first you don't understand it, then it bewitches you. See, every piece has a feather on it,—a different feather! She has wrought some fancy about her own name into this tea-table, I'll venture. Oh, I see! No, I don't; I don't see. I suppose we're not expected to see. That rose-curlew on the creamer is like—a singing-leaf, I think."

"Perhaps so," moaned aunt Chloe. "But have you seen the vegetable-dishes? Not a handle that a servant could get hold of if her thumbs were all fingers. And that rep in the parlor, poor child, *may* last her through the summer. And when I told her how easy it was to slip down newspapers—and I'm sure you can get them up again while the door-bell rings, and a housekeeper can't begin by counting a little trouble like that—but if I'd proposed plated spoons it couldn't have been worse. Not that I've said much about it to her father; for he is so over-worked, and it never does to worry a literary man: they weaken down under it like a baby under the whooping-cough. But when I come into this house, and think of those two, I am—I am very much troubled," said aunt Chloe, stiffening suddenly at the discovery that one slow tear had rolled into the Japanese tea-pot. "Now, while she was painting all this china, she might have learned to set white-bread, at least with milk; and the yeast I could have looked after. Mr. Ostrander may dine off painted feathers a while; but he's too literary to like it long. No men are so fussy about what they eat as those who think their brains the biggest part of them, though my brother is very patient, and easy to pacify. And poor Avis knows no more what is before her than if she were keeping house with little stones and broken crockery in a huckleberry-pasture on a Saturday afternoon."

"There's a baker," said Coy soothingly, "and Mr. Ostrander is very much in love with her." But in her heart she shared aunt Chloe's anxieties more acutely than she found it worth while to allow. Coy had a delicate loyalty about expressing them. She did not talk much about Avis, even with John himself: she wished to spare Avis the sting which pricks the brightest hours fate yields to some of us,—the knowledge, that, behind the shield we hold before our dazzling happiness, a prudential committee of our friends sits indorsing—whether in our temper, health, income, complexion, or the nature of things—a grudge against our delirium. Coy reverenced the severe old canon which bids us rejoice in the joy of the soul we love.

Mr. and Mrs. Ostrander came with the laggard March sunset. Avis moved about the house radiant and unwearied as a Hebe: even the dust of travel seemed to glitter on her. Coy and her husband, the professor and aunt Chloe, remained, at her wish, to dedicate the pleasant tea-table. Certainly there was never a pleasanter. And the bread was aunt Chloe's. Avis presided dreamily. The room was alive with color. She felt rather than perceived the rose-tint of the linen, the bronze prism on the peacock's plume which encircled the cup that she lifted to her lips, the Pompeiian red upon the walls, the mellowed meaning of the Japanese coloring upon the lamp-screen, the flutter of the bright ribbon at her own throat, the luminous presence of her husband's face. She lifted her eyes to him timidly for the first time across their own table. Life put a finger on its lips like a child with a secret to tell. Love was a mystery that went deepening before her. She stood with one foot on an untrod path that broadened to the sun. She shrank from the advance, nay, even from the existence, of unexplored joy. She was afraid to be so happy.

He found her, when, at an early hour, their friends had left them to themselves in the silent house, in a daydream in the middle of the parlor, just where she had bidden her father good-night. He came and stood beside her; but he, too, found it difficult to speak. He was silenced with joy: to find words for it was a task sacred and slow, like selecting an earthly lily for an angel to carry into heaven. He did not try, it seemed, and for that she liked him better; for he said only presently,—

"Are you too tired to go over the house to-night, Avis? Will it not be pleasant to see how it all looks at first? And in the morning I must get to college early."

She felt grateful to him for the easy commonplace words as they wandered up and down, hand in hand, through "that new world which is the old." She wondered how women ever became used to their husbands, and spoke of them indifferently, as Mr. Smith or Mr. Jones.

This home—their home—lifted its walls gravely about her like a temple; and this man whose wife she was, ministered therein a high priest, before whom her soul trod softly. She had never perceived before how solemn a thing it is to found a human home. Most of those experiences which make the whole world kin must become personal to become interesting. The truism was now the discovery.

Avis had contrived, it was impossible to say how,—for never did a bride take possession of a house, knowing so little what was in it,—to stamp her individuality with a delicate but distinct definition upon her home.

"It is like going from flower to flower," said Ostrander, as they strolled from room to room.

On certain points Avis had been stringent. Whatever the vague necessities in the matter of tin-ware, aunt Chloe should not put a scarlet cricket or a purple tidy in the same room with a maroon curtain. His library was a harmony in green and gray. The little room upon whose windows the buds of the elm-tree tapped was a melody in blue. In her own room Avis had gathered the shades of the rose. The little house was a study in color. To the young man, coming out of the cold spaces of so many homeless years, it seemed, that night, like a new and glowing science, which it would take him as long to command as to possess the mysterious nature of his wife. Both awed him. He watched her with held breath as she moved, gentle with the new domestic touch and stir, that sat so strangely on her. She breathed color, he thought, as other women breathed pale air.

Avis left him presently to look over some matters for his morning class, and herself strolled about the house alone. It was one of the small surprises of life to her to find herself stroking the curtains, and patting the pillows, like other women whom she had seen in other new houses; to see that her hand lingered upon her own door-knobs even, with a caress. The thrill of possession, the passion of home, had awaked itself in a sleeping side of her nature.

In her own room there was a very fine East India hammock, woven of a lithe pearl-white cord, much favored for this purpose by people of ease in tropical countries. Avis put it there, because, against the color of the walls and drapery, it had a peculiarly delicate and negligent effect, grateful to her in the confined house. Above it, against a deeply-stained panel, stood her own Melian Venus.

She flung herself into the hammock, and yielded to its light motion idly. As idly she thought of her future, of her work, of the sphinx in the cold, closed studio. Not to-morrow, perhaps, but some day, she should convert her delight into deeds.

It seemed to her a necessity simple as the rhythm of a poem, or the syntax of a sentence, that the world should be somehow made nobler or purer by her happiness. By and by she should know how to spell it out.

Her husband called her presently from the foot of the stairs, and she stole down to him with a beautiful timidity. She did not tell him what she had been thinking: she felt as if he understood. This is what it is to be happy, to believe that our thought is shared before it can be spared.

She had exchanged her travelling-dress, while she was up stairs, for a loose wrapper, over which she had thrown a shawl—a crape shawl—that he had never seen. He put his hand upon it, and said,—

"You do not often wear this color, Avis. What do you call it?"

"It is carmine."

"It looks like a live thing."

"It is one of the colors made from the cochineal," said Avis. "I have always fancied that they throb with the life that has been yielded to make them. Do you like it, Philip?"

"Like it? How should I know? You are in it." She blushed gently: she was glad he thought the carmine suited her; she loved it too well to wear it at hap-hazard. One of those subtle fancies which the happiest woman does not expect to share with the man she loves, came to her just then. She would not wear this color except for him. Her soul seemed filled with fine reserves, winding corridors of fancy, closed rooms of thought, deep recesses of feeling, which she curtained from him by a lofty instinct.

The nature of the wife withdrew itself with a deeper than maidenly reticence. She feared lest her great love should put into his hands the key to a fair palace in which she would that he should be forever an expectant guest.

"What are you thinking, Avis?" he asked her suddenly. A certain contraction of her forehead which he did not know, and the familiar throbbing of the temple, arrested him.

"I was thinking," she began, and hesitated.

"Are not your thoughts to be mine, love?"

He drew her to him slowly. In the rich color of her loose drapery she had the poised, reluctant look of the fine Jacques rose.

"I was only wondering," she said. "I was thinking that there are women in the world whose husbands have ceased to love them. I can think of nothing else like that."

"You could never, under any conditions, be one of those women," murmured the young husband rapturously.

"I?" said Avis, looking for the moment perplexed. "I was not thinking of myself. I was sorry for the poor women. But I would rather be such a woman than such a man. I begin to be sorry and glad about many things, in many strange ways, new ways of which I never thought. Philip, two people who love one another might almost make the world over, it seems to me. Joy is so strong—we are so strong. God will ask a great deal of us."

"If he asks he shall receive," said the young man solemnly. He was impressed with her reverent mood: he assimilated it so perfectly, that he could have thought it was an impulse of his own which she rather had perceived and reflected. He asked her for a Bible, and himself suggested that they have prayer. With an agitated voice he sought God's blessing upon their home and upon their love.

They talked no more of lesser things after this. Avis moved about hushed and happy; she stirred, putting his books and papers in order upon the table. He watched her with eyes beaten faint by love.

"You must not tire yourself to work, dear love," she said. She had never called him so before.

Shivering like a cremona upon which a discord had been struck, Avis started, when at the newly-painted door of the new gleaming room, there fell a sudden knock. It was the new "girl." Ostrander had forgotten that there was anybody in the house but themselves. Avis looked at her in gentle perplexity. It seemed to her a remarkable breach of good manners, that the woman should have come at all; and when she said,—

"An' what is it yez would lave me to get for your breakfast?" Mrs. Ostrander could have dismissed her on the spot.

Philip Ostrander now plunged into his life's work with the supreme vigor of joy. His ambition took on the colors of his emotion, and fired feverishly. He assumed the drudgeries of his position with the fervor of a far more conscientious temperament; and its excitements took on the character of a thrill. His really brilliant but phosphoric nature strengthened into honest flame. He was at that time in his life a marked and splendid illustration of the cohesive power of a great love. His own wife failed sometimes to fathom the almost pathetic movement with which, in those days, he would turn to her, when he came home from the lecture-room over-wearied, holding out his still thin hands, and ask her to strike a few chords for him upon the piano, saying, as he did so,—

"Harmony, harmony! Avis, I am spent for a touch of harmony."

And when her eyes only asked him what he meant, when she had satisfied him as she could, with her repressed, rich touch, he would answer that the boys had tried him, that something had jarred, that there was a discord in him.

"And you," he said,—"you quell it all." And then he spoke no more; but to himself he said, bowing his forehead on her yielding hair, "Who am I, that I should win her?"

He was then, at least, as that man should be who has gained the allegiance of a strong wife,—an awed and humble man.

Then his professional work began to partake of the gravity of his happiness. Professor Dobell brought to his daughter from the green-room of the university a report of her husband's present popularity and prospective power in the college, which excited her like fine wine. For a little while that seemed to her, added to all the other elements of deep emotion in her new life, as much excitement as she could sanely bear. Her own work she deferred resuming from day to day, but neither from that syncope of the will, nor fever of feeling, which threatens the integral purpose of a woman first intoxicated by the deification of herself, that grows from ministry to the man she loves. She reasoned herself through her honeymoon and its succeeding weeks with a steady eye. The studio was not in order; and she chose not to put into her picture— this one picture, at least—any element less permanent than repose. She decorated the dados in her hall contentedly: the sphinx could wait.

A tender sense of justice, possibly, mingled itself with this course. She had not treated Philip so well before their marriage, that she need accentuate her haste to pursue her personal aims and wishes now. Each lingering sign of physical weakness in him smote her with a rich revenge. She watched the lessening pallor of his temples with a hidden remorse of which she dared not trust herself to speak. Sometimes she stole up, and kissed the still prominent and beating vein across his forehead, darting like a vanished thought then from his outstretched arms, and silent afterwards for a long time. One day, sitting beside him in the full light, she lifted his hand, which was whiter than her own, in both her sensitive, healthful palms, and brought her lips to it with her slow and delicate, deepening touch. Then, when he restrained her, she sat crimson. She could not have said whether she was more afraid of, or more savage with, herself. She had never thought before that she could care to kiss her husband's hand.

But in these days she felt herself wasted with unsatisfied sorrow for all that she had cost him.

For him, he sat blessed and blind with love. He remembered when his daring fancy had first asked itself, "What will her tenderness be?" Her lightest endearment, he thought, meant more than the abnegation of other women's souls.

A little thing chanced at this time which gave Avis a deep pleasure, and which threw a certain glamour, even in her husband's own eyes, over his brightening popularity in the college.

During the two years of travel and study which had preceded Ostrander's connection with Harmouth, it had befallen him, one Leipsic vacation, to find himself so exhausted with the term's work, that his German physician ordered an immediate sea-voyage. Ostrander, never loath to yield himself to a new sensation, readily threw aside the laboratory life marked out for that summer, and joined a fellow-student on one of those aimless expeditions so alluring to a young, unanchored fancy, shipping on a trader, which, for aught they cared, might have been booked for the Chinese Seas or the River Styx. It chanced that they were driven by gales out of their expected course, which skirted the South Seas, and found themselves in the Paumotu Archipelago,[3] somewhere in the track taken first by the Wilkes Expedition,[4] and thereby opened since to navigators and missionaries. They anchored for some cause, one day, off an island to the north-east of Tahiti,—a small coral island uninhabited by man. Ostrander and his friend rowed out, overcome by an emotion which they were still young enough to try and express to one another, and beached their boat upon this maiden shore. But Ostrander, after the first thrill had spent itself, wandered away into the heart of the place, finding himself as unable to share the impression it produced upon him as he would have been to share the heart of a woman with another man. He plunged on from beckoning thicket to beckoning thicket, reeling like an intoxicated creature. When he came to himself, he was in a wild place alone. It was on the bank of a small stream, fair but fearful to him. The virgin repose of the trees, the startled look of the strange flowers, the retreat of unseen and unknown creatures rustling through the undergrowth at his approach, solemnized the nature of his delight.

Suddenly, as he sat reverent there, a bird—the island was peopled with rare birds—settled slowly over his head, and alighted on a cactus near him. It was a large creature, snow-white, and dropped like an angel from the burning sky.[5]

A tide of feeling half terror, half joy, overswept the young man, sitting there with upturned face, gone white to the lips' edge.

Perhaps there was not a young scientist in the world but would have risked years of his life to be in Ostrander's place at that moment.

The name and nature of that bird were unknown to science; and the young man knew it. It seemed to him as if Nature laughed in his face. She held out this one sequestered, shining thought of hers, this white fancy that she had hidden from the world, and nodded, crying, "Catch it if you can! Classify my unwon mood in your bald human lore. Marry my choicest tenderness to your dull future if you will. See, I have waited for you. I have kept my treasure book from the eye and hand of other men. Yours it shall be, yours only, yours, yours!"

As for the bird, it stirred circling on the scarlet cactus. Ostrander grasped his gun, dropping to his hands and knees. The bounding of his heart delayed his shaking aim.

He sought to calm himself. His future lay balanced upon that long, shining, shuddering barrel. To capture that bird was fame: so at least the situation presented itself to the young man. When we are young, nothing seems quite so likely to happen as glory. He grew pale, with faint finger on the trigger. The bird stood perfectly still.

One day in the class-room it occurred to Ostrander to tell this story. When he had reached this point he paused, shaken by the retrospect of one of the most muscular emotions that his life had known.

"Gentlemen," he said, "the bird stood still. It turned its head and looked at me: its eyes shone with a singularly soft, pleased light. I lowered the gun. How could I fire? I crept towards it. It was a beautiful creature. It did not move: I thought it was gratified at the sight of me. It acted as if it had never seen a man before: I do not suppose it ever had. I crawled along; I stretched out my hand: and yet it did not fly. I touched it—I stroked it. With this hand I stroked that magnificent, unknown creature. It did not shrink. I took out my knife, opened it, laid it down. The bird looked at me confidingly. I put the blade to its throat; but it would not stir. It trusted me. Gentlemen, I came away—I could not kill the bird."

For a moment after the young professor told this story, his repressed feeling extended itself, like the shade of a powerful cloud, upon the class; and then the boys broke into a passion of cheers that out-rang till the old college walls trembled like a being surprised by something in its own nature that it had never perceived before. Ostrander had become the demi-god of the term.

He came home to his wife, that afternoon, much moved by this little experience. He called her several times, and, receiving no answer, sought and found her in their own room. She was in the hammock under the Venus. The weather was warm, and she was lightly covered with a white muslin *negligée*. The instinct of the English tongue has done no better yet than to level the artistic possibilities of this garment to the word "wrapper." As she lifted her head at his knock in her poised way, and, slipping from the hammock, stood to receive him, holding the long white folds of her dress, he looked at the Venus behind her, and said,—

"How like you are to one another! And I have known you so long, and never thought of it till this moment. Turn your head—so. There. Yes.—What were you doing love, when I came in?"

"I was at work."

"At work?"

"Thinking where I had better put—what I shall do about the studio?" said Avis.

"Oh the studio!—yes. We must attend to that to-morrow, immediately," said Ostrander lightly. He was thinking about the bird and the boys. He began at once to tell her about it. Her face flushed with a divine light. Nothing could have happened to *her* which would have so kindled her tender eyes. If the sphinx, standing with her patient face to the wall in the closed studio, had herself put on the wings of immortality that summer afternoon, would the woman have turned her proud head to see her fly?

They sat down side by side, like children, in the hammock. Avis touched the floor with the tip of her slender long foot; she lifted her arms timidly, and wound his hair about her finger; they looked in one another's eyes through a sweet distance, like Cupid and Psyche through the dark.

Philip Ostrander that day saw his future as the people saw the face of Moses, shining so as it must be veiled. They had been four months married, and his wife was as sacred a marvel to him as on the day when he first touched her reluctant hand. Not one charm of the bud was missing from the glory of the flower.

Deeps beyond the lowest deeps in her nature were yet unwon. His manhood gathered itself to be worthy of their mastery. He felt himself to have taken a supreme lien upon an exhaustless joy.

CHAPTER XIV

> *"The primal duties shine aloft,*
> *like stars."*
> —The Excursion.[1]

"It's the drain, mem, as is playin' the fool on me, bad luck to it!"

Mrs. Ostrander's third "girl"—the third that is in point of continuity, not in contemporaneity—met her at the front-door with these portentous words. Mrs. Ostrander, radiant from an hour in her old studio in her father's orchard, came in, shutting out the August morning, and repeated with a perplexity which would have had a touch of the superb in it, if it had not been something at once too pitiful and too ludicrous,—

"The—*drain!*"

"The kitchen-drain, mem, as has refused ontirely to take the clane tea-leaves from the sink, but casts them back upon me hands, the vagabond!"

"I did not know there had to be—drains in sinks," said Mrs. Ostrander with an expression of recoil, "I never examined one. Could not ours be fixed to work without? What must we do about it, Julia?"

"Yez must have a man to it, mem," said she of Erin,[2] with a sweet superior smile.

"Very well," said Mrs. Ostrander with a sigh of relief. "We will send for a carpenter at once. Mr. Ostrander shall attend to it. You can go now, Julia. Is there any thing more you wished to say?"

"It's the chramy-tartar I am lackin' for me cake, mem; and the butter is out against dinner: but that is all, mem, barrin' the limon for the pies, and the jelly-strainer, as they slipped me mind when the grocer come, being up to do the beds, mem, at the time; and the hole in the pantry-windy that lets the rain upon the flooer-barrel, as yerself complained of the mould in the biscuit. That's all I think of at the minute, savin' Mr. Ostrander's company."

"Mr. Ostrander's company?" blankly from Mrs. Ostrander.

"It's meself as well-nigh forgot it till this blissid minute, on account of ironin'-day and the breakfast so late, ye'll own yerself, mem," penitently from Julia. "But it's himself as left word wid me while yez was gone, as there would be four gentlemen to dinner."

"Have we—I suppose we have dinner enough in the house for four gentlemen?" asked Avis a little nervously. She liked Philip to feel that his friends were welcome; and she had thought, with a certain scorn, of families that were injured by the appearance of a guest on ironing-day. She was sure that a narrow hospitality must indicate either a narrow heart or a dull head. Any family in a university Faculty must, of course, be expected to receive largely and irregularly. Avis was quite used to this. But she had never been able to understand why aunt Chloe found it a necessary condition of this state of things to make the puddings herself. The political economy of any intelligent home implied a strict division of labor, upon which she was perfectly resolved not to infringe. A harmonious home, like a star in its orbit, should move of itself. The service of such a home should be a kind of blind intelligence, like a natural law, set in motion, to be sure, by a designer, but competent to its own final cause. Besides, as Philip had said, she had not married him to be his housekeeper.

"It's the pound and half of steak for the two of you we has," observed Julia peacefully. "An' the butcher had gone before Mr. Ostrander let on a word about the gintlemin; and college gintlemin, mem, eats mostly awful."

It was not much, perhaps, to set herself now to conquer this little occasion; not much to descend from the sphinx to the drain-pipe at one fell swoop; not much to watch the potatoes while Julia went to market, to answer the door-bell while the jelly was straining, to dress for dinner after her guests were in the parlor, to resolve to engage a table-girl to-morrow because Julia tripped with the gravy, to sit wondering how the ironing was to get done while her husband talked of Greek sculpture, to bring creation out of chaos, law out of disorder, and a clear head out of wasted nerves. Life is composed of such little strains; and the artistic temperament is only more sensitive to, but can never hope to escape them. It was not much; but let us not forget that it is under the friction of such atoms, that women far simpler, and so, for that yoke, far stronger, than Avis, had yielded their lives as a burden too heavy to be borne.

That one day wore itself to an end at last, of course, like others of its kin. It was what Avis had already learned to call a day well wasted. She was so exhausted, what with the heat of the weather and the jar of the household machinery, that she scarcely noticed her husband, when, after their guests had gone, he came in to the cool darkness of the parlor, and threw himself in the chair beside her to say easily,—

"Tired, Avis?"

Everybody knows moments when to be asked if one is tired seems in itself a kind of insult, and to be asked in that tone, an unendurable thing. But it was not in Avis's poised and tender temper to drizzle out her little irritations as if they were matters of consequence. And her husband's greater physical delicacy had already taught the six-months' wife the silence of her own. She replied, after a moment's pause, that she should soon rest.

"I am sorry to have you concerned so much in this domestic flurry," began Ostrander. Avis turned her head with a slight contraction of the brow. To have left the colors without the drying-oil upon her easel, and surrendered her whole summer's day to the task of making one harmonious fact of the week's ironing and four round, red, hungry alumni, and then to have her moderate, but at least gracious and orderly success called a "flurry," was one of those little dulnesses of the masculine fancy which she was loath to admit in Philip,—Philip, whose fine perception, and what might be called almost a tact of the imagination, had always from the first been so winning to her.

"It must not be," proceeded her husband with some deepening sincerity in his affectionate tones. "We must have better-trained service for you."

"We must, I think,—I have been thinking it over to-day,—have more service," replied Avis. "It seemed as if Julia ought to take care of two people. And there are your college-debts to be got off, whatever happens; but I cannot think it right to get along so any longer."

"Certainly not," said Ostrander promptly: "you must have what relief you need, my dear. Do not burden yourself to worry over those debts. At most, as I have told you, three thousand would cover the whole, and a part of that is already cleared."

Avis did not answer. This point of the debts was rather a sensitive one between them. Philip thought he had explained it all to her before their marriage. Avis thought he had not made it quite clear. Of course she dimly understood that he had incurred pecuniary liabilities for his education, like other young men in America, whose belongings and beginnings were unendowed. But her way would have been to have straightened all that before incurring the risks and obligations of a home. Still, with Philip's good salary, and her own little income that fell to her from her mother,—and surely when she herself was well at work,—there need be no trouble about it. And, of course, if Philip thought he explained it to her, he must have done so. It was she who had been dull. She argued this slight point with herself sometimes with an earnestness which she could not justify to herself, without a glance at some far, crouching motive set deep like a sunken danger in her thought, at which it did not seem worth while to look scrutinizingly. Any thought of her husband which was not open as the mid-day to her heart and his, was beneath the respect of attention. Her most distinct annoyance in this, and other little points which might occur to her, was, perhaps, the first baffling consciousness of a woman, that there may be laws of perspective in her husband's nature with which courtship had not made her clearly acquainted.

"It will all come right," said Ostrander in a comfortable tone, turning to go. "And now I must get to college, or I shall be late." He looked back across the long parlor; the closed blinds and dark drapery cast a moveless green shadow upon Avis's face, that made her look pale and ill. Ostrander came back. He had not reached the point of conjugal culture at which a man can go happily away, leaving a shade upon his wife's face. He came back, and said, more tenderly than a husband who has been six months' married may be expected to speak upon an especially busy day,—

"What is it, love?"

"Nothing worth getting late to recitation for, Philip."

"You tire yourself going so far and so often to your father's. We must build you a studio at home, I think."

"I do not get to father's so *often* as to tire myself," said Avis with a slight emphasis, but with a brightening brow. "But indeed, Philip, I begin to be a little impatient for my regular and sustained work. We have changed girls so much—and with all the Commencement company—something has continually happened to embarrass my plans so far. But do not look troubled, my darling. It is not all worth one such look as that."

She leaned to him lovingly; she was comforted by his tenderness; she blamed herself for adding one least anxiety of her own to his crowded cares. When he said that all this must be changed, and that she at least should not be exhausted below the level of her work, if they had to close the house, and board, her heart lightened at his thoughtfulness. Her little difficulties fused like rain-drops into a golden mist. She was sure that she saw her way through them, and beyond them, to that "energy of days" which nature had made imperative to her. When her husband called after lecture, and asked if he might go to the studio with her, and see what she was doing, her heart lifted as it did when they two stood there beneath the apple-boughs, learning love and surrender of the falling blossoms, now so long ago. She looked her future in the face with aspiration larger, because deeper than her maiden days had known. With love as with God, all things are possible.

Avis had that day retouched the sphinx. She turned the easel, and she and her husband stood before it silently. Against a deep sky, palpitant with the purple soul of Egypt, the riddle of the ages rose with a certain majesty which Ostrander may be excused for thinking few hands could have wrought upon it.

Avis had commanded with consummate skill the tint and the trouble of heat in the tropical air. It was mid-morning with the sphinx. The lessening shadow fell westward from her brow. The desert was unmarked by foot of man or beast; the sky uncut by wing of bird. The child of their union looked across them to the east.

"Staring straight on with calm eternal eyes." The sand had drifted to her solemn breast. The lion's feet of her no eye can see, the eagle's wings of her are bound by the hands of unrelenting years; only her mighty face remains to answer what the ages have demanded, and shall forever ask of her.

Upon this face Avis had spent something of her best strength. The crude Nubian features she had rechiselled, the mutilated outline she had restored; the soul of it she had created.

She did not need the authority of Herodotus to tell her that the face of the sphinx, in ages gone, was full of beauty. The artist would have said, "Who dared to doubt it?"

Yet she was glad to have wise men convinced that this giant ideal was once young and beautiful, like any other woman. If there were a touch of purely feminine feeling in this, it was of a sort too lofty to excite the kind of smile which we bestow upon most of the consciousness of sex which expresses itself in women.

A poet of our own time has articulated the speech of one phase of womanhood to one type of manhood thus,—

> "I turn from you my cheeks and eyes,
>   My hair which you shall see no more.
> Alas for love that never dies!
>   Alas for joy that went before!
> Only my lips still turn to you,
> Only my lips that cry, Repent."

With something of the undertow of these words Avis was at this time struggling in the making of her picture. Grave as the desert, tender as the sky, strong as the silence, the parted lips of the mysterious creature seemed to speak a perfect word. Yet in its deep eyes fitted an expectant look that did not satisfy her; meanings were in them which she had not mastered; questionings troubled them, to which her imagination had found no controlling reply.

"It is a great picture," said her husband heartily, after long and silent study. She flushed joyously. Just then she would rather hear these words from him than from the whole round world besides.

"I am not satisfied yet," she said. "The eyes baffle me, Philip."

"They ought to baffle you; they ought to forever: else you would have failed," he answered. "Let that picture go now. It isn't right to waste it on one blessed, unworthy sort of fellow like me. Let as much of the world as has been created fit to understand you, have the sphinx at once."

"I cannot be understood till I have understood myself," said his wife in a low voice. "The picture must wait—now—a while."

"You should know best; but I hope you'll not mistake about it," he replied, yielding himself to the influence of the picture, with only a superficial attention to her words. "That, I have noticed, is the peril of thoroughly trained women. Once really fit to do a great thing, their native conscientiousness and timidity become, I sometimes think, a heavier brake upon their success than the more ignorant, and therefore more abandoned enthusiasm. Why, in reason, should the sphinx wait any longer?"

"Not in reason perhaps, only in feeling; and an artist can never be brusque with a feeling. The picture must wait, Philip—a little longer."

The depth of her tone arrested his scrutiny; and the eyes which she lifted, turning from the solemn sphinx to him, held themselves like annunciation lilies in a breaking mist.

It was not long after this that Professor Ostrander received imperative telegraphic summons to his old home in New Hampshire. His mother lay very ill. A succession of those little distractions incident to young people who have just yielded themselves to the monopolizing claim of their own home, together with the brief trip to the scientific convention which Ostrander had taken at the outset of the vacation, had delayed their longer and more laborious journey up to this time. Avis, upon the reception of the message, said at once that she should go with him. They set out that night, oppressed by a differing weight of feeling, of which neither cared to speak.

They found themselves in the face of a calm, inevitable death, which seemed rather an awe to the son, and an anguish to the daughter.

Avis trod the dreary oil-cloth of the narrow stairs to the sickroom with an acute sense, such as she had never known before, of what it meant to live and die in these dumb country homes. Poor, narrow, solitary home! Poor, plain, old mother, watching so long for the son who had not come. She forced herself to remember with some distinctness how imperative her husband's reasons had been for not coming before. She dismissed the neighbors and old friends who were in attendance, and herself, having sent Philip to rest within sound of her voice, watched out the night—for the first time in her life—alone with a dying face.

She found it a reticent, fine face, on whose gray solemnity sat a strange likeness to the youth and beauty of the son. Towards morning, when Mrs. Ostrander, stirring, spoke, she bent, and kissed her passionately.

"Thank you, dear," said the old lady with a painless, pleasant smile.

"I have lived without a mother," cried Avis, headlong with regret and grief. "I am so glad I am not too late! Now you kiss me, I know what it is like."

"Thank you, dear," came the answer once again quietly. "Is Philip here?"

"Oh, yes! Shall I speak to him?"

"No, do not disturb him," said his mother in the pathetic, un-complaining tone which solitude gives to gracious age. "I would not break the poor boy's nap. And I like to see you. You are my daughter, my son Philip's wife. You made the portrait for me of my son. It was kind in Philip to send me his portrait, because I do not see him very often. You have a gentle hand, my dear. You are a good daughter."

"I am a heart-broken daughter!" cried Avis. "Why did you not send for us? We did not think—did not know—Philip did not understand how feeble a summer you have had. I can see how it has been. You did not tell us!"

"I have had—rather—a feeble summer—yes," said the sinking woman with some effort of speech; "but I have needed nothing. My son has been always a good son. I knew he would come when he could. I did not want to trouble him. I have never lacked for anything. Did you have a pretty wedding, my dear?" Her mind seemed to slip and wander a little with this; for she spoke of Philip's father, dead now these twenty years; and then she called to him, bidding him find the wedding-slippers in the bureau-drawer, that she had saved for her son's wife; then reiterating that Philip had been a good son, and she had wanted nothing, turned to Avis once again, to say apologetically,—

"They had got so yellow, my dear, and I had not seen your foot. Philip thought they would not fit, when he was here, and I showed them to him. I'm glad you had a pretty wedding. Philip thought it was too cold for me to go. He was always careful to think when I would take cold. He was quite right. But I'm glad to know it was a pretty wedding. Raise me up, my dear, and let me look at you again."

Avis lifted her with her strong young arms easily against the pillows, and the two turned to one another. "In the chill before the dawning" something seemed to stir from eye to eye between them, and to crawl cold about the heart of the wife, like a thought created to be of the creeping things forever, to which rectitude of gait and outrightness of speech, were forbidden.

Had Philip—Philip, whose tenderness was like the creation of a

new passion in the world—somehow, somewhere, in some indefined sense, *neglected* his mother,—his old mother, sick and alone?
It was not a question for a wife to ask: it was not one for a mother
to answer. Like spirits, the two women met each other's eyes, and
neither spoke.

Waitstill Ostrander (such was her poetic, Puritan name) died that
night. Her son was with her, tender and sorrowful, to the last. But
a little before the stroke of midnight she turned her face, and
said,—

"He was a good boy—he was always a good son to me. I never
lacked for any thing. Your father will be pleased, Philip—that you
had—a pretty wedding. Now I want—my daughter, Avis." And in
Avis's arms and on Avis's heart she drew her last uncomplaining
breath.

Philip and Avis were together after the funeral, drearily busied
with all the little matters about the house which required the
woman's and the daughter's touch before they left. Avis was standing reverently before an open bureau in their mother's room. She
had just lifted from their old-fashioned swathings and scents of
linen and lavender those sacred yellow satin shoes which had
never ventured to the pretty wedding. Their first smooth, suave
touch upon her palm gave her something almost like an electric
shock. To conceal the intensity of her momentary feeling, of which
she could not just then speak to her husband, she laid them down,
and began to talk of other things.

"Philip," she said, "there was a woman,—a young woman in
gray, I think,—who cried so bitterly at the funeral, that she attracted my attention. Do you remember? She went up and kissed
poor mother on the forehead. She had dark eyes; and I am sure the
shawl was gray. Do you know who it was?"

"It might have been Jane Gray, or Susan Wanamaker, possibly: I
hardly know. Both have dark eyes, and both were neighbors of
mother's," said Ostrander thoughtfully. "Susan Wanamaker was always very fond of her," he added with an increasing interest. "I
think you must have heard me speak of Susan?"

"No, I do not remember that you have."

"I did not have a suitable chance to speak to her," proceeded Ostrander: "I ought to have done so. It was an old friend. All the
neighbors seem to have been very kind to mother." Thus he chatted on, to divert her, of indifferent things. Avis said nothing just
then; but presently she asked,—

"Of course you added your own urgent invitation, Philip, to
mine, that mother should have come to our wedding?"

"Why, of course," said Ostrander. "But certainly she could not
have come. The weather was far too cold, and I really don't know

what we could have done with her exactly. But I was so absorbed then, my darling, that I am afraid I don't remember about it all as clearly as I ought."

In truth he did not; and it was this very fact, perhaps, that Avis brooded over with the most definite discontent. She had half feared, standing there with the poor little old wedding-shoe in her hand, that he would turn to her, flashing across it, and ask her if she thought him capable of a slight to his mother. That he had not even perceived that the circumstances were suggestive of neglect was in itself peculiarly painful to her. His nature had slipped so lightly away from an experience under which her own was writhing, that she felt at a loss to understand him.

She folded the white slipper with tender fingers, to take it home. Perhaps Philip could not be expected to know what a sacredness it would have added to her marriage-day to have worn it. Perhaps no man could. Perhaps this was one of the differences, one of the things that it meant to be a man, not to understand such matters. Gently she tried to think so. But she stood looking across the slope of the near church-yard to the locked, oppressive hills, with a dull pain for which she wished she could have found the tears. When her husband came up, and laid his hand upon her shoulder, stooping to see what she saw, she pointed to the mountains, and said,—

"How lean they look! How parched! And she lived—shut in here—seventy years."

"Don't grieve so!" said Ostrander tenderly. "Poor mother would never have been happy away from them. She always told me so when I asked her."

He kissed her, and went down stairs to see about boxing the portrait for the morning's express.

CHAPTER XV

*"Only the eye of God can see
the universe geometrically:
man, in his infirmity, sees only
foreshortenings. Perspective is,
so to say, the ideal of visible
things. . . . As man advances
towards his horizon, his
horizon retreats from him, and
the lines that seem to unite in
the remote distance, remain
eternally separate in their
eternal conveyance."*

The point at which love ceases
to be *per se* an occupation, is seldom more distinctly defined than
the line which divides the fire of the sunset from the calm of the
upper sky. Avis's love for her work was as imperious as her love for
her husband, and as loyally stubborn to distraction.

Said one of the greatest women of this age, "Success is impossible, unless the passion for art overcomes all desultory passions."[1]
Avis found herself, by dimly shaded gradations, approaching a condition of serious unrest. She was like a creature in whom two gods
warred. Her nature bent, but could not break, under the divine
conflict. Yet at this time she looked across it with firm, clear eyes.
All would come right. These little household obstacles, experience
would disperse. They loved each other,—what could she fear?

The winter passed dreamily. When her husband came home on
the bitter nights, her eyes turned to him full of a trust as unreflec-
tive and as much in the nature of things, it then seemed, as the
trust of the lily in the summer wind. He liked best to find her in
the dark, opaque reds of their little parlor, and in the mood of
the open fire. She sat with her books or her sketching, or in the
shadow at the soft piano. The usual little feminine bustle of sewing he missed without regret. Women fretted him with their eternal nervous stitch, stitching, and fathomless researches into the
nature of tatting and crochet. He rather admired his wife for sharing so fully his objection to them. Avis was that rare woman who
had never embroidered a tidy in her life.

"It is as much of an exhaustion of the nervous centres to my wife to sew as it would be to me," he used to say at this time, "and as much, if not more, of a nervous waste. She shall not do it."

It did not occur to him—how should it?—that Avis's exemption from this burden was a matter requiring any forethought or management; and he expressed surprise on learning, by accident one day, that the price of two portraits which she had painted—her only finished work—that winter, had gone to cover the seamstress's bills. Avis did not chatter about such things. She had a fine power of selection in her conversation (has not some one well said that conversation is always but a selection?) which he admired.

Certain moods befell her that winter, from which he stood afar off. Sometimes, when the wild weather deterred her from the brisk walks which her sturdy, out-of-door habits had made a necessity to her, he found her pacing the house, up and down, from attic to cellar, in a fitful, and what, in a woman of less self-control, would have been a fretful way. He spoke to her, and received courteous but uncommunicative answers. Her eyes had become two beating rebels, for whom his tenderest thought could find no amnesty. Usually, at such times, she retreated to the studio (which was now established, in a manner, in the attic), and worked fiercely till the early winter dark dropped down. Then he would come up and call her, unless he were too busy. If he came, he found her gentle and calm. She leaned upon his arm as they went down stairs.

Avis left the unfinished sketch or painting patiently. She said, "By and by. After a while. I must wait a little." She was still able to allure herself with the melody of this refrain, to which so many hundreds of women's lips have shaped themselves trembling; while the ears of a departing hope or a struggling purpose were bent to hear. Life had become a succession of expectancies. In each experience she waited for her foothold upon another, before finding her poise. There is more than a fanciful symbolism in the law which regulates the drawing of the human form. We must be able to take a straight line from the head to the feet, or our picture topples over.

Women understand—only women altogether—what a dreary will-o-the-wisp is this old, common, I had almost said commonplace, experience, "When the fall sewing is done," "When the baby can walk," "When house-cleaning is over," "When the company has gone," "When we have got through with the whooping-cough," "When I am a little stronger," then I will write the poem, or learn the language, or study the great charity, or master the symphony; then I will act, dare, dream, become. Merciful is the fate that hides from any soul the prophecy of its still-born aspirations.

The winter was over. In the elm-tree outside of Avis's chamber-window a robin was building a nest, with an eye that withdrew it-self like a happy secret. Avis watched the bird with a blind sympa-thy. She held out her hand, and the little creature ate from it after a decorous hesitation. She felt a lowly kinship with the brooding, patient thing.

In May her baby was born,—a son. Avis was a little sorry for this, but she did not like to say so: it seemed a rude disloyalty to the poor little fellow. But when his father asked her if she were not content, she said,—

"If I had a daughter, I should fall down and worship her."

It was a delicate, ailing baby, and seemed at first a mere little ganglion of quivering nerves. It cried a great deal.

"I don't see what the child has to cry for!" said Avis, looking a little offended.

The baby's grandfather was there the day that she said this. He put on his spectacles at the precise angle and with the peculiar rub which he reserved for a pet philosophical problem, and with a lordly reverence took the child's fingers—poor little sprawling an-tennæ—upon his own.

"What Aristotle and Leibnitz and Kant," he said loftily, "would have yielded their lives to know, you ask, Avis, over-lightly. Phi-losophy will be no longer a fragment, but a system, when it has commanded the psychological process by which one infant is led to weep."

Aristotle might have had a chance to find out, Avis thought, if he could have had the pleasure of studying her child for the first three weeks of its life. But the professor watched the child gravely. He had a deep respect for a being who could baffle Aristotle.

"That baby has cried ever since it was born!" Avis wailed one night, exhausted with sleeplessness. "I wish somebody would take it out of my sight and hearing for a while."

"Why, Avis," said her husband, "don't you care—don't you feel any maternal affection for the little thing?"

"No," cried every quivering nerve in the honest young mother; "not a bit!"

Perhaps, indeed, she was lacking in what is called the maternal passion as distinct from the maternal devotion. She was perfectly conscious of being obliged to learn to love her baby like anybody else; and really she did not find the qualities which that unfortu-nate young gentleman developed during the early part of his exis-tence, those which she was wont to consider lovable in more ma-ture characters. She felt half ashamed of herself for being the mother of so cross a baby. She had supposed that children were gifted by their Creator with some measure of respect for the feelings of oth-ers. This child seemed to be as deficient in it as a young batrachian. It mortified her, like an evidence of ill-breeding. Avis had never lived in the house with a baby; neither had Ostrander. Their vague ideas of the main characteristics of infancy were drawn as, I think I may safely say, those of most young men and women are at the time of marriage, chiefly from novels and romances, in which parentage is represented as a blindly deifying privilege, which it were an irreverence to associate with teething, the midnight colic, or an insufficient income.

Avis herself had not escaped the influence of these golden, if a little hazy pictures. While she knew, or supposed that she felt, many things not expected of her, and failed to feel others which it was proper to feel under the conditions of maternity, yet she cherished in her own way her own ideals. But of these she did not talk, even to her husband. These it was only for her child and herself to understand. Over these, as over her wedded fancy, Nature drew a veil like those casement screens, which to the beholder are dense and opaque, but to the eye behind them glitter with a fair transparency through which all the world is seen divinely new. And then motherhood was a fact which had never entered (as in the case of most women) upon her plans or visions of life. It was to be learned like any other unexpected lesson.

But the spring was budding; and in the robins' nest at the window the fledglings chirped; and the tender air stole in on tiptoe; and her strength waxed with the leaping weather; and God made people to love their children: so it must all be well. The kind of dumb terror with which she had lain listening to the child's cry gave place to a calm exultance. Now, in a fortnight, in a week, in days, to-morrow, she could be at work.

To be sure the baby was a fact; but he was matched by another,— the nurse: from so fair an equation it was not too much to expect a clear solution.

She came out into the sunshine with bounding heart. The soul of the spring was in her. Her most overpowering consciousness was one of deep religious fervor. She thanked God that her life's purpose, for which she believed He had created her, would be more opulently fulfilled by this experience. The baby would teach her new words to tell the world,—His sad, wrong world that the birth of a little child had saved. She felt a deepening respect for the baby. She kissed him fervently. It seemed singularly obtuse in him to double up his seriously inartistic fist, and put her eye out with blind and smarting tears.

"I hope you like him, Avis," said Coy a little doubtfully, one day in June. He was so pre-eminently uninteresting compared with her baby, that she really felt some uncertainty on the nature of Avis's feelings; and then Avis said so little!

"Certainly," said Avis, looking up rather wearily from the week's wash which she was sorting,—a snowdrift fatally deepened by all these little garments whose name and nature were still a mystery to her, and, if the truth must be told, produced more a sense of irritation than of poetry on her fancy, since she did not see that her love for her son required that she should know whether the scallop on his flannel petticoat was ironed the wrong way,—"certainly I like him; but I don't understand why, when he is put on the bed, he doesn't go to sleep. It is very inconvenient,—crying so, when it is proper for him to take a nap. Why," said Avis, lifting her grave eyes, "*I find him a great deal of trouble!*"

Coy, who thought it quite in the order of things that her baby should be three months the older, since naturally Avis couldn't get on (she never had) in any real *thing* that had got to be *done* without her advisory council,—Coy gasped, and felt it useless to remonstrate that morning, even about the little shirts which poor Avis was understood to have trusted the nurse to sew.

We hear and think much of the marked days of life, the signal-stations of gloom or gladness, the wedding, the birth, the burial, the day that lent its ear like a priest to love's first confession. One may dare assert that among these

> "Days which quiver to their roots
> Whene'er you stir the dust of such a day,"

there strikes in the lives of most of us one deeper than they all,—that day when we heard the first bitter word from lips which would once have breathed their last to win our kisses. Do you not remember how the sun struck out the figure in the carpet? The refrain of the bird that flew singing past the window? What the pattern of the sofa-cushion was on which you sat gazing? How the Parian Venus tumbled from the bracket, when, going out, he slammed the door? How she swept away to the piano, and the little polka that she played with bent head to hide the tears? You turned that carpet, you covered the cushion long ago, for economy's sake, you thought. Ah, me! It must have been for economy, too, that the broken Venus was never mended, but lies hidden in your bureau-drawer; and let me hear you play that little polka if you dare!

Avis's baby selected one July night, when the thermometer stood at ninety degrees in the heart of the little town, to cry, with a perseverance worthy of so noble a cause, from nine o'clock in the stifling night till three in the exhausted dawn, doubtless for reasons which were metaphysically satisfactory to himself. Philip Ostrander, not finding in them any distinct bearings upon the natural sciences, was, as might be expected, less of an enthusiast in the matter. He took his pillow, and vacated the scene of action. He had some time since reached the stage at which a man first perceives the full value and final cause of the "spare room,"—an institution not created, as we have crudely supposed, for a chance guest, but for the relief of the father whose morning duties clearly require a full night's rest. It certainly was plain enough that Mr. Ostrander could not conduct the morning recitation if he had been kept awake all night; and his weak lung forbade his carrying the baby, Avis said.

The poor girl wore that terrible July out as best she might, in the deepening reserve which motherhood only of all forms of human solitude knows.

On this particular morning she came down late and wan. The fierce, free fire of her superb eyes had given way to the *burnt-in* look of anxious patience, which marks a young mother out from all other young creatures in the world. Her husband sat with a disturbed face at a disorderly table.

"Avis," he began, without looking up to see how she was, "the cracked wheat is soggy again."

Avis for a moment made no reply: she could not for sheer surprise. The husband's tone, breaking in upon her exhaustion of mind and body, gave her something of the little shock that we feel on finding our paper give out in the middle of an absorbing sentence. When she spoke, she said gently, but with some dignity,—

"I am sorry, Philip: I will speak about it."

"And the cream," proceeded Philip, "is sour. The steak was cold; and the coffee will give me a bilious headache before night. I really don't see why we can't have things more comfortable."

"We certainly must, if they are so very uncomfortable," replied his wife with rather a pale smile, striving, she could hardly have told why, to turn the discussion into a jest. "But you remember you didn't marry me to be your housekeeper, Philip!"

Philip Ostrander pushed his chair back without a smile, folded his napkin with the peculiar masculine emphasis which says, I can hold my tongue, for I am a gentleman; but it is doggedly hard work! Then turning, with averted face murmured through his closed teeth,—

"Yes, I remember. I don't know what we were either of us thinking of!"

With this he took his hat and strode away to college, in the sacred summer light, to conduct the morning prayers of a thousand perceptive and receptive boys.

Avis sat for a little while at the uninviting breakfast-table; she tasted the cold coffee, and sent Julia away with her sympathetic if a little bitter tea: she felt too weak to eat. She looked out into the elm-branch, and saw the empty nest which the May robin had left, and dimly thought what an unpleasant look it had, and dimly thought she would get Julia to pull it down. It seemed quite necessary not to think of any thing except the nest. Her eyes burned feverishly. She threw herself upon the lounge, and lay with both hands pressed upon them, still as the coins that press the lids of the dead. Presently she rang the bell sharply, and in a strung, strained voice bade that the nurse be ordered to bring the child.

He came, poor little fellow! looking as wan as his mother, but as innocent of having made himself an unpleasant fact in the family life as a tuberose is of yielding too strong a sweetness. Avis caught him with something not unlike the passionate love which Arria may have felt for the dagger,[2] and hid her broken face upon the baby's neck, as if she would have hidden it there forever from all the world.

When Ostrander came home, he sought his wife all over the house. She was not to be found. The cook said she took her hat and went out an hour since; and the nurse explained, that in throwing back the nursery blinds to give the important message which the cook had forgotten to deliver to the grocer's boy, she had thought it likely it was Mrs. Ostrander as she saw just beyond the top of the cart, turning Elm Street to the beach.

Ostrander pursued her impatiently in the blazing sun. He perceived the flutter of her dress far down against the light-house; and, when he had overtaken her, he found her creeping along in the shadow formed by that great gorge so memorable to them both. She did not see him or hear him, and so crawled along in an aimless, dreary fashion which it gave him a nameless terror to see.

Her figure looked so broken, so beaten, and weak, that it for the first time occurred to him that the effect of a little conjugal quarrel upon a nature like that of his wife's was not altogether a calculable one. His own words once spoken in that spot came back to him as he made his penitent way along the purple gorge, looking from torn side to torn side.

"It was a perfect primeval marriage. The heart of the rock was simply broken."

Had Avis wrought herself into that frenzy of wounded feeling in which weaker women have courted death, as a man with lacerated spinal nerves courts the *moxa*?[3] He overtook her without her hearing his light step, and, man-like, trusting to the sensation to interpret the emotion, barricaded her with both arms, and folded her to his shamed and sorry heart. But Avis glided from his touch like a spirit. Her bent figure heightened grandly, and her unwon maiden eyes seemed to look again from a great height, down upon him where she had swept and stood upon the jutting cliff.

Ostrander at that moment felt that to have been permitted to

gain the allegiance of the heart we love, is but the most tentative
and introductory step towards the durability of a happiness whose
existence depends upon our being found worthy to retain what we
have won; and in feeling this he felt deeper than he could reason
into the joy and pain and peril which weld two individual human
souls into the awful fusion which we call marriage.

But he said only,—

"Avis, I was a brute!"

"No," she said bitterly, "you were only a man." Then repenting,
with swift nobility she came to him,—

"Now it is I who am wrong. Forgive me, Philip!"

"*You!*"

He gathered her tenderly. She did not repel him: she was worn
out with the strain of the night and the glare of the long walk. She
did not cry; but she lay in his arms with a dry, sobbing sigh which
alarmed him. He caressed her passionately. He sought her pardon
in the soul of every sweet sign love had taught him in its first dizzy
hours. She submitted quietly, but with an unresponsiveness which
afterwards he remembered with disquiet perplexity.

The scar which an unkind word leaves upon a large love, may be
invisible, like that of a great sin upon the tissues of the repentant
soul; but for one as for the other, this life has no healing.

Avis did not choose to talk about cracked wheat. There were
other things in the world to say. And it was impossible to express,
without giving them both useless pain, her inherent, ineradicable,
and sickening recoil from the details of household care. And Philip,
distraught with his deepening responsibilities at the college, naturally ceased to inquire so often how matters went in the studio.
Avis faced her circumstances with such patience as she could command. A weaker woman lets conditions override her, be the lash a
divine frenzy or a chronic neuralgia. Avis sadly turned the tense
muscle of her strong nature now to secure a gracious home. The
thong which has stung the aspirations of all women, since Eve, for
love of knowledge, ate and sinned, goaded her on. She said to herself, "It will be a matter, at most, of a few months. When I have
mastered this one little house, life waits; and art is long." She
made haste to be wise in wisdom that her soul loathed, to clear the
space about her for the leisure that her patient purpose craved. But
sometimes, sitting burdened with the child upon her arms, she
looked out and off upon the summer sky with a strangling desolation like that of the forgotten diver, who sees the clouds flit, from
the bottom of the sea.

✑ CHAPTER XVI

> *"It is the low man thinks the*
> *woman low."*
> —Tennyson[1]

> *"Thou hast met, found, and*
> *seized me, and know'st what*
> *my ways are.*
> *Hold* ME,—*hold a shadow, the*
> *wings as they quiver,*
> *Hold* ME,—*hold a dream,*
> *smoke, a track on the river!"*
> —Theodore Prod[r]o[m]us[2]

John Rose was one of those people to whom one may surrender a confidence, and never repent it; this is to say, John Rose had a rare nature, and therefore one which educated him for the peculiar draughts upon delicacy of organization involved in the calling of a Christian preacher.

At the outset of his work in Harmouth he had adopted a plan never, to my knowledge, put in use by a pastor in precisely this form, in more than one other instance. Doubtless there are others unknown to me.

The experiment resulted from a chance word of his wife's. Coy, with the grasping capacity for self-exhaustion characteristic of the New-England girl, had married the profession with the man. She always said, "Our work," "Our people," "Our pulpit," and "Our salary." She flew from the nursery to the prayer-meeting, from the mission-school to the Commencement dinner, from the church fair to the Italian class; young married ladies losing caste in Harmouth, if they do not maintain a palpable connection with that sad, forsaken world which has no baby, poor thing! to interfere with its course of reading.

Coy, who had never been considered "religious" before her marriage, and who sorely felt her lack of clear theological acumen, said one day,—

"John, a minister's business is precisely—what? When we talk about saving people, we mean exactly"—

"I don't answer conundrums for any other minister," said the Reverend John, thoughtfully calculating the distance from hand to eye between the baby's head and the ceiling, as he stood playing his after-dinner game of human pitch-penny with that remarkable infant; "but I consider my business a very simple affair. The human animal seems to have been (for what inscrutable purpose, you young porpoise, I'll not attempt to say, and you'll never grow up to prove, if you jerk yourself over my lame shoulder like that) endowed with what we find it convenient to call, for lack of a better term, an immortal soul."

"John!" said wife, in the tone she used at tea, treading on his toes under the table when he propounded some doctrine that savored of laxity, with a conservative supply spending the Sunday.

"What's the matter now?" asked John, giving the baby a double twist that the offspring of any less muscular Christianity would have resented. "Have I said any thing heretical *again* to-day?"

"I—th-think—not. It sounds right on the whole," said Coy anxiously; "but I never know where you'll turn up, John. An immortal soul is all right, so far as it goes, of course, John dear. But the trouble I have with theology is, I never know what is coming next. And your theology especially, somehow, John, is—you know— I like to have you make it very plain, because the baby is usually mixed up in it a little (there! you'll bump her head!) or else, you see—I find it hard to fix my mind when I'm being kissed. If I'd been intellectual, like Avis, I suppose I shouldn't mind. Certainly it is quite true about the immortality of the soul. But old Mrs. Bobley—you know the old lady behind the last pillar, who always cries in the wrong place, with the ironed purple strings to her bonnet—asked me yesterday what I thought were your views as to the precise nature of the ministerial vocation. I told her I'd ask. She said she hoped you realized, for you were so very young, the awful responsibility which rested on a minister if a single soul in his congregation had never been worried—no, never been warned, that was it—by his pastor. I said I supposed so. And then she asked me if I knew a good recipe for Parker-house rolls. But now, John dear, I'll tell you what I think a minister is. He's a kind of a doctor, John, don't you see?—a soul-doctor. I don't pretend to understand about sin (I suppose that's because I've never associated with wicked people); but it seems to me like an awful disease,—like scarlet-fever. People's souls are sick—sick—sick all about us, John. And if you can cure them, you know"—

"Amen!" said John gravely.

"Or if you can only ease them a little"—

"Amen!" said John again.

"Of course I don't mean quite by yourself—unless Anybody—greater—were behind," said Coy quickly, slipping with the characteristic reticence of the atmosphere in which she had been bred, from explicit expression of the more vital elements of religious feeling. "But I've been thinking, John, why shouldn't a minister have an office-system, like a doctor, and be 'at home,' so many hours a day to aching people?"

It was this suggestion which John Rose, in carrying out almost to the letter, had made so memorable a feature in his Harmouth work. He announced not only from the pulpit and in the vaguely polite ways usually thought sufficient to relieve the ministerial conscience, but literally upon his modest door-plate, like a physician of the body, that he who assumed to prescribe for the health of the soul would be within to patients from such an hour to such an hour, making it in due time quietly understood among the heterogeneous population of the town, that he held himself answerable to the call of any cretaure in any lack, were it of a friend or a pillow, were it of Heaven or a dinner, were it of forgiveness or flannels.

In the course of six months from the inauguration of this project, the young minister's heart and hands were overwhelmed with what Coy called the "aching people." The aching people of a place in which the intelligence of society is almost wholly absorbed in the impartment and the reception of intellectual culture, have a certain bitterness in their capacity and ability to ache not to be matched in communities of broader and more human interests.

John Rose received into his healthy young heart, as within the walls of a newly-consecrated temple, these refugees of human fate, on an average perhaps to the number of twenty souls each day. This method of labor brought him into contact with what we are wont to term the "dangerous classes" of society. The walls of that little study listened to strange histories, not often, in the chance of human lots, brought across the threshold of delicate homes. Strange figures not known to the pew-poll of the Central Church skulked in on Sunday evenings, and stood, savage, unkempt, like Centaurs, up and down the crowded aisles. The heavy pew-owners were gratified, and proposed a mission church.

"If these men and women go, I go with them," said John Rose in a deep voice with which his deacons were not familiar. "Turn them out into a mission church, if you will; but you turn me there too."

So the rich and the poor met together in this young prophet's church, for the Lord's sake, who was the Maker of them all. And John Rose bent to his sacred work with awed and humble eyes, seeking only on the knees of his heart to know wherefore he had been found worthy of that fate than which neither life nor death has more glorious to give the Christian pastor,—that the common people heard him gladly.

That supervision of suffering and sinning homes which his theory of Christian service involved, he assumed at the start in person to an extent which experience compelled him to retrench, but which served to form a peculiar tie between himself and his *clientèle.*

He had often invited Mrs. Ostrander to accompany him upon one of these visiting tours at the lower end of the town, and one day she went.

It had been an uncomfortable day. The child had cried a great deal. Company had come from out of town just as she had, for the first time in weeks, locked her studio-door behind her. The weather was extreme; and it was not so easy as usual to be patient with the heat, to which she was, at best, almost morbidly sensitive. They had taken no vacation this year: at least she had not. Her husband ran down to the beach for a week or so, as usual, with a Harmouth party,—the Hogarths and Allens, and so on; but boarding at a watering-place with a three-months' baby is a modified form of human bliss which Avis had felt compelled to decline.

On this evening she was alone: Philip was out on Faculty business. She trod the hot pavements to Coy's home with that restlessness which is the keenest element of physical distress in a New-England July day. Coy was busy: it was something about the mosquitos; but whether they had killed the baby, or the baby had killed the mosquito, Avis did not distinctly understand, and did not offer to stay and discover. The fire of the outer air was preferable to the smouldering atmosphere of the house. She joined John Rose gladly, and they descended into the Inferno in which the dregs of a large town are to be found upon a July night.

It is not to the purpose of this story to dwell upon the sights, which, for the first time in a refined and sheltered life, passed at a town's breadth from them, met Avis's young eyes that night. They were the eyes of a woman tender and true; but they were those of an artist, to whom it had been mercifully given—while her visions were young, inchoate, and quick to dissolve—to be a little color-blind to misery for beauty's sake. It is enough to say that Avis understood that night how the insight of a single hour, like a torch, may flare out across the width and breadth of a life's work. She understood how great men have seen the drawing of great purposes, the body-color of great inspirations, gone false in the revelation of such hours. She understood how Frère[3] can exhaust an inspiration upon the muscle in the cheek of a sewing-girl starving in an attic; and how Millet was exiled from Paris for daring to paint the misery of peasant-life. Certain sights which she saw that night in the tenement-houses of Harmouth pursued her for years with the force of vocal cries. She felt that, when she was at work again, they would syllable themselves, of sheer necessity, in some form. It was still a long time, however, before she recognized in herself what she could presume to call a passion to express the moan of human famine.

"One other case," said John Rose, as they turned from the furnace of an attic-room in which three families dwelt and damned themselves as comfortably as they might,—"just one more, and we will go. Coy bade me be sure and see this woman,—up three flights, across the court, if you can make it? The last we heard of her she could not get about, and so her business was falling behind. But we are not to understand that she was knocked down, and trampled on. She fell. It is surprising how insecure of foot women with drunken husbands, as a class, are found to be. She is a very respectable woman, from the country. I got her a little book-agency a good while ago; and he doesn't get home very often, and so she gets along. And Coy sent her away for a vacation last year. But I'll just run up and ask how it goes with her." At that threshold Avis shrank instinctively, begging John Rose to go in without her.

The woman came out, however, into the stifling entry-way, when the young minister had completed his errand, and gravely said,—

"Will you not come in?"

She was a dark-eyed, rather delicate creature, with a scar across her forehead.

"This is Mrs. Ostrander," said John Rose.

"Yes," said the woman after a pause. "Will not Mrs. Ostrander step into my room?"

"I was a stranger," replied Avis, giving her hand, which the other, after a moment's hesitation, coldly touched. "I did not feel that I had any right to intrude upon you."

"No," said the woman again, "you had not. That is true. But every one is not so ready to see what is right."

An uneasy sympathy with a sorrow, more impressive because so foreign to her fancy, led Avis to turn as she went down, and say in her pleasant, womanly way,—

"If I can be of any use to you, I hope you will some time come to see me as well as Mrs. Rose."

The woman did not reply, but stood and watched them as they felt their way down the dark stairs. She had noticeable eyes; not so much because of their darkness, and they were very dark, as because of their deadness. They seemed either to have lost, or never to have had, the refractive power. They were the color of cold coal when it is in shadow. They were of the sort which give us the uncomfortable sensation of having been once familiar with them, but of having disgracefully forgotten the where or the when. Avis was dully conscious of such a superstition as she crept down the stairs, and out into the oppressive night. She asked John Rose more particularly about the woman, thinking that possibly, when Philip published that text-book which had been coming out so long, but never came, he might be able to put the poor thing in the way of some slight increase to her precarious business. But, when she spoke to Philip about it, she did not succeed in exciting his interest in the matter; and the chapel bell was ringing him away. Her husband's interests in many things seemed to her, somehow, less vivid than they were.

It was while the incidents of the evening spent among John Rose's "patients" were still cut keenly upon her memory, that word was brought to her one morning that a book-agent had called. Something was wrong that day—the baby was sick, perhaps, or she herself was overworn; and she reminded the servant, with some emphasis, of the rule of the house touching the admission of peddlers.

"It's not so much a peddler, ma'am, as a lady," replied Mary Ann, hesitating; "and she's been badly hurt upon the forehead, ma'am."

Avis put down the baby,—she remembered afterwards that the child clung to her with an irritable persistence,—she took his little hands forcibly from her neck, and went.

She recognized the woman at once; the scar, the coal-cold eyes, and a certain dignity that held itself through her meagre dress, as well-developed muscles do through obedient tissue. The woman wore gray clothes, and carried a little agent's bag.

"I am glad you are able to be out," began Mrs. Ostrander at once. "Mr. Rose told me you had been ill. Pray do not stand."

"I prefer to stand," the woman said, waving away the easy-chair which Avis rolled towards her. There was an awkward pause, which her visitor made no motion to break. Avis said kindly,—

"Can I serve you in any way? Have you a book to show me to-day?"

"I did not come to sell you any book. I came to say good-by. I am going away. I wanted to see you once before I go. I am going to Texas. My husband has come home, and taken the notion to go to Texas. The law compels me to go with him, as if I were a horse or a cow.[4] Women don't think of such things when they marry. I've had a hell of a life with my husband."

The woman brought these words out monotonously, as if she spoke of a matter of course; as if she had said, I've walked half a mile, or I have had my breakfast.

"I am sorry, indeed I am sorry for you," murmured Avis, at a dead loss how to conduct a scene like this.

"My name is Jessup," proceeded the book-agent in the same tone,—"Susan Jessup. I didn't like the man when I married him. I loved another man. But I've got long past that. I never told this before. You're wondering why, in God's name, I've told this to you, Mrs. Ostrander. In God's name, then, I don't know! I didn't mean to; upon my word I didn't. Is your husband at home?"

The excitement of this Mrs. Jessup's manner had so visibly and suddenly increased, that Avis found herself faintly disturbed by it, and stood wishing that John Rose were at hand to take care of his own "patients." It was with a perceptible dignity, though gently enough, that she said,—

"My husband is out this morning. I am sorry. Could he have done any thing to help you? Do you wish to see him?"

"No," said the woman abruptly, "he could not help me; and I do not wish to see him. I'm glad he's out. I thought I'd like to know he was out. Perhaps you've heard, Mrs. Ostrander, that I used to know your husband before he was married. My name was Susan Wanamaker. I lived in New Hampshire, in the same town with him."

"Why—yes," said Avis slowly, "yes, I remember. I have heard Professor Ostrander speak of you."

"We were great friends once, your husband and I," pursued her visitor with a narrow look at her.

"I remember to have heard him—to have heard him say some such thing himself," replied Avis. Her lips had become quite dry, so that she moved them with difficulty, and her words went clumsily. A similar stiffness seemed to have settled upon the action of her mind. Contingencies to which she would not have stooped to give a name, pressed in upon her, and seemed to exert a compelling influence upon her speech. She was conscious of choosing her words with a terrible exactness.

"Oh! he's told you, then, has he?" said Mrs. Jessup sharply. "You knew that I once expected to marry him? I suppose some husbands do tell their wives every thing. I never expected that Philip Ostrander would make such a husband."

"We have spoken together of you," said Avis slowly. In the pause of her voice, the baby's cry came from overhead: she put out her hand to hold herself by the chair which her visitor had refused. She spoke to this stranger with the ceremonious reserve which the circumstances would seem to warrant; but that sensitively responsive sympathy of hers, which no personal exigency could blunt, led her on to say—

"You should have told us—my husband and me—that you were so unhappy, in such need. You must have been most miserable, Mrs. Jessup—to have exposed—yourself or me to a conversation such as this. What then—what now can I do for you to make it worth while for either of us that we should—speak in this way?"

"I saw you at the funeral," proceeded the other abruptly, disregarding Avis's words, as if the force of her own reflection had deadened her power of hearing. "I was up there on a visit—to get away from Jessup for a while: I was there with my old friends. I used to be very fond of Mrs. Ostrander. She wanted it all to go on—before I married Jessup: she thought Philip didn't know his mind—he wasn't always apt to. Then, once I met him here in Harmouth, in a snow-storm, before he married you. And once I went to the chapel-church to see you. I don't blame him. Why, I shall see that face of yours till I die! And I'm a woman. *He* was a man. Oh, you think I've come to taunt and torment you! Women do such things. You think I'm an insolent creature!—some of us are. But I'm not that kind. I'm not jealous: I'm only desperate. I'd like to see the man that was worth, down at the core of him—worth a woman's getting jealous for. The sort of life I've led spreads over you like ivy-poison: you distrust the whole lot of 'em because one bad man brushed against you. When I knew him, he was such a handsome boy! Oh, you've got him—and I've got a brute! That's the difference between us. It's a monstrous difference! It's a monstrous difference!"

She unfolded her thin hands from the old shawl in which she had held them wrapped while she stood talking, and, bringing them together at the knuckles, opened their palms, and spread them out slowly and impressively before Avis; as if they had been facts patent to the conversation.

There is a force peculiar to itself in the mere anatomical appeal of an emaciated hand. It is difficult to believe in the grand despair of a person with plump fingers.

Avis felt herself growing paler and paler under this pressure. She tried to speak; but words looked distant and small, too small to be gathered up.

"Married women don't often look happier than you do," proceeded Susan Jessup a little wildly. "I didn't think Philip Ostrander could make anybody look so happy. He got tired of me. I thought he would get tired of every other woman."

"We will not discuss my husband any more this morning, if you please," said Mrs. Ostrander, collecting herself, not with severity, but with a touch of stateliness. "And I think, Mrs. Jessup, if there is really nothing that I can do for you, it will be best for us both to put an end to a scene which—cannot be fully agreeable to either of us."

"You do it gracefully," said Susan Jessup with a bitter smile, which, however, subsided instantly. "When I found what I'd said, I expected to be sent at once. I hope you'll believe, Mrs. Ostrander, that I didn't come here meaning to make trouble. I didn't even mean to speak about it when I came in; and I'm glad he had the grace to tell you."

She turned, with her hand upon the door, lifting her face slowly. Avis saw that it might once have been rather a pretty, uneventful country face.

"I don't know *why* I came," she said rather pitifully. "Why does a woman trust herself to do any thing, when she's beside herself with things she can't speak of? That's the worst of being a woman. What you go through can't be told. It isn't respectable for one woman to tell another what she has to bear. When I saw you last week, I wanted to pull you into my room and cry in your arms; but *I* can't cry."

Some expression of sympathy hung confusedly upon Mrs. Ostrander's lips; but she was not sure if she uttered it. She felt herself turning dizzy and faint, and the wild figure in the gray shawl blurred before her eyes. She remembered, however, holding out her hand, and that the other took it with a passionate movement, and held it for a moment like a screen before the embers of her eyes, before she closed the door, and trod heavily across the hall and out.

Susan Jessup trod heavily; but her heart was at that moment light with a certain noble joy. We hear much of the jealousy and scorn of women among themselves. It is not often that we are reminded of the quickly-flashing capacity for passionate attraction and generous devotion which renders the relation of woman to woman one of the most subtle in the world, and one exposed most to the chance of what we call romantic episodes. This little wretched, excited creature turned her face from Avis with a sense of having divinely outwitted her. She knew perfectly well that Philip Ostrander had never told his wife of that affair; but his wife should never know that she knew it.

That day passed much like other days. Ostrander was very busy; and, if his wife were a shade more quiet than usual, he was not likely to notice her. He dined with John Rose, and ran in for a little music at the Allens in the evening; and it was late when at last, the child being well asleep, and the women of the house in bed, Avis told him that she wished to talk with him.

He said, "What is it, my dear?" He was pacing the room,—their own room—looking more than usually comfortable. He was in his richly-colored dressing-gown, that Avis thought became him. He had an indefinably masculine air of mastery over his circumstances, and enjoyment in them, which it is impossible to put into words, but to which a woman is very sensitive. At that moment, when, drawing his hand easily out of his pocket, he came up and touched his wife under the chin, lifting her face, Avis felt a dull sense of displeasure. It seemed to her excited thought that he touched her lightly, much as he twirled the great blue silk tassel of the dressing-gown, as if she were, in some sense, the idle ornament of a comfortable hour. She drew her face back, and said with grave abruptness,—

"Philip, something has occurred which I must tell you at once."

"Very well, my dear," said Philip, smiling down.

"There was a book-agent here this morning. Her name was Susan Wanamaker."

"Has Susan Wanamaker been here?" said Ostrander, standing still.

"And told me, Philip—in my own house—that she was once engaged to be married to my husband."

Ostrander slowly removed the hand with which he had sought to caress his wife's withdrawing face: the lordly silk tassel itself seemed to shrink somehow, as it hung from his side. He took a step back, and thrust both hands again into his pockets. Avis did not look up at him. At that moment a deep instinct forbade her to meet her husband's eyes. It was as if she thus saved herself and him from some vague disgrace or grief. Whatever it was, whatever it could be, that flitted across them, her husband should never have it to remember that his wife had surprised his eyes by a stratagem. She would almost as soon surprise his soul. When she had thus given him time, she lifted her own, dim with her sweet sense of honor; but in his she saw then only that darting, scattered gleam— the quicksilver look.

In a deep, displeased voice he said,—

"And—*my wife* discussed such a matter with a strange woman, a book-peddler, before consulting me?"

"You wrong your wife!" blazed Avis, springing to her feet, and holding herself grandly. "I am afraid you have wronged me from the beginning. I am afraid you do not see—my husband does not see— what is wrong, and what is right. I don't understand you, Philip."

"I don't see what could have possessed Susan," said Philip Ostrander.

Perhaps nothing in the range of the English vocabulary would have struck Avis so drearily just then as those few words. She could not conceive of any others which would have so emphasized the distance between the temper of her thought and his. It was the sense of this distance and difference which oppressed her to an extent, that, for the moment, obliterated the admission which the words themselves implied.

But with his characteristic quickness, Ostrander's manner suddenly changed. He shook his bright hair impatiently, as if shaking off a temporary annoyance, and, swiftly turning, threw himself upon the lounge, and held out his arms.

"Come, Avis," he said in his usual voice, "come and hear *my* story now."

The slight arraignment of her justice in this appeal, touched Avis's delicate sense of honor. True, she had *not* heard his story. She stirred slowly towards him, and sat down at the other end of the sofa.

"Come," he repeated still holding out his arms. "I can't talk to you over there. No? Well, then; perhaps I deserve it. But upon my honor, Avis, there is so little in this affair, that it never occurred to me to tell you. I suppose Susan Wanamaker *did* think she was going to marry me once. She was eighteen,—a country school-girl: I was just past twenty,—a college-boy. I found I did not love her, and I told her so. Was there any thing dishonorable in that? You see at once, the dishonor would have been in going on with the affair."

"The dishonor lay," began Avis, but stopped. She could not bring her lips to say that dishonor lay in her husband. "The mistake lay," she want on.

"Permit me one minute," interrupted Ostrander, "till you have heard me out. Grant that I had a boy's fancy for this girl: is that such a crime, Avis? Has a man never blundered with a pretty face before? Very well, then. Grant that I did not tell you, and so blundered again. I was wrong: I perfectly admit it. I see it now, if I never saw it before. Poor Susan has made a mess of it, for which I'm outrageously sorry. I wouldn't have had you so mortified for the world! It's a confounded *faux pas!*"

"She does not know," said Avis more gently. "I told her we had talked of you. She thinks you had told me. But the mortification was the least of it, Philip."

The mortification was the most of it on Ostrander's face at that moment. His lips murmured some phrase of relief; but his heart took little comfort in it. Susan was not dull. And Avis's marble rectitude of speech was not calculated to make the most of a matter. Who could have thought that Susan would have turned up in this way? Women needed to be guarded against the accidents of their relations to each other as much as against graver indiscretions; though he must admit that his wife seemed to have held herself with admirable prudence throughout a very awkward position. Poor Avis! How solitary she looked over at the end of the sofa, across the color of the cushion. Ostrander at that moment wished with all his heart that his wife might have loved some better fellow. He wished he had that talent for openness, which a perfectly honorable man may yet lack, but of which he felt the want keenly in an emergency like this. He said with genuine agitation,—

"I was wrong, Avis, quite wrong. I ought to have told you all about that affair. And it's not quite true, perhaps," he added frankly, "that it never occurred to me to tell you. I think it did—must have. But I was having such extra hard work of it to win you,—do me the justice to remember,—and a breath would have blown out my chance. Perhaps the plain truth was, I didn't dare talk about it. You were not in a state to be tolerant of a lot of boyish nonsense. And I knew I had nothing wrong or base to hide from you. And every other woman seemed so far away from me after I knew you!—and all other feeling so false!"

Her husband spoke with a tremulous passion which she did not often look to hear now, in the stress and haste of daily care into which marriage seemed to resolve itself, in which it seemed a man and woman must take their love for granted to save time. She yielded to the stir of feeling like a harp to a hand. When Philip said with a delicate reproach in his voice, "After all, Avis, I think I have the worst of it, *you* have nothing to repent," she crept towards him across the rose-colored cushion with a long, exhausted sigh. She was perplexed at finding herself, at the very moment when her nature had risen most emphatically in rebuke of his, most weakened with the need of his love. Was there always an incalculable element in the radical metamorphosis which wifehood wrought? Was this one of the ambuscades of nature against which a strong woman must perforce go fortifying herself to the end of life? She hid herself—she would have hidden herself from her own consciousness just then—upon her husband's breast.

For him, he bowed his head over her in a solemn and solitary shame. He could not know what was in her guarded heart. He felt that he had in a dim sense lost the right to know. They sat clinging, but separate.

Presently he began to talk to her again of what they had been saying, thinking it most natural and best. He spoke of the night in which he had met poor Susan in the streets of Harmouth; he dwelt upon every detail of the affair which he could recall: the process gave him a late, agreeable sense of candor. He went farther; he told his wife that he supposed he had been a susceptible boy. His fancy, he said, had been a gusty thing till he found her; he had never felt quite sure that he was capable of a permanent feeling, till he loved her. He spoke sadly, as we speak of a misfortune of the nature as distinct from a fault.

Aristotle ranks confidence as one of the passions.

Avis felt rather sorry for her husband, and feared she had been harsh. And then the baby cried, and she went to him; and Philip went down to finish the article on the electric battery.

It was late when he came up stairs again. He found Avis fallen asleep upon the lounge, half wrapped in the shoulder-robe from the hammock: the rose and white silk was fading, like all the other little fancies about the house. His wife's face, too, seemed to have faded with the rest of the bridal brightness. She had thrown herself down with the especial grace which great exhaustion gives to a lithe figure. Avis was too much of an artist ever to choose an awkward pose: she would have writhed under one, he thought, had she been dead. If she had been alone in the universe, she would have thrown that firm hand of hers, upon which no eye should ever rest, with just that slowly-surrendered outline across the happy pillow. Her hand was a trifle worn, too, like her cheek. Her husband stood looking down. There swept and gathered upon his face an expression which it was as well for both of them, perhaps, that Avis did not see. Whether it were most of self-reproach or self-pity, of tenderness or terror, it were hard to say. Whether he the more distrusted himself at that moment, or the more believed in her, perhaps Philip Ostrander could not for his soul's sake have answered.

He stooped and kissed her. He was more in love with his wife just then than a busy man can afford to be every day in the year. Avis stirred, and, lifting her hand, gravely drew his face beside hers on the pillow. She did not tell him that she had not been asleep. She listened to the faint tapping of the elm-bough upon the window; a dreaming bird chirped in its nest somewhere in the summer night; in the sensitive, windless distance, the college-boys were singing Kinkel's "Soldier's Farewell."[5] The wildly-swelling words came up,—

"How can I bear to leave thee?"

The mournful monotone of the frogs piped from the meadows beyond the town, and under all fitful music she heard the chant of the eternal sea.

Afterwards she wondered how it would have been, daring to wish that they had died that night,—they two,—dumb with the sweetness of reconciliation and resolve; nay, they three,—Philip with the boyish love and laughter in his eyes, and the baby sleeping in the crib, and she herself just then content to have it so.

It was Philip who was wakeful that night. Visions which he would just then have gone blind to forget, electrotyped themselves upon the half-lit room. Long odorous country twilights, the scent of honeysuckle about a farmhouse-door, the pressure of confiding fingers on his arm, the uplifting of a young face, the touch of trustful life, pursued him rather with the force of sensations than reflections. With these came other ghosts, incoherent fancies, aimless fevers, nameless dreams. He shielded his eyes from the nursery-lamp, watching the unconscious face of his wife with a fine envy which only a noble soul, or the nobler side of an inharmonious soul, could have commanded. She,—she only of themselves,—he said, was the truly married. He could think of no lesser joy which he would not have sacrificed just then, if he could have brought to her that absolutely unmortgaged imagination which she had brought to him.

He drank the ashes of his own nature in silence, as soldiers swallow in their wine the cinders of their worn-out colors, before unfurling new.

Faint and more faintly in the distance, from the now dispersing boys, the cry came up,—

"Farewell, farewell, my own true love!"

CHAPTER XVII

> *"Men think that it is ungrate-*
> *ful to the Creator to*
> *say that it is the design of*
> *Providence to keep us in a*
> *state of constant pain; but . . .*
> *were our joys permanent we*
> *should never leave the state in*
> *which we are; we should never*
> *undertake aught new. That*
> *life we may call happy which*
> *is furnished with all the*
> *means by which pain can be*
> *overcome: we have, in fact, no*
> *other conception of human*
> *happiness."*
> —Kant

"The worst of it is the babies," said aunt Chloe, giving a severe twist to her flower-pots, that would have estranged the devotion of any thing else than the verbenas. But verbenas are not sensitive: one knows about how far one can go with them. "I don't see but the worst of it always *is* the babies, in this world," she proceeded, and prayed next minute to be forgiven for so unevangelical a sentiment. Aunt Chloe was so stubborn to the advance of civilization, that she still held that the Lord never sent more mouths than he could fill. She would have thought it very unwomanly to confess to Avis her conscious lack of enthusiasm at the birth of this second child. She blamed herself, that in her honest heart poor Avis's experience of motherhood gave her so much more anxiety than pleasure, and attributed it all to the fact that Mr. Ostrander would use homœopathic remedies for the croup. And now—

"Who is going to prepare Avis for this?" asked aunt Chloe, turning her back on the verbenas without ceremony, and standing on tiptoe laboriously to remove a bit of lint from her brother's coat-collar while she spoke: it was not necessary that they should meet each other's eyes. When a literary man is in any kind of trouble, he does not want his women-folks to know too much about it: that, aunt Chloe thought might be easily understood, even in a business family. When the professor said shortly,—

"I suppose I must tell her myself," going out, and letting the wind take the door behind him, she said, "Poor Hegel!" and wondered if the arbutelon overheard her. And then she went to start a lemon-cream for his dinner. She remembered that she gave him lemon-cream the day the president vetoed that plan about the post-graduate courses; and what a comfort it seemed to be to her brother! And then perhaps poor Avis would taste of it; and there really was no hurry about the child's shirts. Aunt Chloe, like the rest of the world, had expended all the poetry of her allegiance upon the first baby. It did not seem so necessary to crochet the edges of things for this one, poor little lassie; and she had put fully five cents a yard less into the flannels.

Mrs. Ostrander's little girl was four weeks old, four weeks that very day, as the professor—Heaven knows how!—chanced to remember on the way to his daughter's house. He was rather proud of himself for thinking of it, and made the most of the little matter. He was nervous over what he had to say. He thought he had never seen Avis looking so poorly. He took the child from her, for she held it rather listlessly across her arm upon the rose-red lounge: he lifted the little maiden upon his knee well-nigh as tenderly as if she had been a leaf from the "Rhetoric" or "Poetic"[1] in the original autograph. When the boy ran in, he gave him a cough-lozenge, and said,—

"And how is Van Dyck,[2]" to-day?" with a sense of unusual originality of expression. In his heart the professor was rather glad that day, that the boy had not taken a family name. Avis had never been heard to express a wish to name her son for his father. She did not try to explain either to herself or to another why this was. We do not always remember that a woman seeks and finds two perfectly distinct beings in one and the same man. For herself, she can afford to love a human creature; for the father of her child she demands a God. That very weakness in his nature upon which she will abnegate herself, which perhaps she will lower the tone of her own soul to idealize into a perversion of strength, she will defy like a lioness in its transmission to her son. But Avis did not talk—even to her own husband—much about her children. There were throes of the soul in her strong motherhood, which it was no more possible to share than to share a physical pang.

When the professor had repeated, "And how is Van?" and asked the four-weeks' baby (in the anxious tone of a man who expects a reply) if she were sitting quite comfortably, he found that he had exhausted his nursery vocabulary; and when he had said helplessly,—

"Are you quite well to-day, my dear?" and when Avis replied that she was gaining slowly every day, his mind proved to be perfectly barren of any further phrases logically consequent upon the premise formed by the morsel of humanity upon his knee. He began therefore, at once, but with a certain hesitation to which Avis's transparent face became magnetically alive,—

"I came for a special purpose to-day, Avis: I want to have a little talk with you about—your husband."

"Van," said his mother immediately, "run into the nursery." She spoke to her two-years' baby in a tone which assumes both intelligence and obedience in the listener. "Mary Ann, take the child—take both the babies, and do not bring them back till they are sent for.—Now, father, what is it? What has Philip done?"

She raised herself upon the pillow with a sharp motion. The deep circles about her eyes seemed to widen, like the circles in the sea into which a blazing jewel is sinking.

"He has not done any thing," said the professor nervously; "and that is exactly the trouble."

"Do you mean," asked Avis in a rapid, business-like tone, "that my husband is not giving satisfaction in the university?"

"Somebody must tell you," pleaded the poor professor. "I thought you would rather—perhaps—it would be I."

"Walk the floor, father," said Avis, after a moment's silence: "you will feel a great deal more comfortable. Don't mind me."

The professor, with a sigh of relief, thrust back his chair, and trode heavily to and fro: the floor of the room shook beneath its faded roses.

"Now," said Avis, after a slightly longer pause than before,— "now tell me all about it. I am quite ready to hear. Stop! To begin with, does Philip know this?"

"N-n–I do not know. Probably not. There has been no direct expression of dissatisfaction made to him as yet. How sensitive he is to the indirect command of the situation, it is not possible to say. There is a committee of the Board in town to-day: that is why I have annoyed you with it. Probably the matter will be taken up at once in some form. I thought you would prefer, and he, that you should be forewarned."

"Thank you, sir!" said Avis in a low tone.

"The trouble is"—began the professor, and stopped.

"The trouble is?" prompted Avis gently.

"That your husband does not attend to his business," said her father desperately. "The department is running behind. It ought to be one of the most brilliant in the college. Under Professor Cobin's day it acquired a prestige, which, of course, makes it difficult for a younger man, *any* younger man. I thought Mr. Ostrander was equal to these difficulties. He is not: that is about all."

"Still I don't understand," urged Avis. "Is not Philip enough of a man for the position? Did you overestimate his ability to start with? In plain words, has not he the brains for it?"

"He has the brains for any thing!" exclaimed the professor irritably, "that he chooses to apply himself to. It is not his ability that has been over-rated."

"What, then?" insisted Avis. "Does my husband *shirk*?"

She brought the ugly word out with a keen emphasis with which it was not possible to parley. "Certainly," she added with a momentary flash, "he is not an idle man: he works hard. Philip is rather overworked than underworked. I think he is always busy. I do not in the least understand where all this activity has gone to, if it has not gone into the department."

"It is not easy to say where it has gone," replied her father nervously. "I doubt if he knows himself. It is not quite fair to call a man a shirk, perhaps, while he is occupied in so many—but, the trouble is, they are not the right directions. He bends himself to too many things. Now it is electricity; now it is magnetism; then it is a process for utilizing coal-gas. Just now it is a new method for blowing up caterpillars—blowing up fiddlesticks! His business is in his class-room. He ought not to see one inch beyond the faces of those boys this five years. He ought to absorb that morning recitation as the old Hebrew prophets swallowed the scroll on which the word of God was written. Every fossil ought to be a poem to him. He shouldn't be able to *say Old Red Sandstone without a thrill!* He should have conquered his lecture-room by this time. There is a soul in science: he should have handled her body reverently for her soul's sake. He should have overwhelmed that class with his inspirations, as the deluges have overmastered the mountains. When every man in it worth educating could get an enthusiasm out of a chip of granite; when a man he'd marked down on examination would huzza for him in the street; when the college papers were afraid to lampoon him,—then he might have taken to his magazine-writing, and his what-not, and the more welcome. *When the college could afford to be proud of him* was the time to let the world know that such a man as Philip Ostrander was in it. Well"— the professor brought himself up short before his daughter's sofa with burning eyes—"I am tiring you, Avis. It is a great pity: it is all a pity."

"Then Philip has done—none of this?" proceeded Avis authoritatively. "He has been impatient, volatile—he has"—She paused.

"He has shirked the drudgery of the class-room," said her father in a lower and calmer tone. "He got weary of it. He has dissipated himself in inconsequent ways. He has no more business to be giving popular lectures on physiology, or writing poetry for the news-papers, than I have to set up a milliner's shop on the college green. It is too bad, too bad. But, my dear, I'm tiring you."

"The trouble," began Avis, hesitating.

"The trouble with your husband, my child," said the professor with something of gathering enthusiasm in his manner, as though he propounded a well-involved metaphysical problem to a rather superior class,—"the trouble is an extraordinary lack of intellec-tual constancy. It—it really is nothing worse, my dear," he added soothingly. "It does not prevent him from possessing all those do-mestic virtues which have doubtless endeared him to you; and I must say," tremulously—"to myself as well. I have been very much drawn to the young man, as to—a—son. After we have adjusted ourselves to this—blow, my dear, something else will open for him. I see no reason for indulging in any undue—regrets. As for yourself"—

"Should Philip resign at once?" demanded Avis in the metallic tone which resolutely suppressed feeling gives to a tender voice.

"It may be—I cannot tell till after the meeting of the Board. It is impossible to say what will be done, or when, about a successor. But it will not be expected that his resignation shall take effect be-fore the end of the year. That will give us six months to look about us in," added the professor rather miserably.

He came and stood beside his daughter, looking compassion-ately at her. He did not seek to offer her a consolation which her nature would inevitably reject. Her lip did not tremble. She had the half-recoiling but wholly patient look of one who was adjust-ing herself to a familiar experience in a slightly altered form. She put up her hand, and said only,—

"Thank you, father!"

And he said,—

"There, there, my dear!"

And then the little boy ran in, with Mary Ann and the baby be-hind him.

Avis gathered both the children in her arms with a quick and passionate motion. Her heart said, "Oh! what have we done? What can we do?" But her lips said nothing at all.

"The little folks interfere with the studio just now," said the pro-fessor awkwardly, coming back when he was across the threshold of the room. He was sick at heart to say some tender word. "If her mother had lived," he thought, "this might somehow have been spared." Whenever Avis was in any trouble, he always said, "If her mother had lived"— The great professor was as unconscious of any logical flaw in this sweet inconsequence, as the lover is of the laws regulating the circulation of the blood in the lip he kisses.

"Yes, papa," said Avis, falling back into the pretty girlish fashion of speech that she had scarcely outgrown before her marriage.

"But as soon as you are about again—and—the little girl begins to grow, we shall have some more pictures I hope, my dear?"

"Yes, papa," patiently. But she said nothing more. It did not seem to help any thing to talk about it. And then the baby began to cry—her little daughter—her woman-child. Avis looked at her, and said, "You too, *you too!*" It seemed to her just then more than she could bear, to know that she had given life to another woman.

When her husband came to her with the news, a day or two after, she had so far adjusted her mind to it, that she was able to receive its announcement from himself in the only way which—long after—she could have recalled without regret.

He came in looking very pale. She had heard him coughing in the hall: the day was damp. He threw himself heavily upon the lounge, and said,—

"Has your father told you what has happened?"

"Yes, Philip."

"How long since?"

"On Tuesday."

"Some way or other," said Ostrander irritably, "I have offended Cobin. He has been more or less cavalierly in his treatment of me this long while. When it's time for a man to die, he never can understand why other men are alive. He opposed me about the museum; he complained of my Star Course Lectures; I haven't raised a point in Faculty meeting this year, that he hasn't voted down. I attribute this disaster entirely to the cause which has ruined so many a young man,—the jealousy of his senior colleague."

Avis made no reply. She could not speak just then. It did not seem a sane expense of words, which, at best, must be hard to choose. She let him dribble on petulantly for a few minutes. Her boy at her knee was vociferously claiming it an evidence of extraordinary maternal depravity, that his little sister was not allowed rubber-boots with which to go to walk with him. The child's voice and his father's chimed together oddly. She stood apart from them,—these two intensely wrought male personalities, with whose clamorous selfism it was impossible to reason. It struck her unpleasantly at that moment that Van might be like his father, if he lived to grow up. She pushed the boy a little away from her, than drew him penitently back.

"What in Heaven's name is going to become of us," Philip was saying, "is more than I can see. The mere mortification of it is enough to kill a stronger man than I am."

"Never mind, dear," said Avis, exactly as she spoke to the child. She came up, and bent over the lounge, passing her strong hand across his forehead and hair, with the magnificent, maternal motions which her fingers had learned more slowly than those of most women, but more passionately. When he said,—

"My head aches horribly!" she stooped and kissed him, and said,—

"My poor boy!"

It was impossible for her to render any thing more reasonable than tenderness to a humiliated man.

"It is hard for you, coming just now," said Ostrander, rather as an afterthought. "I wish the children were not both babies. It's a confoundedly tough thing for a man with a young family to be turned adrift in this way. I should have thought," irritably, "that your father's influence might have prevented it. But it seems he couldn't or didn't exercise it. I shall write my resignation to-morrow, and get it off my mind. Ought you to stand so long, Avis?"

"It does not hurt me;" but she sank wearily down upon the edge of the lounge. Philip did not move to make room for her, but lay with his brows knotted with pain, and his restless eyes flitting about the room. She slipped down upon her knees, and so knelt, crouched and cramped, till the life of her sensitive hand had spent itself upon him.

"The pain is gone, thank you," he said at last politely. Avis rose at once, and took a chair. In these days, if she caressed her husband, it was with a sufficient and distinct reason: the time had tripped by when he expected her to sit within reach of his hand, within vibration of his breath, within the maze of all that sweet young folly which is wiser than the love of the ages to those who love. It was so with all married people, she supposed.

"Whatever," began Philip, "is to turn up next"—

"Whatever we do next, I hope we shall be able to persevere in it," suggested Avis gently. She was not a woman of reproaches. Philip Ostrander's wife never "nagged" him. He shrugged his shoulders now, and said,—

"Perhaps it is all for the best. I was worn out with that eternal class-room," rather sullenly. Then he complained of the draught, and said that he had taken cold, and asked what on earth the baby was crying about now.

Avis's heart brooded over him, seeing him so irritable and weak, as if he had been a wounded thing. She drew a little nearer, and began to plan and purpose for him, as she would for an excited boy who had got into a scrape. She brought the whole machinery of her superb imagination to bear upon their future. She presented it to him in the colors of courage and the ardors of hope. She spoke with a cheer and assurance that rang hollow to her own forebodings. Ostrander warmed at this tremulous fire. He talked of his command of the languages, of his medical education. He thanked Heaven that he had never been a man of one idea; and now, whatever versatility it had pleased Providence to endow him with would serve them through this emergency till another position offered. Avis listened, and said,—

"Yes, Philip." She sat with her faced turned from him.

"Of course, it will be impossible to meet the first annoyance of this by living along here," said Ostrander in a tone that admitted of no reply. "I must get abroad for a month or so at the end of the year; but I think we can manage that. And, as soon as I return, I shall take to lecturing. It is impossible that we should get into a very tight place. I am not sure that the freedom of such a life will not be better for my health. Whenever I get strong enough to go under the harness of all this drudgery again, some other college will be ready for me. At least, a good American can always go West. We won't give up the ship for one blunder, Avis."

He put out his hand to her affectionately; he thanked her for her courage and consideration; he was afraid he had overwearied her in her state of health. His spirits and his tenderness rose together. And Avis to herself said, with a leap of her strong heart, "No, we will give up nothing, not for many blunders." She gathered him under the wing of her great love with a kind of fierce maternal protection; her husband,—the man who had won her lost freedom from her; life of her life, and soul of her soul; hers in his weakness as once in his glittering strength; hers in the fault and folly as in the beauty and the brilliance of his nature; still hers, for still he loved her: nothing could snatch that from her,—her one sure fact, abiding calm above the gusty weather of her life. Philip loved her: let the rest go. Why should she fret?

"It will all come right," she said, letting her hand drop reticently into his. "There are two of us, Philip, to try again."

She was glad to see him catch the glow of her strong spirit so quickly. She smiled when he got up nervously, and walked the room, calculating the expenses of the European trip. It pleased her better, she said to herself, than if he had staid where he was, and stopped to fondle to her. And she never told him, when, her strained nerves being too receptive, she caught the headaches which she had cured.

She threw herself down wearily, and watched him. She thought she could never have noticed before that uncertain curve in his delicate lips; perhaps that little something in the shape of his head, which had always troubled her—was it a deficiency in the organ of tenderness? either the cause or the effect, as Lavater[3] would have put it, of some weakness in the nature? Ah, well! Poor Philip! Her heart assumed a new burden, as if a third child had been born unto her. Was it possible that her soul had ever gone upon its knees before the nature of this man? So gentle had been the stages by which her great passion had grown into a mournful compassion, her divine ideal become this unheroic human reality, the king of her heart become the dependent on its care,—so quietly this had come about, that, in the first distinct recognition of it all, she felt no shock; only a stern, sad strain upon the muscle of her nature. There was, indeed, a certain manhood in her—it is latent in every woman, and assumes various forms. Avis possessed it only in a differing degree, not in differing kind, from most other women,—an instinct of strength, or an impulse of protection, which lent its shoulders spontaneously to the increasing individuality of her burden.

She spoke to her husband out of a deepening self-restraint, down whose solitary corridors she did not suffer herself to look too closely. She bowed to the great and awful law of married story, by which, so surely as life and love shall one day wear themselves to death and calm, we may know that it shall befall the stronger to wear the yoke of the weaker soul.

But late that night, when the wind was high about the house, and the firelight, dying, flung wild shapes upon the walls, Avis got up, and went into the little room where her children were, to think it all over alone with them. She could not sleep. The shadow of their disordered future, of her own dishonored aspiration, of bedraggled ideals, of clambering fears, sat heavily upon her. Her thought flickered confusedly, now upon her own unfitness for the cares of motherhood, now upon the lapse of time before they should have Van's school-bills to pay. Then as the child stirred, coughing slightly, she must sit mourning about it, and wondering what else he had inherited from his father besides his delicate lungs. Then her imagination flew like a bird into a clouded sunrise, across the future of her little daughter.[4] She turned from one little face to the other; she gathered them under her knotted arms half savagely, as if she would shut them in from the chance of this awful gift called life, which she had imposed upon them. It seemed to her a kind of mortal sin that she should have bestowed upon her children a father whom she might not bid them kneel to worship. She felt a sense of personal guilt for every pain or peril that was in store for these two poor little confiding creatures—her children, their children—to be reared in a sick and poor and struggling, and perhaps (Heaven only knew) an inharmonious home.

"Nothing can make this right," she said, and fell upon her knees beside them, constrained by that mute prayer without ceasing, through which all lofty motherhood draws the breath of its strong life.

CHAPTER XVIII

*"The effects of weakness are
inconceivable, and I maintain
that they are far vaster than
those of the most violent
passions."*
—Cardinal de Retz.[1]

*"Ce temps où le bonheur brille
et soudain s'efface,
Comme un sourire
interrompu!"*
—Victor Hugo[2]

It is said that Greenland, five or
six centuries ago, was temperate. Parts of Siberia were once mild.
Sulphur past the point of fusion, at a higher degree of temperature,
consolidates again.

Perhaps most married people reach a point where, for the time
being, they consider their union with each other to be the greatest
mistake of their lives. Fortunate are they who pass this period, as
the younger and more irritable passion may, within a year or two
after the wedding-day. It is the slowly growing divergence, as it is
the slowly gathering attraction, which is to be feared. That tether
galls most terribly from which the satin surface is longest in wear-
ing down.

Avis and Philip Ostrander had been married three years and a
half.

She was thinking of this one night rather sadly, more leisurely
indeed than she might often think of any thing in that careworn
summer. Beneath the pressure of their increasing anxieties and the
more clamorous strain of the nursery, her elastic strength had at
length surrendered. For the first time in her life, she had been dangerously ill.

Stung with the immediate needs of their position, in the heart of
July she had put the new-born baby off her knee, and gone up into
the hot attic studio to finish a portrait. Then came the old and
commonplace story: any woman knows it. Why the children must
needs select that precise time to have the whooping-cough? why
the cook must get married the week before Commencement? why
Philip must just then and there have an attack of pleurisy? why the

New-York relatives, unheard of for years, should come swarming in on class-day? why she herself should come down with diphtheria the evening that Philip's resignation was accepted?—such questions eternity alone can be long enough to answer to the satisfaction of some of us. A fig for the mysteries of fate, free-will, foreknowledge absolute, the origin of species or pre-Adamic man! when in teeth of it all, flat comes the professor with rheumatism, and aunt Chloe even cannot be spared to High Street.

It was very kind in Barbara Allen to make the offer. Really, there was no one else to be had. And Barbara was always kind; she certainly had a genius for the sick-room, as Philip and Avis agreed. Avis accepted the attention gratefully, dropped her household in Barbara's hands as gladly as the escaping soul may drop the dying body, and proceeded immediately to be as ill as she knew how. Her sickness was characteristically intense, and culminated rapidly. Stirring one day, out of the famine of exhaustion which renders that disease, when fatal, a peculiar prolongation of the agony of dissolution, she caught an expression upon her husband's face which absolutely aroused her.

"Philip," she said, "am I going to die?"

"Oh, God knows!" he had cried, before he could be silenced. Avis had not thought of it before. She lay a few moments perfectly quiet. She did not,—like that great creature to whom late happiness brought an early death, to whose genius love was superadded, only that both might mercifully sleep before the conflict of ages should befall which has set these two at odds in women—she did not cry out,—

"God will not separate us, we have been so happy!"[3]

No, not that.

Afterwards she remembered that she did not think about her husband at all. In one supreme moment the whole future of two motherless children passed before her. One of those clairvoyant flashes which sometimes seem to make motherhood a form of prophecy, flared out across these unconscious lives for whose creation she was responsible. Oddly enough the thing presented itself to her in isolated pictures, as if she had been turning the leaves of an illustrated book. She saw Van—a large boy in jackets that did not fit—coming home with his rubber-boots wet: nobody told him to change them, so he had the lung-fever; and the nursing was poor, so he got the cough.

As distinctly, she saw him skulking in from college one night (a moonlit night); he swore as he came up the steps; there was something wrong, but he did not tell his father. Van would never confide in his father. Then she saw her little daughter. Avis was sure that she knew what her daughter was like before the child was a week old,—a reticent, solitary little girl, hating her patchwork, always down by the sea; as full of dreams as a dark night, and as impenetrable,—her daughter, brought up by another woman. There probably would be a step-mother. Rather a pretty woman, Avis thought she would be (Philip's taste was fastidious), well-bred and a little dressy, a member of a Harmouth reading-club, but without a career; probably her bread would always rise; and she would turn the studio into an excellent lumber-room, with every thing done up in camphor, and carefully shaken twice a year on account of the moths.

"Doctor," she repeated, "is it death that is the matter with me?" The baby, as her mother spoke, began to cry from the adjoining room; not crossly, as the boy used to, but with a low, confiding wail. Avis could never be impatient with her little girl's cry. Van, too, came trotting up vociferously, demanding, behind the sick-room door, to be let in and ask mamma why he couldn't get the kitty through the ice-cream freezer. His voice, as his father hushed him, died away rebelliously. A singular upheaval of the moral nature seemed to Avis to take place in herself; something stronger, because more vital than the revolt of the will or the physical recoil against death. Her children assumed the form of awful claims upon her conscience; they presented a code to her, absolute, imperius, integral with the law of God.

"It is wicked" she said aloud, "it is wicked for the mother of two little children—babies—to die. Doctor, you should have told me I was in danger of committing such a mistake. I will not do it. Do you understand? I will not die! Call in my husband. Tell him to kneel down there and pray. God understands about this. It is my duty to live."[4]

Magnificently she set herself moment by moment to conquer death. She counted the dropping of the medicine which she could not swallow, the passing of her pulse, the beating of her heart, the ticking of the watch. She cast the whole force of her nature upon that die. Her will rang iron to the crisis. She repeated at intervals,—

"It is my duty to live."

She continued the struggle for three days, growing weaker. On the fourth she swallowed brandy; on the next her medicine; beef-juice on the next. Every physician knows such cases. "The soul makes her own body," said the great physician Stahl.[5]

Avis recovered rapidly.

Perhaps the inevitable re-actions of convalescence told more heavily upon Ostrander than upon most people. His mercurial sensitiveness to discomforts rose as the excitement of danger ebbed. The annoyances of sickness acted upon him like cologne upon a blooded dog. (If any reader fail to understand the force of this simile, let him put the experiment in practice.) Ostrander had never been able to remain within hearing of the children's cough. Once when the boy was ill, long ago, worn with watching, Avis had asked him to take the baby a while. He said, "Oh, certainly!" and paced the floor with Master Van, who was black in the face with vocal disapprobation of the arrangements, for half an hour. Then Avis heard Philip say through his clinched teeth,—

"*I'll get a nurse for this child to-morrow, if it costs twelve dollars a week.*"

She never asked him to take the babies again.

On this particular night, when it occurred to Avis to lie thinking just how long they had been married, he had come up after tea and said,—

"Nicely to-night, Avis?" And she had said,—

"Thank you, Philip!" And he had asked,—

"If we leave the doors open, will it not rest you to hear a little music before I go out?" And she had repeated,—

"Thank you, Philip!" And then he had said,—

"Pellet makes a mistake using so much camphor in your case," and had kissed her forehead, and gone away.

She tore the bandage off her throat when he had gone. Philip was always fastidious about scents; no wonder this kept him out of the sick-room so much. She felt a little solitary, listening to Barbara's fine execution down stairs, as the twilight came on. But she was glad and grateful to have Philip amused. Barbara was playing the "Adelaide,"[6] then the operas, "Trovatore," "Lucia," "Faust."[7] Everything she touched to-night had the sway of familiarity: every thing was full of arias, of—it was not easy to say what. Barbara was not a woman of strong emotions. She possessed, however, abundant sensitiveness to strong effects.

Avis thought how long it was since her husband had asked *her* to play to him. She remembered the day when he said beneath his breath,—

"What a touch!"

But now Barbara had begun to sing. She sang,—

> "Oh! dinna ye mind, young man, she said,
>   When the red wine ye were spillin',
> How ye made the cup gae round and round,
>   An slighted Barbara Allen?"[8]

Barbara was still playing, when, pliant to the quiet temper of returning strength, Avis fell asleep. When she waked, it was late, and the house was still.

The door was open into the hall. Philip, in coming up, must have forgotten it. He usually came in, but, now that she was so much better, sometimes merely looked in, on his way to the little blue room which he occupied. Avis rose to shut the door: as she did so, she glanced at her watch. It was two o'clock.

The gas in the hall was still lighted; and they could not afford to waste gas in these days. Thinking it a pity to wake the nurse, and feeling her strength rather rising than falling with the exertion, Avis flung over her wrapper a shawl,—the carmine one,—folding it about her face and head, and crept along, hand over hand upon the balusters, clinging with care. Her bare feet made no sound upon the carpeted stairs: not a board creaked beneath her tread she noticed, as she crawled down.

Half way down the stairs, she was surprised to hear the sound of a voice, low and irregularly articulate; no—voices—two. The sound came from the parlor; and then she saw that the parlor-door, too, was open, and that the room was still lighted like the hall.

She was for the moment slightly startled. There was usually a little tramp and burglar panic in Harmouth in the early autumn nights, and usually with some reason. Then she remembered that Philip had said something of an appointment with an Englishman, with a notion about making telegraphy subservient to audible speech. But she crept on to make quite sure and safe, staggering a little, holding by the wall, and so into the doorway.

It was not the Englishman.

CHAPTER XIX

PRO: *"How long remained the fickle true to thee!"*
EPI: *Her vision still is true: 'tis near me."*
—Goethe's *Pandora*

Barbara Allen sat on the piano-stool, leaning backward, one elbow upon the music-rack, and the poise of her pleasant figure resting upon the bruised white keys.

The sheets of music lay scattered about; one or two had fallen to the floor: they lay with disordered leaves. A hand surprised by some momentary disturbance would have dropped them so. Barbara's touch was habitually self-possessed; that of few women more so. Barbara's head was bent. Her bronze curls fell against her cheek, sweeping clean that fine profile from the comb to the curve of the neck. There were traces of agitation upon her face.

Philip Ostrander sat beside her. He had drawn his chair, so that its edge and the edge of the piano-stool collided. The hardly-acquired housekeeper's impulse in Avis noticed this, even at that moment, and she thought how the varnish was getting rubbed.

One of Ostrander's arms was stretched out, his hand resting upon the bass keys. It could not be strictly said that it encircled Barbara's waist; but there was no back to the piano-stool, and Barbara was tired. In his other hand he held, alas! he held her own. There were dimples in Barbara's fingers; she had cool, clear-cut, conscious nails. She had put her hand in Ostrander's, so that the profile of the thumb and first finger was presented to view; a constitutional amendment on nature, which a hand not altogether of the smallest may surely find legitimate. Nature had as yet suffered no such surprise in Barbara as to enable her to forget this; but then Barbara had never allowed a man to hold her hand before.

Ostrander's eyes were fastened upon Barbara's face. They wore the look which a woman accustomed to the admiration of men would feel, whether through the lid of her eye or her coffin. You think you can watch a woman as you will, sir, because she happens to be at the other end of the room? transfigured in conversation with the hostess? netted in the labyrinth of a crocheted shawl-strap? up to the ears of her soul in the poem or the sonata? promising the next polka to your rival? or adoring the Tintoretto, with her cool, round shoulders to you? Do you fancy that you can lift an eyelash that she will not know it, any more than you can pass a comment on the weather that she will not hear?

Barbara's lashes swept her flushed cheek; but she would have seen Ostrander's look through her back-hair.

Ostrander's face wore a peculiar illumination when he admired any thing,—a statue, a picture, or a woman. The corners of his mouth quivered a little, and his lips parted in a smile beside whose silent homage a spoken word would have seemed a definite rudeness. There was a refined, cool light in his eye, too, which Barbara exceedingly admired. She had never seen a man look just like that. His whole bearing was that of one swayed by a delicate intoxication, in which all that was noblest, calmest, and most permanent in himself, deferred to the object which had excited it.

It was this look which his wife—years past, now, there in the garden-studio, when the apple-blossoms fell about them—used to surprise, looking up suddenly from her painting; and then sit lifting her beautiful head gravely beneath it. It was this look which his wife surprised now.

Philip Ostrander was called a man of great discretion in his relations to women. It is doubtful if his most wayward fancy had ever betrayed him into a positive social imprudence before.—What, then, would he have done with Barbara's hand?

When Avis saw him lift it, prisoned there like a bird against his leaning shoulder, she stirred, and would have uttered his name. Her lips made no sound; but her trailing dress rustled upon the floor. Barbara started. Philip turned slowly around.

His wife in the doorway, haggard from her mortal sickness, stood colossal. She was paler, perhaps, than need be, in that red drapery. She gathered it, for it had fallen almost to her knee, in one hand. The other was thrust into the empty air. She had never reminded him of her great Venus as she did at that moment. In the blind action of her arm and figure was something of the same shrinking as of a creature from whom a shield had been torn away. The real or fancied similarity in her features, too, was emphasized by the way she held her head.

By degrees her pallor deepened dreadfully. Her features seemed to grow thin and sheer like a marble medallion of a spirit.

Philip Ostrander looked from her to Barbara's curls; and his eyes dropped like a falling star.

Barbara drew away her hand swiftly. He would not have had her do this: it was an implication which, he began angrily to say to himself, the circumstances did not call for. He roused himself at this, and said in his easy way,—

"Why, Avis!"

But Barbara said nothing.

Avis also said nothing—nothing at all. She advanced a step or two into the room, and in silence pointed to the little Egyptian clock upon the mantelpiece, whose bronze sphinx told the hour,—seven minutes past two o'clock. With the other hand she pointed to the door.

Barbara arose at once. She said she had no idea it was so late; she muttered something about being very sorry, and that she was afraid Avis would take cold. Barbara had never got into such a strait before. She was frightened.

Avis did not stir when Barbara left the room, but stood, still pointing with a grand sweep of her arm to the open door. Perhaps never in her youth and joy and color had she possessed more beauty than at that moment. It is undeniable, explain it as you will, that Ostrander's most conscious emotion just then was one of overpowering admiration for his wife. He felt a kind of terrible taunting pride in her. He did not believe there was another such woman in the world. He could have flung himself at her feet, if he had dared.

His eyes, as hers transfixed them, seemed suddenly to reel; then came on their dead, dense look. He appeared to watch her from a vast distance like a being from another sphere; as a dumb animal watches a human face; or the victim of some pitiable mania regards the sane.

"Don't be offended over a little thing, Avis," he began, collecting himself, stumbling into the weakest thing he could have said.

He wished hotly that she would have burst into reproaches, accusations, into a passion of repulse or rebuke. The woman who does this puts herself at radical disadvantage with most men. Perhaps, mingled with the unworthy consciousness of this little psychological fact, a nobler impulse stirred in Ostrander's heart. Perhaps he knew that he deserved the worst she could have given, and it might have been a certain relief to him just then, to get what he deserved.

But Avis answered him not a word. Her lip curled slightly,—his wife's lip,—curled above him as she stood looking down. A single articulate syllable would have broken the exquisite edge of her scorn; but she did not utter it. He felt under her silence as men may under crucifixion, which does not permit the victim even to writhe.

"You are making a mountain out of a mole-hill," he said irritably, rising with his fugitive look, determined to put an end to this dumb and dangerous scene; "and it is a terrible imprudence for you to be here in the cold. You will have a relapse to-morrow. Let me help you up the stairs."

Advancing, he put out both hands, and would have touched, supporting her. But Avis, with a slight, imperious gesture, waved him away.

"Very well," he said, "have it as you will." He stood to watch her from the bottom of the stairs, anxious for her, till he should see her safely up. She had swept by him with a certain strength, but tottered on the first stair. He sprang and caught her; held her for one moment so impetuously, that his trained ear detected the irregular, sluggish beating of her heart,—a paralytic beat. It alarmed him, and he said hurriedly,—

"You are not fit to get up by yourself. Don't be so hard on a man, Avis!"

But she disengaged herself, and crawled up alone. He followed at a little distance to catch her, if she fell. Thus they reached the landing; and she went on into the faded rose-red room, and shut the door. The wind was rising as she went in. She crawled weakly into bed, and lay with her hands crossed, listening to it. It blew all night fitfully, like the resolve of some great live, lawless nature; but it rose perceptibly from hour to hour. Towards morning it lulled.

In the morning aunt Chloe came over, and Barbara sent up word, that, if she could be spared, perhaps she had better go home. Avis replied that she should like to see her. Barbara came awkwardly enough. She had been crying, and her front-hair was out of crimp. Avis looked at her with gaunt, insomniac eyes: it was evident that she had not slept, but she was quite at ease. She thanked Barbara for all her kindness, and bade her a grave good-by.

Barbara looked sullen for a minute; then a quiver ran through the bronze curls. She began to sob.

"Pray don't," said Avis wearily. "I am not quite strong enough— to—see people cry. But I understand your feeling. It is so dangerous for a woman to commit an indecorum! Society does not excuse her as it does a man. Will you ask aunt Chloe to bring the children up?"

Avis spoke gently. A certain terror fell upon her at finding in her own heart no sting sharper than that of a sad scorn. She had rather hoped that she might find herself a little jealous of Barbara. She hung over her love for her husband as we hang over a precious, diseased life, of which we have not the courage to despair. She fanned it wildly. Better fire than frost! Better the seething than the freezing death! But all her soul was numb. She looked calmly at Barbara's curls and fresh maiden colors and attitudes. She could not be jealous of so slight a thing. With a sickening dismay she perceived that Philip—he too—began to seem to her small and far, like a figure seen in the valley of an incoherent dream. She felt as if she had suddenly stepped into a world of pygmies, and had a liliputian code to learn before she could take up the duties of citizenship therein.

Barbara stopped crying. She stole down stairs with dry, startled eyes. *An indecorum? Society? Excuse?* Barbara repeated the words confusedly. Two weeks ago she would have regarded the supposition that any human lip would ever tell her she had been indecorous, with a pleasant unconcern, like that with which she regarded the habits of the cave-men, or the subject of unconscious cerebration. Barbara thought she ought to see Philip Ostrander at once, and ask him if he thought any harm was done. But he was in the study, and the door was locked. When he came out, he asked where she was, and his little boy told him she had gone.

Now, Barbara forgot to take her sun-umbrella. It was the middle of the afternoon before Ostrander saw it—a pretty purple silk toy—hanging by the clutch of a little ivory hand upon the hat-tree. Ostrander saw it, and thought he had better carry it over to her: he must walk somewhere. Under the circumstances it would be more fitting that Barbara should not come for it; it would be pleasanter, indeed, for Avis, he said to himself: and Avis had expressed no wish to see him to-day. He put on his hat and strolled out, carrying the parasol. A delicate perfume hung about it, something that he had never known any woman but Barbara to use: he remembered that he fancied it when she was taking care of that gunshot wound. Barbara had certainly been very kind to them both. It was not right that his wife's over-scrupulousness should re-act unpleasantly upon her. The least that a sense of honor demanded of him now was to see to it that Barbara should not in any manner suffer from his folly. If he did not guard her, nobody would. No man with a spark of chivalry in him would allow the woman whom he had so unfortunately drawn into a trifling imprudence, to meet the consequences of it unwarned or unshared. Then, too, he would not be misunderstood himself in the affair, if he could help it. If he had said any thing that sounded indiscreet,—and he could not remember that he really had,—it would be better to explain to Barbara precisely what he did mean: there should be no mistake in the thing anywhere. There was no need that any man with a sound head should get into that fog-bank of relations in which men and women were always going astray for simple lack of a clear understanding each of what the other wanted. He thought the sooner he had a talk with Barbara the better.

He went to her brother's house, and she presented herself at once: her eyelids were still delicately discolored, like rain-beaten flowers, with tears. Ostrander did not go in, but stood in the hall, hesitating. He said,—

"Here is your parasol." And Barbara thanked him; and then there was an awkward pause.

"I want to see you—a few moments," said Ostrander gravely.

"There is company in the parlor," replied Barbara, with downcast eyes.

"It is pleasant on the beach this afternoon," urged Ostrander impulsively. It did not seem quite possible now to go home without seeing Barbara alone.

Barbara said, "Just as you like." She got her hat, and they went out in silence together into the hot summer afternoon.

When they reached the beach, he said, "It will be cooler on the water." Nothing but common-places occurred to him.

He pushed down the boat,—his wife's little dory,—and helped Barbara in. She slipped, and he caught her, but neither spoke: she released her hands slowly. An old fisherman stood on the beach, hauling his dirty boat, with a rasping noise, across the coarse gray sand.

"I wouldn't put up that there sail ef I was yeou," he said.

"And why not?" argued Ostrander, glad to have something to smile at just then. Avis and he had always differed about that sail: she never used it.

"You mought as well put spurs onto an angel as a sail onto a dory," observed the fisherman, dogmatically moistening his hands for another tug at his boat. "'Tain't in the natur' of a dory to stand it: there's natur' in boats likewise as there's natur' in fishes and folks. No use rowin' agin tide in none of us. A dory, now, knows what she wants done as clear as yeou do, or the lady. Ef I was yeou, I wouldn't cross her."

"I wouldn't, either," said Barbara.

So Ostrander took the oars. He rowed hard, but composedly, with the long, virile Harmouth stroke. He rowed quite into the heart of the harbor; but few boats were in sight. He drew in his oars, and they drifted beneath the blazing sky. Barbara put up the sun-umbrella, and they sat under it in a purple light. The breeze struck pleasantly across the bay, and the sun dipped. The wind lifted one of Barbara's curls, and blew it softly against his cheek. He looked at her; but she did not return his look. She sat quite still.

"I am very sorry," he began, and stopped. What in the name of reason was he to say he was sorry for? Barbara came to his aid. She turned her head: the wind was at her back, and carried all her hair forward, so that her face looked out of a soft aureola. She said,—

"Avis was very much annoyed."

"I suppose so," answered Ostrander irritably.

"Do you think," asked Barbara timidly, "that any—any thing unpleasant—any harm will come?"

"Harm cannot come where there is no harm," said Ostrander, suddenly remembering that this was the thing to say.

"Certainly not," replied Barbara more courageously.

"The whole world is welcome to hear any thing that I have ever said to you, Miss Barbara," he went on in a confident, clear tone.

"Why, of course," said Barbara.

It seemed for the moment to make quite sure of it, that he should say it, and that she should assent to it. He took up the oars with a sigh of relief, and instinctively, perhaps, made toward the shore, as if it were safer to let this scene end just where it was.

The tide, while they drifted, had turned. He rowed a few minutes in the hot sun, laboriously, and then laid down the oars: he came and sat under the sun-umbrella. Barbara's face looked unusually tender in the purple light. Their eyes met. Necessarily they sat so near, that he could perceive the agitated fluctuation of her breath.

"The man was right," he said in a low tone: "it is of no use to row against the tide."

"Oh, hush!" said Barbara.

It is possible to say a very dangerous thing in a perfectly safe way. Ostrander's readiness both of the lip and of the fancy at once exposed and protected him in the possession of this perilous power. When he said, "It is of no use to row against the tide," he certainly was not altogether thinking of the tides of Harmouth Harbor. But when Barbara not only perceived that he was not, but committed the mistake of letting him know that she perceived it, he fell back at once upon the literal significance of his words. Instinctively he had provided himself with a barricade of such significance. If one trench had failed, he would have withdrawn to another, strictly, in his own view at least, on terms of honorable retreat. This is one of the accidents liable to a lithe mind, and may fasten itself upon a nature of great delicacy; in rare cases, upon one of real rectitude.

Ostrander regarded Barbara with a certain gentlemanly surprise, and saying in his usual voice,—

"However, we will try again," took up the oars. But the tide set sternly against him, and he perceived now how far they had drifted. His friend the fisherman was abreast of them: he sat in the sun, hauling out his nets, still as a figure in the foreground of a marine picture.

"With your permission," said Ostrander after a few minutes' very unplatonic hard work, "I think we will put up the sail. There is not wind enough to trouble a nautilus."

He put it up, and they glided along quietly; the swifter motion at once rested and excited him. When Barbara said, How pleasant it was! his deepening voice and eyes answered,—

"I am afraid it is too pleasant." But Barbara did not say, "Oh, hush!" She knew better this time.

They were sitting so, she leaning over the gunwale like a violet, with the purple light across her white dress, when a slight stir struck the perfectly calm water, as if the feet of an unseen spirit trod across it. Then the whole bay seemed to gather her bright shoulders, and shiver a little. Then the near waves crinkled and curdled, as flesh does with fear.

Ostrander sprang to wrench the little mast out of its socket just as the dory reeled. He was too late.

As he went down, he saw the fisherman leaning, gunwale to the water's edge, the fine lines that his black net made against the sky, and the wreath of smoke from his pipe. Distinctly he thought what a good sketch Avis would make of it.

Then he thought how the bay looked like a lake of blue fire, and how he and Barbara were going into it together. The last thing that occurred to him was, "We have been struck by a white squall."

By the time that he had begun to ascend, he was not conscious of any coherent idea, except that, if he and Barbara were drowned, then and there, together, his wife would believe him a rascal to the end of her life. And then he knew that the mere fact of dying was only an incident in that supreme despair.

He struggled up, and struck out madly. Barbara was clinging to the bottom of the dory. She was calling to him. He seemed a great way off. The water between them—calm now as outworn feeling—was a cold and deadly blue. Once more he thought of the lake of fire, and of those terrible old Bible metaphors that played upon it in such a ghastly way.

He made his way rather weakly. Who would have believed that the blazing summer sea could hold so cold a heart? The fisherman was coming with long, sharp, agitated strokes: the water reeled under his blows. Ostrander's head reeled too. He was growing very cold. A paralytic thickening of the tendons, and stiffening in his muscles, had crept upon him.

"My God!" he said aloud, "am I going to have the cramp?"

Then the boat made a great leap, and recoiled on itself, like a jaguar, and snatched him up.

"You took me before the lady!" cried Ostrander, horror struck.

"The lady doos very well!" said he of the sea imperturbably. "As long as they can screech, they ain't cramped. Just you stay where you be. You mought be took agin—and she's pretty solid. I'll haul her in."

Barbara was hauled in, hand over hand, like a mackerel-net; the dory was righted, and taken in tow—possibly the whole thing had taken seven minutes. The fisherman had not removed the pipe from his mouth.

Ostrander and Barbara sat awkwardly and miserably in the dirty boat. When the fish flopped in the net, and an eel, in the struggle for existence, jumped into Barbara's lap, Ostrander felt as if he were watching the blue-devils in the last act of some second-rate opera. The purple umbrella was gone. High in the western heavens the holy sun peered into their faces. His fastidious fancy revolted from this grotesque, satiric ending to a highly-wrought experience. He would have found it hard to explain why he felt as if it must be, somehow, Barbara's fault. He would not imagine his wife, for instance, in the same boat with an eel. At all events, she would not have shrieked at it. He was surprised to find how it altered Barbara's appearance to have her curls washed straight.

The fisherman took the pipe from his mouth as they grated on the solitary beach.

"Mebbe," he said, "ye'll remember next time not to hurt the feelins of a dory. A dory's like a lady, sir. The man that slights it has to pay for it fust or last. She's tender in the feelins, a dory is."

He had landed them, as chance would have it, just off the lighthouse reef; and Barbara and Ostrander walked up through the divorced gorge together. Barbara did not understand the expression which his face had assumed. She thought him very cross. He, for his part, was not thinking of Barbara at all.

He and Barbara parted miserably enough, at the edge of the town. They agreed that it was better so. Barbara protested that she was not very wet, and preferred to take care of herself. When he said that he supposed it would attract less attention, she assented decidedly. She said she was sorry they went to row. She asked him if he were going to tell Avis. Barbara was thoroughly alarmed.

Ostrander went quickly home. As he passed his wife's room, she called him. The door was open. Avis sat upon the edge of the bed, partly dressed: she had thrown a thick shawl about her, and her bare feet, with which, it seemed, she had been trying her strength, hung weakly, just touching the floor. Something in her attitude— whether it were the weakness or the strength of it, its courage or despair—affected Ostrander powerfully. He stopped in the doorway, feeling disgraced and miserable. He did not cross the threshold of his wife's room. She said rapidly,—

"What has happened, Philip?"

"I was out in the dory, and got struck by a white squall. That is all, except that I had the cramp, and a mackerel-boat picked me up."

Ostrander brought the words out stolidly. He did not exactly mean to appeal to her fear or sympathy; yet he felt conscious of some disappointment that she exhibited no sign of either. She said,—

"Was Barbara with you?"

"Yes," said Ostrander doggedly. His quick sense of irritation rose. He was not going to stand and defend himself like a school-boy. There was a long silence.

"Well," he said, breaking it uneasily, "I must go and get out of these wet things."

"It will be best for both of us," said Avis in a low voice, after yet another pause, in which she had sat with her eyes upon the floor, but rising now, and slipping to her feet, "if this thing is to go on,— if you wish to indulge platonic friendships with other women,— that your wife should not be unnecessarily insulted by it; you would agree with me, I am sure, that I had better take the children, and go to father's for a while."

When he was gone, she crawled back into bed. The words of the woman Susan Jessup had dogged her thoughts that day: "He got tired of me. I thought he would get tired of every other woman." Oddly beside them stepped in that hideous old rhyme of Goethe's,—

"The false one looked for a daintier lot;
The constant one wearied me out and out."

These pursued her like the jingle on the hand-organ that follows us seven squares away. She hated her own heart for giving hospitality to such words.

The children were laughing in the nursery. Birds broke their hearts for joy upon the window-ledge. She shrank as she listened, turning wearily in bed. All sweet sounds in life seemed to have fallen suddenly a semi-tone too high or too low for her, so that harmony itself became an exquisite ingenuity of discord. She seemed to herself like that afflicted musician to whose physical ear this happened; or like that other, who stood alone deaf in the middle of his orchestra.

How could they ever hear—she and Philip now—the perfect music of a happy home again?

She struggled with the unique dismay which overtakes the woman who first learns that she has married a capricious man. Avis thought, that if her husband had committed a forgery, or been brought home drunk, she should have seen more distinctly, at least more clearly, where her duty lay. She was sure that she should have gone on loving him, in fierce proportion to the depth of his fall, till death had resolved all love to elements so simple, that it knew no code of duty, and needed no spoken bond. But then he would have loved her. She could not spend herself for the husband whose tone and touch had hardened to her. She could not cast away the pearls of wifehood: that were to commit the unpardonable sin of married story.

But Ostrander came back presently, manfully enough, to his wife's room. He was startled by what she had said, and touched by the gentle dignity with which she had said it. Then the consciousness of clean linen is in and of itself a source of moral strength only second to that of a clean conscience. A well-ironed collar, or a fresh glove, has carried many a man through the emergency in which a wrinkle or a rip would have defeated him. Ostrander came in, looking very clean and comfortable, shut the door, and sat down by his wife on the edge of the bed. He leaned, putting one arm over her where there was room to support himself, upon his hand: Avis stirred uneasily, and he removed it.

"You have given me no chance, Avis," he began, "to explain myself: I don't see but I must take it."

"What is the use?" asked Avis drearily.

"I don't understand your disinclination to discuss the matter," said Ostrander, flushing slightly.

"There is nothing to discuss," said his wife, turning her head from side to side upon the pillow. "When a man has ceased to love his wife, that is not a subject of discussion between them."

"Upon your own lips rest the shadow from those words!" he cried with an heroic air. "*I* did not utter them. I scorn to deny that I have ceased to love my wife."

"You adopt a singular method of expressing your affection," said Avis. She was terrified at her own words as soon as they were spoken. Roots of bitterness and blight seemed to be fastening upon her soul, like a fungoid disease upon the flesh.

"Well, admit then," said he with a peculiarly winning air of patient sadness, "that my love is not quite the same as it was; that it has assumed, with time, a different form and different force."

"Oh, hush!" cried Avis. She could not help it: the imperious impulse of the woman overswept her. When her husband understated in her ears that which her own voice had underscored, she felt as if she had plunged a knife into a dissolving ghost, and drawn it back, reeking with human blood. All was over now, she thought. They never could look at each other with tender fictions in their glance again. Their four lips had spoken the terrible truth: in their eyes forever would be the memory of it.

"I am sorry," continued Ostrander sadly, "that my peculiar temperament has brought you into suffering. I ought to have foreseen it; but I had more confidence in myself than events have warranted."

"Do you care for—do you love Barbara?" asked Avis abruptly. Her voice rang foreign to her own ears. The whole scene moved on dimly to her, as if they sat on some solemn historic tribunal, weighing the fate of two strangers whose life hung in their trembling hands.

"Love her? *No!*" thundered Ostrander, recoiling.

"What *is* it like, I wonder," asked Avis, "to feel as you do? I am not made so as to understand it, Philip."

"You may thank Heaven you are not," murmured Ostrander, exactly as if she had inquired of him touching the sufferings consequent upon some physical deformity.

"Is it friendship you seek?" went on Avis simply. "My husband was my friend. I needed no other."

"That is your temperament," said Ostrander: "mine is different. I am sorry it is so. I don't know what more I can say."

It is impossible to convey the absence of self-insistence and presence of gentle regret by which Ostrander contrived to transfigure these feeble words: they seemed, as he uttered them, to be the outgrowth of a delicate and forbearing reticence, in itself the index of essential strength. Avis lay for a few moments with a pathetic confusion on her worn face. Her husband made her feel as if she were dealing with an afflicted man.

"It is harder to be subject than the object of an infirmity," he went on. "Do me the justice, Avis, to remember that I must suffer more in discovering that my affection is capable of change than you can in the consequences of such a fact."

"That will do," said Avis faintly, after a silence. "It is a waste of strength for us to talk. We do not understand each other."

"I repeat," he said more earnestly, "that I am sorry for the whole thing. You shall not be annoyed again. Don't take the children to father's just yet!" He leaned over her, smiling; but her soul sickened within her. He had rather expected to kiss her; but the expression of her mouth deterred him. He would as soon have dared to kiss the Melian Venus.

How could he know that a great impulse came upon her to throw herself upon his heart, and sob her misery out? It seemed incredible that Philip could not help her to bear it. They had been so dear to each other—for so long! Then she thought how he would soothe her, and how she should writhe to remember it. He did not love her. He was her husband. Humiliation beyond humiliation lay forever now in his caress. She gave him her hand gravely, like a courteous acquaintance.

She thought, "I would have clung to *you!*" But she said only,—

"Well, Philip, we must make the best we can of it." After a silence she added,—

"We shall always need each other's forbearance, though"— She could not bring herself to say, "though we have lost each other's love." And then Van ran in, radiant and indescribable. He had invited Mary Ann and the kitty to a party. He had been dressing his hair—with the prepared glue.

Barbara that afternoon curled *her* hair, with cheeks hotter than the seething tongs. She had made up her mind that it would be best for her to marry before long. She thought, perhaps, she had amused herself with men about long enough. Barbara was exceedingly disconcerted at what had happened. She hoped there would be no talk: Barbara could think of nothing worse than to be talked about. She had never forgotten herself before. In Barbara's "set" in Harmouth, young ladies did not flirt with married men. Barbara had never been the least in love with Philip Ostrander. But, strictly speaking, it could not be said that she had ever quite forgiven him for not having fallen in love with herself before he married Avis. Yet she knew it was expecting too much of the masculine perception that he should understand all that.

Probably he would go to his grave supposing that she cared.

No more subtly confusing type of woman than Barbara is as yet rudimentary in the world. That man must have a keen and modest eye who will distinguish her vanity from her tenderness, or her love of his admiration from her love of himself.

Barbara thought she should marry a minister.

One day not long after, John Rose ran over to High Street. There was a poor fellow who could not get a scholarship; and Mrs. Ostrander had promised some flannels to those Pinkham babies; and Coy sent over a taste of snow-pudding; and so on. But, when he went away, he put one finger upon Ostrander's arm with a delicate yet deepening pressure. Ostrander followed him at once to the street.

"I suppose you know," began John Rose, hesitating gravely, "at least I thought I had better call your attention to the fact, that Harmouth is very much occupied just now with—that accident in the dory."

"The—mischief it is!" said Ostrander, stopping short. There was a silence, in which the two young men walked up and down in front of the gate. Avis watched them from the windows contentedly. She always liked to see her husband and John Rose together. She thought, or rather she felt, that John's must be one of the golden natures of which it would be possible to say, as was said of one of the grandest of our time—the noblest words, that can be spoken of any human life,—"There never lived a truer friend."

Ostrander put his hand upon the other's shoulder as they walked, and leaned upon it heavily.

"Seriously so, Rose?" he asked.

"Not unkindly so, I think," said Rose thoughtfully; "but there is some unnecessary and annoying gossip. It will soon blow over; but I thought—excuse me, Phil—it would be as well for you to understand it at the outset."

"John," said Ostrander, after a longer silence than before, "if it be possible,—you will help me, old fellow, I know,—I hope my wife may never hear of this."

She never did.

CHAPTER XX

*"Every man has experienced
how feelings which end in
themselves, and do not express
themselves in action, leave the
heart debilitated. We get
feeble and sickly in character
when we feel keenly, and
cannot do the thing we feel."*
—Robertson [1]

In September the college papers announced that Professor Philip Ostrander had resigned the assistant geological chair in Harmouth University, on account of an increasing delicacy of the lungs, in consequence of which his physicians had forbidden all brain labor, and required a change of climate. It was understood that he would sail for Havre next week to spend the winter in the south of France. His resignation was deeply regretted by the Faculty and students. The academic year opened prosperously under the hands of Professor Brown, his successor. Professor Cobin was expected to resign at the close of the winter term.

Professor Ostrander was so feeble, that he had not been present at the Senior Party kindly given by Mrs. President Hogarth at the usual time. He had been as deeply missed in the drawing-room as he would be in the class-room, both of which locations he eminently graced.

Professor Brown was understood to be the man who had recently detected the precise difference between the frontal sinuses in the white and grisly bears. A brilliant career was predicted for him.

> Footnote.—A contributor adds, that he is also the discoverer of the left foramen of the third cervical vertebra of the first monkey who harmonized with the environment. It is needless to say that a Freshman bears the entire responsibility of this grave statement.

After the first strange chill was out of the lonely air, Avis was shocked to find her husband's absence a relief. He had become extremely irritable before he went away. The re-action from his college-work, and from his escapade with Barbara, had added mortification to mortification, under which he weakened petulantly.

Like all untuned natures, he grew discordant under the friction of care and trouble. He became really so ill, that Avis felt that not an hour should be lost in removing him from the immediate pressure of annoyances from which she could not shield him. It was she who passed lightly over the embarrassments and economies under which the projected journey must place the family. It was she who was sure they could get along till the lease of the house was out. It was she who was confident that rest would restore him, and that a future would await him. It was she who remembered the draughts that lurked for him, shaded the sun that dazzled him, cured the headaches that tore him, went away to amuse the children when they fretted him. Philip must have the cream-whip and the sherry, and the canter across country, and Europe, though the nurse were dismissed, and the seamstress abandoned, and the rent paid— Heaven help her!—out of that locked studio to whose cold and disused walls she should creep by and by with barren brain, and broken heart, and stiffened fingers.

Avis took the emergency in her own strong hand. She planned, she hoped, she commanded, she contrived. That intelligent self-surrender which is the supreme sign of strength, expressed itself in her with the pictorial graciousness peculiar to her special gift. She brought the whole force of her professional training to bear upon the shade of dye which might renew a baby's cloak. She made the very shoes that Van wore in those days,—poor little pathetic shoes, badly stitched, perhaps, but of exquisite color, and a temporary defiance to the family shoemaker. If only papa could have beefsteak at breakfast, the omelette need not be in a nicked platter; and a flower or so on the table gave Van a swelling consciousness of hilarious domestic dissipation, which obviated the gloom of absent luxuries.

"I am sorry to have you burdened with such petty economies," Philip had said one day. But he spoke with the polite reserve which had become habitual with him. He was always polite to his wife. He noticed her domestic ingenuities with approval. He said,—

"We never thought you would turn out so comfortable a housekeeper, did we, Avis?" with an absent-minded smile. And then he asked her what she did with his passports, and if she had packed the Calasaya bark,[2] and where was the lecture on "Chalk," which he thought he might have a chance to deliver in England. Avis answered patiently. She thought Philip walked about like a frostbitten man. A certain hardness in his nature, of which she could not be mistaken in fancying herself the especial object, developed itself in a delicate but freezing form, like the ice-scenery upon a window. It was with profound intellectual confusion that she remembered his first kiss. Was this the man who had wooed and won her with an idealizing gentleness which made of his incarnate love a thing divine? To admit it seemed like a challenge to the doctrine of personal identity. One day, spurred by a momentary impulse to leave no overture of wifely forgiveness and yearning unoffered, of whose omission she might think afterwards with that scorching self-rebuke in which all shallow pride shrivels to the bitterest ashes, she crept up to him and began timidly,—

"Philip, this poor old carmine shawl that you used to like so much is pretty well faded out. Do you remember the night when we first came home, when I had it on?"

"Yes, I remember," said Philip distinctly.

"We were very happy, Philip—then."

"Yes."

"Sometimes I wonder," tremulously, "if nothing in this world can ever make us feel so again."

"That," he said, regarding her with cool, distant eyes, "is entirely out of the question." The man whose unapproachable tenderness had spared the life of a dumb bird because it trusted him, could say this—to his wife. His voice had a fine, grating sound. It made Avis think of the salute of icebergs meeting and passing in the dark.

Yet we should see that, apparently, Philip Ostrander was as unconscious of cruelty as the burnt-out crater is of the snow that has sifted down its sides. It was his temperament, he reasoned, to express himself as he felt, and he certainly did not feel to his wife as he did when they first married. He saw no occasion for dwelling upon an ardor which marriage must inevitably chill. Avis's good sense must perceive this. Why should they trouble themselves? The daily annoyances and anxieties which the bond between them compelled them to share were as much, he thought, as either of them could bear just now, without adding any finer affectional subtleties to their burden. He wished with all his heart, he said, that it had been the necessary outgrowth of his nature to love with the poetic constancy natural to his wife. Events had proved that it was not. What, then, could he do? Ostrander pitied himself. He sincerely believed that he bore the heavier end of their mutual sorrow.

And now he was gone,

He had not, indeed, parted with his wife without emotion; but it was a perfectly silent one, like that of a man struggling with feelings ill defined to himself. He had hung over his boy, and clung to him, choking. He was very fond of Van.

His departure left Avis free for a space to wrestle as she might with the inevitable re-action of the last few months. In the calm of her first solitary hours she was chastened to perceive how her married story had deepened and broadened, nay, it seemed, created in her, certain quivering human sympathies. Her great love—so hardly won, so lightly cherished—withdrew upon itself in a silence through which all the saddened lovers of the world seemed to glide with outstretched hand, and minister to her,—a mighty company. Especially her heart leaned out to all denied and deserted women, to all deceived and trustful creatures. A strange kinship, too solemn for any superficial caste of the nature to blight, seemed to bind her to them all. Betrayed girls, abandoned wives, aged and neglected mothers, lived in her fancy with a new, exacting claim. To the meanest thing that trod the earth, small in all else, but large enough to love and suffer, her strong heart stooped, and said, "Thou—thou, too, art my sister."

Avis had been bred to the reticence not uncharacteristic of the New-England religion among its more cultivated, or at least, among its more studious possessors. She was one of those sincere and silent Christians with whom we must look more to the life than to the lip for the evidence of the faith that is in them. The professor's had been a home in which the religious character of his child was taken for granted, like her sense of delicacy. She was expected to be a Christian woman precisely as she was expected to be a cultivated lady: in a matter of course, abundant speech was a superfluous weakness. She had escaped the graver dangers of this training, but not its life-long influences. It was inevitable that the tragedy of her married life should result in a temporary syncope of faith, which it was equally inevitable that she should support in perfect solitude. But to dwell upon this phase of her experience would seem to copy the rude fault of those biographers that break faith with the personal confidence of the dead who can no longer protest.

With a terror for which I do not feel at liberty to find speech or language, Avis watched departing love shake the slow dust of his feet against her young life. With a dread which shook to the roots of belief, she perceived that her own slighted tenderness had now begun to chill. That Philip should cease to love her—this could be borne. There was a worse thing than that. All was hers while she yet loved him. She wrestled with her retreating affection as Jacob of old wrestled with the angel till break of day.[3] She struggled with that which was greater and graver than the sweet ghost of a ruined home. She fought for her faith in all that makes life a privilege, or death a joy.

No argument for the immortality of the human soul seemed to her so triumphant as the faith and constancy of one single human love.

· · · · · · · · · ·

"Mamma, has papa gone to Jerusalem?"

"No, my son. Mamma has told you a great many times where papa has gone."

"Jesus went to Jerusalem!" said Van with a reproving smile, quite gentle, and a little sad, as if his father had been caught in the omission of some vital religious duty. "But after I got frough crying, I fought I'd like to have him go. I'd rather kiss you myself, mamma. I don't like another man to do it. I'll have a wife of my own, when I get big enough he needn't fink!"

"There, Van; that's enough for now. Don't you see I am very busy painting? I can't kiss little boys *all* day. Run away now."

Van disappeared, not without something of the reluctance of a jealous lover drawing his first breath of bliss in the absence of his rival. Van's love for his mother was one of those select and serious passions which occasionally make the tie between son and mother an influence of complex power. She must be a woman of a rare maternal nature who will supersede in the heart of a man the mother who is capable of inspiring in the boy a love of this controlling and sensitive kind.

Scarcely had the palette-knife struck the cobalt to the Naples yellow, when the studio-door shivered, stirred, and started with a prolonged and inspiring creak. Van admitted his little nose on probation into the crack, and heaved a heart-breaking sigh.

"Mamma," very sweetly, "now *Philip* is gone, I suppose I may call you *Avis*, mayn't I?"

"Shut the door, Van."

His pretty mamma had an unhappy habit of expecting to be obeyed, which was a source of serious disorder to Van's small system of philosophy. He shut the door in—nose and all—with a filial haste and emphasis, the immediate consequences of which fell heavily upon both parties in this little domestic tragedy. When the outcry is over, and the sobbing has ceased, and the tears are kissed away, and the solid little sinner lies soothed upon the cramped and forgiving arm, where is the strength and glory of the vision? Where are the leaping fingers that quivered to do its bidding in the fresh life of the winter morning hour?

"Run away, again, Van: mother must go to work now."

"Mamma," faintly, "I've sat down on—somefing—soft. I'm all blue and colors, mamma, on my sack behind. I didn't know it was your palette, mamma. I didn't mean to. Oh! I'd rather not. I'd like a shair!"

"Mamma," presently from behind the locked door, "I want a piece o' punky-pie."

"No more pumpkin-pie, to-day, Van; and you mustn't talk to mamma through the door any more."

"Oh!—well, mamma, a *piece* o' punky-pie will do. I've had the
sherries. I've had twenty-free or nineteen canned sherries. Me and
the baby eat 'em. I eat the sherries, and she eated the stones,
mamma. I put 'em down her froat. She needn't have cried, I don't
fink. So I want a piece o' punky-pie."

Silence succeeds.

"Mamma, can't you kiss little boys *all* day? Not very *dee* little
boys, mamma?"

"By and by, Van. Run to Julia now. Run and play with your little
sister."

But Master Van stoutly maintained that he did not wish the society of his little sister. He thought his little sister had bumped
her head. He should axpect mamma would want to unlock the
door, and find out. If he had the mucilage-bottle, and papa's razor,
and the pretty purple ink (and the kiss), he would go and find out,
and never come up stairs any more.

"Mamma," by and by, "do you love my little sister best of me, or
me best of my little sister? I should fink you'd rather let me in and
tell me 'bout that.

"O mamma!" once more persuasively, "I want to say my prayers."

"To-night, Van, at bed-time."

"No, I want to say 'em quick vis minute. If you'll let me in to say
my prayers, I'll go straight down and see if Julia's got the cookies
done."

Love in the guise of religion, as ever since the world was young,
carried the yielding day before him. With despair in her heart and
the palette fresh from its service as a cricket in her hand, Avis ad-
mits the little devotee. Plump upon his knees upon the drying-
oil—in the unutterable background of that sack—drops Van, and
thus waylays the throne of grace,—

"O Lord! please to not let boys tell lies and say he's got a jack-
knife and a pistol in his pocket when he hasn't either one which
a boy did to Jack Rose and me this morning O Lord Amen. . . .
Mamma, I fink it was one of the Plimpton boys. *Now* will you kiss
me, mamma?"

And so, and so, and so—what art can tell us how? O golden
winter morning! your coy heart is repulsed forever; and when from
the depths of the house, sweeps, like a scythe upon the artist's
nerves, that sound which all the woman in her shrinks to hear,—
the cry of a hurt baby,—Avis with a sigh unlocks the studio-door.
There is the problem of ages in that speechless sigh. Van, all paint
and patience, like a spaniel lies curled upon the floor, with his lips
against the studio-door. The stout little lover, faithful in exile, has
lain and kissed the threshold till he has kissed himself asleep.

The rare tears filled Avis's eyes as she lifted him; and then Julia brought the baby, and the bump, and the brown paper. And there she was sitting, pinioned, with both children, patient and worn, with the bright colors of her paints around her, and the pictures, with their mute faces to the wall, about the room (there was a hand-organ, too, playing a dismal little tune somewhere down the street), when an impatient knock preceded a nervous push to the unlatched door, and, with the familiarity of art and age, her old master presented himself upon the scene.

Frederick Maynard stood still. He did not immediately speak. He looked from child to child, from both to her, from her to the barren easel. The dismal hand-organ below set up a discordant wail, the more pathetic for its discord, like all inharmonious things. The baby had pulled down Avis's pink neck-ribbon and her bright hair. The tears lay undried upon her cheek, whose color slowly stirred, and scorched her lifted, languid face.

"You see," she said, trying to smile, "how it is."

"I am not here to see any thing," answered the drawing-master shortly. "What have you done this week?"

"Nothing."

"Last week? The week before?"

"Nothing at all. Only the sketch for the crayon that you see. And I have begun to give drawing-lessons to Chatty Hogarth. Mr. Maynard, once a visitor came into Andrea del Sarto's studio. It was after his marriage. He was dabbling away at some little thing. He looked up and said, 'Once I worked for eternity: now I work for my kitchen."

"Confound the kitchen-work!" cried Maynard savagely. "Kitchen-work, indeed! Crayon portraits, I should think! Drawing-lessons if you dare! You—you! Why, I am sixty years old. I have never got a picture into the exhibition but once. There was a quarrel among the directors, and one fellow put my landscape in to spite another—but I've never thought the less of the landscape. And here are you with your sphinxes and your sphinxes—why, New York has gone wild over you in one week's time! Every studio in the city pricking up its ears, and 'The Easel' and 'The Blender' in a duel over the picture to start with. May Heaven bless them for it! Drawing-lessons, indeed!"

"Pray tell me," said Avis, growing very pale, and putting the children down, lest her faint arms should drop them,—"pray explain exactly what you mean. I do not understand. I have never heard from the picture since you sent it to New York. Has anybody noticed—will anybody buy my sphinx?"

"No," said the drawing-master with a short laugh. "I don't think anybody will buy the picture—just yet. Not immediately, that is. The trouble is, you see"—

"I expected trouble," sighed Avis patiently. "I am used to that. Don't mind telling me. *I* don't mind."

"Why, the only trouble is," said Frederick Maynard, "that the picture was caught up the second day out."

"Caught up?" asked Avis faintly.

"Engaged—bought—sold—paid for. The sphinx was sold before Goupil⁴ had held it forty-eight hours. Mind you don't let Goupil photograph it. You can't afford to photograph a fledgling. *You* have a future. 'The Easel' says it is a work of pure imagination. 'The Blender' says it shows signs of haste."

"'The Blender' is right," said Avis with returning breath and color. "That child in the foreground—the Arab child looking at the sphinx with his finger on his lips, swearing her to silence—do you remember? I put in that child in one hour. It was the day"—

She checked herself. Her husband himself should never know the story of that day—he would not understand. It would not have been to him as it was to her, coming down that morning, not a month after he had sailed, to find the dun for those college debts. Avis had the blind horror and shame of most delicate women in the presence of a debt. Her stinging impulse had been to discharge this without telling Philip or her father. Upon the spot she drew up an order for the sale of some bonds of her own, upon whose proceeds the family were in part dependent for the coming year. Fortunately she had not to deal with stock or real estate, which the wife cannot sell without the husband's consent. Avis did not know this. She knew nothing, except that she was grieved and shamed, and vaguely in need of money. She flew to the studio, struck the great sphinx dumb with the uplifted finger of a child, and sent it desperately from her before the cool of her frenzy fell.

"You are to make no more portraits, you understand," said Frederick Maynard, stumbling over Van, and narrowly escaping sitting on the baby as he went out. "You'll never be a portrait-painter. You must create: you cannot copy. That is what we lack in this country. We have no imagination. The sphinx is a creation. I told Goupil so when I took it on. He bowed politely. And now he comes asking for a photograph! You—*you!*—life is before you now. And I am sixty-three years old."

But Avis put her hand in his with a patient, unresponsive smile. She looked very gentle in her falling hair. The children clung to her. The light lay gravely on the studio-floor. She could hear the faint pulse of the sea, whose mighty heart beat between her and her husband, throbbing upon the frozen shore. The hand-organ in the street wailed on.

"Life is behind me too," she said gently. "It was before my marriage that I painted the sphinx. Don't be too much disappointed in me, if there are never any more pictures. Oh, I shall try! but I do not hope—do not think. We all have our lives to bear. If I, too, were sixty-three, perhaps—there, hush, my little girl!—perhaps—I should not—mind so much"—

"It seems to me," interrupted the drawing-master, winking resolutely, "that it can't be quite right for those children to look just as they do. Isn't there something a little peculiar in their expression?

Van was ingeniously trying to cut his throat with the palette-knife, and it would have been impossible to accuse the baby of not trying to swallow the tube of Prussian blue.

The year ran fleetly. Van was ailing a great deal that spring; and in the summer her father was ill. Thus, in the old, sad, subtle ways, Avis was exiled from the studio. She could not abandon herself to it without a feminine sense of guilt, under which women less tender may thrive callously, but at whose first touch she quivered with pain. She was stunned to find how her aspiration had emaciated during her married life. Household care had fed upon it like a disease. Sometimes she thought it an accession to her misery, that still, straight forever through the famine of her lot, its heart beat on, like that of the nervous physique, which is first to yield, but last to die. Then she wished, with all the wild, hot protest of her nature, that the spirit of this gift with which God had created her—in a mood of awful infinite irony, it seemed—would return to Him who gave it, that the dust of her days might descend to the dust in peace. She wished she were like other women,—content to stitch and sing, to sweep and smile. She bowed her face on the soft hair of her children; but she could not forget that they had been bought with a great price. She thought of the husband whose love she had mislaid, and counted the cost of her marriage in the blood of her soul.

·   ·   ·   ·   ·   ·   ·   ·   ·

"Mamma, I'm most damp and a little wet." Van, one sharp afternoon in September, said this hilariously. He and Wait had been to swim. They'd been to swim in the hogshead. Julia wouldn't put Wait in; but *he* got in. He got in like funder, while she went to tell of him. Then she came back and pulled him out. But there weren't any fishes in the hogshead, and he'd rather have his feet shanged now. What was the matter, mamma?

"O Lord!" said Van, kneeling, swaddled in his mother's rose-colored shoulder-robe at his prayers that night,—"O Lord! I know you've got a great many little boys to fink of; but I hope you'll remember I've got a sore froat."

And now what was the matter, again, mamma? Somefing was always the matter, Van thought to-day. He wished there had never any such day been born.

"*Lo!*" echoed the heart of the mother, "*let that day be darkness; neither let the light shine upon it. As for that night, let darkness seize upon it. Lo! let that night be solitary; let no joyful voice come therein.*"

With the frosty dawn the child lay very ill. Before another night an acute form of pneumonia had developed itself. Sensitive from birth, the boy's lungs succumbed with only a frail struggle. For fifteen days and nights his mother hung over him in her strong, dumb way. Then, perhaps, she first understood the solemn depth of the tie, which, through all distance and all difference, all trial and all time, binds any two human creatures who have bestowed life upon a third. In this awful language of bereavement which God was setting her ignorant youth to learn, her own loss seemed to her but the alphabet of agony. Her heart yearned with unspoken and unspeakable throes over the father of her child. That this must be; that the lips of his first-born should grow cold without his good-by kiss; that Philip, somewhere wide across the world, should that day be strolling and laughing in the sun, not knowing,—this seemed to her the very sense and soul of her sorrow. She saw him go chatting with a group of sight-seekers down a bright street, idling in a chapel at the mass, buying a ticket for the opera, twirling a lady's fan beneath a chandelier, praising the claret at the hotels, drumming with his finger to the music in the beer-garden, stopping at the toy-shop windows to decide what he would get for Van, writing notes, perhaps, to the little fellow (he wrote to Van a good deal) at that moment; while the boy struggled on her nerveless arm, to turn and say,—

"Mamma, will papa come walking in?"

"Some day, Van, some time."

"Will he come in at the front-door, mamma, to kiss his dee little boy?"

"O my darling! Some time—somewhere—yes."

"I fought I heard somebody at the front-door, mamma."

"It is the wind we hear, Van."

"Can't papa get home on the wind? Can't papa—walk—on the wings—of the wind? God did. I fought papa could, mamma."

. . . .

"Mamma, do you love my little sister best of me? or me—best"—

Best, oh, best, that moment, Van, of all the empty world!

CHAPTER XXI

"There above the little grave
Oh! there above the little
grave,
We kissed again with tears."[1]

The wind was high about the house. Aunt Chloe and the professor had left her at last alone to sit and listen to it. The baby slept. The women had gone sobbing away. The windows stood wide to the bitter dark in that room up stairs. The child's bed was straight and still. It was a wild night for the little fellow to be lying out there—his first night.

Avis was almost sorry that night that they had laid him so near the sea; for the sea was high too, like the wind, and thundered heavily, even here, sharp through the sheltered house. He had always been a wakeful baby, quick to start and shiver in his naps. She could not rid herself of the feeling that the noise would disturb him. The imperious mother's habit of three years and a half of nervous care was strong upon her. She could have dashed out and hushed the voice of the almighty deep, lest it should wake the child.

Pursued with this and a horde of the irrational impulses of solitary grief, Avis sought refuge in her first attempt to write to the boy's father. The arm upon which Van had lain, with imperfect intervals of relief, for fifteen days and nights (it had been only in one position that the child could breathe) refused to hold the pen. She wrote with her left hand, a faint and feeble cipher. She told him what there was to tell, sparing when she could, striking as she must. She begged him not to let this make any alteration in the plans which his state of health should suggest as wisest and best for them all,—they who were left,—they three. She hoped he would not allow any impetuous image of loneliness at home to hasten his return before the time which he had selected as desirable in itself, and urged upon him that a part or the whole of his second winter should be spent in those kinder climates which would perfect the growth of his now really grafted strength. Of herself and her own loss or lot, she wrote but little. Of the solitude in which she bore the burden laid on two, she did not speak. Of her unshared fears, her unkissed tears, she could not tell. She was an unloved wife. She could not woo her husband.

As she wrote, the wind went busying itself impetuously as a

lawless feeling, with the calm of the house. It beat upon the ear with a slow, increasing throb, like the purpose of an advancing tide. At short intervals the roar uprose, as the "third wave" rises on the coast, and splashed upon the walls and roof. About the doors and windows unpleasant sounds set in steadily: Avis tried to think that they were like the sobbing of the shingle on the shore. She could not, would not, must not, think—wild night, be so merciful as that!—that she may not think what else the wind is like.

She had finished and sealed her letter. She had sealed the letter, and laid it down, and was turning to step and see if her little daughter on the sofa by her side slept warm, when, in the swelling of the storm, the front-door blew violently open.

She sprang to shut it, latching the door of the room behind her. As she stepped into the hall, the light went out. Rain blew in upon her face. She groped her way to the door, pushing it feebly—she was so worn—against the resistance of the wind. The solid oaken panel baffled her as if human hands had been behind it. If a human voice had called her,—

"Avis?"

Swift as the superstitions that we would not, if we could, disown, flashed the memory of the little lover, calm out there in the discord of the elements, stealing up with brimming face to say,—

"Mamma, now papa is gone, I suppose I may call you *Avis?*"

Avis could not have denied a genuine shock, when, stretching out her hands, inch by inch along the wall and still defiant door, they fell in the dead dark upon an arm of flesh and blood.

"Avis, what is the matter? Where is the light? Do let me in, and shut this superhuman door! There! Have I frightened you? I thought you would know when you heard me speak. Do let us get out of this hideous dark!"

"*Philip!* O Philip! yes, let us get out of the dark!"

Her own words appealed with an entreating significance to her own ears at that moment as they went groping together to the light. He had caught her in his nervous arms; that, she said to herself, was a matter of course. He first found the latch, and staggered in. The room was warm, and seemed to palpitate with light. The baby on the sofa slept peacefully. The books—it was his study—turned their familiar shoulders to him, and their open faces looked from the table where his wife's sealed letter lay.

"Writing to me, were you, Avis?" He started on the purposeless instinct that leads one to open the unsealed letter that he will not read, as nature leads a dog to hide the bone that he does not want. Avis, in passing the table, hit the envelope with her drapery sleeve, and it fell into the waste-basket.

"Never mind!" he said uneasily. "What do we want of letters now?"

Then in the full light she saw how rain-beaten and haggard he was.

"Let me help you with your coat, Philip," gently. "And wait— Oh, how wet you are! Your slippers are just where you left them. I have let nobody touch them all this while. See! And the fire is warm." Like a child she led him; like a child he submitted. She would not question him or chatter now. It was plain that something had befallen. But trouble could wait. Care was too old a friend not to be put by. He had come. Her husband had come back to her.

He flung himself down in his old chair in his old way. His breath came short. He began at once,—

"I was horribly sick in London. I've had two attacks of hemorrhage. There was no time to let you know. I got to Liverpool, and took the first steamer. I was afraid I shouldn't get home."

"But you got home, Philip!" her voice snapped with a wiry cry. "You are here, you are here!"

"Thank God, yes!"

He laid his head back, and closed his eyes wearily. When Avis stirred, he put his hand to detain her. The color came into her hollow face.

"Must you go?" he asked softly.

"Only to see about supper for you, Philip. You are faint, you see; that is all," decidedly,—"only faint. A good hot supper and a long night's rest will set you right." She brought the words out so pathetically, "a long night's rest,"—she who had not rested for so many nights,—that his attention was at once attracted to her appearance. He sat up, rousing with the nervous rapidity natural to him.

"Avis, how you look! Have you looked like that ever since I have been gone?"

"We have had sickness in the house," she said quietly.

"Sickness? Where is Van?"

"Van is asleep, Philip," after a well-nigh imperceptible pause.

"And the baby? Is that the little lady, that bundle on the sofa? Can you bring her to me, Avis? I am stronger now,—stronger already. I want to kiss one of the children. I meant it should have been Van first. I thought about it in the cars. But never mind. I want to see the lassie. Let me see: we named her after mother, didn't we? Does she look like any of us, Avis? Does she look like you? You didn't say when you wrote. You didn't say much about yourself. But I was glad to hear so much about the children. It did me good. Now let me see her—let me see the baby."

Avis brought the child, so gently that she did not wake. She drew a chair up, for she could not stand, and sat down beside her husband with the baby on her knee. As she did so, his unstrung voice went strolling on,—

"How the wind does flog this house! I'm glad to be at home; glad we're all safe under shelter together. It sounds as if there were a child shut out there, crying to be let in. But *our* little folks are warm. Your hands tremble, Avis. Are you quite well?"

"Quite well; only tired, Philip. Shall I see about the supper now?"

"No, not now. I don't want supper. How the little thing has grown! Are you as fond of her, Avis, as you were of the boy? You used to say you were afraid you should love the girl the better. Has Van grown so I sha'n't know him? Little rascal! I've kept the tintype you sent—see—in my wallet. I've carried it all about. I was sorry you couldn't afford a photograph. I showed it to some people in Paris—some ladies. They called him a beautiful boy. No, please, Avis, don't go. Indeed, I cannot eat. What has become of that little teapot we used to make tea in, right here over the fire, so long ago? The first year, don't you remember" (half fretfully, for Avis did not answer), "when I used to come in tired from Faculty meetings—after everybody else was in bed? You used to make it—kneeling by the fire—on that cricket. I think it was a Japanese teapot. Is it broken? Can't we have that?"

"If you want it, Philip, surely. I can find the teapot. Can you hold the baby? or shall I take her back?"

"No, I'd rather hold her. Don't be gone long, will you? You can't think how it is to get home, how it looks,—the fire, the books,—and to see you moving about. You can't think what a fool it makes of me," laughing boyishly. "No man knows what it will make of him, till he has tried it. A whole year travelling alone; and to be sick among strangers! Oh! I thought I should never get back, nor see the children, nor— Oh, it is so pleasant, so pleasant! And I am pretty weak yet. Don't laugh at me. When I've had the tea,—but be sure you get that teapot,—I shall be a man again. I'm nothing but a mass of nerves and seasickness, and sore lungs, just now—it was so cold on the steamer! When I've had the tea, I can see Van, can't I?—No, that was the cricket, this one. Move it a little. You used to kneel on this side. Yes, that is the very teapot. I wonder if it will taste as it used to. I don't see why nobody wrote me how thin you had grown. Oh, I am so tired! It is so pleasant here, so pleasant!"

Thus he wandered on. Avis made the tea, and they drank it together: his eyes followed her. The child slept upon his knee.

"When the trunks come—I'm as bad as a child: I can't wait to show you what I've got for Van (do you remember how we never could wait with our Christmas presents—you and I—those first years? how we used to come skulking round to show them to each other beforehand, and how you laughed at me; but you were the worst yourself). There's a doll for the girl; but I stumbled on such an amazing French notion for *him:* I expect you'll never forgive me. It's a little fire-engine, Avis,—really an exquisite toy. I don't know but he'll be setting us all on fire, little villain! There's something for you, too, somewhere. That's the only pleasant part of going away,—getting ready to come home. A man never knows what his home's worth to him, till he's turned his back on it. I got Van a 'Pilgrim's Progress' too,—the best copy I could find in all London. It took me three days to select that book. I want he should have something to remember his father by, that he'll value when he is a man, and I am"—

He broke off. It has been said that the soul, which has always some influence over the muscles, has none over the blood. Avis supposed that she might betray, but had no conception of the fact that she emphasized, the character of what she was enduring. Rings of blackness slowly enlarged upon her face, like the shadow of an advancing storm upon a writhing lake. But she sat with her head turned from him slightly, bent, like a Mater Dolorosa,[2] over the baby whom she had taken into her own arms.

"Better, Philip, now?" She must say something.

"Oh, so much better—so much stronger! I don't know but it will make a live man of me, after all, coming home. Really, Avis, I don't know but that was all I needed. It's such a mistake, this sending sick people philandering all over the world alone. A sick man wants his fireside, and his books, and familiar ways, and all his little silly, selfish comforts, and not to have to take his slippers out of a trunk, and a Japanese teapot, I believe," he rose, laughing hysterically, "and—some one to make the tea on a cricket by the fire; and his— Come, Avis, now let us go up and see the boy."

"Are you quite strong enough yet, Philip?"

"Yes, yes, yes!" impatiently. "Don't fret over me. I can't wait any longer. Take me to see Van at once."

"Are you sure, Philip, that it is best—to wake Van to-night? He sleeps—so soundly"— She struggled for controlled speech, blindly beating about with the mad instinct of love, which would fain believe that to save time is to save suffering.

But now she turned her face, and its mortal color swept upon him. Slowly, then, it extended itself to his own, as if they had stepped hand in hand—she leading and he leaning—into a half-lit world.

"Avis, how many nights did you tell me you sat watching?"
"I did not tell you, Philip."
"You flit about me like—the shadow of a bird that I cannot see.

You defy me, you escape me, as the dying escape the living. I have never seen you look so. It has been coming on a long time. Somebody should have told me. And here I am—a burden, a wreck,—a broken-down fellow, on your hands. It seems a hideous irony in fate to throw the care of a consumptive on such wasted hands. Let me look at them. Don't be afraid. I will not hold them longer than you like. If there were any thing else to be done—anywhere we could go! I could fight hard for life, I think. That's half the battle, they say. It doesn't come natural to a man of my age to sit down and die, like a weasel in a trap. If you had been with me in France—if I hadn't gone alone,—but what's the use in dissecting old blunders? A blunder's a blunder, and done with it, only we'll do better next time, if we can—eh, Avis?"

If there were an undertone of symbolism in his words, it was too slight, perhaps, to expect her to recognize it. He watched her with his blind gaze; but he watched her constantly. She was used to it in these days: Van used to watch her so, after he had been taken sick. There had been no "scenes" between Avis and her husband since he had come home. They were neither of them quite strong enough for that. They lived on and on, as those live who know that one touch of mutual recognition, nay, even of self-recognition of certain emotions, will bring down upon them a land-slide of gnarled and knotted things, whose upheaval would tear the roots of soul and body. They cultivated that dullness to their own capacity of feeling, which, when thoroughly acquired, amounts to a sixth sense, and becomes an element of character more powerful than the feeling itself. The divergence between them had been too wide for them to resume that superficial comprehension of one another, and that crude standard of affection through which the initiatory phases of married life revolve.

Avis did not think that her husband was going to die. But come life or death, come love or loathing, they should be honest with themselves, they two, to the heart's core now. She devoted herself to his invalid wants with the infinite tenderness as natural to her as her sweet and even breath. But he said to himself sometimes,—

"She would do as much for a hurt dog." For her, she moved about uncertainly. She seemed to herself like one who listens to the interlude in some nameless music, some long symphony whose chords strike all around the world.

All the while she was conscious of crouching like a tigress to save his life.

One day, as he went pacing the house importunately; coming in now and then to lay the incoherent plans and hopes of disease before her; running to her with every sore mood, as Van used to run with every scratch; wondering, should he try Colorado, the South,

California, that place in New Jersey people called the Nice of America, electricity, mesmerism, inhalation, Spiritualism, or the prayer-cure?—she put down her work (her reluctant fingers took many nervous and extremely irregular stitches in those days), and said,—

"Philip, suppose *I* decide this matter for you?"

"I wish you would!" he cried, stopping short. "The most humiliating aspect of sickness is the irresolution it produces. A man's brain becomes a shuttlecock. Mine is sore—what there is of it now—with surging to and fro from plan to plan. And something we *must* do. I won't die without a tussle—yet."

"It is out of the question, Philip," quietly,—"your dying, I mean. That we will not contemplate for a moment. But we will not risk a Harmouth winter just now. Shall you feel at rest to leave it to me,—what we do, and how, and all about it? Shall you feel the confidence in my judgment which will be necessary to the success of any plan?"

"I do not know how a man could have reason to feel more confidence—in any creature," he said in a low voice, throwing himself on the lounge beside her. He was wondering with solemn shame what kind of a fellow he should have turned out, for instance, if he had been obliged to provide good judgment for two. At that moment he was thinking, perhaps for the first time quite distinctly, what a rock in the topography of a man's life, what a corner-stone of granite in a human home, is the nature of a strong wife. All that was strong in himself stood, as column stands to column, in proud comradeship to it. All that was weakest of him leaned upon her with increasing naturalness, as if upon some mysterious maternal power, as we all of us, soul of man and soul of woman, lean alike without dispute or shame, upon the mammoth motherhood of Nature.

After a silence in which she too, perhaps, went her own way into unspoken and not unkindly revery, they resumed their conversation gently.

"Then, Philip, if you leave it to me, we will go South. You've tried climate and solitude: now we'll try climate and l— and care."

"Very well, Avis. And the baby?"

"Aunt Chloe will take the baby."

"Very well, Avis. Do you propose to beg, borrow, or steal?"

"Father and aunt Chloe were anxious to help us. But"—she hesitated.

"Of course. Father and aunt Chloe are very kind. I think, however, I will open a sanitarium as soon as we get—somewhere. I shall be quite able." He began to pace the room again, with blind and bitter feet.

"But Philip—it will not be necessary, I think. I forgot to tell you. While you were gone a piece of luck came to us. I sold the sphinx. And I have just arranged with Goupil. He is to photograph it. There is a demand for the picture. We shall have money enough this winter. I thought perhaps—I hoped—you would like it better so." But she faltered.

When he spoke, which was not for some minutes, he said in a low voice,—

"Was it best for you, best for the picture, to let the photographs go?"

"Not best for the picture," said Avis, with her instinctive honesty, "but best for me, best for us all now. And there is indeed nothing to regret. I shall not paint another picture—at present."

"Why not?"

"Let us not talk about it, Philip"—she whitened slowly about the mouth—"I—can't discuss it." But she collected herself at once; and, when he began to chatter about the sanitarium, she listened with the patience which we lend so readily to the sick, blessed beyond all small or selfish joy if we may indulge at any cost the weakness which was once the thorn in the flesh of our days.

But, when she had left him alone presently, Ostrander sat with knotted brows. He was thinking about the sphinx. Avis's success—mutilated though it was by care and trouble, nay, most of all, by his own failure—contrasted rather bitterly with his own drooping fortune. Was it possible for a man to be jealous of a woman, and that woman his own wife? The noble color burned Ostrander's sunken face. "Before I sink so low as that," he said, "it will be time for me to die."

CHAPTER XXII

PRINCE: *"Enough. The memory*
of the past be razed."
MARIA: *"Are you a God?"*
—Kotzebue [1]

Delicate as the marriage of
shades in a Florida shell, is the tutelage which prepares the eye of
the traveller for the soul of the Florida sun. They yielded themselves
to it, like children to a teacher. Solitude is a stern master, and will
have from us all some form of surrender. Theirs, for they journeyed
quite alone, taught them, first and above all else, what the anxious
brain, and wearied body, and breaking heart most blindly buffet and
most thirstily receive—the influence of atmosphere.

It was to Avis one of those subtle experiences whose suave surprise lends a new outlook to the possible evolution of character
from the probable novelty of scenery in the life which is to follow
this, when, from the narrow windows of the cars she overtook the
widening of the infinite Southern heavens, day by day.

Upon the palette of the sky relaxing Nature spread her colors, as
the human artist does, deepening from the pallor to the flesh.
Their last Northern sunset was cold, polished, and perfect as a
pearl. The first Virginia dawn unfolded like a tea-rose leaf. Down
through the great barrens the passion grew: eternal fire sat sen-
tinel upon the low horizon of Carolina; Georgia took up the torch,
and ran with it, like a will-o'-the-wisp, from swamp to swamp,
swift to the everglades, where Florida kneeled in purple and scarlet, like a queen who was crowned in prayer.

"And the evening and the morning were the third day." [2] Avis,
half to her husband, more to herself, said this dreamily as they put
the first foot upon the white-hot sand. She was a little sorry when
she had said it. The words bore her imagination captive at once
into that powerful old Bible allegory, in which the love of married
man and woman was found the last and greatest, as it was the most
intricate, of God's creative acts. She had no doubt that Philip's
fancy was as swift as her own to go wandering, (ah, how home-
lessly!) led by her chance word so, and that to him, as to her, the
broad bosom of the St. John's River unveiled itself with a fantastic
mockery, as the wave of the river of life may have flashed through
parting boughs that the wind beat when exiled eyes, over shamed
and shrinking shoulders, yearned to Eden.

For Philip's fancy was never dull; and in their early married days they had dwelt much in that delicate, visionary world, in which imaginative lovers find the keenest and the most permanent (because the most varied) stimulus to joy that human feeling knows. These little fables, phrases of their courtship and bridal years, rushed upon her memory that day, through the blazing hours of their sail down the river to the Ancient City by the Sea.[3] Tricks of speech or eye or smile, daily ambuscades of love, all the tactics of the heart that she had long forgotten, presented themselves to her thought persistently. Dead days stalked by her, as the dead trees stalked down the strange and silent shores,—days whose dawn and twilight, whose midnight and whose noon, unfolded each a new petal in the solemn flower of love. Scenes that she could have stunned herself into forgetting, emotions which she would have thought it incredible that she could revivify, pursued her. Her past arose with its grave-clothes on. Her buried tenderness confronted her with the awful immortality given to love, and to love alone, of all births bestowed upon the breathing soul. She had not thought ever to remember, even in heaven, where memory must be the shadow by which we read the dial of joy, hordes of these things that began to oversweep the defiance of her self-defensive calm.

She felt a certain petulance with the surroundings which wrought this mood within her. She did not remember in any of her wanderings to have so quarrelled with the introspective influence of travel. She reminded herself that she had not come to Florida to grow maudlin with drugged sentiment. Her thought stepped out like a disembodied spirit, and took a survey of herself, as she sat there on that boat,—a hollow-eyed woman, past her first youth, economically dressed, come thirteen hundred miles to nurse a consumptive husband—as was clearly her duty—through the winter. She glanced about the boat, and wondered if they looked like the other married people there, she and Philip,—pale, fretful couples, fatigued with the dust, the jar, the heat, the homelessness, of travel; fatigued, above all, she thought, with each other; as if marriage had become to most of them an eternal evening party, in which each believes himself to be of all men most miserable, but gets him into his white gloves conscientiously, lest society strike him from her calling-list.

Like those two young people, for instance, on the after-deck near her; they could not be out of their twenties, poor things, yet clearly there was no longer any splendor in the grass, or glory in the flower, of life, to them. She was the invalid, irritable, and a hard, ill-controlled cougher: he was tired out; their children were with them, and hung about, crying for their dinner. The sick woman complained of every thing, and wished they had never come to Florida. Her husband looked on, poor fellow, in the perfect silence in which the husband of a weak woman, unless he be the weaker of the two, learns to shelter both himself and her. They made a dull, realistic Dutch picture, sitting by themselves, miserably on the hot deck. The very cinders on those people, deep from three days' car-travel, seemed to Avis somehow to accentuate the emphasis of their plain and disenchanted lot. She forgot that she and Philip were just as black.

She wondered what Philip was thinking. He had strengthened, rather than weakened, with the effort of travelling; sitting out on the platform of the creeping cars in the wonderful Georgia weather, hour after hour, like a boy on his first journey; drinking down the froth of the sunlight as frozen men drink wine; chatting with the captain on the little boat, and laughing—she could hear him laugh. It struck her with a certain slight bitterness, of which she was thoroughly ashamed, poor girl! as she sat there alone, that he could laugh like that; that he, too, was not driven by the Florida scenery into small, cynical visions of his neighbors, seeing all life and all love in the Claude Lorraine[4] of their own darkened story. It did not occur to her just then that it was not easy to foretell where a fine influence, in particular a tropical influence, would drive her husband—in a state of mental isolation like this that had befallen them both—to the captain, perhaps, precisely, or to that very cross couple on the after-deck, whose little boy he was now leading away to the wheel-house so tenderly. Philip could be very tender when he would; God had never made a tenderer man. He brought the boy to her presently,—a pleasant little fellow. The tears were still wet on the child's now radiant cheek. Avis stooped and kissed them away, as she would have brushed a speck from a flower. But, when she lifted her face, her husband was watching her, and, as their eyes met, both filled. The child ran back to his parents. He sat down beside her.

"He is about the size of"—

"Yes, yes," said Avis quickly.

"And did you notice, Avis, a little something about the eye-lashes?—some trick or turn? I thought him almost like, at first. But nobody is like Van, I think.—Avis, do you see what a miracle it is? How I bear this journey? Is there room for me here? I don't want to crowd you. We are going to get in late, the captain says. We shall see the sunset and the moonrise, this first night, in this solitary place."

His voice sunk to a certain solemnity as he drew nearer to her, and they leaned over the deck-rail to watch the shadows gather on the water and the pathless shore.

His face, too, as his wife borrowed a look at it in the struggling light, had settled into a solemn cast, like beautiful hardening clay. His sunken eye swept the long untrodden shores, the opaque water, the beckoning sky. This, then, was Florida, where he was to get well, or—

"What is it, Philip?"

Indefinable as the gradation by which the pall of the thickets melted to the blazonry above the forest-tops was the motion with which she stirred towards him. Uncertain as the leaning of the light upon the perturbed river, to whose heart no eye could see, was the impulse of the hand which he held—groping a little, for it darkened now—to hers.

"I was thinking," he said, "that we have never been in such a solitary place. You don't mind our watching the moonrise together? We haven't done such a silly thing—for so long!"

He laughed rather nervously; but for her, she did not trust herself to speak. On either hand the forest glided by,—the awful forest in which no man trod. The river, like all things which seem to enlarge as they become absorbent of light, broadened beneath the rising moon. The fine outline of the pine-fronds and the blurred gray tendrils of the abundant moss made the sole change of accent in the level horizon; and this itself acquired a depressing quality, like that of a sweet but monotonous voice. Their little boat hung, the only sign of breathing life, pivoted in a trinity of isolation, a wilderness of water, forest, and sky. As the moon rode higher, the people on the deck hushed one by one, families gathered in silent groups, and the tired children slept. The woman who coughed so crossly had gone below.

Instinctively, as they rounded into the desolate landing at Tocoi,[5] Avis crept nearer to her husband. There was something of superstition, perhaps, in the repressed shudder with which she shrank from the innocent outline of the clumsy little train that waited for them. She was so tired, that every thing took a symbolic form to her. Her swift, outreaching sympathy gathered in all the other women who had trod this dreary shore before her, homeless, anxious, and careworn, battling for a husband's life. It seemed as much of a wrench to the reason to believe that beyond that eternal forest an unseen sea could beat, as, in our earthlier moments, it seems to the finest spirit among us, that life can leap again beyond the everglades of death.

As they cut their awed way through it, looking out from the wide doors of the rude car, Ostrander said,—

"I am sure I never was in quite such a lonely place in all my life; were you, Avis?"

"Never, Philip."

The simple question was lightly asked, the quiet answer quickly given; yet both fell silent, as if their lips had learned the words of some grave and embarrassing confession. Avis trembled beside her husband, sitting there in the dark car. He put his hand upon hers: it was the first time for a long while. Her pulse bounded so that he removed it. His wife was not a woman to be won lightly for the second time. Caresses could not transfigure for her the nature that had once defaulted to her. No hysteric feeling, warm to-day and chilled to-morrow, could restore to her the shores of reverence upon which her own unfathomable tenderness had surged. Integral and individual as her own must be the allegiance which would be found worthy to renew the exhausted tide of wedded joy. Thus he thought, with sad, abundant pride. He would not have had it otherwise with her for their joy's sake. They two, alone there, seemed to him to stand separate and strange, bringing a soul-sickness deeper than the body's hurt to the healing of this new and gentle land.

When they had got into their hotel that night, he lay and watched her quite silently. He was, after all, more exhausted than he had thought. When she had ordered up his tea, and dismissed the waiter, he asked her, too, to rest. She thanked him for his thoughtfulness, but moved about, busying herself for his comfort, in the little, brightly-lighted, barren room. There was an open fire-place, and a log of light-wood burning in it. She stirred through the resinous, red air, in her gray dress anad soft lace: she had not put on mourning for her boy. She knew that her husband was watching her; but she did not know what a sweet shyness was upon herself, upon her averted figure and unresponsive eyes.

She came and sat down by him presently; the light-wood faded quietly on the hearth. Their neighbor, the sick woman from the boat, was fretting faintly in the adjoining room. It seemed very still with them, and sheltered.

"Are you resting, Philip?"

"Quite rested. And you—are you content? Are you glad we came—this long distance—by ourselves?"

"When we have heard from the baby, we shall be quite content, Philip. There will be letters to-morrow, perhaps."

"How strange it is, Avis—being together so—without the children. We have never travelled alone before, like this, at least, since our wedding-journey. Had you thought of that?"

"Yes, Philip," after a pause.

"It is so pleasant—to me. Do you like it, Avis? Sha'n't you find it a terrible drag, shut up with a whimsical sick fellow for so many months?"

She lifted her face to check him for the idle question, and with it her strong, warm hand. He bowed his head reverently, laying his pale cheek upon it. Her own flushed like a girl's; but she said nothing. Thus, still clinging to her, the sick man slept.

Avis's hand grew numb: she did not move it. She sat on in the dark, for the fire died. The poor woman slept, too, in the next room. She heard the sounds of summer through the open window in the strange December air. In her married life she turned a noiseless leaf.

Ostrander was not without his full share of the prejudices common to men who have received, at whatever remote period in a life which has run counter to it, the education of the medical school. He had an array of opinions upon the sanitary effects and prospects of the State of Florida, with which he treated his wife, boyishly enough perhaps, as the wisdom of his selection seemed to make itself manifest in his own case. Avis heard him with relaxing eyes. As he gained in strength, the tension of care loosened a little in herself. Nerve by nerve, and muscle by muscle, it seemed, her watchful body yielded to the absence of demand upon its resistance in the unassertant air.

The poor girl was almost in as much need as he of the atmosphere in which sorrow seems an infringement of a newly discovered law, and care a crime against an hitherto unguessed, but here unguarded and undiverted love.

They settled themselves in a yellow, old coquina house: there were orange-trees about it, kneeling with their amber lamps; the windows of their room looked to the warm brown water; strange birds swayed by in the flushed air. Ostrander was excited by every thing: he ran in and out like a child. He kept coming up to her, and saying,—

"Avis, don't you think we shall like it?"

When they had been there a day or two, he told her those people from the boat were of their fellow-boarders. Avis idly asked if he knew their names.

"Oh, yes!" he said, "it's a French name,—Smith." Then, when they both laughed merrily, she wondered at the lifting of her heart. It reminded her of how it was on their wedding-journey, when they found each other so amusing, and laughter leaped so lightly to their happy lips.

One day he drooped a little with a cold, or some of the slight hinderances which stay the motion of the spheres for the invalid and those who minister to him; and then he began to worry about the prospects of the family if he should fail, after all, to get up again.

"I should be surprised," said his wife in her quiet way, "if I could not support this family, whatever happened. If you fret yourself sick, I shall certainly have to do it."

"Do you really think you could?" he urged anxiously. "It would be such a relief to think—to know!— You could, if any woman could. It would be so different if you made it a point, if every thing bent to it. Once you might have done any thing you would. What a future you had, Avis, when I came in your way! I don't know how to make you believe—that I didn't mean to blight it all."

"I know, I know, Philip." But her breath began to shorten.

"It's a pretty hard thing, after all, when a man and woman have actually married, not to let things go like the rest of the world," he said, looking up rather helplessly. "But perhaps, if I had helped you more—cared and planned— I don't see how it all came about. We didn't mean it to be so when we married, did we, Avis?"

She did not answer. Her thoughts rushed back through the veins of all those years, like driven blood. She put her hand to her throat. She felt choked, as if with a physical congestion. A passion is a passion, be it of the intellect or of the heart; and a denied aspiration dies, perhaps, more dumbly, but never less drearily, than a denied love.

"Avis! Have you minded so much? And I have been so absorbed— and did not see. Why, my poor girl! Why, Avis!"

For Avis, taken unawares by his tenderness, hating herself for the weakness to which, in all their married life, her husband had never seen her yield before, burst into a paroxysm of the terrible tears which lie in wait to avenge themselves upon all opulent self-control.

CHAPTER XXIII

"I ride from land to land,
I sail from sea to sea,
Some day more kind I fate
may find,
Some night kiss thee."
—Spanish Ballad [1]

The escaped, longer than the uncaptured emotion stands at bay. Ostrander was conscious that it required very different elements of the nature to woo the bruised affection of the wife from those which had won the hard surrender of the maiden's love: the one thing might be done by the complexity, the other only by the force, of character. With the unappeasable self-regret born of the self-knowledge which only the nearest relations of life can create in us, he thought of that drooping calyx of reverence in his wife's heart, which all time might not now be long enough for the dew of his gathered and gathering fealty of feeling to refill. In his stronger moments he kneeled before his lost ideal of himself, as the select three [2] kneeled upon the Mount of Transfiguration before a vanished God: in his weaker ones he tried to forget it. In the first he despaired of her; in the other he yearned for her. Her allegiance without her respect taunted him; her tenderness without her trust shamed him. Ostrander's love for his wife had been the supreme fact of his life. In his expressive medical phrase, he recognized it as one of the proximate principles of his soul. No other woman, or so he believed, could have commanded so long, or reclaimed so autocratically, the tissue of his elastic fancy. He was at a loss how to approach her gentle and devoted calm. He mourned his own crippled power to command in her that idealization which is the essential condition of the love that woman bears to man.

Regret, which had been sentiment at home, was sentience in Florida. The sunlight fell in golden showers, through which they trod athirst. All the colors of life deepened in this prismatic land. They walked with joined hands, but averted faces. The splendor slept upon the warm, strange water, upon the mosaic of shell-strewn sand, the green pulses of the orange-leaves, the veiled crimson heart of the banana-blossom, the bursting mood of the pomegranate; but neither saw that upon the cheek of the other the same glow lay.

One day he said something, carelessly enough, about a beautiful Parisian whom he met at this time last year; and then, turning, he surprised the slow color climbing his wife's face. He came close to her at once, and said with a certain gentle authority,—

"Avis, look at me, please. So; that will do. Now listen. Once before, when I spoke of people I had met, you looked like that. It was the night I came back, sitting by the fire at home; even then,—*that* night. Grant me at least the justice of remembering that a man doesn't make a fool of himself—in such a way—more than once; and believe that I had the brains to profit by a bitter lesson, if you cannot give me credit for the heart. Even if you cannot see—that other women,—if you do not know"—

He turned (they were strolling on the beach), and impetuously began to walk the other way. After a moment's hesitation, she followed, and overtook him.

"You forget, Philip," she said, "how long a scar throbs in a woman's flesh. But indeed I've never meant to remind—or taunt you about any thing."

"I wish you would!" he cried hotly. "I wish you had! I think I should feel better if you would out with it, and tell me what a contemptibly weak fellow you thought me—if you would say the very worst."

"Oh, hush!" said Avis in her rich maternal voice. She did not say there was no worst. That was not true. She only put her hand upon his arm, and spared him with strong silence.

When he came to think it over, he blessed her for it with all his heart. He felt that he could not have borne to hear his wife *say* what he knew she had *thought* of him. On the other hand, he would have shrunk from a superficial tenderness—ignoring facts too keenly present in the minds of both—as from a kind of gruel adapted to invalids and children. Silence, more kindly and more intricately than any speech, he began to hope, would now interpret them to each other. He would strive to make himself worthy to use the deaf-mute alphabet of fine souls. He fancied that she leaned a little upon his arm in walking home that day: it was a bright day, and he had felt quite strong.

They walked on the narrow sea-wall, where two only can tread abreast. She looked very young and girlish that day, in her palmetto hat and white linen dress.

When they came in, the boarding-house dinner-bell was ringing, and the people in their light clothes collecting merrily; the little boy who looked like Van ran up with orange-buds for Philip; the noon surged in across the veranda in a tide of light and heat; unfamiliar tropical perfumes were in the air; and the December roses nodded at the windows. Avis had a confused festal feeling, as if the people and the roses, and the light and the child, had waited for her and Philip to come in.

She bade him go on without her, that he need not spend his strength to climb the stairs; and herself ran up lightly. She tossed the ribbons about in her drawer to choose a fresh one, a golden one, as near the shade of the sunlight as she could find. She held it against the shimmer on the wall, laughing, to try the match. She plunged her hands and face into the cool water; her own eyes looked back to her from the glass, dewey and sweet, as she brushed the damp rings of her hair.

"Do I look still so young?" she thought. In the next room she could hear their neighbors with the French name. The sick woman was berating her husband bitterly—it was something about the soup. Avis turned round, standing alone there, and stretched her arms out solemnly as if she would yearn through the solid wall to gather the poor creature in. Her heart cried out to those strange people,

"You—it is not too late for you—save your love! Oh, save your married love!"

That was Christmas week. She and Philip went out and ransacked the little curiosity shops together, to find something for the baby. There were three letters from aunt Chloe that week—and the child was well. Their hearts lightened, and the stress of anxiety to which the happiest earthly parentage must bow an aching shoulder yielded kindly for them. Bereavement and sickness, peril and separation, slipped by them in the golden weather, with a suggestion of the solemn sweetness with which care may seem to elude rather than escape us in Heaven.

Ostrander said,—

"I believe I am going to get well."

On Christmas Eve they started out to the little churchyard beyond the city gates, whose impressive ruin, cut against the setting sun, said to both that of which neither spoke. They sat down by one of the graves,—a child's grave, nameless and deserted.

"See, Philip!" said Avis in a low voice, "the mounds here are strewn with shells, instead of the flowers that one sees elsewhere: but this poor little fellow has none; I will go and find some." She wandered off alone, while he sat and watched her from his solitary place. The light fell fast; the massive face of Fort Marion darkened down upon the little beach where she strolled in sweet, searching attitudes, that lent so much gentleness to the courageous contours of her figure. It was almost dark when she came back to say,—

"I could only find a few poor little dull things; but they will do."

She stooped, and laid the shells in the form of a cross, according to the custom of the quiet place, upon the grave. "I am sure it was a little boy," she said.

Then, for it darkened steadily, they went in silence home. Just before they reached the house, Ostrander said abruptly,—

"Avis, all the time you were on that beach, I saw the boy."

"The child from the churchyard?" asked Avis, smiling, to humor a sick man's fancy, but wishing that she had not left him so long in that malarial place.

"No—Van. I didn't mean to tell you; but I think I had better. I saw Van quite distinctly."

"Are you sick, Philip?" asked Avis, stopping short.

"Perfectly well. Not so well this winter, and I never had one of these optical illusions before in all my life. My mother used to have them, and they tell some amazing stories about my grandfather's last sickness. I have often wanted to experience a touch of the thing, to see what it is like. It is very strange."

"What was it like?" asked Avis a little uneasily, but walking on. She drew her hand a trifle closer through his arm, and joined her fingers upon it: she used to walk with him in that way, now long since.

"He came out of the water," said Ostrander, "and ran along the beach. He had his little Christmas stocking in his hand. You did not see him, and he pulled at your dress."

Involuntarily Avis cried out: there was a certain terrible realism in her husband's quiet words and the curious, scientific interest of his tone.

"Then you turned round, and he took hold of your hand. I saw him put one of the shells in his stocking. He had on that little blue sack aunt Chloe gave him, with white buttons. Then he ran along again, and waded into the water. I saw him quite plainly. He"—

"What did he do, Philip?" asked Avis in a voice of awe; for Philip paused.

"He beckoned to me. He beckoned to me twice. Then you came up the slope, and, when I looked again, he was gone. Positively, for the moment my breath came hard, and I was a little faint and sick when you found me.

"There is some nervous inaction of the retina. I had one such case in the hospital before I graduated. I believe I'll read up a little on it to-night. Avis, do you know I haven't coughed once for three whole days?"

It was on Christmas that he said abruptly, coming out from mass in the gray cathedral into which they had wandered, "If I die before you, don't expect me to chatter about what I'm thinking,—on my death-bed, I mean. It won't be my way. I know what I believe, and you know, and I don't believe any thing so thoroughly as that, if I get into the other life on any grounds, I shall take somehow a pretty fresh start,—I need it, God knows! more of a start than I'm likely to get here now. Sometimes I wonder if He'll take the trouble to make over such a half-moulded fellow. I don't know whether I'm worth it, upon my soul! Now," he added, "I couldn't have said that a month ago, when I really thought I was going to die. How amazingly natural good luck is! I am as used to getting well as if I had never been sick."

But, when they had come home, he turned to her rather sadly,— "An ailing man talks so much about himself!—as if people could care."

His wife did not answer for the moment; then she crept up, and put her hand upon his hair, passing it to and fro. He remembered the first time she ever did this,—one winter-day before they were married, when his head was reeling with pain; and how aunt Chloe came in, and just how Avis looked, standing over him, shamed and sweet. He wondered if she remembered too. He thought what a subtle bond is the bare community of memory given to those who pass their lives together; how eternal is the vicinity we give to the soul that we suffer to share our memorable joy or grief or peril.

Impulsively he put his hand out, and drew his wife down upon the arm of the chair; but he felt her tremble, and so released her. She stood for a minute uncertain: he did not touch her again, and neither spoke. All the brilliant ingenuity of Ostrander's nature drooped before the task of wooing an estranged wife. He got up awkwardly, and said that Smith baby was crying again; and then he and Avis sat down at separate windows, with their faces to the sultry Christmas night.

But after this he fell into a low, discouraged state. He suffered a brief attack of pleurisy, and complained of the shortness of his breath. He maintained that the air disagreed with him, and that they should move at once.

Mr. Smith expressed a desire to join them, on the ground that Mrs. Smith found her hands cold in Augustine. The little party wandered up and down the river, as Florida parties will, subject only to the caprices of its invalids, touching here and there for a day or so, at hotels or sanitariums, as the restless fancy took them, and absorbed in the exhaustive and enlivening discussion of fogs and fever. After a week or more of this, Avis induced her husband, who was growing scarcely paler than herself, to bring it to an end.

"You're right," he said faintly. "It is killing us both. We will spend the winter at the next landing."

This happened to be Pilatka.[3] Here, therefore, they yielded their search for the impossible, and by windows that scanned the great river, drew breath, and missed the sea.

Mr. Smith drew breath and halted too. Mrs. Smith was sensitive to the alligators, and was of opinion that another night on board boat would strike to the pneumo-gastric nerve.

Here Ostrander fell first into calm, then lethargy, then energy.

The new year blossomed unguardedly. He submitted himself to the regal weather. In the fine quality of the cooler season he gained daily. He ceased to cough. He chatted with the other recuperating invalids about the hotels and shore, bringing home magic tales of the healing genii in the flower-burdened air. He found a Massachusetts college-boy with a bronchial cough, sick with grief at dropping behind his class. He began to tutor him a little in his Greek. Avis saw that he colored with pleasure when the hour came for the lesson. The poor fellow was overwhelmed with a pathetic joy to be doing a man's work again.

When the professor wrote from Harmouth, one day, that he had heard of an opening in a Western college, which his son-in-law's complete recovery might throw in his way, he said excitedly,—

"Father is very good. But really, Avis, I don't know but we can do better than that. We might start a boarding-school in Florida—or, if that, wouldn't work, the sanitarium would."

Avis, painting orange-blossoms for aunt Chloe, said only,—

"We will see, Philip."

She could not more have quarrelled just then with the characteristic effervescence of his returning strength, than she could have revised and annotated her little boy's prayers. She had so long stood, strained, staring death out of countenance for Philip's sake, that his very weaknesses had grown sacred to her; as the faults of Lazarus may have become to the tender eyes of Mary.[4] With that superlative vagueness through which we see the exceptions taken by another to our own force of character, Ostrander was perhaps conscious of this.

One night in January, there befell a warm and wonderful moon, which impelled all the unresting stream of tourist life into the open air. Ostrander was especially stimulated by the stir, the chatter, the scented wind, the Southern sky. He begged Avis to go with him—away, he said, from all these people—for a row upon the river. He would manage the boat himself at first. She said nothing: it was her delicate tact that the limits of his strength should come as a discovery to the invalid, rather than a dogma from the nurse. In a few minutes he yielded the oars to her with a sigh. She took them in silence, and in silence they rose and fell upon the bright resistant current.

Avis, as she rowed, turned her face to the forest, whose peaks of blackness rose on either hand. The river pierced them like a bright defile, narrowing as they entered it. She thought how the light lay on the sea, beating beyond over there at the left, deep miles across the untrodden tangle, where the long bar leaned out that makes the entrance to the St. Augustine Harbor one of the most perilous feats known to the navigators of the American coast. She and Philip seemed shut in here, and secure, on the patient river. Perhaps some poor sailor yonder on the unseen sea came at that moment, daring his fate,—the most cruel that the mariner's chart can know,—the resistance of shifting sand. They were safe,—they two. She leaned over to look into the stream: she blessed its passionless, contracted current. She had called the St. John's River humdrum sometimes by daylight, a tame story, nothing to be done with it but follow it to the tiresome end; now it stretched, transfigured and electric. The sky seemed to stoop with the undue burden of its stars. The moon hung high, and the water rose a little under the warm wind. A few boats only quivered in sight,—so few as to express rather than relieve the phantasmal solitude of the place: their colored skippers cut like ebony carving about the rigging. Indistinct voices drifted from them, and sunk again, as Avis and her husband beat up the narrowing shores alone.

She beached the boat presently. They met no one, and walked silently upon the coarse white sand, close to the water's edge. Avis said,—

"This river is like that old book of Carove's, about the soul. It seems to be a story without an end."

He sat down after a little while; for his capricious strength flagged. Avis wandered up and down, dim as a nereid upon the shore: he could hear the grains of sand crackle beneath her feet. There were now no sails in sight upon the uneasy current. Between the forest on this hand, and the forest on that, the river lay desolate. The dead trees upon its banks wore winding-sheets of moss; they stretched their boughs across the separating stream: those that stood shoulder to shoulder interlocked branches in a manner in which it was impossible not to see a pathetic and at the same time grim likeness to human gestures. In the half-lights, sky and shore and river alike grew fluent and foreign, till whether one walked upon the stream, or sailed upon the sand, or sank upon the clouds, the truant fancy wondered, with a kind of happy terror, such as that soul might feel which first escaped the body on a moonlit night.

It was a spot to drive the lonely from each other, and to draw the loving near.

Ostrander's figure, where he sat solitary, melted and formed in the gray uncertainties of the air. As his wife stood, turning hither and thither, she was not sure where she had left him. He seemed to have vanished from her. She turned back with beating heart. He watched her coming through the unreal light.

The moon was full in his face; with his head upon his bent, thin wrist, he sat with lifted eyes. She sat down beside him. They could not see the lights of the little town. They were quite alone in the visionary place. Without speech and without touch, Avis was made aware that the moment had become a crisis for them both. She dared not look at her husband.

It seemed to her that one careless breath now would completely disorder her self-control. Whether she should go flinging her arms above her head, and leaping down that unsubstantial shore, re-sistant of him; or whether she should spend herself upon him with a storm of long-repressed feeling, which she was scathingly con-scious would not facilitate that intelligent comprehension of one another in which she believed that their sole hope of future hap-piness must lie,—this five-years wife, acquainted with bereave-ments, worn with care, and flayed by anxiety, could not trust her-self to guess.

"Avis," said her husband suddenly, "we won't have any scene or bother about it; but there *is* something I want to say to you."

"Very well, Philip," gently.

"I don't know that it's of any use, either, to talk about it," mused Philip uncertainly. "Most things are better let alone between people who— I wonder if you think a man's worst is the real of him, Avis? There—hush! Don't try to answer such a question. It doesn't de-serve an answer. But what I *want* to say is this, It does seem to me that there must have been something in me worth loving, or you wouldn't have cared for me in the first place.

"Things might have been worse," he added, lifting his head a little; "and all that—these elements of character that you loved are real: they are not dead. If you would think of this sometimes!" he said rather pitifully.

He looked up across the uncertain shadow that her tall figure cast between them. His wife had risen, and stood over him with streaming eyes and choking speech. That very intelligent com-prehension of one another seemed no nearer to her than ever. Was it possible, after all, that people might be happy just to love one another, without understanding any thing about it?

"I cannot seem to make up my mind to bear it," said Philip Os-trander, not without dignity, "that my wife should not respect me enough to love me."

Then in the unreal light she stooped to him, crying out patheti-cally; but what she said, or if she said any words, neither he nor herself could at that moment tell. He held up his hands. In the un-

real light it seemed to him as if she bent from a great height to
restore to him the married kiss which he had lost. But he did not,
or he dared not, draw her to his level.

The moon waned, and they went home. The river was deserted.
The wind was high; but the current bore them powerfully on. Avis
rowed sturdily, and they did not talk. The lights of the little town
nodded to welcome them. On either hand the kneeling moon
slowly veiled the colossal face of the wilderness.

They talked a little when they had come home, in that small
surface-mood to which the deepest wedded romance lies so near,—
as to whether she had rowed too far, and if he had taken cold, and
why Mrs. Smith did not cough to-night, and if the evening mail
had come, and how aunt Chloe had the baby well asleep by this
time,—little lassie! their baby, thirteen hundred miles away,—and
how she would have grown when they got home, and if she would
know them, and what they should take her. But Ostrander watched
his wife with restless eyes. How resolute her rich motions about
the half-lit room! He was growing half impatient with this motherly kind of affection she gave him. It was no comfort to him that
he knew it was the best that he deserved. Beside her quarried loyalty his own frailer instincts had never seemed to him smaller and
sadder than they did that night. Never before had he perceived the
spiritual dignity of constancy; perhaps—since it is precisely in
proportion to the loftiness of a truth that personal humility is req-
uisite to its apprehension—he had never before distrusted himself sufficiently to perceive it. Her love, he thought, like the statues of Angelo,[5] had been struck out at the beginning from the holy
marble; his, like the work of lesser sculptors, from the experimen-
tal clay.

"Shall I light the lamps?" she said at last.

"Don't you like it better as it is?" he asked doubtfully.

"Perhaps so—yes. Do you want any thing, Philip? Is it time for
your medicine? There! I have not rung for your glass of milk. Let
me call Jeff."

"Please not ring—now. Can't you sit and rest a little? You must
be very tired."

"Just as you like, Philip."

She stood in the centre of the dim room, uncertain for that moment. The light from the unlatched door fell in. The halls were
deserted and still. Outside, in the peculiarly dense and appalling
shadows that follow the foliage of orange-trees upon a moonlit
night, the white flowers hung wearily.

"I have been such a care," he said tremulously through the dark,
"for so long! You have borne so much, Avis, and so patiently! Now
I'm getting well, don't you think I'm fit to take my share of things?

Oh, come here, and let us talk about it! Come, my poor girl, poor girl! Don't you *know* how tired you are?"

Perhaps it was the words; perhaps it was the tone. Change and sickness had not jarred the quality of Ostrander's rare voice. It affected his wife just then like those strains of music which a heavy heart is more hurt than healed to hear.

A torrent of memory overtook her. Bound emotions began to struggle in it. All the repressed suffering of a woman to whom it has been given to carry her husband's nature, as she has lifted that of her children, through a lonely and laborious married life, seemed to come sweeping over her, wave upon wave, in a tide to which she could see no end.

He expected that she would come up and take his face between her hands; call him her poor boy perhaps, in that maternal way of hers from which he knew at that moment his manhood would revolt; and what would happen next he could not possibly foretell.

But, like a fascinated girl to her lover, Avis, in the dim room, turned and crept to him. His starved arms shook as they closed about her. He prayed that only his ideal of himself might touch his wife at that moment. She put up her hand to his cheek in her old way.

"Oh, I am so tired!—tired out, tired out. Don't talk to me—oh! there is nothing to say. It was a good while—pulling along alone— and I thought you did not care."

CHAPTER XXIV

*"'Tis most true, two souls
. . . Let them suffer
The gall of hazard, so they
grow together,
Will never sink."*
—John Fletcher[1]

*"Discords quenched by
meeting harmonies
Die in the large and charitable
air;
And all our rarer, truer, better
self—
That better self—shall live."*
—George Eliot[2]

They seemed to themselves now to have become the discoverers of the State of Florida. Above them widened new heavens; below them a new earth leaped.[3] Lonely and awed as lovers, they wandered about the forests and the shore. He was boyish about having her with him. She shared his walks, his drives, his sails. He drooped if they were parted for an hour. His breath and color deepened; his recovery presented itself to them as a foregone conclusion.

He talked a good deal,—more often of their future, sometimes of all that they had put behind them. He would come up excitedly and say,—

"If we don't make it work at the West, Avis, what then? Shall you be contented to come back here? You and I could be happy here forever; couldn't we? And we could educate the girl ourselves." Then she would listen, smiling, and put up her hand, and say nothing: she liked better to let him talk and go dreaming. And he, reverently turning his cheek, still hollow as it was, upon her palm, would slide intently on.

If his health gave way again at the West—but of course he meant to try it faithfully; that was understood. If the climate proved too irritating, or the class-room drudgery—but he thought he should know better how to manage that another time. Still it was a comfort to know, that, if worst came to worst, they could return, and start the sanitarium or the boarding-school. It would be quite practicable to find a suitable housekeeper: Avis should not be exhausted by that. Or, if that failed, there was the orange-business. He was convinced that there was room for a large orange-grove even here; and, farther up the river, a little Northern pluck would work a miracle any day. They might do worse than to take to orange-culture; though he preferred his profession in itself considered: he thought, too, it would be a pleasanter life for her; he wanted, above all, to make it a little easier for her now. Ostrander did not notice how scanty were his wife's answers to all this, her smile was so rich, her surrendered hand so voluble.

As for Avis, she heard him without annoyance or dispute. She would have been uneasy if Philip had undergone a transfiguration like a hero in a novel, in which his weaknesses were sublimated, and his faults idealized beyond her recognition. She would have distrusted a grand metamorphosis as in itself but another form of a capricious and curious self-delusion.

It seemed to her the great triumph of her life that she could love her husband just as God had made him. And that Philip, being Philip, could come leaning in this pathetic way upon her love,—the sure, strained love of five married years,—this seemed to her just then more a prophecy than a fulfilment of hope. After all, what was this one world, to souls which had been joined together by any tissues too firm for the attrition of time to tear? At best a root beneath a forest of experience. Perhaps (she thought) those married men and women were better fitted than they knew for the permanent character of a spiritual form of society, who, at the end of one life passed together, could intelligently desire to renew the relation in a second.

When he talked of herself and her work, her reserve deepened. He spoke much of both. It was,—

"Avis, when you get to painting;" or, "Avis, one thing I mean to make sure of, that you shall be hampered no longer in your own plans;" or, "Why have you done nothing new this winter, Avis?" or, "Now all goes well with us, dear, we shall see you famous."

She said,—

"Yes, Philip." Why argue the matter? She knew how that would be. And she could not have said she did not care. She did not cheat her clear nature by telling herself or him that she found in her married lot vicarious atonement for what she had missed. A human gift is a rebellious prisoner, and she was made human before she was made woman.

But she thought it mattered less to her than it did once,—all this lost and unquelled life. They had saved the life of life, they had saved their wedded love: the rest could be borne.

One day she could not ride with him, there being a burden of home-letters and little accumulating feminine tasks, which she performed less nervously alone. It was the morning, too, for a spelling-lesson that she gave their waiter in the boarding-house (a handsome mulatto boy, to whom both had taken a fancy), whenever the state of Jeff's intellect or dining-room permitted. They compromised (for she did not like Philip to go alone) upon the company of their neighbor Smith. Smith was down on the wharf; and he would find him, if she wished, and they would ride a little towards the swamps, and return when they were hungry. He held her hand, and chatted a good deal about it. He had taken a slight cold for a day or two past, and clung to her, quickly depressed, with more than usual dependence. It was, "Avis, don't stay long down stairs." "Coming back soon, Avis?" "Would you just as lief sit here?" "I can't see you, there by the window."

This morning, when he had gone as far as the gate, he came back. She was standing on the veranda, as it happened, quite alone, in her light dress, and the low, dark outline of her hair: he came back, and kissed her again, and said she must not miss him. She watched him walking down the narrow road,—the road like a "river of sand." He turned, and nodded to her: the wind struck his bright hair. He looked flashing and fresh to her, as if she saw him for the first time in her life. He drew her with that subtle fascination which Nature takes a fitful delight in bestowing upon some creatures as a substitute for strength, perhaps,—shall we say?—as an index of undeveloped strength. Avis followed him with a girl's blush and a wife's eyes. Her heart went to meet that Indian summer of married life, which, after the rain, settles down upon the purple air.

It was towards noon, that, having put her morning's work well behind her, she went down stairs to find the boy Jeff. On the landing she met—with his baby in his arms, and his boy at his coattails, and his wife calling to him to come back and shut the door—the patient form of Mr. Smith. She stopped to say,—

"Did you not meet my husband this morning?" with an unconscious change of color.

"Oh, yes!" said Mr. Smith; "and I wanted to go with him: he had a pretty marsh-pony. He's a fine rider, your husband. But you see, Mrs. Smith has had a bad night. She says it's the worst she's had. And the baby's got the colic; and the girl eat too much breakfast; and the boy—let me see, what *is* the matter with the boy? Oh, yes! the boy chopped off the end of his finger with a hatchet. But maybe, if the nurse hadn't had the sick-headache, I might have brought it about," added Mr. Smith, with a pensive and powerful effort of the imagination.

Mrs. Ostrander went on, and gave Jeff his lesson. Philip would be in to dinner, she hoped, since he had gone alone; or he might have easily found company among the sporting-men about the hotel. He did not come home to dinner; but this was not unusual. Often they had ridden till late in the afternoon, returning with the breeze which set in from the river, he saying, as they jogged along in the happy weather, "How glad I am you came!"

She settled herself restlessly to some long-neglected sketches: it was difficult to remember when she had passed an afternoon alone before; she sat in the strange silence, with flushed cheeks. Mrs. Smith, in the next room, had brightened a little; and her husband could be heard gallantly telling her how well she looked. The people began to collect in the parlor and on the verandas. Jeff came up to ask if Mr. Ostrander's dinner should be kept hot any longer, his main argument being, that, as they wanted the oven for the supper, Mr. Ostrander must have dined with a gentleman. The shaded room began to cool about her; it was time to open the blinds to the breeze from the bay; it was time for the sensitive shadow of the jasmine to deepen across the tea-rose-tree, and the sharp edges of the orange-leaves to grow blunt to the eye that was strained with peering across them to the empty road—it was time for Philip Ostrander to come home.

Steps upon the sand; manly steps enough, impetuous and ringing, as of one who hurried up to say, "Did I frighten you getting back so late?"—The jaunty hotel waiter looks up as he goes by; the light flares on the big seal-ring he wears; he has a red sea-bean upon his watch-guard; he lifts his hat to the quadroon cook, who is opening oysters in the orange-grove below.

Steps upon the sand. He will be sure to watch the windows through the opening in the clump of fig-trees. By leaning out across the ledge a trifle,—not too far, because the guava bough sweeps up,—one can see him turning. How poetic is this Southern light upon long Saxon hair! and in a man, a smile is rare, like this for which a woman waits, with color spent, and breath in leash, and head bent low to listen, her cheek upon her two hands stretched palm to palm.—Why *will* the tourists go to walk upon this street? It is the hour for the veranda and the shore, the forest and the yacht. Impossible to understand why anybody should want to wade across this sand. She leans upon his arm with a pretty color,— a superficial thing, over-dressed and simpering. How can a woman love a man who carries his cane like that? His gloves are too light. There is a blue heron's wing upon her bonnet. They whisper together. They laugh and nod. The orange-tree casts a long shadow over the fence, through which they pass, leaning and still. They do not note the length of the shadow. They do not care if it grows late.

Steps upon the sand. It yields slowly to a weary foot, overtasked perhaps, in wandering about the marshes, or a trifle lamed upon these awkward stirrups; he will limp up to the gate; it will be a minute's work to bound from the window, to clear the stairs, the veranda, the yard, to stand panting and strong; he will lean upon her shoulder as he did in the meadow once at home on a September noon; he will stoop and say, "Was I gone too long?"—The old woman was a slave. She cringes as she walks. Her head is bent well-nigh at right angles from her shoulders. Her turban is made of the MacGregor plaid. Her fingers are yellow; the third knuckle on the left hand is mutilated. It is a sickly sight. The child with her is an octoroon. She has blue eyes, and ties her hair with a lavender ribbon. The child says it is supper-time. One must be very strong and happy to watch these people.

Steps upon the sand. Ah, there! How dull is fear! what a dotard is anxiety! Of course he would ride the pony home. They are short clean steps, very clear and pleasant for a marsh-tackey's foot. It is not wise to look any longer through the rift between the fig-tree and the guava. To wait a little for a relief from over-pressure were the gentler and the gladder way. The pony will come shying to the gate, a little obstinate, wanting to get to the stable, bruising the rider's leaping foot gently against the fence. She will wait and meet him at the landing—there are so many people down below. As he stoops, he will laugh a little, touching her beneath the chin. Her lips, already stirring, say, "You shall never go alone again."

The sportsman rides well. The young fellow is fitted with white gloves. He is fresh from a hunting-trip up the Oclawaha or the lakes. He is in a hurry for a civilized supper. His horse is white too, and he rides fast. There is a shower behind them. Horse and rider bound before it. Children, unseen behind the guava-trees, cry that it is thundering. The air blackens down upon the river; the little yachts take in their sails; the surf stretches out its arms; the wind gets him to his solemn feet; the orange blossoms break and blow in, beating about the darkening room. In the confusion the supper-bell rings shrilly, and the people on the veranda scatter, laughing, from the rain.

"Better let her go," said Mr. Smith.

"You couldn't petrify her to stay at home, sar," said Jeff. Jeff had learned that word in the spelling-lesson that morning: he had not had an opportunity to use it in good society before. Jeff was very fond of Mrs. Ostrander. He felt that it would be a comfort to her, under these anxious circumstances, that he should acquaint the other boarders with some evidence of his proficiency under her educational attentions. For similar reasons he stopped, and said distinctly,—

"Mis' Ostrander, I don't wish to be personal; but have you got a postage-stamp?"

By that time all the boarders were upon the veranda to see them start. Jeff felt a little jealous of Mr. Smith. One driver—at least a driver who could spell petrify—was enough for any lady; and that they should meet Mr. Ostrander directly, every boarder in the house was well agreed. It was agreed, however, that Mrs. Ostrander would feel relieved to start and find herself well upon the way towards her husband, who was later than an invalid had better be upon a stormy night.

It was still raining lightly; but the restless clouds gave promise of a moon, whenever they should yield the wild field to which Avis uplifted her young face. The scant lamps of the town dwindled, nodding like old acquaintances to the passer; knots of brightly-dressed tourists flashed by; the faces of the great hotels and little shops turned their blazing brows away.

Avis was perfectly familiar with her husband's usual haunts, and she directed her course at once towards the heart of the swamp. She sat quite still: the two men talked in low tones, as if in the presence of a sick person. Once Jeff tried to draw her into conversation. He said,—

"Mis' Ostrander, what I want to know is, how you done go spell Aggymemnon." Jeff thought this would be a comfort to her: he prided himself upon the delicacy of his comprehension of Mrs. Ostrander. He did not know a boy in the hotels who had so handsome a lady; and he knew a good many boys who had eight at a table the winter through. In his heart Jeff was much out of patience with Mr. Ostrander; he expected to find that he had taken too much; that and consumption were the only things which ever happened to Northern gentlemen in Pilatka.

"Don't you think," suggested Mr. Smith, hesitating, "that I had better first take out the horse and reconnoitre a little? Jeff will stay and take care of you."

Avis turned her face towards him in the faint, perturbed light: she did not speak.

"Drive on, Jeff," said Mr. Smith, with a sigh.

It was now between eight and nine o'clock. The moon, as they entered the nave of the forest, came climbing into sight uncertainly, like a woman tripping on her robe. The beaten clouds sank towards the river, which it was no longer possible to see. Faintly as a spent breath, as they rode in between the pines, Avis fancied that she heard the invisible waves upon the invisible shore.

It seemed at first supernaturally dark within the woods. Optical illusions flared for a few moments before her eyes; she saw words stamp themselves and melt upon the air, and when she would read them, they were the words which Dante saw upon the lips of hell.[4] This excitement subsided as soon as she had accustomed her eyes to the shadow. She had been there once before—with Philip—upon a brighter night; but they had not ventured far: he feared the malaria from the swamps. Her courage grew more rational as the great beauty of the wilderness closed in about them. The moon was now clear, and the light leaned in, sweet and sane, upon the gently resistant shadow.

As they advanced, sickening odors stole up; beyond the patrol of cedars the swamp lay skulking. It would soon be necessary to conduct their search on foot. As they stood calling, the mocking-birds began to answer them.

Jeff wished he could see her face. He came up, and touched her on the sleeve. He felt that Mr. Smith could not be expected to understand the necessities of the occasion. Mr. Smith had not put the chair up to the table three times a day for those two. The mulatto's yellow jaws began to work.

"Oh, Mis' Ostrander, I got him now! I done got him on the way before we tie the horse. I got Agamemnon right easy in my mind at last. H-a-g, Ag, g-y, gy, Aggy"—

But Agamemnon was too much for poor Jeff, and choked him mercilessly in the swallowing. Jeff shrunk back. He thought she would have been so pleased. He might as well let Mr. Smith comfort her now.

But Mr. Smith fell back a little too. Mrs. Ostrander gently pushed him by, and took the lead in silence, beating down the Spanish bayonet which tore her feet. In the moonlit opening the purple poison from the swamp had a clean color, like blown snow. Her slight figure seemed to wrestle with the dumb, unwilling darkness as she bent into it.

Dawn comes with the reverent and delicate touch of a lover to the Florida waste. That night his arm stole with what seemed especial gentleness about her heart. It had been such a peaceful and womanly night! There had been no wind or rain, no blindness, and no horror. It was quite warm too: even a sick man might breathe the air in safety. Avis had not tottered for an instant in her resolute hope. She should find him. God was merciful.

As the moon dipped, a strange shrill bird awoke and chirped, and slept again. Gliding creatures began to stir, and skulk away, like evil thoughts before clean eyes, or terror before joy. The lampblack of the distant shadows leaned to purple; the nearer undergrowth grew gray. Looking to the sky, one saw that it changed color like a cheek. Suddenly then, the tops of the pines yielded, and each green needle fired. The fine outline of the cedars revealed itself sinuously, like Etruscan screens of old gold wire. The loath moss stirred, and showed bluish white. The wild oranges seemed to tremble, like conscious creatures to whom the sun was plighted first. The rose-curlews moved, tall, slender, and haughty: they looked less like birds than breathing roses. Avis, looking up, saw one rise, glad as a departing soul, and hover, burning to be gone, upon the air. Below him the light stole but slowly to the level where a human face might lie expectant of it.

She pushed her way into the thicket, spreading her hands out, it was still so dark there. As she did so, she was conscious of being confronted by a close pair of gentle, puzzled eyes. She stopped short, and flung her hands before her face.

"Jeff!" she cried, "it is the marsh-pony!"

The light was now deepening fast, and the two men instinctively and authoritatively drew the woman back.

From the moment of finding the horse, she had begun to tremble, and when they spoke to her she obeyed.

As they beat about the opening, Jeff looked back over his shoulder. The mists of the damp place were turned red and rich, and through them he saw that she had fallen on her knees. She looked like one bathed in a scarlet flood.

Then the live-oak bough swept in between them, and Jeff, for he could not see, went stumbling on. . . . The white man and the mulatto looked at each other.

"Sir," said Jeff, lifting his head after a silence, "I've set the chair for 'em for most two months; and there was the writin' and the spellin' as she was so good. She would suspect me to be the man of us two to tell her. It ain't your fault, sir, that you can't be looked to understand her feelin', sir, so well."

She had risen from her knees when he met her. She made no sound, but staggered: she still had her hands before her eyes. Jeff came up; he touched her, cringing, on the sleeve.

"O Mis' Ostrander dear! he didn't take too much—he only took a bleeding. And he says we was to break it to you easy, and that he's glad to see you, ma'am, and has been done expectin' you, and that you're not to mind—and O Mis' Ostrander! now I think if you was to stop a minute—just easy where you stand—and spell a little—it would clar your mind out. He don't look so bad as some doos—but if you was just to stop—before you sees him—it's only jest behind the live-oak yonder—Mis' Ostrander dear"—

·   ·   ·   ·   ·   ·   ·   ·   ·

The daybreak sought them out gently. In the pathless forest whose solemn purpose no man knew, they clung to one another, and thanked God. He had been merciful. Care and change had done their worst. Beaten life had given challenge to their love. They could bear the incident of death. In that hour they were less grieved because they must be parted, than blessed because they loved each other.

She had found him lying quite peacefully, expecting her.

As she knelt, gathering his head upon her breast, the sun arose upon the wilderness. In the splendor he looked young to her, and a future in his face returned her gaze. He felt her arm and her warm breath, and smiled boyishly. "It is hard to believe—that a man can die—here," he said. He turned his cheek, and hers touched it. He asked her not to move.

He had not suffered much, he said, nor long. And he felt sure she would come; he had not doubted for a moment—it was a pretty long night; but he knew she was not far. Once he thought he heard her. And the pony wandered off—it was more lonely after the pony went. But she must not mind. It had been warm and bright; and it had not been hard. Nothing had been hard—but the chance—if she had been too late, that would have been pretty hard. But he knew that she would come.

Then he asked her to lift him a little more upon her arm, and if he tired her too much. After that he seemed to sleep lightly: he upheld his face as if he drank her abundant health. When he awoke, he said,—

"Avis, do you remember—once—how you said that you would like to die?"

"Hush my darling!—yes."

"Love, if I ask it, will *you* kiss *my* breath away? When I speak again, will you kiss me on the lips?"

"Oh, my darling! oh, my darling! Yes."

. . . .

"*Avis!*"

When she lifted her face, the rose-curlew hung overhead, palpitating with joy.

The two men had long since withdrawn into the forest.

CHAPTER XXV

"A dream of man and woman,
Diviner still, but human;
Solving the riddle old,
Shaping the age of gold."
—Whittier[1]

Upon the shores of the river as she went home, the young fine fronds were thrusting aside the unfaded leaves. The forest stood in a pale and tender fog of green, as if an unseen artist had blurred it with a blender, perhaps to deceive an over-wary eye as to his real intent in touching it at all. There was something at once unutterably delicate and urgent in the advance of the deathless spring upon the deathless summer. The eye leaned upon it with the relief which it finds in sunset, sunrise, zenith, fire, or sea; in those things only which bring the thought face to face with what is unfathomable. The heart bowed before it, quickened to ask, "Where shall I find eternity without resurrection?"

She travelled alone, tearless and excited. She felt strong and strained. As yet she was filled less with a sense of loss than love. Philip seemed quite near,—nearer than when it had been possible to be conscious of any imperfection in himself or in their union. Only his ideal visited her heart. She was not without a strange, exultant sense that now she never could see a weakness or a flaw in him again. Life might try her cruelest, she could not fret them now. She thought of him with something of the proud and peculiar triumph of the widowed girl, who kneels to the vision of the man whose wife she never was, to learn to reverence him by one blind thrill the less.

Unheard, he seemed to her tense mood to speak to her as she rode solitary; and his voice had the tone of the wooing and the bridal time. Unseen to her soul's eyes, he journeyed with her; and his face had the look of its first youth and the beauty of its noblest hour. Their relation seemed to her to run on quite uninterrupted. He leaned over her shoulder to read their undivided life. He had but turned a leaf before her in the story without an end.

Aunt Chloe was sitting in the twilight with the little girl asleep across her generous arms. The geraniums in the windows were all pink that year. Aunt Chloe watched them while she hushed the child.

242

The professor walked rather feebly up and down the silent study. He had been saying to his sister that he was growing old, he thought, and that the house seemed lonely. He stopped to right the picture of Sir William, whose fresh gray cord had twisted on its polished hook, and wondered who had taken Locke's Understanding[2] from the left elbow of the mahogany sofa, and if Professor Brown would call again to see about that pet chemist of his who was marked so low on intuition, and how long it was since they had heard from Avis, and what it meant that we were having such a merciful spring, and said how green the grass was, even now, upon the yard. And then aunt Chloe heard the gate click; and, when they both looked out across the pink geraniums, Avis, in her widow's dress, alone, was walking up between the blades of grass.

Aunt Chloe went out and led her in, asking no questions, and saying no word. She led her into the study, to her father, and put her baby into her arms, and went out and shut the door. And then Avis drew in her breath, and shook suddenly, and so began to cry.

No solitude is so solitary as that of inharmonious companion-ship; and, beside certain other phases of her life, her present one seemed at first to Avis to lack the essential qualities of loneliness.

It was with that vivid belief (which has the character of con-sciousness to imaginative minds) in Philip's watchful and intelli-gent sympathy, that she directed her energies to the object which her marriage and its consequences had interrupted.

She opened the garden-studio while the apples budded, and there she staid patiently for a year. They questioned her little or none; and she worked in an absolute taciturnity, not characteristic of her sweet and kindly temper, which was quick to sacrifice an instinct of reticence to one of consideration for the feelings of a friend. Aunt Chloe knew there was a portrait of little Jack Rose, and suspected a picture for the exhibition, and tried to remember that it showed a lack of acquaintance with life to be hurt by the conduct of the afflicted.

When the year was out, Avis one day locked the studio, took her little girl, and went to find her father. She crossed her hands, and stood before him, much in the attitude in which she stood on that June morning when she read "Aurora Leigh." Only now between her folded palms she held the fingers of the child. She said,—

"Next week, father, I shall go into the Art School, and teach, and I think I can get a private class besides."

"Do you suppose," asked the professor after a sad silence, "that your mother would think this to be best, my dear?"

More largely, perhaps, than a smaller man, the professor's sympa-thy yielded what his intellect grudged. He felt that he had made one of the concessions of his life in intimating to his daughter her mother's possible approval of her personal ambitions, or regret at their obstruction; since, of course, when his daughter had married, it was to be assumed that she yielded the tastes and occupations of her maidenhood, like other women—like her mother before her. But the professor could not argue with the eccentricities of an afflicted child. His daughter's frosted future chilled him like some novel defect in the laws of nature; as if the sun should elect upon whose roof it should shine, or the rain pass him by to visit his neighbor's field.

"It is of no use," said Avis wearily, "my pictures come back upon my hands. Nobody wants them—now. They tell that my style is gone. Goupil says I work as if I had a rheumatic hand—as if my fingers were stiff. It is true my hand has been a little clumsy since— Van—But the stiffness runs deeper than the fingers, father. Never mind; don't mind. We've given it up—Wait and I; haven't we, Wait?"

"I don't understand you," said the little girl distinctly. Avis's daughter was a logical little body, clear-headed, speaking only when she had something to say. Wait did not understand what it was that had been given; did not see that any thing had been given to anybody (it certainly was not grandpa's hour for the cough-lozenge), and preferred not to allow herself to be compromised on any matter on which she was not perfectly clear.

Her mother stood looking blindly down. Wait pulled at her dress unnoticed.

"Your little daughter speaks," said the professor.

Wait stood patiently—a sturdy lassie, with straightforward eyes and a healthy temper of her own—aware that she was not of much importance to her mother just then, but perfectly able to bide her time. Avis continued to look down with her eyelids half closed; it did not seem as if she saw her. Something as elemental in Philip Ostrander's wife as the love of their child, required her attention at that moment. She wondered how it would have been if she had cared for him in some other way,—like some other women; if she had been made of tougher tissue; if her feeling for that one man, her husband, had not eaten into and eaten out the core of her life, left her a riddled, withered thing, spent and rent, wasted by the autocracy of a love as imperious as her own nature, and as deathless as her own soul. But she would do it all over again,—all, all! She would never love him by one throe the less. Avis stretched out her arms into the empty air. She did not know how to express distinctly, even to her own consciousness, her conviction that she might have painted better pictures—not worse—for loving Philip and the children;[3] that this was what God meant for her, for all of them, once, long ago. She had not done it. It was too late now. And

Wait was watching her with resolute, critical eyes, tugging at her hands now, with lip put up; would have cried, if she had been a baby like Ave Rose.

Avis turned with a supple motion, and snatched the little girl. "I have my child!" she cried.

She thought of this more often after that: all was not over, the child had her life to live. The parental resurrection came to Avis, as other forms of tenderness had done, slowly, but with passionate intelligence: she seemed to herself to be the first woman in the world who had said,—

"My child shall not repeat my blunders;" or,—

"What does it all matter, if my child may be spared my sorrows?"

Wait developed with the rapidity of most solitary children, quite in her own fashion.

When she was four years old, her mother came to aunt Chloe one day, rigid with dismay.

Aunt Chloe sprang, dropping the cotton-flannel for the beneficiaries. "Is it her fingers? or her throat? Oh! did I leave the oxalic acid out?"

"I asked her if her doll was asleep," gasped Avis, "and she said, *'Hush mamma! It has been the object of my life that she should not know she was a doll.'*"

"Her forehead is too full," said the doctor; exactly as if he had not said it to every other mother on his list that morning. "Keep her out of school till you are convinced she is a dunce. Turn her out of doors with no more restriction than a cricket."[4] One mother on the list at least obeyed him, and one elected lassie was let loose upon the wide Harmouth fields and shore. Before she could read a line, Avis's daughter was a splendid little animal.

At this point the mother's heart withdrew, and took counsel of itself.

It must be clearly remembered that Avis had been reared in social and intellectual conditions whose tendency is strictly to the depression of novelty in conduct or opinion. There are always phases of progress vital enough, perhaps, to their little coteries of prophets or disciples, competent, even, (Heaven forbid that one be dull of imagination about any remote forms of humanity!) to their own organisms, circulation, heart-throbs, possibly, which the life of a university town can hardly be supposed to enter upon its curriculum of interests. Religion, sex, race, class, or whatever, looks for no recognition of its discrowned state from the centres of scholastic culture. The moral evolution comes slowly to the intellectual specialist, as faith to the physicist, or doubt to the poet, or geometry to the artist. Phases of thought quite familiar to most thoughtful people to-day, forms of advance pressing silently against thoughtful and thoughless, now alike, Avis had been trained to regard with the calm curiosity with which a free-thinker tries to regard a Christian,—a being, in the nature of things, of inferior culture, because cherishing a superstition which is, in the nature of things, barbaric.

As free from the compression of any agitating influence or upheaval as if she and Wait had been sitting sheltered on a summer-day in a convent-garden, side by side among the sultry flowers, while the music from the altar sounded on, and the sweet veiled women passed with holy feet, Avis, with her earnest eyes, and tender mouth, and tired brows, found herself face to face with the future of her child.

She found herself in the sensitive state of one who has made a gradual but radical change of climate. Horizons with which her own youth was unacquainted, beckoned before her; the hills looked at her with a foreign face; the wind told her that which she had not heard; in the air strange melodies rang out; uninterpreted colors gathered about the rising of the sun: her own chastised aspiration looked humbly out upon the day whose story she should never read.

We have been told that it takes three generations to make a gentleman: we may believe that it will take as much, or more, to make A WOMAN. A being of radiant physique; the heiress of ancestral health on the maternal side; a creature forever more of nerve than of muscle, and therefore trained to the energy of the muscle and the repose of the nerve; physically educated by mothers of her own fibre and by physicians of her own sex,—such a woman alone is fitted to acquire the drilled brain, the calmed imagination, and sustained aim, which constitute intellectual command.

A creature capable of this command, in whom emotion intensifies reflection, and passion strengthens purpose, and self-poise is substituted for self-extravagance,—such a creature only is competent to the terrible task of adjusting the sacred individuality of her life to her supreme capacity of love and the supreme burden and perils which it imposes upon her.

A man in whom the sources of feeling are as deep as they are delicate, as perennial as they are pure; whose affection becomes a burning ambition not to be outvied by hers, whose daily soul is large enough to guard her, even though it were at the cost of sharing it, from the tyranny of small corrosive care which gnaws and gangrenes hers,—such a man alone can either comprehend or apprehend the love of such a woman.

No man conceives what a woman will do or dare for him, until he has surprised her nature by the largest abnegation of which his own is capable. Let him but venture the experiment, if he will find himself vanquished by her in generosity to the end of the sweet warfare. Then first he knows what he has won; for then only does she suffer him to know. It is not till then, that reverence and surrender radically begin their life in her. Nay, then, he is the man, he only among men, who understands what a woman's tenderness is. With her, he is a crowned creature; but with him she is a free one.

Avis was a careworn woman; and, like most people with whom life has dealt intensely and introspectively, the pressure of the advancing upon the retreating generation touched her personality more than her philanthropy or philosophy. Were there subtle readings of the eternal riddle astir upon the desert? Had the stone lips of the sphinx begun to mutter? God knew; and the desert knew— and the dumb mouth.

For her, she had her child. It would be easier for her daughter to be alive, and be a woman, than it had been for her; so much as this, she understood; more than this she felt herself too spent to question. She folded her arms about the little girl, and laid her cheek upon her hair, and closed her eyes. She had the child, she had the child!

Once, sitting with Coy in the parsonage-parlor, the two women fell to talking of matters of which they did not often speak. Coy had the immense power of incommunicativeness sometimes found in simple and even impulsive women in whom a kind heart supplies the place of a deep imagination. For years now, with Avis, Coy's instinct had kept her close to the surface of the immediate. She felt it to be natural, that there was always something not to be talked about in Avis's life: it was the way with women like Avis, to whom things happened. Nothing had ever happened to Coy— except John and the children.

Coy had three children: they were not kept out of the parsonage-parlor any more than the sun or the air. Coy's children did not tire her: she looked radiantly at Avis across the brisk Babel in which they sat. Coy wore a morning-cap with purple ribbons. She had some pink ones, but took them out for the baby: she wondered how it was that people minded growing old. They talked a little that morning about the geological professor and his new book. Avis spoke calmly of the great gratification which the trustees found in his success. They spoke of the people who rented the house in High Street, and how they had built an L, and cut down the elm-tree, and altered the porch. Then Coy spoke of Chatty Hogarth's Odyssey Club, and of the poem Mrs. Hogarth had written for the Denominational Weekly.

"She asked me how my *babe* was yesterday," said Coy. "I never want to know another thing about a woman than that she calls a baby a babe. I hope she won't suffocate the Odyssey Club. But they say there are some fine law-students in it—rather young, though, I should think. And the girls that are coming along, study Greek, and are really very pretty, Avis,—that stratum just below us, you know, that were flirting with freshmen when we were engaged. Look out, Avis! Wait will cut herself putting Jack's screwdriver into the baby's dimple." Then they talked a little about Wait, and a little about John and the children, and then they spoke of Stratford Allen's housekeeper; and when Coy had told her how comfortable she made him since Barbara went, and how glad everybody was that Stratford was so well cared for, and how much good he did with all his money, and how many fine pictures he had in his house, she said she supposed Avis knew that the woman's name was Jessup, and that she came from Texas, where her husband had got shot.

"And of course, you've heard," said Coy absently, "that Stratford bought your sphinx last winter?" Coy spoke lightly; but her own voice sounded to her as if she had said, "He bought your soul." She rather wished she had said nothing about the sphinx. She hurried on to speak of Barbara, who had not married her minister, but only a New-York businessman: it was a trial for a Harmouth girl, but Barbara bore it well.

Then she talked a little of John and the children, and after that she spoke of the last alumni meeting, and said that John said the wish to put up the monument in Florida originated with the members of Professor Ostrander's first class,—the men who were under him in his opening year at college; clever men, John said, and that they spoke of Philip with emotion.

And then, by way of variety, she talked of John and the children a little more.

"You seem to keep pretty well," said Avis, after a silence, "with all your care, Coy."

The words sounded superficial enough. Coy felt that Avis would rather be taken on her own level, and answered carelessly,—

"Pretty well, Avis. There's about so much bother in everybody's life, I suppose. Some people take it in high tragedy. I take mine out in the mumps. I own my married life would have been happier if they hadn't *all* had the mumps while John was in Philadelphia, and Sarah laid up with her broken ankle, and Deacon Bobley out on a heresy-hunt, and the American Board—as nearly as I understand it—destined to become bankrupt, unless it could pay off its debt out of our church. I own so much, Avis. And besides I'll tell you—I never told it before (Ave, run away with Jack and Wait, a minute), there is one thing I must admit: I do *not* like to ask John for money. There! But that is all, Avis."

Was it all, indeed! It was a peaceful, pleasant story. As the children shut the door, it seemed very still suddenly in the parsonage-parlor: the sun was upon the worn carpet and the playthings, Coy's sewing-chair, and little garments lying half-made, and purple ribbons, and upon the baby in her lap.

Coy looked up from her sewing, and saw Avis sitting there, and watching her; as the country, wasted by civil war, pauses to look off upon the little neutral state.

A spark sprang into Coy's incurious, gentle face.

"It is nature!" she cried. "Explain it how you will."

"But I," said Avis in a low voice, after an expressive pause,—"*I* am nature, too. Explain me, Coy."

Coy did not answer. It was to be expected that Avis should be more or less unintelligible. But, when Avis turned presently to go, she kissed her, looking up with puzzled, affectionate eyes. Then she lifted the baby a little higher on her neck, and went into the study to talk to John.

"Somehow," said Coy, "I am always more sorry for Avis when I go away and think about her than I am when I sit and talk with her."

"Poor girl!" said John Rose.

As they stood in the window, leaning together, Avis, in her widow's dress, in the color of the morning, passed by, leading her little daughter by the hand.

When they were at home that day, more silently, perhaps, than usual, Wait in the corner, with her picture-books, and her mother sitting with crossed hands and vague eyes, the child came up, and said in her distinct, impressive fashion,—

"Mamma, I cannot read this story till I am old enough; but it is a pretty story, and I want to hear it. The man has a yellow saddle, and his horse is red. Read me what he had a red horse for, and where he went to; read me why the saddle is yellow; read me—read me— read me till there is no more to read."

Wait stood leaning a little, and stroking the back of her mother's hand with the palm of her own. If anybody had noticed this, she would have stopped; but mamma understood about such things. She did not talk and make a fuss.

Avis took the book, and read. She sat with her profile towards the child.

"Sir Launcelot rode overthwart and endlong in a wide forest, and held no path but as wild adventure led him. Then Sir Launcelot looked round, and saw an old chapel, but could find no place where he might enter. And as he lay, half waking and half sleeping . . . he saw . . . the holy vessel of the Sangreal pass him by. So thus he sorrowed till it was day, and heard the fowls of the air sing. . . .

"Then the hermit led the young knight to the Perilous Seat; and he lifted up the cloth, and found there letters that said, 'This is the seat of Sir Galahad the good knight.' This is he by whom the Sangreal shall be achieved. . . .

"Now, the name of the young knight was Sir Galahad, and he was the son of Sir Launcelot du Lac."[5]

❦ EXPLANATORY NOTES

"Now, all the meaning of the King was to see Sir Galahad proved": see Thomas Bulfinch, *The Age of Chivalry* (1862), chap. 19, "The Sangreal, or Holy Grail." Phelps feminizes and updates the Grail Legend: Lancelot parallels Avis; Galahad, Wait, her daughter; the Grail, woman's spiritual achievement and self-development (see pp. 249–250).

CHAPTER I

1. Harmouth: a place name formed perhaps upon *Har*vard and Dart*mouth*, each an established New England institution of higher education for men only.
2. This verse and those that follow in this chapter are from Edmund Spenser (1552–1599), *The Faerie Queen* (1596), a work dedicated to the fame of Elizabeth I. Verses quoted appear in Book I, Cantos 2 and 3. Book I tells the legend of the Knight of the Red Cross, champion of Una or Truth. In Cantos 2 and 3, the Knight is parted from Una by fair falsehood or Duessa, who teaches him a sad lesson; Una, protected by a lion, seeks and regains her knight. Passages quoted are from canto 2, stanza 31 and canto 3, stanzas 11, 12, 26, 30. The episode of the Red Knight, Una, and Duessa foreshadows the plot of Avis and Philip.
3. Antonio Allegri da Correggio (1494–1534), the Italian painter, created a sensuous depiction of the mythical Io, the White Goddess of the moon and alleged paramour of Jupiter, Roman Father of the Gods.

CHAPTER II

1. Themistius (317?–388?), Greek rhetorician and philosopher, whose work shows the continuation of pagan Greek thought in spite of Christian hegemony.
2. Geoffrey Chaucer (c. 1340–1400), from "The Squire's Tale,"

ll. 87–88, in *The Canterbury Tales* (1387–1394), a tale of a deserted lady, in which all the actors become birds.

3. home missionary boxes: boxes filled with items for the poor and ready to be distributed by volunteers from a church's home (as opposed to foreign or overseas) missions.

4. Melian Venus: Aphrodite of Melos, a statue named for the island in the Aegean Sea where it was discovered in 1820; it now stands in the Louvre Museum in Paris, more familiarly known as the Venus de Milo, one of the prime examples of Hellenistic art.

5. Jean Ingelow (1820–1897), British poet popular with American readers. Also author of novels and children's stories. See chap. 13, epigraph.

6. Mme Récamier (1777–1849) in Jacques Louis David's (1748–1825) picture hanging in the Paris Louvre: hostess of a noted salon frequented by such French writers as François-René de Chateaubriand (1768–1848), Mme de Staël (1766–1817), Charles-Augustin Sainte-Beuve (1804–1869) and Benjamin Constant (1767–1830).

CHAPTER III

1. Faust (16th century): German doctor memorialized in literature, especially in Goethe's (1749–1832) *Faust* (1808, 1833), where he is depicted as a seeker after knowledge, saved by the love of young Margaret.

2. Abélard (1079–1142): French cleric and tutor to Héloïse (d. 1164?), who bore a son by him.

3. Petrarch (1304–1374): Italian poet noted for his sonnets and vernacular lyrics inspired by Laura (d. 1348).

4. Dante (1265–1321): Italian poet of *The Divine Comedy*, memorial of his love for Beatrice (d. 1290).

5. John Milton (1608–1674) wrote *Paradise Lost* (1667), a major blank verse epic in English, telling of Adam and Eve's fall from Paradise. Phelps would mock his patriarchal views in her humorous *An Old Maid's Paradise* (1879) and *Burglars in Paradise* (1886).

6. Samuel Taylor Coleridge (1772–1834) wrote "Kubla Khan" (1816), a poem he claims was the result of an opium-induced vision.

7. "bird-like": *Avis* is the Latin word for *bird*. The expression *rara avis* often refers to a rare, extraordinary, or otherwise outstanding example. Phelps uses the imagery here to suggest a similarity of circumstance between mother and daughter. The image of a caged bird is frequent in women's writing, appearing as well in the nineteenth-century song for a woman's voice, "I'm just a bird in a gilded cage." (See Ellen Moers, *Literary Women* [1976], pp. 245–251.)

8. "Under the shadow of His wing shalt *thou* abide": A variation of Ps. 17:8 ("hide me under the shadow of thy wings") and 91:1 ("He that dwelleth in the secret place of the most High, shall abide under the shadow of the Almighty").

9. Sir William "The Wise" Hamilton (1788–1856), philosopher at the University of Edinburgh, influenced by Kant. Dobell fancies that he resembles Hamilton. See also pages 28, 33–34.

CHAPTER IV

1. Alfred Lord Tennyson (1809–1892), from *Queen Mary* (1875), Act II, Scene 2. Here Sir Ralph Bogenhall addresses Lord William Howard, a fellow supporter of the Queen, regarding the determination of their colleague Thomas White to support her against insurgents.

2. *Aurora Leigh* (1857) by Elizabeth Barrett Browning (1806–1861) is a blank verse novel. It presents the dilemma of the creative woman (here a poet)—how to live and work creatively in a society that claims she cannot—and permits both Aurora's resolution of this dilemma and her successful achievement. Phelps herself read *Aurora Leigh* as a girl; see her autobiographical *Chapters from a Life* (Boston: Houghton, Mifflin, 1896), pp. 65–66.

Aurora justifies to herself the poet's role as compared with that of "common men." Throughout Avis fights to define herself against the "Angel in the House" role of perfect domestic cheer and competence in which she has no interest. Unlike "Fanny Fern," (Sara Payson Willis Parton, 1811–1872) in *Ruth Hall* (1855)—where an author exemplifies perfect feminine homemaking skills, Avis believes she has different obligations—namely, the development and practice of artistic skills.

3. Adapted from *Aurora Leigh*, Book I, ll. 879–880.

4. "The June was in her, with its nightingales." Adapted from *Aurora Leigh*, Book II, ll. 10–11: "The June was in me, with its multitudes/Of nightingales all singing in the dark."

5. *Critique of Pure Reason*: published in 1781 by German philosopher Immanuel Kant (1724–1804).

6. From *Aurora Leigh*: The original reads "'Who love my art,/ would never wish it lower/To suit my stature'" (Book II, ll. 492–494). Aurora defines herself against her cousin Romney's skeptical and critical estimate of her capacity as a poet and against his narrow view of her possibilities as a woman.

7. Francesco Saverio Altamura (1826–1897), Italian art/painting teacher, working predominantly in Florence and specializing in historical scenes.

8. Thomas Couture (1815–1879), Parisian painter and art teacher. Louisa May Alcott's sister May apparently found Couture "too absorbed in his own work to give [students] more than casual criticism" and thus refused to pay "a high price to this master" (Caroline Ticknor, *May Alcott: A Memoir* [Boston: Little Brown, 1928], p. 234).

9. Soddoma, usually spelled Sodoma: Sienese painter (1477?– 1549), whose fresco "The Marriage of Alexander and Roxana" (c. 1512), located in a bedroom of the Villa Farnesina in Rome, depicts a highly erotic Roxana, being disrobed by cherubs as she waits on the edge of a bed while another cherub pulls Alexander toward her.

10. King Cophetua: In the ballad "King Cophetua and the Beggar Maid" (oldest extant version, 1617), the king—having disdained women all his life—glances from his palace window one day to see a beggar maid who instantly so enthralls him that he marries her.

11. Madeleine: The Church of St. Mary Magdalene (also Miriam of Magdala) in Paris, in the style of a Greek temple, sits at the end of one of the grand boulevard vistas from the Place de la Concorde. A Magdalen is a reformed prostitute. See Luke 7:36ff. and chap. 8, no. 8.

12. "amber intaglio": undoubtedly an allusion to "The Amber Gods" (1860) by Harriet Prescott Spofford (1835–1921), a story that Phelps credited with having a "subtle influence" upon her. (See her "Stories That Stay," *The Century* 59 [Nov. 1910], p. 119.) Spofford is noted for her use of jewel imagery. The amber beads of the title cast an inescapable spell upon a beloved woman, to the benefit of the beads' owner and at the woman's expense. Such will be the effect of this face upon Avis.

13. "amber god": See preceding note.

CHAPTER V

1. "gorge within the cliff": Here the landscape is depicted as a female body. Note the imagery of marriage and motherhood as well as the "purple" "flesh" of this "cleft" (46). Phelps is daring in the sexual implications of this 1877 passage. (See Ellen Moers, *Literary Women* [1976], pp. 254–264.)

CHAPTER VI

1. R[obert] K[elley] Weeks (1840–1876), from the poem "The End" in a series called "With Men and Women." The quoted stanza

appears between one concerning the songs and one concerning the loves that remain ideally out of reach.

2. Balder: Norse sun god, sacrificed to regenerate the world.

3. sphinx: See chap. 6, no. 14; chap. 7, no. 3; chap. 8, n. 9 for a discussion of its significance to the novel.

4. Ludovisi Juno: a head one-meter high of severe beauty, part of a colossal Roman statue after a fifth-century B.C. Greek original; so-called Ludovisi for Louis XIV of France, whose collection now appears in the Roman National Museum.

5. "Then she departed into her own country by another way": adapted from Matt. 2:12, where the Three Wise Men obey God's warning and so depart after presenting gifts to the Christ child.

6. Antinous (c. 110–130): beautiful youth favored by Roman Emperor Hadrian (76–138), who had him immortalized in many statues.

7. Belvedere: possibly the Belvedere Torso in the Vatican Museum in Rome, so-called for the Vatican courtyard in which Clement VII (1523–1534, papal reign) placed it; or more likely, the Apollo Belvedere, also in the Vatican, considered a central monument from the Hellenistic age of Greek civilization.

8. Frederick Robertson (1816–1853), liberal Anglican theologian.

9. John White Alexander (1856–1915), eminent portrait painter in the United States.

10. Lachrymae Christi: an Italian white table wine.

11. rose: typically stands for love in floral iconography.

12. "the pretty thought about the growing of the grass": a reference to Dorothea, ill-fated wife in George Eliot's *Middlemarch* (1872), who "is discovered in a fit of weeping six weeks after her wedding." Eliot goes on to observe:

Some discouragement, some faintness of heart at the new real future which replaces the imaginary is not unusual . . . If we had a keen vision and feeling of all ordinary human life, it would be like hearing the grass grow and the squirrel's heart beat, and we should die of that roar which lies on the other side of silence. (Chapter 20)

See Phelps's 1873 letter to Eliot about Dorothea, quoted in Introduction, pp. xvii–xviii, and Chap. 7, note 2.

13. "hero in the old mythology": Siegfried of the Nibelungenlied who captures Brunhild, Queen of the Walkyries.

14. "dumb, protesting goddess . . . to the glare of day": refers to the sphinx. In 1863, American painter Elihu Vedder (1836–1923) completed "The Questioner of the Sphinx" (now in the Boston Museum of Fine Arts), which depicted only the head of the sphinx in view above the sands, as it appeared to nineteenth-century trav-

elers. The sphinx is supposed to have asked of man: "What goes on four legs at dawn, two legs at midday, and three legs at sunset?" But the riddle for Avis is how to be both woman and artist. See also Phelps's essay, "The True Woman," in this volume.

15. "the humming of the bees in the wigelia-bush": Worker bees or drones are males, the wigelia blossoms, female. Phelps works in an established tradition of women's imagery, one that includes Emily Dickinson's and Margaret Fuller's use of the bee as male marauder, the flower as female depleted by the male. (See Wendy Martin, *An American Triptych*, 1984.)

CHAPTER VII

1. George Eliot [Marian Evans] (1819–1880), from "Armgart," scene 2, in *The Legend of Jubal and Other Poems* (1870). In this dramatic poem in five scenes, the heroine Armgart (a singer) has to choose between her erotic love for a man and her self-devotion to her own artistic development, and decides in favor of the latter. Phelps and Eliot exchanged a series of letters on this subject. Phelps's letters are in the Beinecke Rare Book and Manuscript Library, Yale University; Eliot's are published. See note 2, below.

2. marriage as profession: See letter of Phelps to George Eliot, 26 February 1873 (The Beinecke Rare Book and Manuscript Library, Yale University) regarding Dorothea in *Middlemarch* (1872), who thought her marriage would give her noble work to do in the world but whose husband was only older, and not wiser, than she. (Quoted in Introduction, p. xviii.)

3. "I can dare": For the first Smith College commencement in 1879, Phelps wrote a poem "Victurae Salutamus" (Latin: "On the brink of victory, we women salute you"), which she closed with these lines: "Ideal of ourselves! We dream and dare./Victurae salutamus! *Thou* art dumb." Again, Phelps alludes to women's inability to speak, a sphinxlike dumbness, at the same time that she sounds a call to action—to "dare" (See her collection, *Songs of the Silent World and Other Poems*, Boston: Houghton, Mifflin, 1885, p. 99).

4. A check payable to her father, not to Avis, is "more convenient or agreeable . . . to cash" because women were not expected to handle money or finances. Phelps exposes the drawbacks of such practices in *The Silent Partner* (1871), in "Hannah Colby's Chance" (*Our Young Folks*, 9 [Oct.–Dec. 1873]) for juveniles, and in such essays as "What They Are Doing" and "Women and Money" in *The Independent* 23 (1871), 17 and 24 August respectively.

CHAPTER VIII

1. Charles Blanc (1813–1882), from *The Grammar of Painting and Engraving*, chap. 6, entitled "The methods peculiar to painting force themselves upon the artist as soon as he invents his subject, and conceives the first image of it."

2. "summer of battles": These Civil War battles date the events of the novel as beginning in April 1861, when Avis is twenty-six years old.

3. Vatican, Pitti, Louvre: art galleries respectively in Rome, Florence, Paris.

4. Verses from "The Battle Hymn of the Republic": written by Julia Ward Howe (1819–1910), a Boston resident, who headed the New England Woman Suffrage Association in 1868. Howe also edited *Sex and Education* (1874), a collection of essays favoring higher education for women and including an essay by Phelps.

5. "*Eau de Fleurs d'Oranger*": French for "Orange-Flower brandy," an eau-de-vie or clear, strong alcoholic beverage. In *Chapters from a Life*, Phelps notes that her father read her the writings of Thomas De Quincey (1785–1859), who was especially noted for *The Confessions of an English Opium Eater* (1822), in which he discusses his habit.

6. "self-articulate hour": Avis's self-induced experience of her unconscious and of her sense of being a woman in history and in society. Like the heroine in Phelps's *Confessions of a Wife* (1902), this vision leads Avis to an appreciation of sisterhood with all women. For her male characters, such visions—as in *The Gates Between* (1887) and *Avery* (1902)—or such illness—as for Philip in this novel—leads to man's recognition of his inhumanity to woman.

7. "Isis went seeking Osiris": Egyptian myth in which the goddess Isis, the Giver of Life who gradually absorbed the qualities of all goddesses, seeks her son and consort Osiris; Isis wears red apparel, as does Avis, suggesting their affinity; see *Avis*, p. 117.

8. "full of women": *Cleopatra*, Egyptian queen, and beloved of Julius Caesar and Mark Anthony; *Godiva*, Gothic goddess who appeared naked on May-Eve and blinded any who peeped at her; *Aphrodite*, Greek goddess of Love and counterpart of the Roman Venus; *St. Elizabeth*, thirteenth-century Hungarian martyr, who died from wife-abuse; *Ariadne*, a Cretan moon-goddess and consort of Dionysius; *Esther*, the Hebrew counterpart of the Egyptian Ishtar or Queen of Heaven; *Helen*, who went to Troy with her lover Paris and thus caused the Trojan War; *Jeanne d'Arc*, burned at the stake as a witch in Rouen in 1431 and canonized in 1920; *Magdalene*, the Mary beloved of Jesus; *Sappho*, poet-priestess of the Greek Isle of Lesbos, ruled by women devoted to serving Aphrodite and

Artemis; and *Cornelia*, second-century B.C. Roman widow and mother of the Gracchi, the two sons who were her "jewels."

9. Sphinx's "riddle of ages": See chap. 6, n. 14 for riddle. The sphinx exists in varied representations. The oldest are female: woman's face and breast, lion's body, bird's wings, as in Oedipus. Later Egyptian sphinxes are male: lion, hawk/vulture, or cobra. A sun god—infant-like at sunrise, powerful at noon, and enfeebled but creative at setting sun—the sphinx is a symbol of rebirth, royal power, and benevolent guardianship. Its winged version ties it to Avis (bird). In the poem "The Sphinx" (1879), written for the graduating class of Abbott Academy (a girls' secondary school in Andover, Massachusetts), Phelps depicts a sphinx of lion's heart, "eagle's wings," and "woman's eyes" (*Songs of the Silent World and Other Poems* [Boston: Houghton, Mifflin, 1885], pp. 97–98).

10. vivisection: During the 1890s, Phelps with her husband sought to have laws enacted by the Massachusetts legislature to control this practice. In her writing she uses vivisection as an image for a husband's callousness toward his wife. See Kessler, *Elizabeth Stuart Phelps* (1982), pp. 110–112, 116.

11. Sèvres specimen: French porcelain of highest quality; choice.

12. "a revival already since he was settled": A minister could gauge his effect once settled in a congregation by whether attendance revived as a result of his preaching. Phelps's grandfather Eliakim Phelps (1789–1880) was especially attuned to this mode of self-evaluation.

CHAPTER IX

1. Robert Browning (1812–1889), from "Pippa Passes" (1841): a verse-drama line from a song concerning the sowing of love's seeds, which can be expected eventually to flower.

2. John Fletcher (1579–1625), dramatist, and likely William Shakespeare (1563–1616), co-author, from *The Two Noble Kinsmen* (1634). It is based upon Chaucer's "The Knight's Tale" and concerns a rivalry between two cousins for the love of fair Emilia; after a duel the victor wins her.

3. Mrs. [Anna Brownell Murphy] Jameson (1794–1860), English travel, art, and history essayist.

4. nasturtiums: patriotism in floral iconography.

5. "physical ruin and helplessness": a pattern existing in both British and American fiction by women. Men are blinded in Charlotte Brontë's (1816–1855) *Jane Eyre* (1847) and Barrett Browning's *Aurora Leigh*, both read by Phelps.

CHAPTER X

1. Robert Browning, from "Paracelsus" (1835), a verse drama. Paracelsus speaks, having just explained that God should "elevate the race" as a whole and "make no more giants" among humans.
2. "like—death": In Phelps's heavenly Utopias of 1883 and 1887, female characters feel with comparable ironic reversal, "To be dead was to be dead to danger, dead to fear. To be dead was to be alive to a sense of assured good chance that nothing in the universe could shake" (*Beyond the Gates* [Boston: Houghton, Mifflin, 1883], p. 72) and "'They call this death. Why, I never knew what it was to be *alive* before!'" (*The Gates Between* [Boston: Houghton, Mifflin] 1887, p. 152).
3. Battle imagery weaves through these pages as the "war between the sexes" reaches its climax. Indeed, Avis also experiences an inner "civil war" between her two natures—the woman socialized to sacrifice, the human being expecting to grow and to achieve.
4. heliotrope: a flower symbolizing "devotion and faithfulness" in nineteenth-century floral iconography.

CHAPTER XI

1. H[elen Maria Fiske] H[unt Jackson] (1830–1885), fiction writer and poet, friend of Emily Dickinson, from "Vintage," in *Poems* (1894). The wine that she gives in the five-stanza poem is her eternal love. (Note the wine imagery preceding, p. 107). Jackson's novel *Mercy Philbrick's Choice* (1876) concerns a poet's choice between her poetry and a lover: she chooses the poetry over him.
2. Dugald Stewart (1753–1828), a student of Thomas Reid (1710–1796), who founded the Scottish common sense school of philosophy. Stewart, whose complete works exist in eleven volumes, firmly established common sense philosophy.
3. "Reid on Aristotle": "A Brief Account of Aristotle's Logic," an essay first published in the second volume of *Sketches of the History of Man* (1774), edited by Henry Home Kames (1696–1782).
4. "*Et in Acadia ego*" (Latin): "And I am in Arcadia." Arcadia: a rural paradise or idealized region, after a Greek state noted for its forests and for its devotion to Artemis (Diana to Romans), goddess of nature and of birth associated with the waxing moon. In Sir Philip Sidney's (1554–1586) *Arcadia* (1590), true lovers are united in the end. Professor Dobell seems to have such an ideal state in mind here as he sees his wife in his daughter.

5. The Adelaide: a piano concerto attributed to Mozart.

6. Fee-jeeans: Fiji Islanders, likely intended as an exotic culture to which one is indifferent because it is uncomprehensible.

CHAPTER XIII

1. Mme [Sophie Soymonof] de Swetchine (1782–1857), from *Writings of Madame Swetchine*: A Russian expatriate living in Paris, she knew Mmes Récamier and de Staël. She was noted for the saintliness of her life with respect to its piety and good works.

2. Jean Ingelow from "Married Lovers," in *Poems*, v. 2, a poem in which a husband asks his wife to leave her work and come enjoy the world with him.

3. Paumotu Archipelago: perhaps alternate spelling for Tua-motu Archipelago near Tahiti.

4. Wilkes Expedition: Charles Wilkes (1798–1877), American naval officer and explorer, set off in 1838 for the South Pacific, explored Fiji and Hawaii, and returned to New York in 1842, having circumnavigated the globe.

5. rare white bird: In Sarah Orne Jewett's (1849–1909) "The White Heron" (1886), a young girl is unable to "tell the heron's secret and give its life away" to a young man from the city, bent upon adding to his collection of stuffed birds. Authenticity rules Jewett's story, but not so Phelps's. She treats Philip's narrative with irony: he is less heroic than his students think him, given his limited perception of Avis.

CHAPTER XIV

1. William Wordsworth (1770–1859), from "The Excursion" (1814), Book 9, l. 238. The line occurs in a discussion of the *common* needs of all, in spite of differences among human beings.

2. "she of Erin": Irish servants frequent Phelps's fiction. Ever sympathetic to the help that one woman supplies to another's liberation from drudgery, Phelps depicts with humor and feeling the plight of household servants. See her juvenile *Mercy Gliddon's Work* (1865); and three adult works—*Old Maids and Burglars in Paradise* (1886), *The Successors of Mary the First* (1901), *The Man in the Case* (1906)—all of which contain portraits of lively, self-possessed maids. The 1901 work is both a tribute to such workers and a plea for their rights. Here the servant comments as much upon a wife-mother's plight as her own.

CHAPTER XV

1. "Success is impossible, unless the passion for art overcomes all desultory passions." Possibly George Eliot, given Phelps's view that she was the greatest novelist of her time: in a 1 Dec. 1876 letter to George Eliot, Phelps calls her "the novelist of this century."
2. Arria and the dagger: Accused of conspiring against Roman Emperor Claudius, Arria's husband was condemned to death by suicide; when he hesitated, Arria stabbed herself, explained she had no pain, and handed the dagger to her husband.
3. *moxa*: a woolly mass made from leaves of Asian wormwoods, works as a cautery when ignited on the skin; or other substance so used.

CHAPTER XVI

1. Alfred Lord Tennyson, *Queen Mary* (1875), Act V, scene 2: Lady Magdalen to Alice concerning Philip, whom Mary dotes upon although he does not "see beyond himself."
2. Theodore Prodromus (c. 1166), Byzantine writer and poet, employing a wide range of genres.
3. Charles Theodore Frère (1814–1888), a French painter, who was among the outstanding exponents of Oriental themes during the Second Empire.
4. "the law" and wives: The 1870s feminist reforms included equalizing the relations between wife and husband, by providing wives with rights they did not have. Legally wives were one with their husbands and had no separate status. Drunken wife battering (see p. 160 above) figured large in the rationale of the temperance movement.
5. Johanna Mockel Kinkel (1810–1858) wrote the well-known "Soldier's Farewell," as well as the operetta *Otto der Schutz* and *Acht Briefe an eine Freundin über Klavierunterricht* [Eight Letters to a Woman Friend about Teaching the Klavier] (1852).

CHAPTER XVII

1. "Rhetoric" or "Poetic": classic works of Greek philosophy by Aristotle.
2. Van Dyck: the name of Avis's son, apparently after Flemish portrait and religious artist, Anthony Van Dyck (1599–1641).
3. Johann Kaspar Lavater (1741–1801), noted for his work on

physiognomy, or the determination of character from a person's outward appearance.

4. "imagination . . . future . . . daughter": In *The Angel over the Right Shoulder* (1852), Phelps's mother depicts a mother bending over a sleeping daughter and wishing to "shield that child from the disappointments and mistakes and self-reproach from which the mother was then suffering; that the little one might take up life where she could give it to her—all mended by her own experience" (p. 22). See Kessler, "A Literary Legacy: Elizabeth Stuart Phelps, Mother and Daughter," *Frontiers* 5 (3) 1981: 28–33, for a discussion of this literary relationship.

CHAPTER XVIII

1. Cardinal Jean François Paul de Gondi de Retz (1613–1679), French clergyman and politician, enemy of Mazarin, from *Memoires, seconde partie*.

2. Victor Hugo (1802–1885), French poet and novelist, from last two lines of "Regret" (Feb. 1821), first published in *Odes et poésies diverses* (1822). The lines mean: "This time when happiness sparkles, and suddenly disappears,/Like an interrupted smile!"

3. Charlotte Brontë, upon her deathbed, to her husband of nine months, Arthur Bell Nicholls (1817–1906), according to Elizabeth Gaskell (1810–1865) in *The Life of Charlotte Brontë* (1857). Phelps listed Brontë's *Jane Eyre* (1847) among the four best nineteenth-century novels by women, others being *Consuelo* (1842–1843) by George Sand (1804–1876), *Uncle Tom's Cabin* (1851–1852) by Harriet Beecher Stowe (1811–1896), and *Middlemarch* (1872) by George Eliot. See brochure for "The Greatest Woman Novelists and their greatest books" offered by the Booklovers Library (1901); in Library of Congress, PN 3401/.W6.

4. "It is my duty to live": Compare the words of Phelps's mother to Phelps's father during her final illness, as he reports them, namely, "*Now, my duty is, to live*" (Austin Phelps [1820–1890], "A Memorial of the Author," p. 99, in *The Last Leaf from Sunny Side* by "H. Trusta" [pseud. for Elizabeth Stuart Phelps, 1815–1852]).

5. Georg Ernst Stahl (1660–1734), a physician who theorized that the soul controls the function and structure of the body.

6. Adelaide: See chap. 11, 5.

7. "Trovatore," "Lucia," "Faust": operas containing popular arias sung by heroines ill-fated in love, namely Leonora in "Il Trovatore" (1853) by Giuseppe Verdi (1813–1901), Lucia in "Lucia di Lammermoor" (1835) by Gaetano Donizetti (1797–1848), and

Marguerite in "Faust" (1859) by Charles Gounod (1818–1893).

8. From the Scottish ballad "Barbara Allen." First mentioned in Samuel Pepys's *Diary*, (1660–1669). "Barbara Allen" is probably the best known ballad of Western Europe. The story tells of Sweet William who, though he toasts other maids as this verse states, dies for love of Barbara Allen. Hearing his death knell, she grieves and dies herself. A red rose and briar grow from the respective graves.

CHAPTER XX

1. Frederick Robertson. See chap. 6, note 8.

2. Calasaya bark: a quinine source, used medicinally for influenza, neuralgia, debility; also in tooth powders or throat gargles.

3. Jacob and the angel wrestle one night of his journey homeward, at the end of which he receives the name Israel. See Gen. 32:24–32.

4. Adolphe Goupil (1806–1877?): a nineteenth-century printer-publisher.

CHAPTER XXI

1. Alfred Lord Tennyson, from "The Princess" (1847–1851), Part I, ll. 257–259, the final lines of the concluding song. The song concerns a couple who have quarreled, then kissed and made up before they come upon the grave "where lies the child/We lost in other years."

2. Mater Dolorosa: Latin, literally "sorrowful mother," often used to refer to representations of Mary with the body of the crucified Christ across her lap.

CHAPTER XXII

1. August von Kotzebue (1761–1819), German dramatist and politician, from the play *Hugo Grotius* (1803), Act 3, scene 11.

2. "And the evening and the morning were the third day": Gen. 1:13, the creation of land from the waters, a sequence culminating in the creation of Eve and Adam in Eden.

3. Ancient City by the Sea: likely St. Augustine, Florida, oldest city in the United States, founded in 1565 to protect Spanish interests against French colonizers.

4. Claude Lorraine (1600–1682), French landscape painter noted for his manipulation of atmosphere.
5. Tocoi: a town on the St. Johns River, near St. Augustine.

CHAPTER XXIII

1. John Gibson Lockhart (1794–1854), English lawyer and literary critic, from "The Wandering Knight's Song" in the Cancionero of Antwerp, 1555, in *Ancient Spanish Ballads; Historical and Romantic* (1841). The last of its stanzas is the epigraph.
2. "select three": Peter, James, and John. See Matt. 17 and Mark 9.
3. Pilatka: now spelled Palatka, a town on St. Johns River.
4. Lazarus, brother of Mary and Martha, brought back to life by Jesus. See John 11 : 1–44, 12 : 1–5.
5. "statues of [Michel] Angelo" (1475–1564): masterpieces of the Italian Renaissance.

CHAPTER XXIV

1. John Fletcher, from *The Two Noble Kinsmen* (1634), Act II, scene 1. The full passage reads:

> Certainly,
> 'Tis a main goodness, cousin, that our fortunes
> Were twines together: 'Tis most true, two souls
> Put in two noble bodies, let 'em suffer
> The gall of hazard, so they grow together,
> Will never sink; they must not; say they could,
> A willing man dies sleeping, and all's done.

2. George Eliot from "Oh May I Join the Choir Invisible" (1867), ll. 19–21, 30, in *Poems*. Eliot's verses concern the immortality possible for the best that lives in each of us.
3. "new heavens": allusion to "I saw a new heaven and a new earth" (Rev. 21 : 1), the disciple John's vision of a "new Jerusalem," the new heaven, earth, and Jerusalem becoming metaphors for visions of Utopia, the good society of humanity's deepest hopes.
4. "words which Dante saw": At the beginning of canto III of "The Inferno" in *The Divine Comedy* (1302?–1321?) by the Italian medieval poet Dante Alighieri (1265–1321), the pilgrim-narrator, as he passes through the door of Hell, sees written above it these words:

I am the way into the city of woe.
I am the way to a forsaken people.
I am the way into eternal sorrow.

Sacred justice moved my architect.
I was raised here by divine omnipotence,
Primordial love and ultimate intellect.

Only those elements time cannot wear
Were made before me, and beyond time I stand,
Abandon all hope ye who enter here. (trans. John Ciardi, 1954)

CHAPTER XXV

1. John Greenleaf Whittier (1807–1892), from "My Triumph" in *Miriam and Other Poems* (1871). The poem addresses the "triumph" of daily living in the face of oncoming death. A friend of Phelps, he often wrote her to express enjoyment and understanding of her work.

2. Locke's Understanding: *Essay concerning Human Understanding* (1690) by John Locke (1632–1704), in which he developed his theory of the *tabula rasa* (blank slate), that the human mind is born blank, rather than with innate ideas, and that experience of the five senses leads to knowledge.

3. "better pictures . . . for loving . . .": Phelps's view that Avis was not imagining the impossible is based upon the experience of her own generation of women artists. Some few did escape stereotypic outcomes. Alice Barber [Stephens] (1858–1932) became more successful than her artist husband, Charles H. Stephens. Several other women who trained at the Pennsylvania Academy of Fine Arts also married, but none of these seem to have raised children.

4. "Keep her out of school": The "out of doors" policy also occurs in several books by Louisa May Alcott. See *Little Men* (1871), chaps. 1, 2; *Eight Cousins* (1874), chaps. 2, 3, 22; *Jack and Jill* (1880), chap. 23. For outdoor health advocacy in other children's literature of the period, see R. Gordon Kelly, *Mother Was a Lady* (Westport, Connecticut: Greenwood, 1974), chap. 5 "At Home in the Country."

5. The story of Sir Lancelot and Sir Galahad: The source of the quotations is Thomas Bulfinch, *The Age of Chivalry* (1862) chaps. 19, 20. For a discussion, see note to title page.

Contexts

THE TRUE WOMAN

by Elizabeth Stuart Phelps

from *The Independent* 23
no. 1193
(12 Oct. 1871):1

Whatever the secret motives of opposition current in the heart of society to the "New Departure" in the history of woman—and that the secret motives outnumber the professed arguments it is well for us not to overlook—the most palpable obstacle which we meet is an enormous dummy to which has been given the title of the "true woman."

The "true woman," we are told, desires and seeks no noisy political existence. To the "true woman" the whirr and bustle of public life are unattractive. A "true woman" honors the homely virtues and appreciates the quiet dignities of household life. She is no "true woman" who cannot find in the "sweet, safe corner . . . behind the heads of children" scope for her activities and content in her adjustment to them. A "true woman" will shrink from the rough contact of the world. The "true woman" instinctively merges her life—social, political, commercial—in that of her husband. When this transient excitement is over, the *"true* woman" will outlive and outshine it—a testimony to the "reform against Nature" and herself. There is something of the monotony of the refrains in the old ballads, or of the pathos contained in the chorus to the woes of those celebrated lovers, "Vilikens and his Dinah," in the regularity with which this phrase is chanted in our ears.

"The true woman" of popular speech is the gauntest scarecrow ever posted on the rich fields of Truth to frighten timid birds away. A touch of amusement dashes across the pity with which we see them—for we see them every day—drop and die of hunger rather than face this phantom's eye. When we have poked the empty ribs of the creature and wrenched away her hollow wraps, and found the broomstick and the stuffing, it is not incomprehensible how she could ever have passed for flesh and blood, only because it is the fashion of the world to crown its most evident shams and found dynasties of its most potent deceits.

To say that the empty and powerful figure to which we have attached this royal name is patched up by men, and by those women who have no sense of character but such as they reflect from men, and that it is made of dreams and heartache, tears and weakness, blindness, mischief, mistake, and wrong, and dullness more difficult to cure than wrong, is to state one of those propositions whose proof does not add much to its potency. If he [   ] read its enigmatic letters he will be little the wiser should he stand and spell them out.

In truth, this entire notion of regulating the position of women by conformity to an established ideal of womanly character is, both in theory and in practice, almost without the bounds of sober argument. It is an impertinence and an absurdity. The womanly character is no more the property of the world—to count, weigh, measure, bottle, label—than the manly character. Every time that a man assumes to indicate to a woman the character of her "sphere" he offers her an insult. To use that homely phrase which has no graceful counterpart, it is none of his business what her sphere is.

Woman is not man's ward. Man is not woman's guardian. Man is incapable, even if he were called upon to do so, of competently judging for woman in the adjustment of her "place" in society. Indeed, if one wisdom must decree for two, woman is far better qualified to regulate the position which shall belong to man. He is not the enigma to her which she must always be more or less to him. His force is more comprehensible to her than her fineness is to him.

But these nuts we may crack at our leisure; there is meat enough in them. For the present, it is enough to remember that a thorough and equalized independence of each other's control is the only premise to a healthy exercise of that mutual dependence upon each other's forbearance which must exist between the sexes; and, that any theory of life which means, in crystal, that man's work and position are what he chooses for himself, while woman's work and position are such as he chooses for her, is unworthy either of the intelligence or the Christianity of times like these.

But, beyond and above this, it is to be understood that nobody knows as yet what the womanly character is. Our ideals of it are, *par excellence*, fictitious and contingent. The traits which we attribute to it we have just as much reason to consider inherent in it as we have to consider duplicity and dishonesty inseparable from the negro character; no more. It will not be in this generation that we can presume to any acquaintance with the character of the American freedmen. It will not be in this generation, nor in the next, that we can justifiably assert that we have any acquaintance with what it is in the "nature" of woman to do or to be.

Woman's "nature" was all but born dumb. She has hitherto communicated with us only by signs. She has had no speech nor language. When times are ripe and days are due, and the live coal of her future shall touch her lips, we may then listen, if we would learn something of her "nature." Nature has a wise sullenness, a shrewd sulkiness of her own, by which she defends herself when in durance. Character bides its time patiently; but it blossoms only in freedom as wide as the air and as strong as the light.

We cannot be reminded too often that the history of the world has been, so far, the history of brute force; that by sheer muscle man took the right of way, and through simple lack of sinew woman yielded it; that the moulds in which womanly character has run have been those of necessity, not of choice—feudal, not republican; reflective, not original; expedient, not instinctive—and that it is not the least of their mutual misfortunes that woman, as well as man, has become so effectually bewildered on the subject of her own traits and aptitudes that she is largely unaware of any distinction between man's direction and her destiny.

In the conduct of the world's affairs, hitherto, woman has been always experimented upon. Like the "first child," all the blunders of the human family government have been wreaked about her head. We manufactured a model of womanly excellence—and that means the model most to man's convenience—and dragged the sex to it with a persistent, complacent, stupid, and stupefying good faith, which is to-day the greatest obstacle in the way of our perception of the important circumstance that we really know next to nothing of what we are about.

"The true woman," I maintain, earth has never seen. Her beautiful feet are upon the mountains; but only the echo of their stepping stirs the air. When might has ceased, once and forever, to constitute right; when the weak things of the world confound the mighty; when the lion lies down with the lamb; when the law and love of Christ have successfully opposed the great Rule of Fineness to the Rule of Force; when women are admitted to their rightful share in the administration of government; when, from the ballot to the highest executive honors and uses, they shall be permitted fairly to represent, in their own characters, the interests of their sex; when every department of politics, art, literature, trade is thrown open, absolutely, without reservation, to the exercise of their energies; when the state ceases to expend a dollar more for the education of its boys than of its girls; when public sentiment not only does not deny to them, but imposes upon them, a standard of intellectual culture not one whit inferior to and in no wise differing from that imposed upon men, as well as a standard of physical strength, and an education to it, which will compel them to forsake their present confinement to the deadly drain of what we term "domestic employments"; when public taste selects for them a dress fit for a healthy Christian to wear; when just about two-thirds of the educated practicing physicians of the world are women; when marriage and motherhood no more complete a woman's mission to the world than marriage and fatherhood complete a man's; when important changes have swept and garnished the whole realm of household care; when men consent to share its minimum of burden with women, and women are qualified and eager to keep pace with men in public usefulness; when men are as chaste as women, and women as brave as men; when self-reliant men become unselfish, and unselfish women self-reliant; when through family, church, and state woman the equal of man herself disowns and exiles woman the subject, and when generations have brought the laws of inheritance to bear upon such a race of women; when children and children's children have perpetuated their struggling strength, and dropped their lingering weakness—only then can we draw the veil from the brows of the TRUE WOMAN. Only then shall this sad Sphinx—who lost her crown and received her curse for the love of knowledge, yet who has woven out of her love to man the web of earth's purest dreams and holiest deeds—unclose her marble lips and lift her weary head to take her well-earned blessing.

Fair as the moon, clear as the sun, and terrible as an army with banners will be the face which, out of the desert of her long watch and patience, she will turn upon the world.

FOUR

CONTEMPORARY

REVIEWS OF

THE STORY OF AVIS

"New Books," *Philadelphia Inquirer*
(31 October 1877)

As a piece of literary work this story is as good as anything Miss Phelps has yet produced. In many particulars it shows a marked advance in artistic workmanship. The characters are projected with greater power and developed with a more consummate subtlety than in any previous work of the author, while there is no want of dramatic interest, and the story is constructed with a skill that must hold the attention of the most superficial reader. But, in one respect, and that a most important one, the story of "Avis" is a disappointing book. As though with a prescience that foresaw and forestalled criticism, Miss Phelps has taken exception to the word "morbid;" but there is none other that so well describes the sentiment that dominates her latest book. It is morbid through and through, and in saying that we mean that the author represents unhealthy and abnormal moods of mind and emotions as being natural and typical. She draws an "Avis," and from her history deduces generalities, glittering but unsound. The book makes upon the reader an indefinable but most melancholy impression. There is that about its moral atmosphere suggestive of an air sick and heavy with strange and cloying scents. Now and then Miss Phelps lets in a whiff from the outside work-a-day world, but only often enough to make the contrast more overpowering. The book is a psychological study of the exceptional. Its heroine, "Avis," is a woman by herself, and an artist to wit. Against her instincts, and contrary to her determination, she allows herself to be beguiled into a marriage, and throughout the book the author has unmistakably shown it to be her opinion that she had done better to have remained single, a dangerous lesson to preach, and no less dangerous than untrue. Great pains have been taken by the author to elaborate the character of "Avis," but she remains, in spite of all, a mystery, vague and unreal. She has many troubles, but the reader's sympathies do not readily go out toward her. One feels that she must have been an uncomfortable person to have round the house, and although her husband, "Ostrander," certainly behaved very badly, that he had much to contend against. "Ostrander" is cleverly drawn, but the cooling of his love for his wife is too abrupt in its development. Miss Phelps has a leaning toward abruptness, and makes considerable demands upon the intelligence and patience of her readers. But, whatever may be its faults, the "Story of Avis" is a remarkable book, full of psychological power and subtle sentiment. On sale by Claxton, Remsen & Co.

"Literary Notices," *The Woman's Journal* 8 (15 December 1877): 400

The Story of Avis, by Elizabeth Stuart Phelps, is one of the most remarkable books which has this season come to our table.

In this story Miss Phelps raises the question more and more asked by women, whether marriage, in the case of a woman, is compatible with the pursuit of other strong ruling tastes.

Avis Dobell, the heroine of the story, is an artist of decided talent, with a permanent distaste of and apparent incapacity for details of other practical things.

After six years of patient, hard study abroad, her teacher assured her that in two years she can "make an established reputation." She returned to her home, still oblivious of common practical details, but with the great absorbing love of her art. Then came Philip Ostrander to sit to her for his portrait. Then began the love-scenes, which are drawn with masterly skill and strength. The end is marriage, which also puts an end to the artist's career, and even spoils her capacity for her special work.

The story is told with great power, with artistic skill, and with unflagging interest. The fine word-painting, the subtle analysis, the philosophical discussion, the delineations of character, and the high meaning of the book, will give the story of Avis a permanent place in English literature.

Miss Phelps did not close the book without a description of a woman whom it may take three generations to make, who would be "competent to the terrible task of adjusting the sacred individuality of her life to her supreme capacity of love, and the supreme burden and perils which it imposes." She also sketches the man, "who only among men understands what a woman's tenderness is. With her, he is a crowned creature; but with him, she is a free one." Boston, J. R. Osgood & Co.

L[ucy] S[tone]

Harper's New Monthly Magazine
56 (January 1878): 310

We can not think that such a novel as *The Story of Avis* (J. R. Osgood and Co.) is altogether a wholesome story. Miss Elizabeth Stuart Phelps has certainly taken to heart the criticisms which have been made on some of her other writings. No one will accuse her of slighting her work in this her last publication. There are no careless passages in it, no marks of haste, no writing for the market, no hurry-scurry to catch the fall trade. It is fully finished in all its parts, sometimes perhaps a little too finely finished, as though the language of passionate feeling had been fashioned with too great a thought of artistic perfection. But it is the product of a true poet, of one who sees into the heart of nature—sees into the heart of woman too, if not into the heart of man. Avis is a fine character; Philip Ostrander is exceptionally and unnaturally weak. The story is intensely though purely passionate and dramatic. The passion may not be untrue to nature altogether, but it is at least open to question whether this is the kind of interior experience which it is desirable that our young girls should have portrayed before them as the ideal of true love.

"Gail Hamilton's Criticism," *The Woman's Journal*
29 (30 March 1878): 99

After six columns of adverse criticism, Gail Hamilton* closes her review of "The Story of Avis" by stating that "the faults of the book, glaring as they are, are superficial—wholly so in their origin, chiefly so in their extent. The merits are in its substance and spirit, and for them all who believe in a high standard and aspire to the great living should be profoundly thankful." Belonging to this class, it shall be my pleasant task to try partially to repay a debt of gratitude to the gifted author by a review which shall touch only the merits of the book, its faults having been already so thoroughly discussed by almost all critics, that it is unnecessary here to re-state them.

As in some persons one forgets untasteful dress, irregular features, and even poverty of expression, because some mental or spiritual power lying back of all and overpowering all makes external imperfections of no account, so in this book, where there is not only an all-prevading atmosphere of purity, sweetness, and earnest

* See Introduction, n. 68.

purpose, but also an idea, a thought—something for the brain as well as the soul, the faults which in a lesser work would be glaring, are rendered insignificant.

In one sense, it is not a great work. It is not likely to outlive a single generation, being eminently for the present time. And whilst it is so little beyond the average public sentiment of to-day that the author runs no risk of social martyrdom by reason of progressive opinions on any subject, it is enough in advance of ordinary thought to lead a great many women for the first time to consider seriously their duties and responsibilities. To this end the dramatic form in which it is written is admirably adapted, as those who are most in need of its suggestions would not be reached by the didactic style of representation. It is the story of the evolution of Woman. The mother, with only the longing for something more than marriage and maternity alone could give; the daughter, going a little farther, taking her destiny a little more into her own hands, bearing public sentiment, persuading her father to give her the education her soul craved; believing that there was a conflict between the love of art and the love of man; struggling, agonizing to preserve her freedom and her art, and finally yielding to the man whom her imagination had crowned king, but who was unworthy of any love from such a woman. When his moral weakness and mental instability became gradually apparent, "her heart assumed a new burden, as if a third child had been born to her." Was it possible, she asks herself, "that her soul had ever gone on its knees before this man?" And the reverent love was gone, and in its place came a tenderness which had in it a large element of pity. And so her genius was buried but not lost, for it rises again in her child, in whom we already see promise of the ideal. She is to attain to the fuller knowledge of the meaning of a woman's life, and will understand how to develop instead of crush her divine inheritance.

It is not intended to show the incompatibility of art with true marriage. Had Avis married her ideal, she would have painted far greater pictures than would have been possible to her before. Had the man who won her love really been what she believed him to be, she would have gone to him without hesitation; for there can never be a conflict between true love and anything else. But this is a story of life as it is, and how often do we find great men or women fairly mated? The equal marriages are in ordinary life, not extraordinary. Coy may marry and be happy, though "nothing ever happens to her but John and the children," and her only trouble is a disinclination "to ask John for money;" but Avis must take her only satisfaction in training her child to a completeness of Womanhood.

Philip is a fair illustration of a good type of the average man; above him, somewhat, in personal attractiveness and mental attainments. "Having brains enough to do anything, he chose to do nothing." "Dissipating himself in inconsequent ways;" a creature of impulse rather than principle, whose faults were more negative than positive. The only really commendable thing mentioned in regard to him is also negative—that he was not envious of the superior attainments of his wife. "Before I sink so low as that it will be time for me to die," he said, when tempted to jealousy by the contrast of her success with his own failure. He could trifle with the affections of women to an unlimited extent, and then pride himself on his virtue, because he went no further; was not bad only because he had too much taste to desire self-indulgence in vicious practices. He could neglect his "poor, plain, old mother" shut in by the bleak New Hampshire Hills, patiently waiting for the son who forgot to come; only forgot, that was all. Irritable when overtaken by misfortune, and inclined to blame everyone but himself for his failures; incapable of rising to high, moral or spiritual thought, except when carried by the magnetism of his wife's enthusiasm, to which for the moment, he would so thoroughly respond as to imagine it to be his own conception. To the end, he rested in her strength taxing her tenderness, which he at last becomes conscious of not deserving, and realizing, as far as he could realize, the great wrong he had done her, finally died in her arms, leaving her less lonely in his death than in his life. She could now love the ideal she had once worshipped and could think with an "exultant sense that she could never see in him a flaw again." She could even be glad for all that had been, even though her genius had been sacrificed, for had she not her child, her woman-child, who should realize all her aspirations, who should not fail as she had failed?

All the characters are real. We know the good, old Professor John, Coy and Barbara. We have traveled with the Smiths in Florida or elsewhere, but we will only stop to speak of Aunt Chloe, who deserves notice as a type of woman who does much of the necessary work in the world with very little return; who makes the material basis, without which genius cannot do its perfect work. For though Art is not incompatible with marriage, it seems to be impossible to unite it with domestic drudgery without killing its noblest aspirations.

It is understood that no man can pursue an ordinary business life and attain any degree of perfection in Art; why then expect it of a woman? The secret of the success of many a man lies in the fact that some woman has devoted her life to attending to his material wants and has thereby enabled him to give all his strength, mental and physical, to his chosen profession. All honor to these Aunt Chloes, by-and-by they will find their proper level in the world's estimation, and their work will be acknowledged to form the solid foundations on which the generations rest.

In closing, I quote the passage which seems to me more than any other to indicate the purpose and thought of the book, and to show how high an ideal of womanhood, the author is capable of conceiving.

"We have been told that it takes three generations to make a gentleman; we may believe that it will take as much or more to make a woman. A being of radiant physique, the heiress of ancestral health on the maternal side; a creature forever more of nerve than of muscle, and therefore trained to the energy of the muscle and the repose of the nerve; physically educated by mothers of her own fibre and physicians of her own sex; such a woman alone is fitted to acquire the drilled brain, the calmed imagination and sustained aim, which constitute intellectual command.

"A creature capable of this command, in whom emotion intensifies reflection and passion strengthens purposes, and self-poise is substituted for self-extravagance; such a creature is competent to the terrible task of adjusting the sacred individuality of her life to her supreme capacity for love and the supreme burdens and perils which it imposes upon her."

Brooklyn, N.Y., March 18, 1878.   M.L.C.